SYDNEY'S SILVER LINING

The story of America's most important
water polo team and the journey
to the greatest game in history.

KYLE UTSUMI

Foreword by John Tanner
Edited by Mark Hernandez and Kim Krueger
Drawings by Julia Hermann

ISBN: 978-1-48357-203-1

Photo credits: pp. xii,xiii: United States Olympic Committee. Used by permission. All Rights Reserved; p. xv: Water Polo Scoreboard, Volume 4, Number 6, August 1989; pp. xx, 76, 104, 134, 228, 235: Photos by Max Gardner; p. xxiv: Photo by Adam Lyon. Used by permission; pp. 2, 168, 199, 313, 331: Photos by Kyle Utsumi; p. 8: Water Polo Scoreboard, Volume 9, Number 1, January/February 1978; p 18: Photos courtesy of Dion Gray; p. 36: Photo courtesy of Pat Jones; p. 65: Water Polo Scoreboard, Volume 9, Issue 6, October/November 1994; pp. 200, 211, 242, 282: Photos courtesy of Ellen Estes Lee; p. 252: Photo by David Gonzales, David Gonzales Photography. Used by permission. All Rights Reserved; pp. 266, 292, 314, 328, 332, 336: Photos courtesy of Maureen O'Toole; p. 350 Photo courtesy of Randall Utsumi; pp. 356, 373: Courtesy of the author.

For Mom and Dad

In Memory of Dennis Fosdick

Sydney's Silver Lining Backers

OLYMPIAN
Walter Price

PLATINUM
Greg & Robin Canonica

Sydney's Silver Lining Backers

GOLD

Maureen Eger • Stanford Water Polo Club
Cooper, Sawyer, Esther, James & KT • Randy & Lea Utsumi • Castilleja School Water Polo
Allison, Hailey & Eli • Ellen Estes Lee & Family • USA Water Polo
Guy Baker & Michelle Pickering • Scott Blake, Nordic Water Polo • The Hendrickson Family

SILVER

Susan Ortwein • Gabriella, Madison, Susan & David Lewis
Chris, Dawn, Kay & Andrew Fleischner • The Ruano Family
Bonnie, Chad, Justin, Cassidy & Shane Papa • Menlo Water Polo • The Bressie Family
The Zafran Family • The Denney Family, University of California at Santa Barbara
The Mandema Family • Ryan, Jill & Bruiser Utsumi • Phil, Sue, MJ & Luke Johnston
University of Michigan Women's Water Polo Team • The Larko Family
Gabe, Nico & Mateo Golomb • B. Brent Bohlender, Modesto-Stanislaus Water Polo
Alex Nice • The Klein Family • Kai, Kekoa, Pono, Wendy & Craig Rosenberg

TABLE OF CONTENTS

TIMELINE

1976

- August 22: First United States Women's National Team game, versus Australia, Honolulu, Hawaii

1977

- December 26-29: Commerce Internationals, Commerce, California

1978

- August 18-28: Women's water polo debuts as exhibition at FINA World Championships, Berlin, West Germany

1979

- June 29-July 1: Inaugural Women's FINA World Cup, Merced, California

1984

- July: Exhibition game versus Australia at Pepperdine University Olympic water polo venue, Malibu, California
- July 19-22: FINA World Cup, Irvine, California

1986

- August 14-22: First official Women's FINA World Championship, Madrid, Spain

1994

- September 1-11: Pat Jones pushes "Women for Sydney 2000" campaign at the FINA World Championships, Rome, Italy
- Women's water polo included on NCAA Women's Emerging Sport list

1995

- February 11: International meeting for women's water polo, attended by the United States, Australia, Canada, and Holland, Amsterdam, Netherlands
- October 10-15: International meeting for women's water polo at FINA World Cup, Sydney, Australia.

1997

- May: Demonstration by Australian women's water polo players at Sydney airport and confrontation of FINA President Mustapha Larfaoui, Sydney, Australia
- October 29: Women's water polo added to Sydney Olympic Games
- November: First girls' division at Speedo Cup (now Champions Cup)

1998

- January 8-17: FINA World Championships, Perth, Australia
- March: Guy Baker hired as head coach, United States Women's National Team
- May 21: First training session of Women's National Team under head caoch Guy Baker
- July: European trip to Pančevo, Yugoslavia, Budapest, Hungary, and Zeist, Netherlands
- December: Inaugural Holiday Cup, Los Alamitos, California

1999

- May 24-29: FINA World Cup, Winnipeg, Canada
- December 9-13: Holiday Cup, Los Alamitos, California

2000

- February: Training trip to Zeist, Netherlands
- April 22-30: Olympic Games Qualification Tournament, Palermo, Italy
- June: Training trip to Sydney, Burleigh Heads, and Kawana Waters, Australia
- July 4-9: Holiday Cup, Los Alamitos, California
- July 14: Sendoff to Sydney, Stanford, California
- September 15-October 1: Olympic Games, Sydney, Australia
- September 23: United States women win silver medal at Sydney Olympic Games

2001

- May 12-13: First Women's NCAA Water Polo Championship, Stanford, California

2003

- July 25: United States women win gold at the 2003 FINA World Championships, Barcelona, Spain

2004

- August 13-29: Olympic Games, Athens, Greece
- August 26: United States women win bronze medal at Athens Olympic Games

2008

- August 8-24: Olympic Games, Beijing, China
- August 21: United States women win silver medal at Beijing Olympic Games

2012

- July 27-August 12: Olympic Games, London, Great Britain
- August 9: United States women win gold medal at London Olympic Games

2000 Women's Olympic Water Polo Team

Robin Beauregard
Huntington Beach, Calif.
#10 • Born 1979

Ellen Estes
Novato, Calif.
#5 • Born 1978

Courtney Johnson
Salt Lake City, Utah
#13 • Born 1974

Ericka Lorenz
San Diego, Calif.
#3 • Born 1981

Heather Moody
Green River, Wyo.
#9 • Born 1973

Bernice Orwig
Anaheim, Calif.
#1 • Born 1976

Maureen O'Toole
Long Beach, Calif.
#7 • Born 1961

Nicolle Payne
Cerritos, Calif.
#11 • Born 1976

Heather Petri
Orinda, Calif.
#2 • Born 1978

Kathy "Gubba" Sheehy
San Diego, Calif.
#12 • Born 1970

Coralie Simmons
Hemet, Calif.
#6 • Born 1977

Julie Swail
Placentia, Calif.
#8 • Born 1972

Brenda Villa
Commerce, Calif.
#4 • Born 1980

Rachel Scott
Bainbridge Island, Wash.
Alternate • Born 1975

Guy Baker
Head Coach

Chris Duplanty
Assistant Coach

Ken Lindgren
Assistant Coach

Michelle Pickering
Team Manager

If you want to go fast, go alone.
If you want to go far, go together.

– African proverb

Women's FINA Cup Squad

     This is the first time in the history of the Women's FINA Cups that there has been a full slate of teams. This fact is very encouraging for the further development of international water polo. There is now a continental championship in Europe and a strong and becoming stronger program. The next steps for the United States and the Western Hemisphere are to continue to promote the sport and to work toward including women's water polo in the Pan Am Games, the counterpart to the European Championships – then on to the Olympics.

     For many of the young women now participating in water polo, this is a dream which may be realized by 1996. If not then, these young women will have to join others who have tried – and progressed – but who have had to step aside and allow younger women to take up the cause in the water. Eventually, and probably inevitably, their common dream of women's water polo in the Olympic Games will be realized. The strength and quality of play of all the participating teams in this year's FINA Cup go a long way to realize this dream.

– *Water Polo Scoreboard*, Volume 4, Number 6, August 1989
FINA World Cup, Eindhoven, Netherlands

Foreword

The Perfect Game

Grown men, faces painted, green afro wigs in place, inflatable kangaroos under their arms, chanting, *"Aussie! Aussie! Aussie! Oi! Oi! Oi!"* circled the Sydney Olympic Swimming complex hours before the opening sprint of the 2000 women's water polo gold medal game. One hundred years in the making, the Olympics' first team sport finally had a women's competition. Australia was the perfect place for it to happen at least in part because their team had qualified to compete for that inaugural gold medal. Seventeen thousand people, all ages, most with no real water polo background, were about to experience an epic drama. I'd played in or coached thousands of water polo games, but this was going to be different.

Australians don't need an instructional manual for how to look or act at a celebration. They don't search YouTube for role models on what to wear or how to cheer. They follow their instincts. A game without precedent demanded a packed stadium of fans unfettered by rules.

For an opponent, there could have been none more appropriate than Team USA: women's water polo's first global championship host, the team whose path to Sydney had been the most grueling, and the program with whom the Aussies shared the most history and respect. Put simply: a dream matchup.

All preliminary round games and semifinals had been played at the Ryde Aquatic Leisure Centre. As the name implies, it was an intimate but modest Olympic venue where the warm-up pool included a 720-degree water slide. Five miles away from the primary venues of the Sydney Olympic Park, Ryde epitomized water polo – fun and friendly, but hidden away. Three thousand water polo-savvy fans jammed in there every session of competition, but it was as though the athletes were preaching to the choir, out of view of the Olympic Flame. This game, on the other hand, would be played in the 17,000-seat Sydney Olympic Park Aquatic Centre, in the pulsing center of Games activity.

Coaching in my third Olympics – after serving as an assistant coach with the U.S. Men's Olympic Water Polo Team in 1992, and as a member of the 1996 U.S. Olympic Swimming Advisory Staff – I knew my credential entitled me to premium seating in the Olympic Family area. As it turned out, my VIP status got me a spot so far from the field of play that I could hardly distinguish our players. But that seat location also meant this was water polo not as a marginal sport played in front of friends and family, but as an Olympic centerpiece matchup. All eyes were on this game. Women's water polo would be the center of the Olympic universe for the next 90 minutes.

The confluence of who, what, and where set the stage for a sublime event, one that even veteran observers could hardly believe. Bob Ryan, the legendary *Boston Globe* sportswriter who had covered every major sporting event in the world, called the Sydney women's water polo gold medal game a distinctly enthralling event. It was the perfect venue, the perfect audience, and the perfect matchup for the perfect Olympic story. And Kyle Utsumi is the perfect person to tell this story. Kyle wrote about, promoted, and coached with or against every one of the people involved, starting long before the ball dropped on September 23, 2000.

As a lifelong Olympic dreamer, Kyle had the ideal disposition, discipline, and determination to become an Olympian. Unfortunately he didn't have Ellen Estes' wingspan, Bernice Orwig's eggbeater, or Brenda Villa's vision, so he had to "settle" for becoming one of the world's foremost water polo coaches and journalists.

His coaching resume is comprehensive and esteemed. He has coached high school and college; age group and senior club; and youth, junior and senior international teams, guiding everyone from 10-year-olds capping up before competing in their first game to Olympians standing on the podium after competing in their last. His trophy case includes a collection of global championship medals, and high school, club, and college championship plaques, rings, and trophies. Most recently, he was a vital part of Stanford's run of four NCAA titles in five years.

His water polo journalism career is equally noteworthy. As media director for USA Water Polo, Kyle covered all facets of the sport in the US in addition to many international events. He has traveled the world, to places popular and obscure, inspired by his passion for water polo, and driven by his intellectual curiosity. Kyle has been obsessed with Olympic history, unearthing buried stories and piecing together the twisting trajectories that make Olympians' journeys so compelling.

At Sendoff to Sydney, the final US match before departing for Australia, Kyle orchestrated a reception for the Stanford Girls' Water Polo Club players to introduce "their" Olympians, the thirteen Team USA (and Team Russia) superstars whom they had been researching at Kyle's behest. So long had these women trained and competed in almost complete obscurity; they were stunned that the Stanford girls knew about their journeys to the brink of Olympic participation.

That Olympic participation culminated in the gold medal game in Sydney. These women, who'd fought their way to the top of our sport without benefit of heroes or role models to embrace or emulate, entered the water focused only on fighting for gold. I am grateful that Kyle, a person so deeply knowledgeable in and passionate about our sport, has brought this story to light. Guiding the narrative as carefully as any team he's ever coached, Kyle brings the competitive masterpiece that the United States Olympic Team crafted that September night clearly into view. And he reveals the members of the Sydney team as the heroes they'd never had, and women's water polo as the purest of all Olympic sports.

– John Tanner
Head Coach, Stanford University Women's Water Polo
Three-time Olympic Coach

1996 Stanford Water Polo – 13-and-under Junior Olympic team

Prologue

Twenty years ago, in August of 1996, I coached the Stanford Water Polo Club's first-ever 13-and-under girls team at USA Water Polo's Junior Olympics. I had just returned from the Olympic Games in Atlanta, where I worked media at the water polo competition. That first 13-and-under team included several little sisters (including three sisters from one family!) who had older brothers and sisters who played water polo.

For all of them, it was a beginning. A first summer of water polo, their first JOs – and in an Olympic year, just like this one, when the Games will take place in Rio de Janeiro. If they watched Olympic water polo on TV, though, they watched only men. That JO team played several of our games at Santa Clara University, where there was a men's varsity team, but not a women's.

By the time this first 13-and-under group graduated high school, the landscape of possibility in their sport had evolved dramatically. Over the course of the next six years, an explosion of opportunity came about, starting with the addition of women's water polo to the Olympic Games in October of 1997. One month after the announcement of women's water polo in the Sydney Olympics, several of those first 13-and-unders competed in the first girls' division of the Speedo Cup.

When those girls played in the 1996 Junior Olympics, there were twenty collegiate women's teams with varsity status. By the time the youngest on the team graduated from high school in 2004, there were fifty-nine. In 2001, the first NCAA Championship for women's water polo took place, up the road from Santa Clara University, at Stanford's Avery Aquatics Center. That inaugural tournament featured four teams – the 2016 version, ten.

Women's water polo transformed in the years following the 1996 Junior Olympics. Those girls on my team were the last to watch an Olympics without having female heroes to cheer. The handful who went on to play college water polo had an NCAA Championship to compete for. Meanwhile, JOs has become an example of why the United States Women's National Team is never – and will never be – at a loss for its next crop of talent. Compared to the eighteen teams that competed in the 13-and-under division in 1996, the 2016 JOs will feature over 100 girls' teams in the 10-, 12-, and 14-and-under brackets.

That 1996 13-and-under team was a groundbreaking one for our club, but they are seldom referred to as such. At the 2000 Sydney Olympics, the thirteen athletes who competed for the United States made history as trailblazers in women's water polo. They were our first team to compete for the ultimate prize in international sports – the Olympic gold medal. At the time, it was all very new. Women's water polo was booming, and continued to do so rapidly – so rapidly, in fact, that the next generation of stars quickly took center stage not years after Sydney, but months.

And one thing we learned as women's water polo thrived in our country is that we are not short of young female stars. At the London Olympics in 2012 when the United States finally captured the long-sought-after gold medal, the team's youngest player, Maggie Steffens, took the Games by storm.

This book is a history – a chronicle of those first Olympic stars. They weren't the first to represent United States women's water polo on the international stage – that had gone on for decades before Sydney. But they ushered in a new era, both internationally as the Olympic Games became a reality, and in our country, where young girls now had so much more to aspire to in the sport they loved.

Is the Sydney Olympic Team America's most important water polo team? To answer that question, consider what would have happened had they not overcome their underdog status to *qualify* for the 2000 Games. Hungary, for example, the team the United States knocked out en route to punching its ticket to Sydney, has made three appearances in the Olympics – but is still seeking its first medal.

If the United States weren't playing in Sydney, coverage here would have been scant, and the establishment of Olympic role models would have been delayed at least until Athens in 2004. When young athletes dream of sports glory, those dreams are about proving to the world they are the best – at the Olympic Games. The Sydney team gave American girls the opportunity to see themselves in that position – as future Olympians.

The ability to dream big is so critical. None of the players from my original 13-and-under squad went on to become Olympians – so few in our country ever will. But they all played for their high schools. Several played on collegiate teams. A few competed for the NCAA Championship.

Sydney's Silver Lining tells the story of the 2000 Olympic Team and the individuals who made it a unique group. The book features the diverse backgrounds of the Sydney team members – without each, they would not have become the team they did. Once together as the first women's Olympic Team, they had a lot of work to do, and not a lot of time to do it. They were in uncharted waters, but finished their journey together with one final effort in an American sports lover's dream scenario – squaring off against a longtime rival in front of a record crowd, playing for Olympic gold.

Optimists will find a silver lining in any outcome. In the case of the 2000 Olympic Team, it doesn't take an optimist to see the impact they had on future generations of their sport.

They are the single team upon which women's water polo in America is built.

The 2012 Olympic champions – August 9, 2012

1

THE JOURNEY

2012 Olympic Games **Brenda Villa**

From the top of the Olympic podium, Brenda Villa scanned the crowd. She spotted her mother Rosario and father Ines, her brother Edgar, and her niece Bella, all of them beaming, clutching small American flags. She studied their faces. She saw no tears, just smiles spanning from ear to ear. She nodded her head, silently communicating *We did it* to them with the gesture. Her eyes, curiously dry, moved on, taking in more faces. They paused ever so briefly at the sight of every American emblem to see if she knew the owner. Moving on, they inspected the festive decor of the arena, lingering on the large Olympic rings and the jagged "London 2012" emblazoned on the far wall.

Standing hand-in-hand with her teammates, she felt Olympic rookie Melissa Seidemann's periodic squeezes of joy to her right. To her left stood Beijing Olympic teammate Lauren Wenger, a look of relief and accomplishment radiating from her face. On the other side of Seidemann was Heather Petri, a 12-year partner in Villa's quest for gold, spanning four Olympic Games. More than once, their eyes locked. After more than a decade of sharing both joyous and bitter tears, there were none today. No words were necessary. Their eyes spoke volumes.

Taking it all in, Villa shook her head in disbelief.

The journey that brought her to this moment could be measured in years – more than two decades since she had first taken to the water at the pool across the street from her home in Commerce, California. This journey could be measured in miles. Hundreds of thousands of them, crisscrossing the globe in pursuit of perfecting her craft, performing within a team to achieve its common goal.

This journey could also be measured in inches. On the Olympic podium, Brenda Villa and the United States women's water polo team now stood roughly twelve inches above their vanquished opponents from Spain. The Spanish team stood another twelve inches above perennial powerhouse Australia, winners of the Olympic bronze.

Villa had taken her place on those platforms before, adorned with Olympic silver and bronze medals. Now, atop the podium in London, her neck laden with precious gold, those moments seemed years, miles, and mere inches in the past.

London 2012 medal ceremony

As the notes of "The Star Spangled Banner" powerfully graced the natatorium, Villa's eyes tracked the path of the American flag as it slowly rose skyward. Right hand over her heart, she opted to lip sync the words, while others softly sang the tune. Three times, she had stood on the Olympic podium, listening to the anthems of her opponents. In those moments she was already calculating in her head how she would make sure to hear her own in four years' time.

This time, there were no future considerations. Instead, she allowed her mind to drift to the past.

As her eyes sought familiar faces in the seats, her mind was a blur of people who had traveled with her on this journey, over years filled with both triumph and disappointment.

She knew that she shared the London podium with countless others – Olympic teammates from Sydney, Athens, and Beijing, as well as teammates whose careers simply did not line up with the opportunity to be Olympians. Teammates and coaches from all stages of her long career were with Villa in that moment.

This particular journey was arduous, and upon reaching its ultimate destination the outcome was golden.

But the larger journey for the sport of women's water polo to the Olympic Games started long before Villa and the newly crowned Olympic champions stood tall on the London stage.

@@@@@@

In the mid-1970s Ines Villa and Rosario Chavez immigrated to the United States from Mexico. They met through relatives and a short time later married and started a family in Huntington Park, California, with the arrival of their oldest child, Edgar. Two years later, the Villa family welcomed a daughter, Brenda. When she was six months old, the family made a move that would put Brenda on a path unimaginable to Ines and Rosario at the time. They took up residence in the City of Commerce, in southeast Los Angeles County. The Villa family was complete with the birth of Uriel eight years later.

Ines, an only child, grew up playing soccer, a love he would pass on to his children. Rosario was the eldest of eleven children, and often acted as a second mother to her siblings. Spending time cooking, cleaning, and babysitting left no time for playing sports herself, although she was always drawn to soccer and the beloved team from her home country. Her parents' passion for soccer defined Brenda's sports world growing up.

When they got older, the Villa kids, along with all the children in the neighborhood, got to play soccer and many other sports at the local Rosewood Park. Youth competition in the City of Commerce was centered around the four city parks, each of which had a team for every sport. The teams competed in widely popular leagues for softball, volleyball, flag football, and soccer.

Young Brenda loved anything that had to do with sports and spent every moment of her free time at the park. Once her schoolwork was done as required by her mother, Brenda was free to go to Rosewood. A social butterfly from the moment she learned to talk, Brenda found friends flocking to her every time she arrived. The precocious girl knew everyone and was often the center of attention.

Brenda remembers playing every sport, whether she was an official member of the team or not. Making her way from one end of the park to another, she would crash practices. Passing by the flag football field on her way to the pool, she often joined in the fun.

Her friends would urge her to join the team, but while Brenda loved throwing the football and running free on the field, she always declined. All sports gave her enjoyment, but Brenda had found the one that was her love.

When Ines and Rosario Villa moved to Commerce, they had no way of knowing the impact the indoor pool right across the street from their new home would have on the lives of all of the Villa children, most famously, their daughter Brenda.

Having never learned to swim herself and harboring a fear of the water, Rosario was eager for her children to learn to become water-safe. Edgar and Brenda completed swim lessons, and soon after, Edgar started playing water polo. But Brenda, though eager to tag along with her older brother, was not allowed to join.

Rosario's reservations about letting her daughter play with the boys – as there was no team for girls at that time – were rooted in her culture and her own childhood, in which she lacked the opportunity to play sports. The physicality of water polo and the swimwear were two additional factors that were foreign to her own upbringing, adding to her hesitation.

Not to be left out, Brenda deployed a tactic she had mastered in order to change her mother's mind: she annoyed her about it constantly. When Brenda was eight, Rosario relented and let her daughter join the water polo team.

"She could see that it was fun, and my brother loved it," Brenda said. "Once I started playing, she saw that I had fun and that I was just as good as all the boys, so I think that's what put away all her reservations about me playing this sport."

The joy she found in the pool launched Brenda on a unique journey of opportunity and achievement. She dove headfirst into the life of an aquatic athlete: born at the right time, raised in the right place across the street from the Commerce pool, given opportunities to chase dreams that were unknown to female water polo players before her.

Brenda was born in 1980, a year in which no American water polo player, male or female, would compete in the Olympic Games – the boycott of the Moscow Games dashed the gold medal hopes of the United States men's team. Her childhood and beginnings in the sport occurred during an era of strength for the United States men's Olympic teams: silver medals in Los Angeles and Seoul followed by a fourth-place finish in Barcelona brought attention to the sport and instilled pride throughout the water polo community. But there was no women's water polo team to cheer for at the Olympics, no female heroes to watch playing her sport on television during the quadrennial global celebration of sport.

Brenda's journey started at the right time. Sydney would be the right destination.

☺☺☺☺☺☺

For those fortunate few who reach the top of the Olympic podium, the view is accompanied by a highly charged mixture of emotions. In mere minutes, the mind races through time and over distance – reliving extreme triumphs and joy as well as bitter failures and moments of staring down challenges that seem impossible to conquer.

In the sport of women's water polo, many athletes and administrators worldwide set out on a journey – sometimes fighting alone, sometimes side-by-side with others equally committed to the cause of equity – to see the game they loved gain inclusion to the Olympic Games. Having waited on the sidelines for a full century after men's water polo debuted at the 1900 Olympics, the 2000 Games marked a triumph for those tireless pioneers and for the sport itself, as a field of six women's water polo teams made history in Sydney.

Brenda Villa's quest for Olympic gold included near-misses in Sydney, Athens, and Beijing. Villa and teammate Heather Petri were the only women in the world to own three Olympic water polo medals, an accomplishment that represented the sustainability of women's water polo in the United States as much as it did their longevity. In 2004, the team returned just over half of its roster from the previous Olympics; in 2008, a team with ten Olympic rookies entered the Beijing Games as the favorite for gold. At three consecutive Olympics, the margin of defeat was paper thin – but the factors fueling over a decade of consistency in the women's program combined to finally put the Americans at the top of the world in 2012.

With the United States' victory in London, Villa reached the peak of her Mount Olympus. She completed a journey which, despite an impressive haul of hardware in three previous Games, had yet to reach the pinnacle of the Olympic podium.

As her eyes soaked up the colorful pageantry around her, her ears filled with the tune she had yearned for so long to hear, the weight of Olympic gold pulling down like an opponent grabbing her cap strings. Brenda Villa smiled. Never one to be at a loss for words, at this moment, she was speechless.

This journey was complete.

Indio Aquatic Club – 1976 Junior Olympic champions
Guy Baker, back row, third from right

2

A HARD PILL TO SWALLOW

1999 FINA World Cup **Guy Baker**

Water polo is hard.

Learning to play at a young age has myriad difficulties. It helps to be equipped with certain skills when a player decides to take the plunge. Strong swimmers, especially those who have trained and competed, have a base to quickly build on. Basketball players may bring some conceptual understanding of spacing, post play, player-to-player and zone defensive concepts, and the fast break. Those who have soccer experience have been versed in spacing the field, defending a goal, and using ball movement to attack a defense and, ultimately, a goalkeeper. Baseball and softball players arrive with strong arms and potentially proper throwing mechanics.

While being at home in the water is surely an advantage, many swimmers grow up doing just that – swimming. With double practices and focus on training at a young age, some youth swimmers never branch out to land sports. And for the land sport athlete, things change drastically in the water. Leverage, balance, and basic athleticism can be quickly compromised when one is suspended and submerged without the reassuring attachment to land.

In water polo, holding is commonplace – so much so, that it often goes unpunished by the referees. Holding an opponent's suit, or getting a grip of a wrist or arm, can be advantageous, but also makes for a high-contact sport. The physicality of water polo is on par with sports such as wrestling, football, and the martial arts. Of course, none of those take place in an environment with participants' heads so unprotected and at the same time so close to being submerged and deprived of oxygen.

Throw in the use of only one hand and the lack of in-field markings and water polo can be confusing and frustrating to young players, their parents, and anyone else interested in learning the sport.

Aside from the requisite jokes about horses, the most common questions from the uninitiated center around depth of the water and time spent treading. The root of these inquiries is clearly, "How would I possibly survive this sport?"

Many veteran water polo players would admit they possessed some, but not all, of the necessary skills or conceptual understandings when they were first drawn to the sport. While there are naturals who dive in and excel, even they have to continually add to their toolkits and make significant strides in at least one major set of skills to survive and advance their game to the next level.

Unlike many popular sports, water polo is hard to practice on one's own. Kids across the country grow up spending hours at the local park or a field at a nearby school, fielding grounders, running pass routes, shooting a thousand free throws. Hitting a tennis ball against a wall or a garage door. Practicing with a parent, or a friend. Unsupervised, until the sun sets and the ball becomes a dark shadow, and even then, the work is fun, and the junkies will continually find a way hone their talents.

Water polo isn't like this. When experts talk about needing ten thousand hours to master a skill, the learner can, in most cases, decide to put in extra time, speeding up the process. Relative to other sports, not only are the hours harder – they are harder to get. Pool time is scarce. Goals are expensive. Setting up a water polo course is difficult. And it's not a solo activity.

There are very few shortcuts to becoming a great water polo player.

Indio, California, sits in the Coachella Valley, just east of Palm Springs in Riverside County. With a motto of "The Place to Be" and the nickname "City of Festivals," the city is widely known as the site of the annual mid-April Coachella Valley Music and Arts Festival.

Distanced from the water polo hotbeds of Orange County and Los Angeles, Indio has produced standouts in both the men's and women's game. Charlie Harris played for Indio High School before going on to star at USC, where he was team captain as a senior. Harris was a member of the 1992 Olympic Team which finished fourth in Barcelona. Indio was represented in women's water polo in every FINA World Championship and Olympic Games from 1982 through 2008. Laura Laughlin played on the 1982 and 1986 teams; Amber Drury competed in 1991 and 1994 before coaching in 1998, and Guy Baker was head coach of the United States from 1998 through 2008.

Baker (Class of 1979), Laughlin (Class of 1980), Harris (Class of 1981), and Drury (Class of 1988) are all enshrined in Indio High School's Athletic Hall of Fame.

When he entered high school, Baker figured his main sport would be basketball. While he did star on the basketball court, named MVP of both the freshman and JV teams, his athletic career took a detour in the summer before ninth grade when Dr. John Lowell, coach of the Indio High School water polo team, sought him out to play goalie. After checking that water polo wouldn't conflict with high school basketball, Baker put on the goalie cap and started learning a new sport.

Fear of the ball proved to be an insurmountable shortcoming, however, and Baker's time in the goal was short-lived. In his first game as a field player, Baker found he enjoyed the aggressiveness and the fact that he could foul his opponents with virtually no consequence, unlike on the basketball court. Enjoying the field much more than having balls thrown at him, Baker looked forward to his first season on the freshman team.

But before the season began, several seniors got kicked off the team, making it necessary for Baker and several other freshmen, including Lowell's son, Cal, to play on the varsity. The freshmen got tons of playing time, and while they didn't win many games, the young team gained plenty of experience.

The tough year in the win-loss column paid immediate dividends. Lowell had big plans for his up-and-coming team, and despite the losses during the high school season, he was a master of motivation, setting the players' sights on long-term goals. In the summer of 1976, Lowell led the Indio Aquatic Club's 15-and-under boys to an upset win over perennial powerhouse Newport, to qualify for the Junior Olympics – a feat that Baker remembers as a highlight of his early career.

Indio Aquatic Club traveled to Albuquerque, New Mexico, for the AAU Junior Olympics. Unlike the modern JOs, at the time, the tournament included only five teams, each the winner of their regional qualifiers. A basketball player throughout his youth, Baker found traveling out of California a new and thrilling experience. The farthest he remembered ever traveling for basketball was to Riverside, certainly never leaving the Coachella Valley.

The round-robin competition began, and the upstarts from Indio cruised through their schedule unscathed. They would face fellow unbeaten Mission City Water Polo Club of Santa Clara in the final match, a de facto championship game.

The Indio boys got off to a great start in the final but found themselves tied with Mission City entering the fourth quarter of play. Lowell, an assistant coach on the 1968 men's Olympic volleyball team in Mexico City, never played water polo himself. But his coaching philosophy was anchored by belief in defensive pressure and superior conditioning. In the final quarter against Mission City, with the JO title on the line, these tenets provided the edge Indio needed. They shut out Mission City while striking for the game-winning goal with less than a minute on the clock for a thrilling victory. Baker credits Lowell's recipe for success as a major influence on his own coaching philosophy.

By the time Indio had finished celebrating their national championship, the next part of Lowell's grand plan was in place – a trip to New Zealand the following summer. But there was plenty of work to be done at home before heading overseas. While still featuring a young lineup in the fall of 1976, the Rajahs of Indio High won the Ivy League, knocking off league power Riverside Poly. Although Indio failed to reach the semifinals in the CIF playoffs, their progress was significant enough that Coach Lowell knew his program was right on track to reach its longer-term goals.

The next step – getting the team to New Zealand – would provide Lowell's boys the opportunity to bond together through travel, while getting a taste of international competition. The trip required creative fundraising. In an effort to raise money, the team partnered with a radio station that ran out of a hotel in Indio. While the station broadcast all over the desert, the water polo team conducted a swim-a-thon in the hotel pool. With each lap representing a mile, the boys set out to swim 7,000 laps, roughly the distance from Indio to New Zealand. They swam in shifts, camping out overnight, starting on Friday afternoon and ending mid-day on Saturday. The whole time, their efforts were being broadcast on the radio, resulting in donations of nearly $20,000 from the desert community of 19,000 residents.

The swim-a-thon made the team near-celebrities. The people of Indio knew about the water polo boys that won a national championship and were now going to travel overseas. Everyone on the team got passports for their first international travel. It was unheard of in the small town. Baker described life in the desert as, "You're in the desert, you stay in the desert. People in the desert weren't doing those type of things." The community saw the water polo team as constantly on the move, playing in Orange County, in the LA beach cities, and around the world. It was exciting to the boys and to the people of Indio.

Lowell was proud of the community involvement, writing in a 1978 *Water Polo Scoreboard* article, "Not only did we make the trip, we went in style with team blazers and a sendoff by the mayor."

The boys from Indio traveled for three weeks. Two were spent in New Zealand before a week in Australia and finally two non-water polo days in Tahiti. Baker called it "the absolute experience of a lifetime."

But Lowell's plan was still in motion, and the high school season would be his next masterpiece. The now-seasoned Rajahs stormed through their league and barged their way to the CIF-2A finals. The project Lowell began three summers before was complete when Indio won the 1977 CIF title over Orange County power El Dorado. Indio went on to the silver medal at the 1978 JOs and a CIF runner-up finish in Baker's senior year. Dr. John Lowell built Indio into a player on the water polo landscape.

The coach's ability to build a program with long-term vision had a lasting effect on the one-time goalie whom Lowell plucked off the basketball court. Guy Baker had listened and learned from Lowell. The mentor's influence in no small part gave Baker the blueprint to be a program-builder himself.

☉☉☉☉☉☉

When it came to qualifying for the 2000 Olympic Games, it was clear that for the United States women, there was a route that could be considered its "best chance." Not quite a shortcut, but a route to qualification based on continental representation. The first chance to qualify would be a duel waged between North American neighbors Canada and the United States.

Winnipeg, Canada, provided the backdrop for the dramatic battle to claim a spot in the first-ever Olympic field. At stake in the 1999 FINA World Cup were continental bids for the Americas and Europe. The highest-finishing team from those continents would join host nation Australia in the 2000 Games. Featuring the world's eight top-ranked teams, the World Cup was a fitting site of the first Olympic qualifying event.

While the United States and Canada were in the same preliminary group, the Olympic bid promised to one of the rivals wouldn't necessarily be decided head-to-head in the pool. All that mattered was the final tournament standings, regardless of the outcome of the first round game. It was possible for the qualification to be decided as early as the conclusion of the group stage, if one team reached the semifinals and the other did not. And while the United States women grabbed the upper hand with a 6-5 victory over Canada in the group stage, their fate ultimately proved to be a rematch with Canada in the fifth-place game.

With Olympic dreams in the balance, the United States team fell flat, succumbing to Canada by a score of 6-4. The failure to repeat their success of just a few days prior proved costly. The pain of this loss stung every member of the team like none before.

To the glee of its home crowd, Canada had qualified for the first Olympic field in Sydney. The United States players, stunned, remained poolside struggling to process the loss as their continental rival rejoiced in the middle of the tank.

Long after the victors left the pool to continue their merriment elsewhere, United States captain Julie Swail and longtime National Team veteran Maureen O'Toole swam methodically back and forth in the warm-up pool, their strokes heavy with defeat. When Swail climbed from the water, O'Toole was alone, standing in the shallow end, hands on the gutter, eyes fixed forward. The feeling of shock was still fresh, and her mind had not yet moved on to what the team would have to accomplish if their journey was to reach the land Down Under. For the moment, the dream was derailed up north, dashed in Winnipeg.

The United States still had a chance to qualify for the Olympics. The continental bid was universally viewed as the simplest path to Sydney. The Olympic Games Qualification Tournament in April of 2000 was now the only remaining chance for the United States women.

Members of the coaching staff dealt with the reality of this twist in the journey in their own ways. Assistant coach Chris Duplanty ran. Without a word to Baker, Duplanty left the Pan Am Pool and ran back to the hotel, a distance of slightly less than five miles, in his coaching clothes and only sandals on his feet. It wasn't long before he was carrying the sandals: it was easier to run with bare feet.

Baker and team manager Michelle Pickering killed time that afternoon in a movie theater, viewing *Star Wars Episode I: The Phantom Menace*. The movie had a numbing effect that Baker was desperately looking for to deal with the defeat. The film fulfilled Baker's wish to simply get away, without having to talk to anyone or think about the game or the new task ahead.

But the retreat away from the team, water polo, the Canadians, and the future wouldn't last long. In the grand tradition begun in 1979 at the World Cup in Merced, the tournament committee hosted an awards banquet that evening. Although it took a long time to build up the resolve to go to the event, Baker and the team attended. Putting the situation in perspective, Baker knew that a challenge awaited the group, but there was work to be done and time to do it. This opportunity had slipped through their hands, but another was there for the taking.

Baker vividly remembers his thought as he walked into the banquet room: *It's going to change.*

Because it was the first-ever Olympic qualifier for women's water polo, the 1999 World Cup was unique. Around the banquet room, each team sat together at a large table of their own. The setting offered an unforgettable snapshot of the immense gravity this tournament held, like none before it. The emotions at every table were uncomplicated and told the story of each federation as they prepared to leave Winnipeg.

The Dutch were in a celebrating mood. The team still basked in the glow of their Olympic qualification earned the night before, when they clinched the highest finish by a European nation. And they were back on top of the women's water polo world after slipping to Italy in the gold medal match in the World Championships the previous year. The silver medal winners from Australia were pleased with their performance overall, but, as is commonplace among runner-up finishers, showed dissatisfaction with falling just short of the top of the podium after their 7-6 loss in the final. Their quest for gold in Sydney would require more than their current effort.

Italy, the reigning world champion, settled for bronze in Winnipeg, defeating Hungary in overtime to cap the World Cup. But while the most common measure of success on the world level is winning medals, this tournament wasn't about hardware. It was about the Olympics, and the Italians had failed in their mission. The mood at the Hungarian table was understandably dour. The Hungarians had been pushed around by Australia in a 6-3 semifinal loss, ending their qualification bid. Hungary left Winnipeg with no Olympics and no medal.

Without a doubt, the most joyous table in the room was that of the Canadian team. No tournament in history had had a fifth-place prize. Failing to medal meant nothing – fifth place was good enough to make reservations for Sydney. Hours removed from their victory in the pool over the United States, the Canadians were still on cloud nine as the banquet commenced, a perch they would deservedly occupy long after the event was over.

While Russia blew out Greece for seventh place that morning, both teams knew they were far from threatening the front runners, and there was a lot of work to do before either could even begin to entertain thoughts about Sydney.

The United States team sat together at the banquet, enjoying their camaraderie without a trace of moping – their mood buoyed by the extra drink coupons purchased and distributed by Michelle Pickering. Being unified as a team at the banquet was good for spirits, but camaraderie alone couldn't erase the reality of where the team stood after their failure to capitalize on the only "shortcut" they would ever see during this quest to be a part of Olympic history.

"It was a hard pill to swallow," Baker said. "There were a lot of hard pills to swallow during that time."

1978 FINA World Championships – Berlin

3

LOVE OF THE GAME

1976 USA-Australia game   **Maureen O'Toole**
1977 Commerce Internationals
1978 FINA World Championships
1979 FINA World Cup

The greatest American women's water polo career of the pre-Olympic era was nearly short-circuited before it began.

With teams arriving in Commerce in December of 1977 for the first women's international tournament to be held in the United States, the pool of players who would represent the USA awaited their team assignments. In addition to teams from Australia, Canada and Holland, there would be three United States entries. The Commerce Internationals marked the debut of the United States Women's National Team in tournament play.

Sixteen-year-old Maureen O'Toole had recently burst onto the scene, starting on the boys' team at powerful Wilson High School in Long Beach. Already named an All-American at her first women's national championships in Miami, she had speed, athletic intelligence, and no shortage of confidence.

Playing with future Olympian Jody Campbell and the rest of the boys on the highly ranked Bruins varsity, O'Toole thought she was pretty good. So good, she figured, that she was a lock to be named to the A team for the Commerce tournament. As she thought about it more, it crossed her mind that perhaps her youth and lack of experience compared to the veterans in the squad might land her on the B roster this time around.

She was mistaken.

"They put me on the C team," she said, "and I was pissed."

A self-described cry baby, perhaps due to being the youngest sibling in the O'Toole family, Maureen described her indignance at the decision.

"I went home to my mom that day and I said, 'You know what, Mom? They put me on the C team. Can you believe that? I quit.'"

Janice O'Toole's reply was simple.

"Oh, you quit?"

"Yep," confirmed Maureen before storming up to her room, steaming.

She spent all night thinking about her assignment to the C team. In the morning, her mind firmly made up, she went downstairs, and asked Janice for a ride to Commerce.

"My mom said to me, 'Oh, I thought you quit,'" Maureen recalls. "That's how my mom was. She was so great. She stayed out of it, but not really. I had to tell her, 'No, I'm not quitting.'"

Little did National Team coach Stan Sprague and his coaching staff realize, their decision provided the motivating factor that Maureen O'Toole would use at the Commerce Internationals and throughout her storied National Team career spanning more than twenty years.

O'Toole credits the setback for changing her as a person and a player. She accepted her selection to the C team but vowed to never put herself in that position again. At the Commerce Internationals, she set out to prove the coaches wrong. She carried this attitude with her for the rest of her career.

"I was going to show everyone that they had made a mistake," O'Toole recalls. "I was going to work harder than everybody else in the world, because I was going to be the best player in the world, so nobody could ever question it. It started right then and there."

Once the tournament began, O'Toole quickly made her point. Despite the USA "C" team suffering lopsided losses to the powerful Canadian, Dutch, Australian, and USA "A" and "B" teams, she was named to the All-World Team at the conclusion of the competition. The women's water polo world was put on notice that the young Maureen O'Toole intended to be a force to be reckoned with for years to come.

☺☺☺☺☺☺

Growing up in the Naples community of Long Beach, a young Maureen O'Toole spent almost every day of every summer either in the water or on it. An avid swimmer coached by legends Skip Kenney, Don Gambrill, and Jay Huneke at the local club called Phillips 66, she was also sailing Alamitos Bay from age seven. Maureen and her older siblings Mike and Colleen all had their own Naples Sabots and raced for the Alamitos Bay Yacht Club.

An accomplished sailor, Maureen also raced 505s and Lido 14s, winning the national championships in the latter when she was fifteen.

Soon after she was introduced to water polo at age thirteen by her first coach, Gary Robinett, sailing, and swimming took a back seat. She immediately loved the game and the social aspect that made it more appealing than swimming up and down the black lines. O'Toole remembers learning to play water polo with Sandy Vessey and Jody Campbell at Long Beach City College.

When Kelly Kemp started a girls team in Long Beach a couple of years later, O'Toole took her first water polo trip to Nationals in Miami, and she was hooked. But there weren't high school water polo teams for girls, so she kept playing other sports in addition to playing water polo whenever she could.

In junior high, O'Toole was a dedicated swimmer who also loved joining in on all sports with her brother, Mike. Every day after school, she could be found playing football or basketball or whatever the boys were doing. At school, she ran track and played volleyball. O'Toole figured she would go out for the volleyball and swim teams when she started high school at nearby Woodrow Wilson Classical High School, more commonly known as Long Beach Wilson.

O'Toole and her friend Becky Black, whom she met through sailing, went out for the volleyball team in the fall of 1976. After one preseason practice, the two were walking home when Bob Gruniesson, the JV water polo coach, pulled over in his car and asked them why they hadn't been to the pool for water polo practice. Gruniesson knew about O'Toole and Black and had expected they would join the high school team.

The girls reported that they were in the midst of volleyball tryouts. They were flattered by the invitation, but truthfully, they didn't want to play on the boys' water polo team. Starting high school figured to be enough of a transition, and they were hesitant to join a boys' sport at the same time.

Gruniesson encouraged the girls to rethink their decision, guaranteeing they would have fun and be successful as well. The feeling of being wanted was enough to change their minds, and the two girls left volleyball behind. O'Toole credits Gruniesson not only for steering her to the pool that fall, but for making her experience a life-changing one.

"When you play on the guys' team, it starts with the coach," she said. "The coach has to respect you and give you respect. For me as a girl out there playing with boys, I had to be like one of the guys and not expect to be treated any differently. I got respect from my coaches and my teammates, and therefore, from everybody else."

O'Toole played hard against the boys and expected they would play hard against her. She was determined to be treated just like one of them in the water.

On the JV team in her first year at Wilson, O'Toole showed a talent for the game that was enhanced by the fundamentals taught by Gruniesson. The skills that she learned at Wilson formed the backbone of her own coaching philosophy, and she knows how fortunate she was to have elevated her game under the tutelage of first Gruniesson, and then varsity coach Rick Jones. And she is grateful for the leadership of her coaches, who made playing on the boys' team a joy and, as promised by Gruniesson, a success.

Soon enough, respect for O'Toole's water polo talents reached far beyond Long Beach. She would gain worldwide recognition representing the United States in international competition from 1977 through 1994, when she retired after the FINA World Championships in Rome. Although women's water polo made incremental gains in gender equity throughout her career, the sport itself fell short on respect within the aquatics community. Without a spot in the Olympic Games alongside men's water polo, the women's game found little support. When it was clear that the 1996 Olympics in Atlanta would not be the first to include her sport, O'Toole bid farewell to the National Team and the international game.

◎◎◎◎◎◎

The United States and Australian women's water polo teams have been locked in a rivalry from day one of their existences. Over the course of the Olympic era, the two nations have clashed twice in the semifinals and once each in the bronze medal and gold medal matches. International training partners bonded through common language and similar water polo philosophies, the United States and Australian women have built a familiarity and friendship that began with an unplanned matchup in the middle of the Pacific Ocean in 1976.

That year, the first Women's National Team from Australia arrived in Honolulu to compete in the U.S. Women's Senior Outdoor Water Polo Championships. Australian Pat Jones led the charge to establish an Australian Women's National Championship in the early 1970s and played an instrumental role in arranging the selection and travel of the historic inaugural Australian squad.

Being close to the administrators at the top of the Australian Swimming Union (ASU), Jones knew she wanted to see the Australian women travel overseas, just as the men had done for years. Always with an eye toward making women's water polo legitimate and official, Jones told ASU officials she wanted the team to wear the Australian pocket, referring to the nation's coat of arms with its recognizable emu and red kangaroo.

With the pocket properly embroidered on their official blazers, Jones was pleased with the credibility that came along with the symbol. "We had arrived," she said. "We weren't just this ditzy team going away, and 'Who do they think they are?' No, we were a real representative team. I was quite proud of getting them there."

The championship featured eleven teams, hailing from California, Arizona, Florida, Washington, and Hawaii, plus the Australian entry. Merced coach Flip

Hassett, the National Chair of Women's Water Polo, commented that this field was one of the strongest in history, noting that the reigning Indoor and Outdoor National Champions had never been entered in the same tournament. Fullerton (FAST) "A" and North Miami Beach held those titles, and along with Hassett's Merced "A," Commerce, Arizona's Red Devils, Rogers Water Polo Club of Washington, the University of Hawaii, and local squad Windward "Y," were eager to match up with the visitors from Down Under.

According to Hassett, the only superpower club not in attendance was Cincinnati.

By the time the tournament reached the semifinal stage, the cream had risen to the top. FAST narrowly beat North Miami Beach in one semi, and Australia outlasted Merced in the other. The gold medal game featured an international matchup with the United States' best club facing off against the visiting Australian women. Fullerton, coached by Stan Sprague, got off to an early lead, although the teams waged a defensive battle throughout the first half. The action picked up in the third quarter, and the scoreboard showed a tie with one quarter left to play. After trading goals early in the quarter, two quick strikes by FAST's Kerron Cozens and Sue McIntyre provided the winning edge, as the American team prevailed to claim the tournament title.

Australian coach Paul Gair declared the experience a success, stating, "It's the first time a girls' team has gone outside of Australia as a National Team to compete in a major tournament. We combined girls from about six of what amounts to your states, and since this is our winter, most of our kids were on holidays from competition."

But before the visitors went into full holiday mode in Honolulu, a historic game took place. The first clash of Women's National Teams from the United States and Australia was an unplanned addition after the conclusion of the tournament.

"Basically, we just decided, 'Let's stick in another game,'" Fullerton coach Stan Sprague said.

Sprague and Flip Hassett approached the tournament organizers with the idea to stage a National Team game and met with an enthusiastic response.

The two coaches put together an American all-star team based on performances during the recently finished Nationals.

"We just said, 'Okay, let's just put these girls together and let's go have a game and see how we do,'" Sprague said.

On August 22, 1976, two days after the conclusion of the U.S. Outdoor Nationals, a rivalry was born. Coached by Sprague and Hassett, a United States women's team hit the water against Australia for the very first time. The contest was played under FINA, rather than AAU, rules, officiated by American Doug Arth.

The athletes selected to play for the United States relished the opportunity to join forces against a foreign foe. Dion Gray remembers the excitement amongst the American players. "We thought it was awesome to be able to play with the cream of the crop. Just take our top players, play together in an actual game. We thought it was a really big deal," she said.

In a low-scoring affair, the teams traded a goal apiece in the first quarter. The second quarter began with both teams defending for the entirety of the 45-second shot clock. The Aussies broke through first in the frame, drawing an exclusion against the United States' Nancy Bishop and using all but fives seconds of their 60-second player advantage before Sue Reaburn beat goalkeeper Lynn Taylor. The United States responded quickly, as Vaune Kadlubek earned a penalty and cashed it in herself. The score was tied 2-2 at the midway point.

Kadlubek continued to dominate the center position, scoring twice in the third quarter to put the United States ahead. A power-play goal by Carol Angland cut the margin before the end of the third. The United States opened the fourth quarter with increased intensity on the counterattack, producing a goal by Bishop to open up a two-goal lead. The ensuing Australian possession earned a penalty and a chance to close the gap, but American goalkeeper Gray thwarted the attempt, and the United States piled on goals from Kristi Shepard and shortly after, a fourth by Kadlubek.

In its debut as a National Team, the United States earned a 7-3 victory.

The teams locked horns again in the afternoon, this time with an expanded United States roster. The eleven All-American selections who played the first game had first half duty, while the eight tournament Honorable Mention picks would gain international experience in the second half. Hassett wrote in *Water*

Polo Scoreboard, "This format enabled as many of our players to participate in an international game and to gain exposure and stimulate interest from the rest of the American women's teams."

As the National Championship-winning coach, Sprague was put in charge of the American team. The United States motored to a halftime lead, but Australia's offense came to life in the fourth quarter, as the visitors rallied for a 6-5 win and a split of the two-game series. Kadlubek led the series in goals with five, followed by teammate Debbi Decker's four, while the Australian pair of Angland and Debbie Handley tallied three each.

This friendly meeting in Hawaii served as the precursor to countless colossal clashes between the United States and Australia. An important relationship began, setting the stage for bigger international events and critical steps toward credibility for the international women's game.

@@@@@@

At the end of 1977, Sandy Nitta brought the women's water polo world to Commerce, California, for the Commerce Internationals, the largest tournament of its kind to date and the first women's international tournament in the United States. The United States fielded A, B, and C teams, and the Australian National Team returned for its second tour. Powerhouse Sainte Foy from Quebec headlined a large contingent of clubs from Canada. Other entries from north of the border included North Montreal, Manitoba, British Columbia, Ontario, and CAMO from Montreal. The tournament also featured the first visit from European women's teams, as Dutch clubs De Robben and Zwemvereniging DSZ accepted Nitta's invitation. A fifth country, Mexico, rounded out the international entries. Club teams from Commerce and the University of Arizona completed the 16-team field.

Nitta, who swam the 200 breaststroke as a 15-year-old in the Tokyo Olympics in 1964, initially presented a tournament budget of $250 to the City of Commerce to cover cake and punch for the teams at a post-tournament party. The city council, however, was intrigued by the idea of bringing teams from three continents to Commerce. They saw the opportunity to create a special event for international guests, and they seized it. The council approved providing housing, meals, and local transportation to the teams. A committee planned trips to Disneyland, the Tournament of Roses Parade on New Year's Day, Tijuana, and popular shopping locales. Including an upgraded post-tournament dinner-dance for all the foreign teams, the budget for Nitta's brainchild reached $68,000.

Commerce Internationals

FIRST U.S. INTERNATIONAL WOMEN'S TOURNEY

Following an official opening ceremony with all the participants at the City of Commerce's 25-yard shallow-deep indoor pool, the competition kicked off. The tournament produced two undefeated teams heading into the final day of games, Sainte Foy and the Australian National Team, who had played to a draw. Competition for the top three spots was tight, with Sainte Foy emerging victorious over USA "A" in the last game of the round-robin format. Sainte Foy star Sylvie Dion clinched the title with a desperation shot from near mid-pool that nestled in the upper left corner with four seconds remaining on the clock. Australia took the silver without a loss on its record, having drawn with both Sainte Foy and USA "A."

Dion's dagger just before the buzzer turned the United States' fortunes from gold to bronze, as a tie would have been enough to claim the tournament championship. USA "B" rounded out the top four. For coach Claude Lavoie's Sainte Foy team, the Commerce Internationals title was a signature accomplishment in the midst of an unbeaten streak that lasted from 1972 to 1980.

While international competition was in its nascent stage, the teams from Holland brought a wealth of water polo experience. The DSZ club featured veterans of up to seventeen years who had played together for many the majority of their careers. The oldest player in the tournament was De Robben's 45-year-old Dicky Kloek. An Olympic backstroker in the 1948 London Games, Kloek began playing water polo in the late 1940s. "All the girls played water polo then, mostly swimmers who were keeping in shape," she said.

Their first encounters with North American teams proved somewhat surprising to the Dutch. Kloek explained that until coming to Commerce, they had no knowledge of the different styles of water polo being played by the Canadians and the Americans and were surprised by the amount of physicality, especially at the center position.

"We do not play that way in Holland, and we are not used to it," she said.

The *Water Polo Scoreboard* report on the tournament noted the strength of Sainte Foy's outside shooting and Australia's "smooth and disciplined" game. Australian coach Paul Gair received compliments for his dignified coaching style in stressful situations, and his team was called the "sentimental favorites, largely because of the professional behavior of the coach and the team."

While coming within seconds of winning the tournament championship, the American players, led by Fullerton's Sprague, were learning the intricacies of competing as a National Team, as opposed to with their club. *Water Polo Scoreboard* reported, "For those who belong to the team-playing-together theory of excellence, vs. the all-star approach, this U.S. squad was proof positive that a team of all-stars, gathered together at the last minute, does not have the quality of togetherness that is desirable at moments like these. Had the girls had months to practice, instead of days, the result might have been different."

An All-Tournament Team was selected – in essence, the first-ever "All-World" Team. Australia's Carol Hudson was named Most Valuable Player.

Teammates Judy Darbyshire and Debbie Handley joined Hudson on the All-World Team. Sue Bow, Kristi Shepard, and Sue McIntyre represented USA "A." Sainte Foy's Sylvie Thibault, Johanne Gervais, Dion, and goalkeeper Lyne Thivierge received All-World recognition, as did De Robben's M. Renshoff. The Second Team featured goalkeeper Lynn Taylor and Kadlubek of USA "A," as well as athletes from Montreal, Mexico, DSZ, De Robben, and Commerce.

The final spot on the All-World Second Team was earned by Maureen O'Toole of USA "C." As she had vowed when she was placed on the C team, O'Toole proved she belonged amongst America's best.

@@@@@@

"FLASH! Women's Water Polo may enjoy a new distinction. There is talk among the upper echelon of having women's matches at the 1978 World Championships in Berlin on a trial basis."
– Water Polo Scoreboard, July/August 1977

Women's water polo made its FINA World Swimming Championships debut in Berlin in 1978 on an exhibition basis, joining the aquatic disciplines of swimming, diving, synchronized swimming, and men's water polo. Prior to its addition to the Berlin program, an international women's match took place at Belmont Plaza in Long Beach as part of the men's Can-Am-Mex international series in 1977. The match was intended to show the FINA Technical Water Polo Committee (TWPC) delegates present for the men's tournament that women's water polo was worthy of a place in FINA events. When the Canadian federation declined to send a National Team because of the cost, Claude Lavoie's Sainte Foy club raised the money and traveled to Long Beach for a single game against the United States. The home team prevailed, 3-2. The attendance of Sainte Foy paid dividends, as the demonstration led to the TWPC recommendation to hold a women's exhibition tournament in Berlin.

The inclusion at the World Championships, albeit as an unofficial event, was an important step toward being recognized on the international stage, and many supporters of women's water polo put the Olympic Games squarely in their sights. The "Big Four" nations of women's water polo – the United States, Australia, Canada, and Holland – attended; the host West German team rounded out the field.

The first major travel by the United States Women's National Team was led by head coach Stan Sprague and team manager Jennie Jacobsen. Everyone paid their own way for the trip to Germany – staff included. No one in the United States' travel party had any significant travel experience when their flight from Los Angeles to Frankfurt took to the air.

After a total travel time of over thirty hours by plane to Europe and train through Germany, the team arrived in Berlin. From the train station, the sixteen Americans walked forty minutes to the hotel, luggage in tow. Walking into the hotel like zombies at 11:00 p.m., eager for showers and a nice bed and pillow, the team had to put those thoughts on hold when the hotel couldn't find their reservation. With everything finally sorted out and rooms assigned, the United States women's water polo team had finally arrived at its first World Championship.

The next day, the women's team received their tournament credentials with the rest of the United States athletes at the official delegation hotel. They enviously admired the team gear from sponsor Arena distributed to all the athletes except for women's water polo. Despite this disappointment, the water polo team was thrilled that their credentials granted admission to any of the aquatic events, including swimming and men's water polo, as well as free transportation by subway or bus throughout the city.

In the days leading up to the competition, the athletes had practice sessions at different pools around the city and explored Berlin in their spare time. They were pleased by a delivery of Arena bags and t-shirts, and by the invitation to dinner with all the American athletes before the opening ceremony. As the entire U.S. delegation began marching en masse toward the stadium entrance, the men's water polo team manager approached Jennie Jacobsen and told her there could be a problem with the women's team participating since they were not official participants in the World Championships. Jacobsen emphatically responded, "No way, we are marching!" Without hinting at a potential problem, she raced up and down the line of women's water polo players telling them to keep walking and to enjoy the historic moment.

The opening ceremonies took place in the Olympiastadion in Berlin, with 100,000 seats, mandated by Adolf Hitler to outdo Los Angeles' Olympic Stadium of the 1932 Games. At the 1936 Olympics, spectators in the Olympiastadion, including Hitler, witnessed Jesse Owens' four-gold-medal performance in track and field.

"We were super excited to go and be part of it," Dion Gray recalls. "The most amazing thing was going to the opening ceremonies and being in the Berlin stadium, which has so much history. And to have all the athletes, spectators, flags, and we're participating. Marching in as a country, that was crazy. This was like the Olympics for us."

While marching in the opening ceremonies was a highlight remembered fondly by Gray and her teammates, the exhibition status left the women's water polo logistics a notch below World Championship level. Women's games were scheduled for after the men's slate was finished for the day. Very few spectators remained on hand to view the women's matches. Late schedule changes to the women's tournament on the eve of the competition caused further logistical difficulties for the teams.

In the water, the competition was fierce between the top four teams, with a young West German entry far behind in experience and skill. The tournament opened with Australia blanking the hosts, who had practiced for roughly two hours together prior to their debut, 33-0.

Australian captain Betty Anderson, a veteran of the inaugural USA-Australia match two years prior, recalled her first world championship outing. "Some of them were possibly playing their first or second tournament ever, coming up against a very strong side. I was embarrassed because Stan Hammond, who was coaching us at that stage, did not do anything by halves and he made us slaughter these poor German girls."

The following game for West Germany was not much better, as the powerful Dutch prevailed, 28-0.

The United States took a different approach with its overwhelmed opponent. While they peppered the net with twenty-six goals, coach Stan Sprague conspired with goalkeeper Gray to get the home team on the scoreboard.

Pretending to go for a block, Gray let one slip by, to the glee of the West German side. "They were ecstatic that they scored a goal in the World Championships. I remember them just being happy," Gray recalled.

Among the traditional powerhouse nations, goals were at a premium, and the margin for error was slim. The United States opened its first competition in Europe with a resounding victory over neighbor Canada behind three goals by Simone La Pay. Following the win, the United States enjoyed a bye day, returning to the pool on day three for a key showdown with Australia.

Now in their third year of competing against one another, the United States and Australia had begun to develop familiarity in both personnel and tactics. With similar styles focused on defensive pressure, speed, and counterattacking, the teams played evenly throughout the contest. After trailing 1-0 after the first quarter, Maureen O'Toole tallied twice in the second to give the United States the lead at halftime. Early in the third quarter, her third goal of the day increased the lead, but Australian stars Debbie Handley and Cathy Turner evened it up before the end of the quarter.

Both teams played staunch defense to begin the fourth, but Australia broke through, with goals from center Jennifer Morris and another by Turner, to capture a 5-3 lead. O'Toole brought the United States back to within one with a six-on-five goal, but the Americans were unable to convert a last chance with a player advantage in the final minute, falling by a score of 5-4.

The United States bounced back from the disappointing loss by easily dispatching West Germany. The win guaranteed the United States of a medal heading into the final match of the tournament, and gold was still within the team's reach.

The matchup was one of American quickness against Dutch strength. The United States held the advantage at halftime, but the experienced Dutch thwarted all offensive attempts in the second half and pulled even for a tie. The result was enough for Holland to claim the title of women's World Champion, with Australia winning silver and the United States bronze.

The demonstration of women's water polo at the multi-discipline FINA World Championships had been a success. Not all of the experience was equitable to those of other athletes, including the men's water polo teams, but the women had taken the first step onto the world stage.

Neither the United States nor Australian women were lodged with their main delegations, or with the men's water polo teams. The Australian women stayed in a youth hostel with a curfew. The American women made their own accommodations at a local hotel. The Australian women, who were not included in their country delegation in the opening ceremonies, joined their fellow athletes, including their rivals from America, in the closing.

Sprague summed up the opportunity and its relevance to the movement to elevate the status of international women's water polo: "This was an exhibition idea as a way to see if women's water polo was ready to go to the Olympics. This was really early on, and I think a lot of us were a little bit naive at that point. If we handled it differently, we might have gotten women's water polo at the Olympic level sooner. I don't know. But we had to do it then to start getting the seeds planted."

@@@@@@

The seeds were in the ground, and the next blossom of growth would be a return of international women's competition to United States soil. At the Commerce Internationals in 1977, individuals from several nations formed a committee of sorts, to push forward the women's game internationally. A major part of its strategy was to hold one major international women's water polo event each year.

Following the success of the World Championships in Berlin, the 1979 event was slated for Curacao, to be run by the Dutch federation. A last minute change, however, put the event in the hands of newly appointed United States National Team head coach Flip Hassett and his Merced club boosters. The Merced College pool was the center of the women's water polo world from June 29 through July 1, as six teams from five nations competed in the first women's FINA World Cup. New Zealand was the newcomer to the lineup, which otherwise included the four pioneering nations of women's water polo – the United States, Australia, Canada, and the Netherlands. The United States entered both A and B teams.

Although the men's inaugural version of the FINA Cup had just taken place in Rijeka, Yugoslavia, two months prior, the women's event initially was not sponsored by FINA – in fact, the organizers paid a fee to use the name. But the price was a logical one to pay in hopes of bringing the women's game closer to the Olympic conversation.

"We just did it," recalls Sandy Nitta, referring to organizing the tournament without FINA's helping hand. "In fact, we had to raise money. It cost us $10,000 to use the name FINA, and the fundraising we did at the tournament, t-shirts and stuff like that, went to paying FINA to use that name."

The event was supported whole-heartedly by the local community, and interest spread throughout the San Joaquin Valley. As in Berlin, accommodations were not posh, but the teams were appreciative of their lodging options. Nearby Castle Air Force Base offered inexpensive housing for the Australian and Canadian teams, while the teams from Holland and New Zealand stayed in local motels.

The American team enjoyed the home cooking of local families who offered their homes to the twenty-two women of the USA "A" and "B" teams. The community made fast friends with the players, showing up at practices, loaning out their family cars, and keeping everyone very well fed.

Social events included an official reception for team officials and FINA representative Henny Keetalaar of Holland, a cocktail reception, a farm-style BBQ at Lake Yosemite, and a post-tournament awards banquet for all participants.

Before the games began, the opening ceremonies took place, and each coach received a key to the city from the Mayor of Merced, Robert L. Hart. After an official welcome from FINA representative Keetalaar, the action commenced. In the pool, the competitors were now quite familiar with each other. Many had faced off against one another in Honolulu, Commerce, or Berlin in previous years. The familiarity raised the level of intensity, as individual and national pride and the quest for global supremacy spurred on the athletes and teams.

With only three days to play five games, there were two rounds played on both Friday and Saturday. The United States got rolling on Friday with an easy and expected win over New Zealand in the morning before an exhibition against USA "B" in the evening session.

On Saturday, the teams returned for another two games each in the baking heat of the Merced summer. In a critical tilt, the United States and Holland waged a back-and-forth affair. Maureen O'Toole fired in the tying goal with 30 seconds to play, earning the Americans a tie against the European power. The United States finished the hugely successful day by dispatching Canada. The standings heading into the final round saw the United States tied with World Champion Holland. Australia sat just behind in third, still in contention for the World Cup title.

The United States and Australia opened the final day of the World Cup with a display fitting of the burgeoning rivalry. Needing a victory to keep its gold medal hopes alive, the United States responded quickly to an early deficit and used an offensive outburst to regain the lead. Three goals in the final two minutes of the second quarter put the United States ahead, 4-2. The team maintained this cushion throughout the third quarter and extended the lead to 7-3 in the fourth. A late rally by Australia came too late, and the United States closed out an 8-7 victory.

The United States knew their hopes for the gold medal were alive, depending on the result of the final game of the tournament, between Holland and Canada. For the Dutch, a victory would seal the World Cup championship. A tie or loss would hand the title to the host United States. While anxious about the result being out of their hands, the American women were pleased to avenge their loss to Australia in Berlin – the team's only defeat of 1978.

The United States watched in earnest as Canada sped to an early lead over Holland. The interest turned to joy as the Canadians poured in goals while holding the powerful Dutch offense in check, resulting in a 7-3 win. The 1979 World Cup ended in triumph – the community of Merced embraced the sport of women's water polo; the international competition was superb, and the host United States was on top of the women's water polo world, capturing gold for the first time.

Returning to the top of the podium would be a quest picked up by multiple generations of players, coaches, and administrators over the ensuing years. It would take much longer than anyone could imagine while basking in the glow of gold in the hot Merced afternoon.

Australian women demonstrate at the Sydney Airport – May, 2000

4

THE FIGHT

Julie Swail

Gubba Sheehy

Like most girls, Brenda Villa played 10-and-under water polo on a co-ed team. She was just as good as the boys – bigger than them, too, at that age. When she moved to the 12-and-under team, she was teammates with her brother Edgar and many of her friends who were boys. And for some reason, one of the best offensive water polo players of her generation began her career as a goalkeeper.

Villa suspects it was because she was a girl and the boys wanted to score goals. Looking back, Villa finds both pros and cons to the time she spent guarding the net at a young age. Being in the goal allowed her to watch the action unfold in front of her, to which she attributed her exceptional vision as her game developed. On the negative side, any time her team lost, she took the blame, no matter how the defense played that day.

While she had fun playing on co-ed teams as a 10- and 12-and-under, the Junior Olympics was her favorite tournament of the year because it was a chance to play in the girls-only divisions.

"I remember being really excited playing on an all-girls team because then you could really shine," she said. "It was exciting. But then I realized, if I was going to play in high school, it was back to playing on the boys' team."

Villa looked forward to playing in high school because schools like UCLA and Stanford had recently gone varsity and were offering water polo scholarships. Knowing how difficult it would be for her parents to pay for college, she set her sights on raising her game, hoping to catch the attention of college coaches. She didn't mind playing on a boys' team – she had done that for her whole career.

Villa arrived in high school with more fanfare than the average freshman, having been featured in *Sports Illustrated for Kids* the summer before her freshman year.

"That was definitely something that people liked to talk about," she said. "I could only imagine some of those teammates thinking, 'Really? There's a girl, and they're making a big deal out of her, and she's going to play on the boys' team.' Then you just play, and it's all about water polo. Who cares what gender you are if you can play?"

She tried out for the varsity at Bell Gardens High School and made it, joining two other girls already on the team. Her most vivid memory of the year was Bell Gardens' season-ending loss in the playoffs to Peninsula High School. "We made it to CIF, and we're playing in the second round. We lose, and of course it's my fault because they dropped off the girl," she said.

Years later, Villa found out that Peninsula's goalkeeper was Olympic silver medalist Merrill Moses – who confirmed that the game plan was, in fact, to drop off the freshman girl.

During her high school career, Villa always had a least one other female teammate. While the girls could prove themselves for playing time through skill and ability, one area where they were held back was in strength training. By the time she was a senior, she was going to National Team training camps and felt that she would benefit from developing her strength.

"My male teammates were lifting weights and doing extra training," she recalled. "Our coach wouldn't allow the girls to lift weights with the boys. He said it would be a distraction. It was never an option. I remember asking if I could, because it was something that would help me."

Competing on the international level as a smaller player, she wanted to make sure she could hold her own physically.

The solution was to have Villa and the girls do more band work. When she arrived at Stanford as a college freshman, she could barely bench press the bar. She took gentle ribbing from assistant coach Susan Ortwein.

"I had never lifted weights in my life," she said, smiling.

☙☙☙☙☙

Years before Brenda Villa followed her brother into the pool, Leanne Barnes did the same as a university student in Melbourne in the late 1970s. Improving steadily, she eventually gained selection to the Australian National Team in 1978. Barnes described herself as "a bit of an activist" during her university days. As she was training for the 1980 World Cup, to be contested in Holland, the controversy over the Moscow Olympics was hitting close to home. Barnes trained with men who were members of the Australian Olympic team. While the Australian team voted to compete in Moscow, one player stood by his principles and withdrew from the team.

The only player from the state of Victoria on the Women's National Team, Barnes fielded questions about her own intentions, and her political views of the Soviet Union and the Olympics.

"People wanted to know what I was going to do. Was I going to go to the Olympics?" Barnes said. There was an assumption that, having reached the Australian National Team in an Olympic sport, she would be on her way to Moscow that summer.

Many were surprised when Barnes replied that women's water polo was not in the Olympics.

The more she talked about it, the more she felt a flame inside of her. Barnes began a crusade for gender equality in Olympic water polo, fueled by a thought that kept gnawing at her: *This isn't right.*

The journey of international women's water polo from its roots in the late 1970s to the bright lights of the Sydney Olympic Games was a long one, through a maze of bureaucracy with disappointment lurking around every corner. In the early days, a small but dedicated band pushed for growth, setting the stage for the battle for gender equity. Sandy Nitta and Jane Hale from the United States, Claude Lavoie from Canada, Thea de Wit of the Netherlands, and Paul Gair and Pat Jones from Australia were among the coaches and administrators who vowed to increase the legitimacy of women's water polo by creating an international calendar that matched the men's as closely as possible.

In 1978, de Wit formed the committee which pursued the creation of a women's exhibition at the World Championships in Berlin. She was named Chairman, Secretary, and Treasurer of the Women's Promoting Committee of FINA by Honorary Secretary Bob Helmick. As a member of Ligue Européenne de Natation's (LEN) Water Polo Committee Promoting Women's Water Polo, de Wit was instrumental in the increase of women's teams in Europe. At every chance, she brought media attention to women's water polo through interviews and press conferences. Every FINA Technical Water Polo Committee meeting saw de Wit calling attention to the Promoting Committee, urging a room full of men to support the sport by supporting the women around the world who played water polo.

Leanne Barnes joined the cause in 1982, soon after her National Team career ended. A year later, she joined FINA's Women's Promoting Committee. The agenda was clear: Olympic inclusion for women's water polo.

Barnes found the committee work falsely encouraging. Time and again, the gender equity group was promised that women's water polo would be a priority, and individuals within FINA pledged their support in person, only to turn their back when called on for action.

Despite bouts of despondency, Barnes and the committee members always rallied each other to bounce back. "Even when things weren't moving in a positive direction, we would say, 'We're going to just keep on going,'" she said.

Women's water polo was contested at the 1982 FINA World Championships in Guayaquil, Ecuador, once again with exhibition status. Despite a successful tournament, hopes of raising interest for women's water polo in the 1984 Los Angeles Olympics were short-lived. The competition in Guayaquil, won by the Netherlands, while spirited, still included only the four pioneering women's water polo nations. Growth in participating countries on all continents was emerging as a clear necessity before FINA would take women's water polo seriously.

Another issue centered around semantics. The Women's Promoting Committee focused its message on the fact that women's water polo was an event, not a sport. In the Olympics, the sport of aquatics, overseen by FINA, includes multiple disciplines: swimming, diving, synchronized swimming, and water polo. A women's competition would be an additional event in the discipline of water polo, within the sport of aquatics. The distinction was critical. Adding an event to an existing Olympic sport was an entirely different – and more feasible – pursuit from adding a new sport. Water polo was already in the Olympics. The women simply wanted their own event.

With this definition in place, the working group then set out to identify other Olympic events which lacked gender equity. What they found was the women's marathon. After years of lobbying and rebutting chauvinistic ideas that women risked their health competing in endurance races, the women's marathon was approved as a new event by the Executive Board of the IOC in February 1981 with the aim of contesting the race for the first time at the 1984 Olympics in Los Angeles. In September, the IOC voted on and approved the Executive Board's recommendation and the women's marathon became a reality. Barnes and her fellow members of the Women's Promoting Committee cited this case to FINA in their letter-writing campaigns and face-to-face opportunities. In terms of strategy and pecking order, acquiring FINA's support was priority number one – ahead of any dealings with the IOC.

One idea to get a foot in the door was to seek inclusion in the Los Angeles Olympics as a demonstration event – similar to the status of women's water polo at the 1978 and 1982 World Championships – as opposed to a medal event.

Beginning at the 1912 Olympic Games in Stockholm, host nations could decide to include demonstration sports to their particular Olympic program. In most cases, demonstration sports were culturally popular in the host nation or geographic region. The 1912 Stockholm games featured glima, traditional Icelandic wrestling. Other cultural examples include korfball at the 1928 Amsterdam Games, budō at the 1960 Tokyo Games, and Basque pelota in Barcelona in 1992.

Women's water polo actually made its first appearance at the Olympic Games in 1920, when the Antwerp Olympics featured an exhibition between two Dutch teams. Anthony Bijkerk located two references to the event, complete with reference to the chief intention of introducing women's water polo into the Olympic Games as a full-status event.

> On 5 July 1993, I found the answer on the very first page of the Official Yearly Report from the (then) Netherlands Swimming Association for the period 1920-21, which states (Bijkerk translation): "With great pleasure we may refer in this report, which has to be short even on this particular point, to the water polo demonstration match, played in the swimming week of the Olympic Games and which was initiated by the 'Hollandsche Dames Zwemclub' ('Dutch Ladies' Swimming Club') and played by some 14-some ladies from Amsterdam and Rotterdam. We are quite certain, that this exhibition has shown a great propaganda for women water polo and we very much hope, that the International Olympic Committee will honor the request of the Netherlands Swimming Association to include women's water polo in the future program of the Olympic Games."

> I found another clue in the State-Archives in the form of newspaper clippings from the newspaper *De Telegraaf*, which stated:

"Antwerpen, 29 August (by telephone): The last day: . . . Next two ladies' teams from Holland (*sic* - Bijkerk) played a demonstration match of water polo, which was very much to the liking of the public in attendance. In Belgium, women's water polo is not played at all. The intention for this demonstration match was, to try to get women's water polo on the program for the next Olympic Games. "

With the 1984 Olympics hosted by one of the pioneering women's water polo nations – to be followed by the 1988 Games in Seoul, South Korea – the timing of this push for inclusion was crucial.

The Women's Promoting Committee tried to gain support for the addition of women's water polo, but in hindsight, Barnes felt they were "chasing a lot of rabbits down burrows" during that time. "We heard a lot of, 'Okay, you can be a demonstration sport. We'll put on some games, and that way then you've got a chance for getting into the 1988 Olympics,'" she said.

Eventually, baseball and men's and women's tennis got the nod to be contested on a demonstration basis in Los Angeles.

Despite missing out on demonstration sport status for the 1984 Olympics, the best women's players in the world descended on Southern California that summer for the FINA World Cup. The strategic awarding of the World Cup to Irvine, California, allowed the women to take in the Olympic atmosphere in an exhibition game at the official Olympic venue. Women's National Team coach Sandy Nitta, Jane Hale, and Dr. Ralph Hale, among others, put forth great effort to make the game first-class and worthy of the Olympics.

In a matchup fitting of their nearly twenty-year rivalry in the pool, the United States and Australia faced off at Pepperdine University in Malibu. Staged to serve as a dry run for the impending men's Olympic competition, the women got as close to the full Olympic experience as possible.

"It was exciting to play in the Olympic pool," said Nitta. "There was a big enough crowd to make it exciting. We got to use the locker rooms, and the gymnasium right next door, where we had our team meetings. The introductions were really nice; it gave the feel of almost being there."

Maureen O'Toole recalled mixed emotions from the experience.

"The place was packed, and we're playing a big rival; it seemed that everybody was really enjoying it," she said. "It was really exciting, so we thought for sure it was going to be in the next Olympics."

From the time she was a kid, O'Toole wanted to compete in the Olympics. For a long time, she thought she would be an Olympic swimmer, before she became more involved in water polo. One of the world's biggest stars in her sport, O'Toole waited in vain as one Olympiad after another passed by without the inclusion of women's water polo.

"In 1984, we were happy to be a demonstration; it seemed they were going to add it for 1988," she said. "Then they didn't. 1992, again, we went through the whole thing. We thought for sure they would add it, and they didn't. 1996, it was in Atlanta; so we're like, 'Oh, yeah, they're for sure going to add it here,' and they didn't. That's when, after the 1994 World Championships, I retired. It was a bummer because I always wanted to go to the Olympics – I went through '84, '88, '92, '96, and never got the opportunity."

O'Toole noted the emotional high of playing in the Olympic venue in front of a great crowd; yet clearly, women's water polo was not the equal of the men's game. "It was kind of embarrassing," O'Toole said. "Like, yeah, well, we're not really part of this."

The World Cup in Irvine, held at Heritage Park, now known as the Woollett Aquatic Center, saw the rivalry between the United States and Australia reach a new level. For the first time in history, the two nations met with a world title at stake. The opening match of the World Cup resulted in a 5-5 tie between the two sides. The strength of each was confirmed when both the United States and Australia defeated Holland in the following days – relegating the two-time defending World Cup champion Dutch to the bronze medal game against New Zealand.

As they had in the tournament opener, the United States raced to an early lead over Australia in the championship game. Leads of 2-0 at the quarter break and 4-1 at halftime put the United States in position to reclaim the title of world champion for the first time since 1979.

"We were the best conditioned team that year," Nitta said. "And then the game clock broke."

In a devastating turn of events, the game was delayed for thirty minutes while officials brought in a replacement clock. Taking the opportunity to regroup and rest, Australia turned up its game when play resumed. Outscoring the United States 8-2 in the second half, Australia cruised to a 9-6 triumph.

The exhibition at Pepperdine and the FINA World Cup in Irvine were fabulous events for women's water polo. The organizers and the group working to gain Olympic inclusion saw the successes of the summer of 1984 as stepping stones to the next stage – pushing for Seoul in 1988. But amid positive feelings of progress, the group ran into a new roadblock related to its call for gender equity. FINA stated that gender equity existed in aquatics at the Olympic Games; synchronized swimming represented the female complement to the men's water polo event.

Another hurdle to overcome was the low number of teams competing at major international competitions. While the United States, Australia, Canada and Holland could be counted on to host and attend events, New Zealand, which had travelled to the United States twice for World Cup events, and 1978 World Championships host West Germany, were the only other nations to have competed in FINA tournaments. FINA made it clear to the Women's Promoting Committee that until women's water polo demonstrated increased participation on every continent, the topic of inclusion in the Olympics was off the table.

Representatives from the committee set to work, spreading out far and wide to encourage water polo federations to include a women's team and to participate in continental competitions. Thea de Wit covered promotion of the sport in Europe. A member of the LEN Bureau, she used the opportunity as a delegate to document the European nations playing in women's water polo events. The emergence of women's programs from Russia and Greece competing in LEN and FINA events was largely due to de Wit's efforts.

Leanne Barnes worked with New Zealand and even India. Jane Hale and Claude Lavoie covered the Pan-Pacific region, documenting the development of women's water polo. The group was building a case for FINA and the IOC; global participation on all continents in an appropriate number of countries was becoming a reality.

The international group met every year at the major competition and kept in touch by fax and letter. "I wish we had the Internet," Barnes said. "It would have all been over and done within a year."

The Women's Promoting Committee then started down the path of pushing their case to FINA. Although women's water polo was not added to the program for the Seoul Olympics, an official FINA Subcommittee for Women's Water Polo was established in 1988. The members became FINA delegates, and as such, found more opportunity to meet with FINA leadership, go to events, and pull together their case. At this time, the committee upped the ante, becoming more aggressive with its timeline. The objective became a debut for women's water polo at the 1992 Olympics in Barcelona, but increasing European interest and participation proved difficult.

Of chief concern: many traditional men's water polo powers were protective of their funding. Their fear was that if women's water polo was added to the Olympics, it would affect men's programs.

"There was also the balance of how many teams would be in the Olympics," Barnes added. "There might be a cut in the number of men's teams able to participate. The Spanish were an interesting one that were so strong in men's water polo that were saying, 'But if we also have women, we'd have to spread our funding.'"

Barnes posed an interesting counter-argument: If water polo continued to be the only team sport in the Olympics without gender equity, would the solution be to drop the sport from the program completely? Perhaps men's water polo could *gain* from the addition of the women.

The hopes for 1992 were eventually seen as a non-starter; host nation Spain was uninterested in bringing women's water polo to the Olympics, as Barnes pointed out. The committee turned its attention to the return of the Olympic Games to the United States. With the 1996 Games staged on a "friendly" continent, Barnes and her colleagues got to work on a strategic plan to gain the prize of inclusion.

"We saw a great opportunity with the United States being able to really push gender equity and getting the program on board," Barnes said.

⊚⊘⊚⊘⊚⊘

In the United States, the 1990s brought great strides in gender equity to the sport of water polo. Richard Foster was elected president of United States Water Polo in 1990. At the time, tensions existed within the organization between the men's and women's international programs. Foster saw a general lack of respect for the women's program.

"High profile people in the federation were highly opposed to the women's sport getting on the Olympic program," he said. "Number one, they just didn't see the athleticism. That was their view. Secondly, they didn't see the participation internationally that would warrant placing the women on the Olympic program. The third reason was they feared that the women would take part of their budget if they were considered equal."

Foster described the state of women's water polo within USA Water Polo in a 2013 interview with *Water Polo Planet*:

> We realized that to be an integral part of the movement, USWP had to "believe" in women's water polo. That might sound odd and simplistic now, given our women's team's current status, but in the 70s and 80s our women's National Team members received very little, if anything, from USWP. Talk about a dedicated group of players: they had to fundraise and pinch their relatives for money to compete on an international level. Many times hotels were either not an option, or they stuck five or six persons in one room. They paid for their own air fares. There was simply a very strong belief that USWP shouldn't be spending money on the women because they weren't on the Olympic program like the men. Almost all of our resources were controlled by the men's program. The general attitude towards women's team was, "Let them play, but don't take any of the

men's money." Before I became president of USWP, one very high-level officer of USWP told me, "Women's water polo won't be on the Olympic program in our lifetimes."

Foster immediately set out to prove that statement wrong.

He found himself facing pressure from a majority of the high-level figures in the sport who opposed increased funding for the women's program. But Foster enjoyed the women's game and respected the people in the women's program, including the staff and the players. A Finance Committee meeting early in his term provided Foster the inspiration to search for ways to increase support from the corporation for the Women's National Team. An impassioned speech by Jane Hale outlined the disadvantages the female athletes at the National Team level faced: the hardships of borrowing money from their families and running fundraisers just to go on trips without any funding from the National Governing Body.

"Jane said they deserved this money just as much as the men do," Foster recalls. "Right there, it kind of clicked in my head. You see issues based sometimes on pressures and sometimes on logic; Jane's presentation, to me, had a lot of logic."

What happened next made a huge impact on Foster and truly set him on the path to change the way women's water polo was viewed within USA Water Polo.

Foster vividly remembers John Felix, Jr. raising his hand to speak. Serving as an Athlete Representative at this particular budget hearing, Felix agreed with Hale, advocating for the women's program budget to receive an increase.

Foster admired the courage to speak up against the popular viewpoint.

"The negative reaction was palpable," Foster told *Water Polo Planet* in his interview, "but from that date forward, USWP believed."

The words from Hale and Felix influenced Foster to join the international fight to include women's water polo in the Olympics.

"I had kind of known this was the right way to go, but this crystallized it for me," he said. "From that point on, I just didn't listen to the people who were complaining about the athleticism, the international level of the game, and how it would affect the men financially. My mind was made up."

The next task for Foster was finding funds. He decided to turn his attorney's eye to the Amateur Sports Act of 1978, poring through the legislation. The Act, signed by President Jimmy Carter, established the United States Olympic Committee (USOC), which in turn could charter National Governing Bodies (NGBs) for Olympic sports. Foster came up with a legal argument for receiving funding for the women's program from the USOC. Absent the status of an Olympic sport, the women's water polo program received no federal funding to that point.

"The theme in the Amateur Sports Act is, if you have a sport that has a legitimate international championship, among other criteria, but that being the biggest one, you should be entitled to funding," Foster said.

His first call was to the USOC's General Counsel.

"He said things that just really flew me off the handle; I obviously said things to him that made him fly off the handle, because it turned into a shouting match."

Foster says the General Counsel acknowledged the mission of the Amateur Sports Act: to support women's athletics. He then proceeded to give examples of sports other than water polo that were the recipients of federal funding.

"I said, fine, I'll just go to our next meeting and I'll tell our women, 'Hey, I know that you should qualify for funding under the Amateur Sports Act. I know that you're playing hard. I know that you deserve that money – but you should feel good about yourself because volleyball players and softball players and track and field athletes, they're getting money and they're female. That should satisfy you," Foster recalls. "And I said that sarcastically to him. He really got pissed off, and I think we both hung the phone up on each other."

The statement that particularly raised Foster's ire was that the women's team could expect funding when they were added to the Olympic program.

Foster argued, "You can't do it that way. You can't just start funding a team and expect the next Olympic quadrennium, they're going to be any good. You've got to support them now, so when they do get on the program, we have a quality team that can compete on an international level. He didn't agree with that."

The next day, Foster's phone rang. It was Harvey Schiller, the Executive Director of the USOC. He told Foster he agreed with him, and pledged to give the women's team funding through the creation of two grant programs which only women's water polo would qualify for.

With some initial funding to cover travel and training expenses and equipment, Foster and the Executive Board began discussions about increasing international support for the movement.

One of the first stops on the road to rallying support in the Americas region beyond the United States and Canada was a meeting at the 1991 Pan American Games in Cuba. Foster and Becky Shaw made a presentation on behalf of the women's Olympic movement.

"In a kind of patting-you-on-the-head kind of response, person after person from Central and South America got up and said, 'We love water polo, and we love women's sports, but this is not the proper sport for women, and for us to be pushing on an international level.' The argument that there was a lack of an appropriate number of nations playing at a competitive level arose once again. It was really disheartening because they were treating us like children," Foster said.

"Then this guy from the Caribbean, whose name I don't think I've ever known, stands up and gives an impassioned speech about why this continent should be backing and supporting the concept of getting women's water polo on the Olympic program," Foster remembers. "He said, '*Women play the game well and deserve our support*.' When he was done, Becky and I stood up and clapped; others followed, and pretty soon this guy had a standing ovation. All those South American and Central American officials who were talking down to us had very sheepish, embarrassed looks on their faces."

Even with growing support in the Americas as a continent, Foster ran into disinterest from the organizers of the 1996 Olympic Games. He urged the Atlanta Committee for the Olympic Games (ACOG) to consider adding women's water polo, but found very little interest – but plenty of financial objections.

"I suggested doing it as an exhibition event," Foster said. "Eight teams, six teams – it couldn't be that much more expensive, and it's really important to the movement. They were just very skeptical."

Foster believes the Georgia-based organizers felt little connection to water polo, creating a road block that was impossible to get around. And, of course, the finances were prohibitive.

"They would keep saying if you add 100 players to the Olympic program, costs rise exponentially with housing and security and so on," Foster said. Placing a call to Anita DeFrantz – a member of the IOC, a USOC Executive Board member, and an ACOG executive – Foster heard that the financial argument was, in fact, valid.

"I said, they're talking like it's going to be a huge increase in expense if we add eight women's teams," he said. "She told me, 'Well, Rich, they're right; it does increase exponentially all of those expenses.'"

In the end, the return of the Olympics to the United States didn't lead to the addition of women's water polo to the program. All of the folks who wanted so desperately for it to happen licked their wounds once again and moved on to the next target: Sydney.

@/@@/@@/@

When it was clear that the Atlanta Committee for the Olympic Games intended to pass on women's water polo, the 1994 World Championships in Rome turned into a pivot point for the United States program. Retirements following the fourth-place finish resulted in only four of thirteen players carrying over to the 1995 World Cup roster. Headlining the departures were coach Sandy Nitta and the world's longest-tenured international player, Maureen O'Toole. Maggi Kelly and Amber Drury hung up their caps after seven years with the Senior Team. The quartet, who would have made multiple appearances at the Olympics in their primes, left the National Team to a young crop of players following their final go-around in Rome.

Julie Swail, a 21-year-old player from UC San Diego, made her National Team debut at the 1994 Worlds. She wasn't counted on for much during the games, but she was given specific responsibilities on the trip.

"I was the baby on the team," she said. "I had to carry the equipment. My job in the water was to egg-beater with Mo's daughter, Kelly."

Swail looked after two-year-old Kelly Mendoza during warm-ups before games.

"I wasn't going to play in some of the games, so Kelly and I would egg-beater," she said. "It was like, if someone gets sick, you'll play. So I was supposed to keep Kelly entertained during warm-up. We traveled almost the entire summer; my legs got really strong."

Even though it was her first trip with the Senior Team, Swail understood the magnitude of the World Championships for the women's game. She recalled the flight home from Rome, when some members of the women's team enjoyed cocktails together. A member of the men's staff commented to them, "You should keep it together – you didn't just win an Olympics."

Swail took exception to the berating tone. The women's team wasn't drinking in excess – for many, it was a celebration of their careers coming to a close.

The men's coach continued, "It's not a big deal – it's World Championships."

"I didn't say anything," Swail said, "but I remember thinking, *This kind of is our Olympics. Does he not realize that?*"

When Julie Swail was young, her mom took her to try out for a soccer team.

"It was so hot, and I was so tired and uncomfortable," she said of the single day spent as a land athlete in her youth. "I was a fat kid. I was overweight, and nothing on land felt good. I couldn't jump. I couldn't even do a credit card jump. I don't even know if my feet left the ground when I attempted to jump. Soccer, I didn't like to run. I did bowling in a summer camp once, and thought, 'Yeah, I can do this. It's air conditioned.'"

Leaning toward indoor activities, she tried ballet at age six – and was done by seven.

"I think it was pretty clear that I wasn't going to be a ballerina," she said.

In sixth grade, several of her friends were ice skating, and Swail figured an indoor sport on ice would suit her well.

"We went, and in my mind, I was going to go to the Olympics to ice skate," she said. "My mom, bless her heart; I don't know how she phrased it gently, but, 'Julie, you're not going to be an ice skater, either. I will give give you money to go ice skate every Friday night with your friends who are going to be the ice skaters.'"

Swail's older sister, Jana, also stayed off land, opting for the water. The two sisters joined the Fullerton Area Swim Team (FAST), where Olympic-great Janet Evans became the world's best. Swail would not be following in Evans' footsteps.

Swail was amused to hear her mom tell stories about her first year on the swim team.

"Apparently, I got kicked out of practice every day," she said.

More often than not, Judy Swail arrived for pickup to find Julie already out of the water. The report from the coach always included screwing around, and playing with the lane lines.

While swimming at FAST, Swail had a partner in crime when it came to goofing off during practice. Whether their coaches at the time saw greatness is questionable – but both Swail and Omar Amr would go on to become Olympic water polo players.

"We would antagonize each other, argue over who was going to go first, touch each other's feet, pull each other, and block each other on the wall," Swail said. "Our coach would get fed up and send us to the side to do a 500 butterfly."

Swail remembers a particular practice in which she was sent off seven times.

"We were both getting in trouble," said Swail. But the two sometimes made the most of the punishment. "We would end up racing each other in the 500 fly. We've had a good laugh about it since then. It's probably why we got to where we did."

Years later, Swail crossed paths with one of the coaches who had put up with her as a youth. In the spring of 2000, while preparing for the Olympics as captain of the team, Swail heard the voice of one of the club swim coaches – a voice that immediately stirred up memories.

"You always recognize your coach's voice," she said. "I'm thinking, 'Oh my gosh, that's Kristy.' There was enough memory in me where I realized, *Oh, man, I hope she doesn't recognize me.*"

By this time, Swail knew she hadn't been a model swimmer – and one recollection came back to her right away.

"I remember swimming long course, and seeing if I could make myself go backwards to see how long it could take me. Here's this one swimmer trying to take six or seven minutes to do a 100, while everyone else is going fast."

For about two weeks, Swail flew under the radar when Kristy was on deck. One day, while sneaking her way to the locker room, she froze at the sound of the voice she recognized from swim practice years before.

"Julie Swail? What are you doing here?"

The quick hellos included Swail explaining that she was training for the Olympics.

"Kristy said, 'Don't take this the wrong way, but you are the *last* person I would have ever expected to make the Olympic team.'" Swail agreed. "I didn't take it personally. I realized how difficult I was back then."

An expert in doing whatever it took to not swim while in the pool, Julie Swail first found water polo as a way to get out of swim practice.

"The coach asked who wanted to get out early," she said. "My hand was the fastest to shoot up."

The club's water polo team needed a player – accepting the offer meant staying a half hour later than usual. It was a good deal to the 12-year-old Swail.

"At that time, it was like, 'Get me out of this black-line swimming,'" she said. "So that was my start. I wasn't good, but it was a lot more fun."

Swail even scored some goals on her first day, although she did it without picking up the ball once. Her strongest recollection of her initial experience was the coach telling her not to pick up the ball, at all costs. So, whenever she had the ball, Swail dribbled. Eventually, she dribbled around her defender and swam the ball into the goal.

"I swam in two or three goals because the goalie would never expect you to swim the ball all the way in," Swail recalled, laughing at the thought. "If I had to make a pass, I would swim the ball over to my teammate. I could swim, so I would just swim the ball to whoever needed it, or swim the ball into the goal."

Stan Sprague, who headed the first Women's National Team, saw Swail and told her mom that he saw potential in the girl who dribbled the ball through the opposing defense. She tried out Sprague's club at Canyon High School in Anaheim.

"My mom took me a couple times; it was fun. I liked it," Swail said. "But there were no other girls, and it was kind of far, so my mom decided I would just keep swimming. I respected that."

But soon after, in junior high, Swail quickly lost interest in swimming. A bad respiratory infection sidelined her for almost half of a year; when she returned to the water, she struggled. Swail contemplated quitting aquatics and looking for another activity, but watching her sister Jana swim on the high school team inspired her to stick with it.

"I saw that I could be good with the high school group," she said. "It was different than club swimming. With this group, I could make a name for myself."

There was another factor motivating Swail to reconsider leaving the pool behind.

"I didn't want to do regular PE."

Fall water polo her freshman year was a natural starting point; with her swimming background, she started on the boys' frosh/soph team. As the sprinter, she would sprint for the ball – then get subbed out.

"But sometimes, you don't score the whole first quarter, so I would get a lot of playing time," she said. "Little by little, I learned and got better."

As a sophomore, Swail received a promotion to the varsity for the CIF play-offs; her junior year, she was a full-fledged member. A defensive specialist, she made up for a lack of offensive firepower with determination at the other end of the pool.

"My whole role was to play defense," she explained. "I could guard one person easily; two people pretty well. Guys don't play counterattack defense – I would counter back and swim between and stunt them. But I had nothing on offense. I was a good passer – not a shooter."

During her junior season, Julie Swail's Valencia High School team took on Irvine High School. An interaction with one of the Irvine boys after the game set her on a path she never imagined. In a complete surprise to Swail, the opponent approached her and said, "You're pretty good. You know, you should try out for the National Team."

Feeling like she had played a really good game that day, Swail thought, "He probably thinks I play like this all the time."

She thanked him for the compliment, and asked about the cutoff time for the 50 freestyle. Swail had heard of a tryout a few weeks before with swim standards far faster than her best. Her opponent said he knew of some of the Irvine girls going to a Women's National Team tryout.

"I said, 'What are you talking about, girls?'" Swail recalled. "That was the first person that ever mentioned it."

Then Irvine coach Scott Hinman, the former head coach of the Women's Junior National Team and Senior Team assistant, approached Swail, encouraging her to try out.

Hinman talked to both Swail and her mother, passing along the phone number of Brent Bohlender, the Junior Team head coach. Hinman repeated his opinion that she had a chance to make the team.

At her mother's urging, Swail made the phone call to Bohlender to inquire about the tryouts.

"This was before email, so I remember calling," she said. "I was so nervous. My mom made me do it myself."

Swail asked Bohlender what her chances were of making the team; she was discouraged by his response.

"It felt like a big investment to go up to Modesto for a weekend," she said. "Brent told me something along the lines of, 'Well, I pretty much know all the players, but I'd love to have you come up; I'll check you out, and if you're good enough, then you'll make it.'"

Swail's immediate thought was, *He's already picked the team!*

Judy Swail, encouraging as always, persuaded her daughter to follow through.

"Let's just go up there and see what you've got."

When she arrived in Modesto to try out for the Junior National Team, Julie Swail had never played water polo with another girl in her entire career.

"I went up there thinking, 'This should be a kick'; I had never seen another girl playing," she said.

Swail couldn't even imagine there would be a full team's worth of girls at the tryout; she was immediately blown away and intimidated, seeing almost 100 girls at the pool. Swail didn't know anyone else. But she remembers an athlete roster that included each player's experience.

"They gave everyone a list at the first meeting, showing their resume," she said. "The other girls all had things on their resume like going to Junior Olympics."

Back at their hotel room, Swail cried. She told her mother she didn't want to try out. But Judy gently convinced her daughter to make the most of her opportunity.

One name on the roster – Nicolle Payne – stood out to Swail, due to the lack of accompanying accomplishments.

"I remember thinking, 'I've got to meet this Nicolle Payne.' At least I had three years of high school experience; she had like one year of club experience. I thought, 'OK, so there is one other person here like me.' She was in the same boat as me. We didn't have any background, or water polo history."

Swail sought out and met the 13-year-old Payne; ten years later, the two would be Olympic teammates in Sydney.

When Bohlender announced the team, Swail learned that she was an A/B.

"I was told, 'You didn't make the A team. But you're not a B,'" she said. "'You're like an A-minus, B-plus.' What does that mean?"

Bohlender explained to Swail, "If you had any offense at all, you could make the A team, but you never look at the goal."

Swail understood, thinking to herself, "Yeah, that's about right."

With the Junior Team tryout under her belt, Swail was pointed toward the Long Beach Ancient Mariners, a masters team with players ranging from their early- to mid-20s up to 50-plus-year-olds. The team was mostly men, but included a strong group of women: Maureen O'Toole, Sandy Vessey, Margo Miranda, Teresa Bixby, and Margo Butler who were all influential on the high school junior. While it didn't do much to increase her offensive confidence, the higher level of water polo led to her overall game quickly developing.

In the summer after her trek to Modesto, Swail got the call for a much more intriguing travel opportunity. An injury to a player on the Junior B team left a spot open. Bohlender made his way through a list of alternates, but none had a passport, or were able to get one on short notice. Eventually, he called the Swail home and spoke to Judy, who immediately agreed to take care of the passport.

"My mom drove me to LA, where we sat all day to get a passport," Swail said.

With expedited passport in hand, she was off to Rio de Janeiro to play with coach Jim McMaster and the Junior B squad. The games were her first-ever with an all-female team, playing against women. For Swail, it was an amazing introduction to international travel. Games were played every night at 10:00, allowing for plenty of time to see the sights of Rio.

"We would get picked up at 10:00 in the morning, and get back at 6:00," Swail said. "We'd just get our suits and go to the pool. We played water polo at night, went to bed, and did the whole thing again the next day."

Playing against women for the first time, Swail found the advantage she had built up from all the time competing with boys. Goalkeeping and physical strength were at the top of the list of differences that made the women's game seem easier.

"All of a sudden, nobody that I'm playing against is as strong as the guys I had been competing with, so I felt much more confident," Swail said.

She recalls a huge improvement in her offensive abilities in the short amount of time she was in Brazil.

"It was so much easier," said Swail. "I thought, *Okay, this is fun.*"

Playing water polo with women in Brazil between her junior and senior years of high school convinced Julie Swail that she loved the sport and wanted to continue to play in college.

"It was really fun to play with other women, or girls," she said. "They passed me the ball, they wanted me to shoot. It was an even more enjoyable sport when I played both offense and defense."

Having seen her sister, Jana, head to Williams College, where she played club water polo, Julie wasn't interested in following her to the East Coast. She received a letter from Harvard, which had varsity status, but the cold weather was the deciding factor.

"What kid in their right mind would say, 'No way would I go to Harvard'?" she said. "I wanted to go someplace near the beach, where I could enjoy myself. So my range was Santa Barbara to San Diego."

At the time, varsity programs existed at Harvard, Slippery Rock in Pennsylvania, Pomona-Pitzer and UC San Diego. Swail looked into the differences between the varsity and club programs; she found few.

"Everyone played everyone else," she said. "The idea was that your college team would get a little more funding if it was varsity, but it wasn't really significant."

Team members at UC San Diego paid for their airfare and hotel costs when they traveled. If the team went to Collegiate Nationals, the school paid for their hotel. If air travel for Nationals was necessary, the team fundraised. Student services such as priority registration and academic support didn't exist.

Her first meeting with Tritons coach Denny Harper convinced Swail that UC San Diego was the right place to continue her water polo career. As opposed to other coaches, who promised to make her the focal point of the team, Harper was more measured in his assessment.

"He told me, 'We have a lot of strong players, so you're going to be playing a supporting role,'" Swail said. "That was so much more attractive to me. I just wanted to be part of the team."

Making great strides in her game at UC San Diego, Swail set her aim on the Senior National Team. She debuted on the Senior B team in the summer of 1992; the following year, she was just on the wrong side of the cut line for the World Cup team. In 1994, she made her first Senior Team appearance, between eggbeater sessions with Kelly Mendoza, at the World Championships in Rome.

With the mass retirement after Rome, Swail found herself all of sudden one of the older players on the team; she was named co-captain with Lynn Wittstock – a duty Swail would handle solo after Wittstock's retirement in 1998.

Her National Team career beginning squarely in the pre-Olympic era, Swail approached her commitment to the team as one piece of a much larger balancing act between a full-time job, full-time training, and fundraising to both travel and compete. As such, starting with her first international trip to Brazil, she always valued learning about the team's destinations, seeing the sights – and eating ice cream or gelato around the world.

"To sit indoors someplace, you lose life," she said. "You lose the passion; if you get out and you're having fun, it just makes it more enjoyable. It keeps you alive."

Swail understands the changes in the National Team, and its pipeline of age group National Teams, that have taken place since her era has passed.

"It's kind of sad that that *Bad News Bears* kind of era is gone," she said. "Everyone is going to come through the ranks of playing club polo and high school polo and college polo. I don't think you're going to get the background diversity that the 2000 team had, ever again."

◎◎◎◎◎◎

One example of background diversity that may never happen again is that of Kathy "Gubba" Sheehy. A swimmer and soccer player in her youth, Sheehy didn't pick up a water polo ball until she was in college.

Growing up in the aquatics hotbed of Moraga, in Northern California's East Bay, Sheehy started swimming competitively at age three. Her mother, Tedra, took her to the pool, where she fell in love with being in the water.

"They decided that they would let me swim in a meet at three years old," Sheehy said.

Lined up in one of the middle lanes, Sheehy started the race, only to turn around and swim back to where she started.

"I wasn't really that advanced yet, and I wanted to swim by the wall," Sheehy explained. "I swam back, got out, and ran to one of the side lanes next to the wall."

Sheehy jumped in and finished the race successfully, to the delight of everyone on deck.

"It was pretty cute at the time, being a little kid," she said.

Gubba Sheehy's parents kept her busy throughout the year with swimming, soccer, and softball.

"They didn't really diagnose it back then, but I had a little bit of ADD," she said. "They didn't really have drugs or anything for that, which I'm actually very happy about, because my parents would just take me to one event after the next."

Sheehy swam in the mornings before school, then played one of her several sports in the afternoons.

"They kept my whole life filled with activities; that helped me get through school," she said.

It was quick thinking on the part of her father, Steve, that got Sheehy onto the soccer field, where she excelled. When she was five years old, Sheehy declared that she wanted to be a ballerina. Steve Sheehy took his daughter to the local ballet school.

"The lady looked at me and said, 'I don't think she's suited to be a ballerina,'" Sheehy recalled. "I was really upset. My dad thought he had to do something, so he took me straight to the field and said, 'Why don't you try soccer?' I fit in perfectly there."

Sheehy rose through the local soccer ranks, and had her sights set on the Junior National Team. When it came time to try out, she found out that despite her ability, her birth date was on the wrong side of the age cutoff. After being told she was on the team, she was dropped because of the new system. Crushed, Sheehy decided to quit soccer altogether. Around the same time, she also stopped swimming, taking time off from sports completely.

Enrolling at Cuesta College in San Luis Obispo following high school, the restless Sheehy found her way back to the pool as a member of the swim team. Known for its strong men's team, Cuesta didn't offer women's water polo. Sheehy got to know the men's water polo team, since they also swam. One of the men's players, Jamie Stuart, was coaching the women at nearby Cal Poly. Stuart convinced Sheehy to join the team. She gave it a try. In a meteoric rise, unlikely to be duplicated in the modern era, she found herself on the National B Team less than a year later.

One aspect of water polo made Sheehy fall in love with the sport – the physicality. On the soccer field, she wasn't afraid to slide tackle; her style was physical, creating contact, and jawing at opponents.

"I felt like water polo was swimming and soccer, two sports I loved, combined into the same sport," Sheehy said. "If you can be physical and get away with it, it can mean you're a smart player. Not looking to hurt somebody intentionally, but gaining an advantage through contact – the good players can do that."

In a departure from many of her teammates' beginnings in water polo, Sheehy competed against women from the start. But in between National Team training camps, she practiced primarily against men, developing her memorable rugged style.

Sheehy and Julie Swail made their B Team debuts together on a trip to Quebec under coach Jamey Wright. Both the Senior National A and B Teams traveled together to Canada, and both players caught the eye of National Team head coach Sandy Nitta.

Nitta knew right away that she had a talent on her hands. She had seen Sheehy play for Cal Poly; what stood out to Nitta was how often she was in the exclusion box.

"I thought, 'This girl is really physical. This is the type of player I need on the team,'" Nitta said. "I picked her for the National Team because she got kicked out so much."

Sheehy remembers Nitta describing her as a Tasmanian Devil.

"I grew up with two brothers that used to beat me up, so I kind of used that as an outlet in the water," she said. "Sandy said it was hard to take a player and make her play physical, but you could take a physical player and tone her down. I was the Tasmanian Devil in the water that she needed to tone down."

The memories of trying out for the junior national soccer team, and the competitiveness she left behind when she quit, motivated Sheehy as she earned the opportunity to play water polo for the United States. Whether the sport was added to the Olympics wasn't a big concern to her as she progressed.

"We were always hoping that it would become an Olympic sport, but I think I was playing more just to be the best," she said. "Trying to beat the other countries and trying to be number one at what you're doing is more how we were looking at it."

When the possibility of women's water polo at the Atlanta Olympics passed unfulfilled, Sheehy was disappointed. But quickly, it became apparent that the fight was about to escalate.

"At that time, it started to buzz around with the Aussie chicks; they were working really hard to get it as an Olympic sport in 2000," Sheehy said. "Obviously, the dream came true."

☺/☺☺/☺☺/☺

In early 1995, Rich Foster, President of United States Water Polo, reached out to the Dutch federation. Foster and the band of women's water polo supporters worldwide looked to host an international strategic planning meeting for the women's Olympic movement.

The Dutch agreed to host the event in Amsterdam, an important location because of its proximity to so many of the European nations playing women's water polo. Foster knew that hosting a meeting in the United States wouldn't draw enough foreign participation; it was also common to ask a friendly federation, like the Dutch, to help with American initiatives such as rule changes or scheduling issues.

On February 11, 1995, Foster and Megan Hernandez, the Chair of United States Water Polo's Women's International/National Committee, arrived in Amsterdam. They were joined by Australian representatives Leanne Barnes and Tom Hoad, and Claude Lavoie of Canada. Kees van Hardeveld of Holland greeted the group.

No one else attended.

Foster and Hernandez traveled to Amsterdam with great expectations; which quickly evaporated.

Despite invitations to every country with a semblance of a Women's National Team, and the relative ease of travel for Europeans to Amsterdam, the lack of turnout shocked and disappointed those in attendance.

"Holland, the United States, Australia, and Canada were the only countries who cared enough to attend," Foster said. "All the Europeans had to do was drive or take a short plane flight. The rest of us had long-haul trips, but all but one person attending were from outside of Europe."

Foster was stunned.

But having traveled so far, the dedicated few rolled up their sleeves and got to work on their objective – establishing a strategy for elevating women's water polo to the status it deserved. After a few hours of dealing with frustration over the lack of attendance, Hoad got the group focused on using the time together wisely. They started by outlining some principles to frame the movement. These principles were also intended to hold FINA accountable for its statements of support for women's water polo.

Hoad and Foster penned a letter addressed to FINA President Mustapha Larfaoui and agreed to send copies to all FINA members. Foster chuckled as he remembered the task of proclaiming the Amsterdam meeting a great success.

"We didn't say anything that was false, although I can tell you the letter was certainly misleading," Foster said. "We knew we had to generate some support, so we talked about having a successful meeting. We said the major water polo federations attended."

The letter outlined the principles adopted by the attendees and announced the next meeting, to take place in Australia during the 1995 Women's World Cup.

"We sent that out," Foster continued. "We didn't say only six people showed up and only one European country was represented; if we were blunt with them, we wouldn't generate any momentum. That letter generated a lot of momentum."

In October, more than fifty people attended the next meeting, held in conjunction with the World Cup. Foster estimates there were thirty or so representatives from nations without a team among the eight in the World Cup field.

The excitement among the attendees was palpable. Foster recalls sitting next to Leanne Barnes, a big smile on her face. "I said something to her like, 'Well, I think we're going to get this done,'" he said. "I think that was really the essence of getting the movement on the top shelf."

☺☺☺☺☺☺

Robed in hope for inclusion in the 2000 Games, the Women's World team points to the 2000 Sydney Olympic Games.

Parting Shots

United States women at 1994 FINA World Championships – Rome

In 1990, Australian Water Polo, Inc. (AWPI) created a Gender Equity Committee, with Pat Jones named chairperson. Its first and only item on the agenda was to put women's water polo into the Olympic Games. At the time, Jones served as manager of the Australian Women's Senior National Team. The father of Karen Wade, Australia's goalkeeper, made a huge banner with a water polo ball and the words, "Women for Sydney 2000." Wade and Jones made sure it was displayed at every venue in which the Australian women competed during that time.

The banner didn't go unnoticed; many times, Jones was asked to take it down.

She never did.

At the 1994 FINA World Championships in Rome, the banner was prominently placed, and athletes from all participating nations wore t-shirts with the same slogan. Tournament officials confronted Jones about the banner and the organized photo shoot of each team to publicize the Olympic pursuit. "They got very angry in Rome and tore the banner down," Jones said, describing the interaction. "One man gave me a bit of a delivery, but it was all in Italian and I didn't understand it. So I just smiled at him."

Following the 1994 World Championships, Jones resigned as team manager; the Gender Equity Committee was no more. She and Leanne Barnes continued to work together, using every contact they had in the cause. Barnes prepared a media package using all the materials that AWPI had produced, as well as a video of the team in training. Thus began a media campaign that Jones maintained relentlessly, in pursuit of the inclusion of women's water polo in the Olympics.

Having shed her official duties with AWPI, and with the resignation of her husband, Bill, from the presidency of the organization at the end of 1996, Jones felt she had the freedom to be as outspoken as necessary to move the cause forward.

In early 1997, opportunity knocked.

Jones read a story in the *Sydney Morning Herald* about a female lawyer who was being bullied by her colleagues. Angered by what she read, and having had enough of being bullied herself by FINA, she decided to take action.

"I phoned the reporter and gave our story, in which I emphasized the unfairness, the struggle and the question, 'Why?'" she said. "I emphasized the word 'why.' Why is our event excluded from the Olympics in a sport that was there from the beginning of the modern Olympics? It is not a new sport, which is a very different situation."

The result was an article in the *Herald*, and Jones' phone began to ring. Radio, television, and news media wanted to know more about women's water polo's situation; Jones knew she needed to keep them interested. She told of previous experiences of rejection, including the incidents with Italian officials at the World Championships in Rome, the tearing down of the banner, and the demand that the teams leave the arena. "The media had already seen the banner, and all the teams wearing t-shirts with 'Women for Sydney 2000.' It was such a good thing that the European teams had the courage to stand up for the cause at that time."

By April of 1997, Jones had done numerous interviews and felt supported by the Special Broadcasting System (SBS) sports division. When she received notice from a contact at SBS that FINA President Mustapha Larfaoui was arriving for meetings in Sydney, Jones hatched a plan to meet his flight to deliver a letter on behalf of women's water polo.

She would rouse the media with a new tack: a demonstration. Although the Senior National Team was not available to take part, junior coaches Phil Bower and Bruce Falson trained more than forty girls in their squads, and they were more than happy to help.

Jones enlisted her husband, Bill, and her daughters, Lisa and Kerry, both ex-Australian National Team players, to make some posters. And she called on Liz Weekes, a goalkeeper on the National Team, to rally the troops.

"Pat told us the date that Mr. Larfaoui was coming in to Sydney airport," Weekes recalled. "She suggested, 'Why don't you organize a demonstration with the girls; it'll create some bad noise about the Olympics, and that'll help your case.'"

Jones was aware that the International Olympic Committee preferred to avoid bad publicity when it came to the Olympic movement.

On April 22, 1997, the plan to gain attention through the media went into effect. "We got a whole stack of us; we've all got cossies (swimsuits) on and banners and everything, and we're all marching up and down," Weekes said. "It was so embarrassing."

Yvette Higgins, one of the youngest members of Australia's Senior National Team, agreed with Weekes one hundred percent, literally echoing Weekes' assessment.

"It was so embarrassing."

Emblazoned on the placards carried by players were the slogans:

Mustapha. We Need to Talk.

Water Polo Oldest Olympic Sport Still No Women. Shame! Shame! Shame!

Gender Equity in F.I.N.A. What a Joke!

You Must Be Kidding Mustapha. Synchro is not Water Polo.

Embarrassing or not, the demonstration met an important part of its goal. News cameras were there, and the coverage put women's water polo on the evening broadcasts. But the players didn't have a chance to speak to Larfaoui; word had reached his party, and he was whisked away by a route sidestepping the general arrival hall. The television cameramen who had been waiting for the FINA president to engage with the athletes instead filmed a lone piece of luggage on the carousel; the newscasters implied that hidden inside was Larfaoui.

"It was funny and worked really well," recalled Jones.

While discouraged by the failure to meet Larfaoui at the airport, the next chance for Jones and the Aussie players came just two days later. Jones was tipped off by her contact at SBS of Larfaoui's attendance at a meeting in downtown Sydney.

"Pat called me again and said, 'There's a press conference,'" Weekes said. Jones gave her the time and location. "Mustapha Larfaoui was going to be there and all the officials for the Sydney Organizing Committee and the IOC and FINA."

Jones and Weekes quickly composed a letter outlining their aims in speaking to Larfaoui about gender equality in the Olympics.

Weekes remembered the letter well. "*Men's water polo was the oldest team sport, and it's getting to a hundred years later,*" she recalled. "*It's about time women's water polo be included.* We had this letter, and there were five of us that went that day to gate-crash the event – Yvette, Bec Shepard, Kirsten Binnie, my sister Sally, and myself."

Weekes' father, Barry, who became a celebrity during the Sydney Games for his role in a television commercial featuring parents playing their child's Olympic sport, accompanied the group in place of Jones, who was committed to a tennis final and couldn't let her partner down.

Weekes recounted the tension she felt that day. "We drove into town, and I didn't really know what I was getting myself into," she said. "I was very nervous; I had to get my dad to pull the car over so I could vomit on the side of the road. I was that nervous about it."

Dressed in Australian track suits, armed with several placards from the airport two days earlier and the letter for Larfaoui, the players made their way to the site of the press conference. The media, alerted by Jones before she headed to her tennis match, were already there, waiting.

"We walked up to the door, and I opened it, and the whole room just looked at me," Weekes remembers. "I nearly didn't walk in; my dad was behind me, and he pushed me in, and my sister followed me with Kirsten Binnie. They followed me in, and they both just stopped. People were trying to push us out, just grab us and push us out, but I just stood my ground and said, '*We just want to speak to Mustapha Larfaoui about why women's water polo is not in the Olympics.*'"

Officials told Weekes and her teammates that Larfaoui would speak to them outside the building, if they left the room quietly. Weekes asked for their guarantee.

"It was all on camera, so we went outside and then the second that meeting was over, everyone just raced outside; there were reporters everywhere. I can't even remember what I said."

@@@@@@

In the critical years leading up to both the Atlanta and Sydney Olympics, the women's water polo movement gained key figures who remained in the fight until the end.

In the United States, Bret Bernard, Women's International Committee Chair, took up the cause. In Australia, Tom Hoad and John Whitehouse, administrators in Australian Water Polo got involved.

"Tom had spent years of involvement having been absolutely dedicated to men's water polo," Barnes said. "He and I were on the Australian board together, and we'd have these constant battles about other issues. But he saw the benefit toward water polo by women being there. We flew to Amsterdam; we met with the IOC delegates; we met with FINA, and we started presenting the case. We were very hopeful that we would get on for '96, but sadly there was an IOC Program Committee in Mexico, and in the lead up to what new events there might be for '96, we were told, 'You're not going to be there.'"

Pushed aside again, Barnes and the committee would not be discouraged easily. They knew that the back-to-back Olympic hosting duties of the United States and Australia were hugely important to the fate of Olympic women's water polo.

It was at this point that the Australians decided to really raise the stakes of the campaign.

"We knew Sydney was coming up, and so we have the official route," Barnes said. "I went to the Atlanta Olympics with Rich Foster, and we took videos. We presented to various people. We had a slogan of 'It's Time,' and we went through that process to really get on that agenda."

Barnes began working in Australia with representatives of the Sydney Organizing Committee for the Olympic Games (SOCOG). John Coates was SOCOG Sports Commission chairman, a SOCOG vice-president, and the president of the Australian Olympic Committee (AOC). Coates had driven the campaign for Sydney's hosting of the 2000 Games, and was well respected in international Olympic circles. Women's water polo had further support from four-time water polo Olympian Peter Montgomery, who was the AOC Vice-President.

"John Coates and Peter Montgomery – I think they looked at the faces of our female players, and just said, 'There's no reason why they shouldn't be playing,'" Barnes recalled.

After years of championing women's water polo – including the first tour to Hawaii of the Australian National Team – Pat Jones became a key figure in the movement, operating from her home in Cronulla, a suburb in southern Sydney.

Concurrently, Coates relentlessly wrote letters to FINA and the IOC – roughly fifty-seven, according to Barnes' count – pushing the case for women's water polo and pushing the numbers.

The numbers were a focal point of the fight. 10,200 was the number at the center of all discussion.

In February of 1997, it seemed that women's water polo had officially lost out on the numbers game. A news report out of Lausanne, the home of the IOC, stated there would be "no women's water polo in the 2000 Olympics." This news came on the same evening that Pat Jones received the Prime Minister's award for contribution to water polo. Jones considered the occasion spoiled.

"The Olympics were getting so big, and there was a cap on the number of athletes at 10,200," Barnes explained. "How would we protect other sports and other events but still be able to have a profile for women's water polo? This is why we had this lower number of women's teams for 2000."

With Coates and Montgomery pushing women's water polo on the official path through SOCOG, Jones and the athletes continued stirring up the media and public awareness.

Coates made good on his promises to women's water polo: on August 22, 1997, the headline in the *Gold Coast Bulletin* declared, "SOCOG support for women's water polo." Olympics Minister Michael Knight announced that SOCOG would support the inclusion of women's water polo, and would lobby the IOC at its upcoming session in Lausanne. Less than two weeks later, *The Australian* ran the headline, "IOC okays water polo." All that was left was FINA's blessing, as the article explained:

> The IOC board said it approved in principle the addition of women's water polo, pending final agreement from the international swimming federation (FINA).
>
> Until now FINA has resisted the idea of adding women's water polo.

But, following the IOC's endorsement, the federation will feel compelled to approve the event during its congress at swimming's world championships in Perth next January.

Barnes, still wary of FINA's reluctance to lower its number of athletes in other disciplines, including men's water polo, began to seek to legal options.

"I got legal advice about taking the message to the Court of Arbitration for Sport," she said. "I'd been working through that legal process, as well. All these things sort of funneled, and it seemed to really up the ante between '93 and '97, and things fell into place."

On his October 1997 visit to review Sydney's Olympic progress, Barnes was prepared to inform FINA President Mustapha Larfaoui that she intended to lodge legal action unless women's water polo was added to the 2000 Games. Barnes modeled the plan after the actions that led to the women's marathon earning a place on the 1984 Los Angeles Olympic program. Because FINA's World Championships, its peak event, featured women's water polo, any legal action taken would have been against the IOC.

The roller coaster of emotion continued during Larfaoui's stay in Sydney. On October 27, newspapers across the country reported Coates' optimism, stating, "he thought the odds were firming that women's water polo would make its Olympic debut at the 2000 Games in Sydney." The headline in *The Mercury* read, "Women's water polo set for Olympic plunge."

But, just two days later, on October 29, a 180-degree turn, announced by *The Sydney Morning Herald*: "FINA sinks women's deal." SOCOG's proposal to FINA, designed by Coates, called for reduction of the number of men in a water polo team from thirteen to eleven – a move that would have freed twenty-four of the sixty-six athlete spots sought by women's water polo.

After meeting with Larfaoui, Coates announced, "Nothing will happen before Perth." The final decision for women's water polo was put on hold for at least another three months.

However, a morning meeting on October 29 that included IOC Executive Board member Dr. Jacques Rogge, John Coates, Michael Knight, Mustapha Larfaoui, and IOC president, Juan Antonio Samaranch, who joined the meeting by telephone from Switzerland, produced the decision Leanne Barnes, Pat

Jones, and countless others had fought so hard for. By the afternoon, Australian National Team members Liz Weekes, Simone Hankin, Bronwyn Mayer, and Naomi Castle were summoned to a press conference in Sydney. Hankin, who worked at a bank at the time, didn't have time to go home to change – she dashed into a shop on the way to buy clothes for the hastily called event.

And just like that, it was official. Women's water polo was in the Sydney Olympics.

Photographers snapped away, capturing the joy and relief on the faces of the Australian athletes. The photos made the front pages of newspapers nationwide – replacing the lasting image of the demonstration at the airport in April. Australians had a new medal hope to support in the upcoming Olympic Games.

"It was one of those processes where right isn't always might," Barnes said. "We were right, and what was happening was wrong; we just felt incensed that the people who made the decisions couldn't see that it wasn't right. John Coates was in a position with that dual responsibility (representing SOCOG and the AOC). He's a very successful lawyer in his own right. He could negotiate on a level we couldn't. We could get in the door, but we just didn't get to have the time to have those discussions. With him and Peter Montgomery and Tom Hoad and John Whitehouse working here with the Olympic Games rolling out in Australia, I think it was what got things over the line."

Barnes and Jones both point to Coates as a "knight in shining armor," who stood by his word to look out for and, in fact, push for, women's water polo in Sydney. Surely, Coates' contributions to the cause were incalculable and invaluable.

But the meeting that produced the final decision to include women's water polo in the Olympics featured all the same men who had been at the negotiating table – unable to reach an agreement – except for one.

Pat Jones believes the final order to FINA came from the very top – from IOC President Juan Antonio Samaranch himself.

When Leanne Barnes' daughter, Amy, was four, she hated water polo. In her efforts to bring women's water polo into the Olympic Games, Barnes would drop off Amy with her grandparents and rush off to do a telephone interview – or leave daughter and husband while heading off to Singapore, or Amsterdam, or Atlanta.

"When I was on television, my parents or my husband would say, 'Mommy's going to be on television. Want to come and have a look?'" said Barnes. "She'd say, 'Nope.'"

Barnes remembers exactly where she was when she received the news she waited so long to hear.

"They were doing an announcement in Sydney," she said. "I got a telephone call, 'Be by the phone at such and such a time.'"

When the time came, Barnes was at the beach with Amy, while her husband Dennis surfed.

"I was just sitting there with one of those big, brick, late-90s phones, and it went off," she said. "And Amy wasn't going to let me answer it. I said, 'I have to answer the phone.'"

She picked up the call; soon tears were rolling down her face.

It was official. Women's water polo would be on the Sydney Olympic program.

"I think that was the turning point for Amy, when she thought, *Maybe water polo is a good thing.*"

For those who had spent years pushing for women's water polo in the Olympics and been through the processes of 1988, 1992, and 1996, it had been an emotional roller coaster.

"In my heart of hearts, I didn't think Australia would let us down," Barnes said. "I thought we had everything lined up."

But at times, she was assured that everything was in place, urged not to worry. At other times, she received sobering reports as information changed. After the ups and downs of decades of work around the world, and the final push at home in Australia, Barnes' odyssey reached its end.

If not for Sydney, she pondered what the next steps would have been.

"I like to think that we would have kept fighting," she said. "I think it became a quest for those of us that were on that journey. There was a resilience there; I don't think we would have given up.

"Would we have had the same reception, the same support from the Athens Organizing Committee? I don't think so. I think the stars aligned for us to have someone like John Coates and Sydney and Australia. You don't know. The thing that's working against all sports now is the cap on the number of athletes. I think it would have got harder and harder. I think our group would have continued.

"I'm glad we didn't have to."

Ellen Estes and Brenda Villa – Sendoff to Sydney, July 2000

5

A NEW ERA BEGINS

1998 European Tour   **Ellen Estes**

On October 30, 1997, the phone rang in Maureen O'Toole's office at Cal. When she picked it up, Sandy Nitta was on the other end of the line.

"Hey, Mo, did you hear?" Nitta began. "They added women's water polo to the Olympics."

In her rush to get out of her Piedmont home that morning, O'Toole had seen a one-line blurb in the *San Francisco Chronicle*; she surprisingly didn't process it as earth-shattering news. Perhaps the buildup of false hope over the years caused her to head out the door without thinking much of the short announcement.

"Is that really true?" she asked Nitta, who quickly got to the point.

"Yeah. What do you think?"

The World Championships, normally a summer event, were scheduled for January of 1998 because of its Southern Hemisphere locale in Perth, Australia. Nitta informed O'Toole that she was returning as head coach for the World

Championships. She wanted her former all-world star to come out of retirement, too.

There was a lot for O'Toole to consider. Her daughter, Kelly, was five years old. O'Toole was the head coach at Cal. She was playing water polo with the men at The Olympic Club in San Francisco when she had time, but she wasn't training at nearly the level of her National Team days. It would require a whole lot of juggling to make a return to the National Team. But it didn't take long for O'Toole to answer Nitta's question.

"At first, I thought, *Oh, man. Oh, no. Can I do this?*" she said. "I'm totally thinking about it for ten seconds, and then, *Yeah. Yeah, I want to do it.*"

The opportunity to cap her playing career at the Olympic Games was too much to pass up. O'Toole wasn't the only retired player to return to the National Team; the lure of the Olympics was strong.

Ready for the challenge ahead, O'Toole knew returning to international competition at age 37 wouldn't be easy. But admittedly, she didn't fully understand the monumental effort she would have to put forth, and the emotional strain she would endure for the opportunity to write a triumphant final chapter to her storied career.

When asked about coming out of retirement in October of 1997, O'Toole drew in an extensively long breath.

"Oh, yeah," she began slowly, with drawn-out words, "that almost killed me."

@@@@@@

The United States Women's National Team had been experiencing a time of transition since the end of the 1994 World Championships in Rome. For women, retirements were common following the World Championships, held in even years between Olympic Games. With no Olympics to aspire to, many female athletes planned their National Team careers around Worlds.

Another factor in the mass retirement after Rome was the realization that the 1996 Atlanta Olympics were not in the cards for women's water polo. Hopes had been high among both athletes and staff that an Olympics on home soil would provide the break they had been waiting for. By the time the World Championships were held in Rome, however, attention for Olympic inclusion had already turned to Sydney; Australian Pat Jones led the campaign, to the distaste of Italian officials. After the United States' fourth-place finish in Rome, National Team icons Sandy Nitta and Maureen O'Toole both said their farewells to the program.

Vaune Kadlubek moved over from the assistant's seat and became the first new head coach of the United States women since Nitta herself in 1980. Without a core of veterans to lean on, Kadlubek turned to youth. Many Junior National Team standouts identified by coach Brent Bohlender and his staff got the call up to the Senior Team, and a period of rebuilding began.

The results at major tournaments reflected the team's growing pains, as well as the arrival of new European nations on the women's water polo scene. Hungary won its first world title in 1994. Italy finished higher than the United States for the first time at the 1993 World Cup and would do so at the next seven FINA events. Russia and Greece also burst onto the stage, consistently besting the United States throughout the mid-1990s.

The surge in the quality of the European teams could be largely attributed to the support the women's game received from the continental governing body of aquatics, the Ligue Européenne de Natation (LEN). With an eye towards making an impact at the first official World Championship for women in 1986, LEN added women's water polo to the European Championships in 1985. That inaugural edition was held in Oslo, separate from the men's tournament in Sofia, Bulgaria. Despite the obscure venue, from a traditional water polo perspective, the move indicated that LEN was intent on raising Europe's profile in the women's game. Eight women's teams participated in the 1985 European Championships. Holland, Hungary, and West Germany won the gold, silver, and bronze medals. Norway, Belgium, Great Britain, France, and Sweden rounded out the standings. The top six finishers qualified for the 1986 World Championships in Madrid.

The next edition of the European Championships in 1987 brought the women's tournament to the same site as the men, in Strasbourg, France – once again elevating the status of the women. Holland maintained its dominance, repeating as European champion over runner-up Hungary. Following its success in Europe, it didn't take long for Hungary to break through to the podium on the world scene.

In 1988, Hungary took the silver medal behind the Netherlands in the first all-European final at a FINA event, the World Cup in Christchurch, New Zealand.

By the mid-1990s, the strength of European women's water polo was undeniable. From 1995 to 1999, the podium at every FINA competition featured two nations from Europe. Australia remained a world power, collecting a medal at each of those events, including gold at the 1995 World Cup in Sydney.

As Europe rose, and the Aussies held onto elite status, the United States women were stuck in the middle of an international medal drought. A pair of bronze medals in 1991 at the World Championships in Perth and the World Cup in Long Beach preceded a steady drop in world ranking. The United States entered the 1998 World Championships as the No. 7 team in the world, a long shot to reach the podium in Perth.

In the months leading up to the World Championships, the triumph of becoming an Olympic event was muted by a transition bordering on chaos for the United States Women's National Team. Changes were afoot; most notably, the resignation of Vaune Kadlubek, and the return of Sandy Nitta as head coach. Maureen O'Toole and Maggi Kelly, both retired since the 1994 World Championships, suited back up with Olympic aspirations. The two veterans brought a wealth of experience to the squad; at the same time, they were newcomers among the young generation of National Team athletes.

Nitta led the team to Perth with the top priority being the top-eight finish required to qualify for the 1999 World Cup, where the first Olympic bids would be awarded.

When the tournament began, the United States women embarked on a roller coaster ride. After an opening-day drubbing at the hands of Russia, the team responded by shocking the host Australians behind a spectacular second-half performance. Although the team fell to Canada the next morning, it snuck into the quarterfinals as the fourth seed from its group. Its berth in the 1999 World Cup was secure.

That feeling of accomplishment faded quickly over the next three days, as the United States found itself bounced from medal contention by Holland, then shocked by a game-winning buzzer-beater against Greece. Facing a strong

Hungarian team in the final match of the World Championships, the United States succumbed, finishing eighth. The ranking was the lowest in program history.

The tumultuous transition took its toll on the team. While the Olympics beckoned, the short period of time between the announcement at the end of October 1997 and the 1998 World Championships in January meant that there was no change to the realities of being a member of the women's National Team. Athletes sold t-shirts to fundraise for the trip to Australia. They worked either full- or part-time and trained on their own in between the scheduled team sessions. Every player put in a tremendous amount of work and sacrifice to be on the team and achieve results as a team – but at the time, the team's older and younger generations were not necessarily on the same philosophical page when it came to the business and mindset of a travel trip.

"You get to travel and play water polo and have these great experiences playing a sport you love," said Heather Moody, who debuted on the senior team in 1995. "But the other component is, I just worked my ass off to raise the money to get here. I'm going to have a good time. A change in the culture was going to have to happen."

The team in Perth was made up of players from three distinct eras of United States women's water polo: long-time veterans who had played under Sandy Nitta in the past, those who cut their teeth on the Senior Team under Vaune Kadlubek but played club water polo in college, and the National Team newcomers whose careers coincided with the explosion of collegiate varsity programs.

The culture clash could be overcome, but it wouldn't happen without growing pains.

Transition was necessary. With the hiring of Guy Baker to lead the team after the 1998 World Championships, transition was unavoidable.

◎◎◎◎◎◎

In March of 1998, a new era for the Women's National Team began. United States Water Polo charged Guy Baker with leading the team to qualifying for the Sydney Olympic Games. Baker served as an assistant under coach Bill Barnett at the 1992 Barcelona Olympics; he had also guided the men's team at UCLA since

1991. In 1995, he took the reins of the Bruins' women's team, newly elevated to varsity status. Baker quickly started filling the UCLA trophy case, sweeping national titles in both genders in the 1995-96 and 1996-97 academic years. The 1998 women's squad was UCLA's deepest yet; it would bring a third straight national championship to Westwood.

The 1998 World Championships, held in January, fell between the men's and women's seasons at UCLA. Baker was in Perth as an assistant for the United States men under head coach John Vargas. When the schedule allowed, he and fellow men's assistant John Tanner, the Stanford women's head coach, watched the United States women's games.

Baker's impressions at the time were that the team was solid athletically but missing a professional look and some measure of seriousness. In terms of personnel, he immediately thought of collegiate players he believed could make an impact on the group.

When he took the helm, Baker's assumption was that the roster would undergo a massive overhaul between Perth and the Olympic Games, less than three years away. In fact, eight of the thirteen players from the 1998 World Championships team went on to represent the United States in the Sydney Olympics.

"My impression coming in was that wouldn't be the case," Baker said. "I thought I was going to come in, and most of them were going to be gone. Everybody going through the process earned their position, but my mindset coming in, I thought that I'd be making a lot of changes, player-wise."

The first practice for the new regime took place at Lynbrook High School in San Jose, California, where thirty athletes were invited to tryout. Reflecting on the mindset of the group at that point, Baker recalled an uncertainty hovering over the athletes from top to bottom. The excitement of the Olympics, and setting out on a mission to Sydney, was palpable. That enthusiasm, however, competed with a fear of the unknown – *Who was Guy Baker, and what would he demand of the team?*

Despite his success with the UCLA women, many in water polo circles considered Baker a men's coach. The decision of the hiring committee to select Baker over National Team pioneer Sandy Nitta didn't sit well with some long-time women's water polo supporters; both Baker and the committee members heard about it in the months after the appointment.

"There had been a lot of coaches who had worked a long time in women's water polo. I understood it," Baker said. "It's a chance to go to the Olympic Games; the committee hired the person who had been three years into women's water polo, just getting started."

If there was uncertainty in the air when the team convened for the first time in San Jose, it wasn't coming from Baker. Never lacking confidence or drive, he was locked in on the task at hand. The road to Sydney was a long one; it was time to take the first steps.

Uncertainty. Anxiety. Chaos.

Those words came to Heather Moody's mind during the coaching and roster changes of 1997 and 1998 and the eighth-place result in Perth. She settled on transition.

"It was transition; I think the state of transition that the program was going through helped Baker's transition, because to go without that bridge would have been too much," she said.

Moody figured the conflict between the past and the present during that time eased the magnitude of change the women's National Team was about to undergo due to its new status as an Olympic event and the arrival of a new head coach.

"If Baker was to step in there without some of that unrest, it wouldn't have worked," she concluded.

Any way one looked at the situation, it had to work. Baker knew that. The players would find out.

By the time Baker got the team together for the first time in San Jose, there were details that were known, and others that were unfamiliar. The United States' path to qualification was clear: place higher than Canada in the final standings at the World Cup in May of 1999. Baker and the team had almost exactly one year to prepare. What was unknown to Baker and assistant coaches Chris Duplanty and Susan Ortwein was detail about their foreign competition, and what precisely they were up against. It didn't matter – in Baker's mind, creating culture was first on his agenda; that required the same approach regardless of what the competition had in store.

The members of the World Championship team received letters inviting them to begin training on May 21 in San Jose. Moody recalled Baker and Michelle Pickering, the team manager, starting the meeting with a tone different than what she had previously experienced in the program.

"They came in, and it was business," she said. "It was a business meeting. It was like, here's the guidelines, here's what you have to commit to, this is your situation; like, boom, boom, boom, boom, boom. We'll be in full-time training; if you can't agree to these terms, then you shouldn't be trying out."

Moody wasn't the only one knocked for a loop by the onslaught.

"This was the first interaction with the new coach," she said. "You're just sitting there, going, *wha...*? It was basically a 'come to Jesus' moment because it was completely different."

The water workout was equally as foreign. Baker had a lot in mind for the first training session. While his impression was that the team had a long way to go, it didn't take long for him to find he had underestimated the situation. Baker admitted his first reaction was, *You've got to be kidding me.* Looking back, he gave more credit to the players and the position they were in. "In hindsight, it's natural," he said. "How would they know what to do and how to do it?"

But at the time, he felt they should know; from that moment on, it felt to Baker that the team was behind. The feeling never passed and served as motivation throughout the journey.

As he walked off the pool deck on May 21, 1998, Baker was by turns anxious and eager; he would have to make some adjustments – fast.

"Fortunately, it was just one practice," he laughed. "We had the whole night to figure out what we were going to do the rest of the weekend."

Despite Baker's stubborn nature, the plan changed in some ways. Rather than push through workouts at his accustomed speed, he slowed down a bit, at the urging of assistant coach Chris Duplanty.

"Dup was great at getting me to slow down," Baker said. "It took a couple years for me to actually understand what he was talking about sometimes. I was always trying to do a lot, and do it fast. If it's in my head, I understand it. It makes no sense to me why someone else doesn't understand it even if they haven't done it. It took me a long time to learn that one."

In addition to swim conditioning, skill work, and tactical play, strength training and fitness were on Baker's list of immediate concerns. The team routine was exact down to the smallest detail. It was a starting point, a clean slate from which the team could craft its image. While the image of strength was a positive for the group, another measure of image received less than enthusiastic response from the athletes.

Committed to approaching high-performance from all angles, the staff conducted body fat tests on the athletes from the outset. Baker attributed early awkwardness and resentment surrounding this practice to his own naïveté. "With a guy, you just say, *This percentage is too high. You've got to get it lower,*" he said. "What's wrong with saying that? Well, there's a lot wrong with saying that when you've got three men and one female athlete, and you're talking about her body fat. What a disaster. What an absolute disaster. Talk about tension."

It was a learning process, one of many for Baker in his early days with the team.

The opening weekend in San Jose was followed up by a training session in Long Beach a week later. When the women arrived on deck, one player's absence was conspicuous. Three-time USWP Athlete of the Year Lynn Wittstock, captain of the 1998 World Championship team in Perth just months before, called Baker during the week informing him of her retirement.

Retiring from the National Team after a World Championship was a common occurrence for the women. At 31 years old following the Rome Worlds in 1994, Lynn Wittstock wasn't quite ready to hang up her cap. But as Sandy Nitta had before her, new head coach Vaune Kadlubek wanted players to commit to four years – the women's World Championship quadrennial.

Wittstock, the team captain since 1987, promised she would stay on for two. But at end of the 1996 Women's Olympic Year Tournament, she saw the turmoil on the team and felt a responsibility to help hold the program together.

"If I quit at that time, it was going to fall to pieces," she said. "It would have caused a snowball effect; I just didn't feel that I could do that to the team. As a leader that people looked up to, if I quit, it would not have been a good thing."

The World Championships in Perth were scheduled for January; that was only eighteen months away. So Wittstock stuck it out. Then in late October came the word of women's water polo's inclusion in the Olympics. Instead of lighting a fire inside of her, Wittstock had nearly the opposite reaction.

"I thought, *Oh, god. I'll try out. Whatever*," she said. Selected flagbearer for the United States delegation at the opening ceremonies of the World Championships in Perth, the 34-year-old Wittstock knew in her heart it was her last major tournament. She kept herself in shape between Worlds and the first training camp with Guy Baker; but she also took a lot of time to consider the ramifications of making a run at the Olympic team.

"My shoulder was locking up; parts of my body were just torn apart," Wittstock said. "Full-time training for two years? I don't know that my body's going to make it. I was ready to be done two years ago – could I hang on for two more years?"

Wittstock had long worked at Blymyer Engineers designing AutoCADs for utility-scale solar, and she felt loyal to the company for giving her the time to play water polo at the elite level. Moving to Long Beach wasn't an appealing option.

Nevertheless, Wittstock drove from Berkeley to San Jose to participate in the first training camp. Although team manager Michelle Pickering purchased a ticket for her to travel to Long Beach for the next session, Wittstock never got on the plane. She called Baker from her desk at work.

"I'm done," she told him. "I'm not coming."

And that was it. The long-time team captain didn't reach out to the team.

"I didn't tell my teammates," she said. "I just didn't show up. There was a plane ticket, and I'm like, *I just can't do it*."

Wittstock made a point to assure Baker her decision had nothing to do with him or the fact that Sandy Nitta was not selected to lead the team.

"People always say about professional athletes, like in the NBA, *You're making all that money. Why are these people retiring? All you have to do is fake it, and you're going to bring home $10 million per year*," she said. "Well, there's no way you can fake it. If you're done, you're done. You can't coast through a practice. You know when it's time. As much as I wanted to keep playing because there was that carrot of the Olympics at the end, I had already hung on for two years. I couldn't do it for two more."

When Baker addressed the team at the Long Beach training session, he previewed the workout, then dropped a bomb. "Lynn's not coming, she quit. Get your suits on and get in."

In another lesson learned, Baker later realized the impact the news of Wittstock's decision had on the group.

"You're sitting there thinking, 'Oh my god, how am I going to make this happen?'" said Heather Moody. "Here's this person with all this experience, a great player physically, she can swim, handle the ball really well, and this coach has cracked her. How are we going to overcome this if she couldn't?"

Ever the team captain, Wittstock also had the best interests of the program in mind when she decided to forego her flight. She considered the summer trip to Europe that was on the National Team schedule.

"At that point, it was a new team," she said. "That was the time to quit if you're going to quit. I thought, if I go on that first trip then I'm taking a spot away from somebody who needs to be there. I'm not going to take somebody's spot for a team that's going to the Olympics. That's just selfish, to me. They needed to get these girls together and get on with the new team."

For Wittstock, a 14-year National Team career ended without the Olympics on her resume. Like many players of her generation around the world, the timing simply wasn't right.

"They finally put us in the Olympics, and I was worn out," she said. "I just couldn't make that last push."

Maureen O'Toole was already a seven-year National Team veteran when Lynn Wittstock joined the team in 1984. Wittstock's departure left O'Toole and Maggi Kelly as the last two players from the 1980s era teams left in the mix for Sydney.

When she decided to end her retirement to pursue the Olympics, the only glitch in her mind was her five-year-old daughter, Kelly. With a strong support network of family and friends in both Northern and Southern California, she confidently took the leap back into international water polo.

"It was a good thing I didn't know what I was getting into," said O'Toole. "Because if I did, I probably would have said no because of Kelly."

A month later, O'Toole was back with the National Team training for the World Championships in Perth. The team's eighth-place finish was eye-opening to the ten-time FINA medalist. As far as her individual performance, O'Toole was the United States' second-leading scorer with nine goals, behind Coralie Simmons' ten. Four years of retirement hadn't eroded her playmaking skills, either.

She arrived at the first tryout with Guy Baker feeling zero anxiety about her position.

"I went to the tryout thinking, *Well, I'm going to make this team*," she said. "I mean, I was the best player in the world. Call it arrogant or whatever; I felt I was going to make the team."

O'Toole and Baker had known each other for years. They coached against each other in three consecutive collegiate championships while at Cal and UCLA. Laura Laughlin, Baker's first wife, was among O'Toole's best friends; the two played together on the National Team for several years.

The first individual meeting between Baker and O'Toole as coach and athlete was anything but a cordial renewal of friendship. Instead, Baker delivered a message O'Toole will never forget.

"Guy called me into the office and told me, *You're old. You're going to be really old at the Olympics, and I don't think you're going to make this team*."

One thought repeatedly ran through O'Toole's mind as she drove home, livid: *All this time I put into this sport; now it's in the Olympics, and I'm not going to get to go.*

She flashed back more than twenty years, to the day she was named to the C team at the 1977 Commerce Internationals. Her approach to this new challenge was exactly the same – she was determined to prove her doubters wrong. "I decided right then and there that I was going to do everything I could," she said. "I was going to take care of myself physically and work harder than everybody else."

The meeting with Baker immediately erased any giddy excitement about the prospects of competing in the Olympics. Her original vision of coming out of retirement, going to the Olympics, and helping the team changed in an instant. O'Toole realized her biggest hurdle was going to be simply making the team – something that had never been a problem for her in the past.

O'Toole now had another glitch to confront.

ᱜᱜᱜᱜᱜᱜ

With the year's FINA event already in the books, the summer of 1998 was free of a major competition. Taking advantage of the rare scheduling flexibility, Baker planned a three-week trip to Europe, lining up tournaments in Yugoslavia and Holland and common training in Hungary. The staff was faced with picking a travel team after just three weekends of practices, two in May and one in June.

In that short amount of time, Baker was focused on articulating the standards of the program and each team member's responsibility to the group when they were apart. Players were sent weight workouts and swim sets to complete on their own. Results were sent back to the coaches, who kept tabs on progress.

Swim testing was a Friday tradition when the team arrived for weekend training. The 3,000-yard test set they completed on the first Friday in San Jose was repeated every time the team was together. The willingness to train diligently when teammates were spread out across the country was crucial to Baker. He had witnessed his first wife, long-time National Team player Laura Laughlin, put in the yardage on her own in order to perform when the team came together. Baker believed players counting on one another to be prepared to make the most of time together created a team connection despite distance.

"The group test set, that's generational," Baker said. "I can't say that we started it, but it was an important part of my program from the beginning and on through the National Team pipeline with the Junior and Youth National Teams."

With his program just off the ground it was already time to fly. After three weekends of evaluation, Baker had to select his first team. One decision in particular caused a rocky start to an important and long-lasting athlete-coach relationship.

ᱜᱜᱜᱜᱜᱜ

The roster turnover following the 1994 Worlds brought an influx of youth into the Women's National Team. Among the fresh faces was Brenda Villa, who debuted as a 16-year-old at the 1996 Olympic Year Tournament in Emmen, Netherlands. Already a veteran of the Junior National Team, she helped the United States earn the bronze medal at the inaugural Junior World Championships, for ages 20 and under, in 1995.

The move to the Senior Team was exciting for Villa; she was pleased to find she could play at that level. A four-goal outburst in one game at the Olympic Year Tournament announced her arrival as a new American star in the making. Armed with that confidence, she followed up her rookie appearance with a breakout performance at the 1997 World Cup in Nancy, France. Villa led the United States offense, netting eight goals in five games.

After her big performance in France, the next phase of the program's transition took place. She recalled her first interaction with returning head coach Sandy Nitta. "Sandy said, *You don't know me, but you owe me,*" Villa said, referring to the program Nitta had established at Commerce decades before. Coaching-wise, the transition seemed smooth enough. But when the team competed in Perth at the World Championships, Villa's offensive output plummeted.

Without seeing a marked reduction in playing time, Villa managed only three goals in eight games as the United States sputtered to eighth place. The return of veterans to the team made a difference – Villa deferred on offense more often. Her looks at the goal were fewer, and came from spots other than those to which she was accustomed. What wasn't a factor was limitation from her new coach, Nitta, who nicknamed Villa "All Day." The high school senior had the green light to shoot, but in Perth the freedom didn't equate to tallies on the scoresheet. Fortunately, Villa had a shooter's mentality; the lack of production didn't affect her confidence in the least. There would always be more shots to make.

With three major senior international events under her belt, and the proven ability to score goals, Villa had carved out a spot for herself in the program by the time Guy Baker took the helm. She was happy to play for any coach; because of her youth at the time, any politics surrounding the coaching change were well off her radar.

She was excited to start playing for Baker but a little hesitant at the same time. On her way to Stanford in the fall, she took notice of the number of players trying out from Baker's UCLA squad. Early on, she also picked up on the fact that he was looking for players with size and strength – two qualities the 5'4" high school senior lacked.

Even so, Villa was confident in her position, thinking to herself, *I was on the team before him. I do have a place here.*

When the team was announced, there was a place for Villa, but it wasn't with the Senior National Team. Baker explained to her that he wanted her to help the Junior National Team qualify for the next Junior World Championships. She would go to the Junior Pan Ams in Havana, Cuba, rather than Europe with the senior team.

"My feeling was she could do that and still get games," Baker said, explaining his rationale. "I was trying to get international competition for as many players as I could that first summer. That was a shock to Brenda."

Villa said it wasn't a complete shock. What angered her the most was the reason. Yes, she was young enough to play on the Junior Team. But so was her longtime friend, competitor, and fellow Junior Team member, Robin Beauregard. A year older than Villa, Beauregard had already played one season at UCLA with Baker, but had not yet joined the Senior National Team. The European trip would be her Senior Team debut.

Villa understood that she wasn't competing directly with Beauregard, a defender, for a position on the team. Nevertheless, at that point, Villa felt overlooked, and that she didn't fit the mold Baker was looking for.

The assignment seemed like a demotion, despite the explanation that she would benefit from playing a leadership role at the Junior Pan Ams.

"I was pissed I didn't make that team," she said, emotion wrenching her face as if it were just yesterday. "It was really frustrating. Guy was our new coach, and I didn't know what he was thinking or what I needed to do."

Feeling uncertain of her position on a team for perhaps the first time in her water polo career, and with the thought of leaving home for college in the fall, Villa was reeling. A former teammate came to her rescue, easing her fears through a written letter. The recently retired Lynn Wittstock reached out to Villa, offering words of encouragement. Wittstock urged her to look at the situation not as a set-back, but as an opportunity.

"Lynn's advice meant so much to me," Villa said. Wittstock, the National Team captain when Villa joined the squad, told her that she had a long career ahead with the Senior Team. "She told me to do a great job at Junior Pan Ams and to prove myself. She said I'd be back where I expected to be soon," Villa recalled.

Wittstock's wisdom came from the beginnings of her own career, when she was a rookie in 1984. Sandy Nitta gave each team member a token; Wittstock received a button with the phrase "Believe in yourself" on it. Realizing that she was projecting a lack of confidence, Wittstock let the gift light a fire inside of her. She vowed to step out of her shell, a message she wanted to pass on to the 18-year-old from Commerce.

It was obvious to Wittstock that Villa possessed phenomenal talent. She was also quiet, despite her uncanny understanding of the game. As team captain, Wittstock had seen Villa "trying to find her spot." She had been in the same place years before.

"I wanted Brenda to know that she was a valuable team member; that her time would come," Wittstock said. "I wanted her to come out of her shell, just as I had."

The button that fueled her fire traveled with Wittstock on every National Team trip for fourteen years. Villa kept the letter all the way to the Olympics in Sydney, a reminder of the captainship of her former teammate and an inspiration when she needed a pick-me-up.

Baker sent Villa to the Junior Team to become a leader. By the 2008 Beijing Games, she became an Olympic captain.

Reflecting on the early process of athlete identification and selection, Baker pointed to the short time frame and the need to name a team. Getting as many players competing in international games was the priority.

"It's an interesting dynamic looking back on it," Baker said. "It's what you see. It's some of your perceptions coming in; as you learn as a coach, you've got to keep your mind open to things, because you come in with perceptions, and then you're projecting that onto what you're seeing. Maybe you're not actually seeing things for what they are."

Baker pointed out the drawbacks of tryouts in selection, noting that the circumstances may not be right for a player to shine, or show what the coaches need to see, and how their play fits into a team.

"All those dynamics were in play," Baker continued. "It was who I was comfortable with at that time."

Baker admits that besides being young enough to get international games with the Junior Team that summer, Villa did not fit at least one of his projections.

"I liked athletic players during that time, and Brenda wasn't the most athletic player," he said. "I was projecting. I took some players who were a good size. I did come from the men's side, and anybody will tell you, internationally, the United States team completely changed physically during that time. I was projecting, *Okay, this player, based on their size and how well they swim and how well they shoot, they can be this position.* Mentally, some of them couldn't do it during that time, or it wasn't the right time, or whatever it might have been."

This particular perception wasn't a new challenge for Villa. While her water polo IQ stood out as special, she started hearing from coaches about her fitness and speed before Baker arrived.

"When I made my first Junior Worlds team at 15, my individual meeting with Brent Bohlender was, *Everything is great, but be aware of your weight*," she said. "To hear that at 15 was hard."

While never overweight as a child, Villa wouldn't be classified as petite for her height. She believes that if she were petite, she may have never made the National Team.

"If I weighed what I was supposed to at 5'4", I would have been pushed around at that level," she concluded.

Villa knew she could compete at the Senior level; she had the experience to prove it. Her problem was proving to Baker that despite not fitting the classic mold of a player with the measurables he was searching for, the value she added in the water was essential to the team's success. Left at home while the Senior Team went to Europe, she would have to wait patiently for her next opportunity. At that age, and when it came to water polo, patience was not Brenda Villa's strong suit.

In July, the Women's National Team headed across the Atlantic for a three-week trip to Yugoslavia, Hungary and Holland. The itinerary was lengthy on purpose – Baker wanted the most time with the team in unfamiliar surroundings, in order to gauge their ability to adapt and learn.

The first destination was Pančevo, Yugoslavia, by way of Budapest. Following three flights to get to Hungary, the team took an eight-hour bus ride to Pančevo. At the airport, they were met by a man who spoke little English. He took their bags, put them in another car and took off. The bus driver didn't speak English; he had not spoken a word. The darkness on the road was impenetrable.

Baker caught assistant coach Chris Duplanty's eye. A three-time Olympian, Duplanty was a veteran of travel to Yugoslavia; he had never traveled like this before. The two coaches, sitting across from each other on the bus, traded a quick exchange.

"Women's water polo," Duplanty said.

"Yeah, you're in," replied Baker.

While the mode of transportation was new to Duplanty and Baker, to the players, everything was normal. At one point in the middle of the night, when he hadn't seen a single car on the road in over an hour, Baker turned around to find team captain Julie Swail awake in the seat behind him.

"He asked, *Should I be at all worried?*" Swail recalled. "I'm like, no, this seems about right. Is this normal for you?" Swail laughed. "It's like he expected a tour bus or something."

Swail assured Baker that this was his new normal and predicted the safe delivery of the team – and their bags – to the hotel. The team checked in in the middle of the night and woke to find their accommodations were far from luxurious.

"It was a lousy hotel with lousy food," Baker said. The men's team sometimes experienced bad hotels in different parts of the world, but Pančevo was a new low.

On the first morning in the hotel, players approached assistant coach Susan Ortwein, concerned about what looked like blood on their walls and ceiling.

Ortwein replied, "Well, there's none in mine."

The room and board may have been below par, but no compromise was made in terms of training. The standards of working while on the road, no matter the amenities, were set on this first journey. Dry-land training took place on an open field beside the hotel where the players had to keep an eye out for all sorts of hazardous items on the ground. The team swam in the shallow end of the pool while other teams practiced. They took extra pool time to swim after their opponents left. Despite less-than-optimal conditions, nothing was skipped training-wise; the attitude became a trademark of the program.

Considering how much each athlete pushed herself to her physical limit, not every player was able to replenish themselves with proper nutrition. Some had trouble stomaching the food; the most seasoned veterans brought a stock of snacks from home. A trip to the store to boost the supply netted a random assortment of edibles.

"Guy gave me $50 to get snacks at the local store; I'm thinking, *This is the best coach ever*," Swail said. "I'm looking for snacks; they have canned beans, canned meat, dry pasta. We got everything that we thought was even remotely snackable."

One player who had no trouble filling up was National Team newcomer, Ellen Estes.

"It was my first trip with the Senior Team, and I got known for pretty much eating anything," she said.

Estes' approach regarding the Yugoslavian cuisine was simple: *I'm hungry. Mystery meat? Sure. If it's not going to kill me, I'm going to eat it. I don't really care.*

"We got these huge sandwiches, with random meat you couldn't identify," Estes said. "And I would be the only one eating them; I'd eat one on the bus on the way to the pool. They would be looking at me like, *Who is this girl that's eating this mystery meat?*"

While the looks didn't bother Estes at all, she did consider the impression she was making on her new coach, Guy Baker.

"He was probably thinking, *Oh, my God. What is she doing? Is she going to be able to play after eating that?*" she said, laughing at the memory.

Estes answered the question with solid performances throughout the Yugoslavian tournament.

"I'd eat that huge sandwich, hop in the water, and go play," she said. "Guy finally figured out, if I didn't actually eat fairly close to playing, I would feel weak and not have enough energy to play."

If her opponents knew Estes needed pre-game fuel to succeed, they might have hidden the food. Estes was on a water polo rampage in 1998; named a first-team All-American at Stanford, she poured in a school record 93 goals on the year. The record still stands, virtually unchallenged in the nearly two decades following Estes' historic output.

At the end of the Mountain Pacific Sports Conference tournament that year, she was approached by UCLA's Guy Baker, the newly appointed National Team coach. Her post-season schedule filled up quickly, as Baker invited her to open training sessions. While the promotion to the Senior National Team was a logical step for Estes – she had competed at the 1997 Junior World Championships in the Czech Republic – it fulfilled a desire she had allowed herself to entertain many years before.

When Estes was a senior in high school, the National Team held a training camp at her club's home pool, Indian Valley College. As club practice ended, her coach, Andrew Morris, had her and a friend stay in the water; the two passed together on the side as the Senior Team jumped in.

"I have pretty vivid memories of them – Coralie, Brenda, Mo, Lynn Wittstock," Estes said. "I remember thinking, *I think I could play with them. That would be fun. I think I'm pretty good at this sport. I wonder if I could actually play with them some day.*"

It wasn't long before she was in Yugoslavia, playing for the National Team – powered by mystery meat sandwiches.

Gary and Carole Estes each passed along a critical trait to their daughter, Ellen.

From Gary, she received athleticism. Always encouraged to play sports and participate in a team atmosphere, he became a collegiate athlete, playing tennis at Grand Canyon University in Arizona.

From Carole, something else that would define Ellen during her water polo career.

"I don't know if you'd call her athletic, but she is super competitive," Estes said of her mother. "People always wonder where I got my competitiveness from. I would say it's definitely a blend; my dad from sports and his athletic career, but it's mostly from my mom. During the holidays we play Scrabble, and it wasn't until recently that I actually beat her fair and square; I think I've won once out of probably fifty or sixty games."

She laughed before continuing, "That one time I beat her, it was the best victory of all time. Competitiveness runs in the family, and it comes from my parents."

Estes grew up in Novato, California, swimming and playing plenty of team sports such as basketball and soccer. Like many of her fellow Olympians, she followed a brother into water polo; but for Estes, it was a younger brother, Brian, who had started playing on the local club. In a twist to the common story of athletes migrating from swimming to water polo, Estes' swim coach was the one who suggested that she take up the sport.

Friday Funday at the Rolling Hills Swim Club in Novato provided the inspiration for a future Olympian. Estes' swim team played water polo every Friday to break up the routine. She quickly found she loved Fridays much more than Monday through Thursday. Her coach saw not only Estes' competitive nature; but the joy that came along with playing water polo.

On her swim coach's suggestion, Estes decided to try out for the high school boys' team as a freshman. Nervous and intimidated, she talked her friend Daisy into trying out for the JV team with her.

"It's freshman year of high school, so it's kind of a big deal; a big transition," Estes said. "We went to the pool deck of Novato High, and we were super nervous to try out and play with the boys. But a lot of the boys were on our swim team, so after the first week of practice, it was fine."

The JV team had about ten girls that year, largely because of the Marin Water Polo Club, which served the whole of Marin County; from the Golden Gate Bridge to the south and Novato to the north. Estes joined Marin the summer between her freshman and sophomore years, enjoying the girls-only practices and summer tournaments.

After Estes played two years on the co-ed JV team at Novato High, Carole Estes and other moms of girls on the team decided it was time for the school to sponsor a girls' water polo team. They took action.

"The feeling was that it was ridiculous," Estes said. "We knew about Title IX. There were plenty of girls – enough to have our own team. We had more than enough to scrimmage ourselves."

The parents approached Andrew Morris, fresh out of college and a former player on the Marin club, about coaching the first girls' team at the high school. Armed with a coach, the girls and moms scheduled a meeting with the Novato High School athletic director.

"We walked into the athletic director's office and said that they needed to either create a girls' team or they'd be hearing from some lawyers," Estes said. "Not in a threatening way, but just, look, there's enough interest. You need to do something about it. We can't not have a girls team."

Sure enough, in the fall of Estes' junior year, she and her friends had a team of their own. Many of the local high schools were making the move to include girls' water polo at the same time, including Terra Linda, Tamalpais, Sir Francis Drake, and San Marin. Marin Water Polo Club was the anchor of the sport in the area, filling the girls' teams at the local high schools. Meeting the requirement of four schools in order to have an official league schedule and championship, the Marin County Athletic League adopted girls' water polo in the fall of 1996.

While girls' high school water polo was also getting off the ground across the Richmond Bridge in the East Bay, the club scene wasn't yet taking off in that area for girls. Several of the most talented players from the Walnut Creek area commuted to Indian Valley College in Novato to play club water polo for Morris at Marin – a one-hour drive each way.

"We had five or six players making the commute three or four times a week for practices," Morris said. "We often had tournaments on weekends. It was a huge compliment, but surprising that there wasn't more going on for girls in the East Bay at the time."

The creation of the girls' high school league along with the growth of the Marin club provided one clear benefit: the female players could more easily draw the attention of the local college coaches, whose programs were rapidly improving as they gained varsity status. In the winter and spring, club teams competed in tournaments with the colleges. Teams like Stanford, Cal, and UC Davis competed against masters teams and age group club teams at tournaments like the Pacific Coast Championships.

"It was a great era, before there were NCAA rules about contact," Morris said. "Women's water polo was a close community in Northern California."

Morris encouraged Estes to try out for the Youth National Team, and she quickly rose through the ranks of the Youth and Junior levels.

"Andrew was so influential in my early career," Estes said. "I think early on, he recognized my competitive spirit and nature. I had experience in team sports and picked up water polo quickly. He realized that I might have a future in the sport."

Morris was right. In the summer after her junior year, Estes began to feel the same about her future in water polo.

"Having played a season with an all-girls' team and club all year round, by the end of that summer, I think I had enough games under my belt to realize I was good," Estes said. "I felt like I was going to be good at my position. You get enough measurements by these different games against all the different clubs playing in California."

Entering her senior year, Estes knew she wanted to play water polo in college, with hopes of that leading to a career in the international game. Calling the era of recruiting "low-tech," Estes remembers writing letters to college coaches.

"Technology has just changed so much," she said. "There was this hard, spiral-bound little book with contact information for all the college coaches. Nothing was electronic. I remember typing up letters, essentially all hard copy, to say I was interested in playing water polo. It was definitely low-tech back in the day; it was harder to make those connections and get visibility outside of your local area."

Estes heard back from Maureen O'Toole at Cal, and Ben Quittner at Stanford. She was greatly interested in both universities; the decision was a tough one.

"If I was going to base my decision on the water polo program at the time, I would have chosen Cal," she said. "The team that would put me in position to win national championships at the time would have been Cal."

The opportunity to play for O'Toole, whom Estes looked up to, was enticing. But Stanford had always been on her radar. Even when her family lived in Oregon, where she grew up, a 10-year-old Estes asked her parents what colleges she should be thinking about. Carole Estes replied, "Stanford."

Estes took recruiting trips to the Bay Area schools, the only two to pursue her for their teams. Once she received her acceptance to Stanford, her mind was made up.

Even as an accomplished high school player who had experience on the Youth and Junior National Teams, Estes was as nervous for her first college game as she had been when she walked onto the Novato pool deck as a high school freshman.

"I think I cried before the game," she said. "I was like, *Oh, my gosh. This is serious; everyone's really good.*"

Estes was good too, as a freshman. As a sophomore, she was great. Her record-breaking year caught the attention of coaches throughout the collegiate ranks, including Guy Baker.

In one of their first one-on-one meetings, Baker focused on Estes' aggressiveness. As an opposing coach, Baker told her that she lost her effectiveness when she let her competitive spirit get the best of her; silly kickouts from being overaggressive or overreacting to physical play benefited only Estes' opponents.

"It definitely took me a while to figure out how to reign in that competitive edge and the feistiness that ultimately made me a good player internationally," she said. "It needed to be at a level where I could contain it, and it could be effective."

That feistiness in the water led the National Team to give a nickname to Estes' alter ego: Andre.

Robin Beauregard, one of the center defenders who matched up with Estes in practices for nearly six years, coined the moniker in reference to Andre the Giant's role as the lovable Fezzik in the movie *The Princess Bride*; "Fezzik is mild-mannered and nice – until something snaps."

"Plus, it was easier than calling her Jekyll," Beauregard quipped.

"She has the sweetest demeanor outside the water, kind of like Mama Ellen," said Brenda Villa. "And then you get into the pool with her, and she's a different person. You would never think that these two personalities were one person. They are, and it takes teammates a while to recognize Andre, and not let Andre affect relationships outside of the water."

One memorable instance of Andre taking over occurred at the 2003 World Championships in Barcelona. The United States was on fire, taking it to Italy in the gold medal match. Estes was in the zone.

"She was tearing it up, unstoppable, creating kickouts, scoring goals," Villa said. "At one point, Guy subbed her out; we were in hostile territory, playing in Spain. The Italians had so many fans, and we were getting booed."

Climbing out of the pool at mid-tank after an American goal, Estes welcomed the boos that rained down on her from the grandstand. Estes – or Andre – looked up at the jeering spectators, kissed her bicep, and waved at the crowd.

"She sees red; then that's all she sees when she's playing," Villa said. "As much as you're in the zone, you still have to make sure that you're playing with your team, that you're following our game plan. She could do it; it's definitely a unique skill that made her special."

@②@⑤@⑥

The tournament in Pančevo included Yugoslavia, the Czech Republic, Great Britain, Hungary, and the United States. The Americans and Hungarians faced off in the finals, with the United States triumphant, 10-8.

Baker thought it was a great start; the win was satisfying for the veterans, who were soundly defeated by Hungary in Perth. Baker kept the Pančevo trophy, a memento from his first international tournament victory. The top of the award was lost over the years, but the base of the trophy, a good solid piece of marble, lives on.

Within months of the tournament, NATO forces began a heavy bombing campaign on the city of Pančevo, targeting an oil refinery, the Utva aircraft factory, and chemical plants.

At the conclusion of the competition, the American and Hungarian teams boarded the bus together for the eight-hour return trek to Budapest. Perhaps peeved at losing to the United States, the Hungarian players sat one to a seat in the front, leaving the Americans to squeeze into the remaining seats at the back of the bus. As they neared Budapest in the darkness of morning, the bus stopped every so often; a Hungarian player got out, hopped into a waiting car, and drove away.

The delay created by the individual drop-offs didn't damper the team's spirit, which received a boost when their accommodations proved to be a solid improvement over the hotel in Pančevo. Housed at the sports training center, on the Pest side of the city, everyone had time to explore before getting back to work. The teams trained together for a week, with practice sessions in the morning and afternoon, followed by scrimmages in the evening. Hungary and the United States were evenly matched, but throughout the week, Baker felt his squad beginning to gain the upper hand on its opponent. By the time they left Budapest, the progress was clear.

The final leg of the inaugural trip of the new era took the team to Holland and the Dutch training facility in Zeist, a town a little less than an hour south of Amsterdam. While it was Baker's first time in Zeist, many of the players, along with assistant coach Susan Ortwein, a former National Team member, were quite familiar with the setup, known to the Americans as "Camp Snoopy" for the lush forest surrounding the small housing units.

The road-weary team was proving its perseverance and grit to Baker; it continued to impress as the eight-team Dutch Trophy tournament began. In group play, the United States defeated reigning world champion Italy, and their travel and training partner, Hungary, to finish atop the standings. A narrow loss to Australia in the semifinals pitted Baker's troops against the tournament host in the bronze medal game.

A strong outing by the United States wasn't enough to overcome the Netherlands, but Baker was pleased with the result.

The trip he had set up as a test of the mettle of his new team netted a first-place trophy, plenty of obstacles in terms of food and lodging, a week of hammering against the Hungarians, swim sets, weight lifting, dry-land training in unusual places, and reason for optimism after the team acquitted itself well against all three medalists from the recent World Championships at the Dutch Trophy.

"Three-week trips are brutal, but we became warriors," Baker said. "Traveling is hard and tiring, but I had to find out what we had there."

Amid a sea of uncertainties, what Baker and the team had at the conclusion of their first summer was a solid base of work which they could build upon. And they had less than a year for that foundation to pay off at the World Cup in May.

Nicolle Payne and Maureen O'Toole – Sendoff to Sydney, July 2000

6

EXPLOSION

Nicolle Payne

Coralie Simmons

Brent Bohlender's office on the pool deck named in his honor at Johansen High School is filled with a history of water polo in California's Central Valley. The first California high school coach to reach 1000 victories in one sport, Bohlender's career spanned four decades. In addition to pioneering girls' high school water polo in California, Bohlender served as the Women's Junior National Team coach throughout a critical period for the women's program. Eleven of the thirteen athletes on the 2000 Olympic team spent time with Bohlender in the Junior ranks.

Team photos cover the walls, and trophies line the shelves surrounding Bohlender's desk – all reminders of his work and success with hundreds of club and high school athletes.

In the 1970s Sandy Nitta pushed for women's collegiate clubs at universities around the country, while Bohlender pushed the high school side.

"Actually, I thought hers was a lost cause," Bohlender said. "Way back then, I thought, college, it's not going to happen. I just kept focusing on high school. We both got the payoff that we wanted in the end, no doubt about it."

In 1973, the Modesto schools, in an action tied to the recently passed Title IX legislation, added girls' water polo as a sport in the Central California Conference (CCC). Four high schools – Beyer, Grace Davis, Atwater, and Merced – formed the original league. After a brief stint at Beyer, Bohlender took the reins at Grace Davis.

For a long time, the Central Valley was the only area in the state with a high school girls' league, leading to a substantial amount of honors for the athletes of the early era. When the California Interscholastic Federation (CIF) announced its 100th Anniversary Fall All-Century Team in 2014, the list included eight female water polo players graduating between 1979 and 1992. Seven of the eight hailed from CCC schools Beyer, Turlock, and Grace Davis. The one exception was Maureen O'Toole, a 1979 graduate of Long Beach Wilson.

"You saw so many Modesto girls on that All-Century list," Bohlender said. "Nobody else played. Whoever our league MVP was was also the state player of the year. There was nobody else playing."

There may not have been any other leagues playing in California, but as early as the spring of 1970, a girls' team began playing at Pasadena High School. Jennie Jacobsen, the team manager of the National Team from 1978 until 1980, was on the original teams at Pasadena High, which went undefeated against local high schools Blair, Muir, and Temple City. In 1973, Kaia Hedlund, who would later be heavily involved in collegiate water polo, was on the first girls' team at Arcadia High School. Hedlund recalls borrowing the boys' equipment and convincing one of the boys to coach. The team received no funding, but the swim coach volunteered to act as the team's sponsor.

By 1977, girls' water polo was fully established as a championship sport in the CCC, but Bohlender wanted to find teams for a girls' tournament. Berkeley High School had a girls' team with eventual United States National Team members Maggi Kelly, Jocelyn Wilkie, and Lynn Wittstock. Berkeley became a regular attendee at Bohlender's annual tournament. Looking to widen the field, Bohlender used the contacts he made as Junior National Team coach. Reed Barnitz in New

Mexico had standouts Heather Moody and Robbie Larson on his club. When Bohlender asked Barnitz to bring his high school team, Barnitz replied that his best players attended different high schools.

"Bring 'em," Bohlender said. "We were probably skirting the rules a little bit."

The same happened with a club from Reno. Then Steve Marsing from Utah brought a high school team that included future National Team member Courtney Johnson. Jim McMaster from Newberg, Oregon, once complained to Bohlender at the United States Water Polo convention about the lack of evaluation of girls from his state.

"Bring your team out," was Bohlender's response. "Then I put him on the Junior Team staff, and then they started coming."

The tournament was eventually dubbed the Western States Invitational. From an inaugural field of eight teams in 1977, the tournament grew to over seventy across varsity and JV divisions. In 2015, the 38th version of Western States took place in nine pools across greater Modesto area.

Over the years, Western States has drawn teams from Oregon, New Mexico, Nevada, Utah, and all over California, including a club team from Huntington Beach in the mid-1990s.

"They came up here with a team that included Robin Beauregard and Dani Bell, and that group," Bohlender recalled. The popularity of girls' high school teams in the Southern California sections was increasing, and Huntington Beach's attendance was a boon for Bohlender and Western States. "That was short-lived, though, because almost right after that, you had CIF starting down there; with different seasons, it killed that connection that could have happened."

Whether or not teams from the different regions of California could play each other at Western States, the biggest girls' high school tournament still represents the rise in opportunity for girls to play water polo in high school – a trend pushed in large part by the explosive growth of women's water polo in the collegiate ranks.

Beginning in the 1970s, women's water polo at the collegiate level came in the form of club competition. *Water Polo Planet* lists Women's National Champions beginning in 1984, when coach Jamey Wright led UC Davis over Cal in the title game. Stanford, UC San Diego, and UC Santa Barbara won the next three Nationals. In 1995, Slippery Rock University of Pennsylvania made its fourth appearance in the National Championship game, and became the first team from outside of California to capture the title of Collegiate Champion. Led by coach Doc Hunkler, the women of The Rock downed San Diego State to reach the pinnacle of collegiate women's water polo.

When Slippery Rock ascended to the top spot, women's water polo was in the midst of an exciting growth spurt.

A 1991 NCAA survey of member institutions' expenditures for sports in both genders found that while undergraduate enrollment was about even, participation and finances were not. Female students made up only 30 percent of the participants in intercollegiate athletics; their programs received about 30 percent of athletics scholarship funds, 23 percent of operating budgets, and only 17 percent of recruiting funds. The findings led to the formation of the NCAA Gender-Equity Task Force.

In 1994, the NCAA adopted the recommendations of the task force, including the creation of a list of emerging sports for women. Nine sports – archery, badminton, bowling, rowing, ice hockey, squash, synchronized swimming, team handball and water polo – were on the original list. Among the requirements for an emerging sport was gaining championship status – a minimum of forty varsity NCAA programs – within ten years. The first emerging sport to achieve NCAA Championship status was women's rowing in 1997. Women's ice hockey and women's water polo followed suit in the 2000-01 academic year, and women's bowling was next in 2003-04.

Sports can be removed from the emerging sport list, though, as happened to synchronized swimming in 2010, when the sport failed to show progress toward the requisite forty teams needed to reach championship status. There are currently four varsity synchronized swimming programs nationwide. The most recent women's sport to reach NCAA Championship status is beach volleyball, which crowned its first champion in May of 2016. Equestrian, rugby, and triathlon are currently on the emerging sport list.

At the time of the task force recommendations, only four women's water polo programs in the country held varsity status: Harvard University, UC San

Diego, Pomona-Pitzer Colleges, and Slippery Rock University. By the 1995-96 academic year, the number skyrocketed to twenty. Two years later, the number reached thirty-two, well within reach of the mandated forty programs needed to hold an NCAA championship.

Instrumental in the expansion of women's water polo at the collegiate level was Daniel Sharadin, of the Office of Collegiate and Senior Programs for United States Water Polo. The office was conceived in 1995 by Bruce Wigo, Mike Schofield, and Monte Nitzkowski, with the purpose of preserving the men's NCAA Championship.

"There was legislation on the NCAA books that said if you fell below a certain percentage of sponsorship, then you lost your NCAA Championship," Sharadin explained.

Men's collegiate water polo was on the cusp of falling below the mandatory percentage level. Also at risk were men's gymnastics and riflery. Wigo, Schofield, and Nitzkowski approached Sharadin, the coach of the Villanova men – a program recently downgraded from varsity to club status. Wigo, the Executive Director of USWP, saw Sharadin's position as Commissioner of the Collegiate Water Polo Association as a good platform from which to lobby for the men's game.

Wigo asked Sharadin to carry on much of the work that Kaia Hedlund had been doing voluntarily at the request of Collegiate Coaches Association leaders Ted Newland and Pete Snyder. Hedlund managed a grant program funded by the USOC and United States Water Polo aimed at adding new men's water polo programs. In his position with USWP, Sharadin continued the dialogue with administrators across the country, lobbying to add more varsity men's programs.

"As commissioner at the time, I thought, 'Well, that's certainly not going to help my cause here as commissioner if we lose the men's championship,'" Sharadin recalled.

He agreed to take the position on the condition that he remain with the CWPA. Wigo quickly agreed; Sharadin pledged to devote summers and off-time between seasons to the cause. His first victory consisted of getting new legislation written that took away the percentage requirement, giving men's water polo a safety margin in case additional schools dropped the sport.

For the first couple years on the job, Sharadin focused solely on men's programs.

"I wasn't really thinking about women's programs," he said. "And then I sat down with Bruce and said, 'You know, we should be doing both.' Remember there was no women's Olympics, so the National Governing Body was having a hard time politically, as to putting money towards developing women's collegiate water polo when there was no Olympic water polo.

"But as you started to see that coming on the horizon, we said, 'We need to do this for both.' That's when I began pushing for both women and men with the institutions."

In October of 1997, women's water polo was added to the 2000 Olympic Games. In April of 1998, Santa Clara University elevated its women's club team to varsity status, to begin play in 1999. In the same month, Cal State San Bernardino announced its women's program, bringing the total number of schools to thirty-seven.

The momentum continued. In June 1998, women's water polo edged ever closer to the magic number of forty institutions. Brown University and George Washington University elevated their programs from club to varsity.

One year after the announcement of women's water polo in the Sydney Olympics, the number of collegiate varsity programs reached its goal of forty teams. Hartwick College, in Oneonta, New York, became number forty in October 1998, prompting Daniel Sharadin to proudly explain the situation of women's water polo and the NCAA Championship process in his monthly report from the USWP Office of Senior and Collegiate Programs:

Great News! The announcement made by Hartwick College to add a women's varsity water polo program in the year 2000-01 brings the total number of women's NCAA varsity programs to 40. The significance means we can now write legislation to request a fully sponsored NCAA Championship for women. Presently, the rules state that emerging sports must have 40 institutions for a period of two years before they can request to have the championship sponsored, but we are going to request a waiver of this rule, based on the fact that we have 40 announced and there has been no other emerging sport to receive a championship since Crew four years ago. Worse case scenario, we are looking at a championship in 2003, while best case scenario at this point would be 2000. In any case, it is no longer "if" but "when."

When women's water polo reached the magic number of forty teams, a Women's Collegiate Committee already had its ducks in a row to ensure the quick adoption of an NCAA tournament.

When Ted Leland was outgoing Chair of the Men's NCAA Water Polo Committee, he and Secretary Rules Editor Ted Newland lobbied the men's committee hard to insert Kaia Hedlund, Assistant Athletic Director at the University of Hawaii, as the new chair. Despite the lack of varsity water polo at the UH campus, Hedlund was an appealing candidate for the position due to the work she had done with men's water polo, particularly her efforts to expand the number of varsity teams.

Hedlund chaired the NCAA Men's Water Polo Committee from 1996 through 2000.

During this time, the University of Hawaii fell in the category of many schools: seeking Title IX compliance while sponsoring a football team. Women's water polo provided an attractive solution.

"Schools were going, 'We have to add a women's sport,' and many had club water polo with a lot of great athletes," Hedlund explained. "The growth began gradually with the expectation that certainly it would gain NCAA status some day."

In 1996, with an eye toward that movement, Sharadin suggested Hedlund form a women's collegiate committee. Given her efforts and involvement at the time, she was well-positioned to play an instrumental role in its formation.

"We formalized the Women's Collegiate Committee that year," she said. Hedlund concurrently chaired both the NCAA Men's Water Polo Committee and the Women's Collegiate Committee. "With my status on the men's committee, I was also working with Barbara Kalbus, who did the work of editing the rule book."

One example was editing the rule book to include language for both genders. With Kalbus writing the text, the men's committee agreed to it. But Hedlund describes the practice as "outside of the regular NCAA structure."

"I mean, it sounds funny, but you know this is coming, so you're thinking, 'How can we do this?'" she said. The women's committee focused on preparing institutions which added women's water polo for the rules and structure of a fully sponsored NCAA sport. "We focused on the NCAA rule book because we wanted the schools to be following the NCAA rules for scholarships and everything else, before we became an emerging sport."

The Women's Collegiate Committee started to mirror the NCAA rules long before reaching the required forty teams.

Hedlund was also a member of the NCAA Financial Aid Committee, and suggested to the Women's Water Polo Committee that their sport have a maximum of eight scholarships per school. The committee was in agreement, and Hedlund finagled it into the legislation.

"We thought that was a good number to encourage the big schools with football to add women's water polo, but not so many that the smaller schools would be disadvantaged, and decide against adding the sport," Hedlund explained.

Other rules such as the defining of the competitive season were added through the Olympic Sports Liaison Committee. Hedlund wrote the text of the rules and worked through edits with the committee. "Once we had all of that, then we were going through the political process. You have to have standing in the NCAA – a lot of that I just kind of snuck through because I was on the men's committee," Hedlund said.

"That was all done so we could say to the NCAA when the time came, 'Look, we've been doing this for years,'" Hedlund recalled. "'Here are our rules. It's already in the NCAA rule book.'"

Women's water polo was included on the list of emerging sports. The organization provided by the Women's Collegiate Committee led to simplified discussions with the NCAA at that time, and throughout the explosive growth of the following years.

"Once we were an emerging sport, you got more schools adding women's water polo," Hedlund said. "And Dan Sharadin and I were both very active in targeting schools – looking at who has a pool, who has swimming. A lot of it was who has football and is going to need to add women's sports."

Sharadin and Hedlund researched the landscape for potential targets. They looked at individual schools, but also conferences, hoping to make a big gain in numbers in one fell swoop. The job required countless conversations with athletics directors, college commissioners, and college administrators – as well as swim coaches and club water polo coaches.

Sharadin figures the most important part of his job was creating relationships at institutions.

"It was based on trying to develop a scenario that's a win-win," he said. "You want it to be a win obviously for water polo by getting the program added, but you also don't want to add a program at an institution that's not going to support it. And you want to make sure that the institution itself is going to benefit from the addition of the sport.

"So, if you add water polo at a place where they really don't understand it, or they're not equipped to support it properly, it's just going to fail," Sharadin continued. "And then you end up hurting student-athletes that get recruited there. It's just a bad situation. I was very much motivated by the idea of creating a win-win situation, making sure that it was going to be positive for both sides."

Sharadin knew that water polo didn't have the status of mainstream sports such as basketball or tennis. He also found that women's water polo faced an uphill battle against women's lacrosse and field hockey. These sports, he learned, had much more traction and were better understood throughout the country. Many of the Senior Woman Administrators making decisions about adding sports came out of the lacrosse or field hockey background in women's sports.

"When they moved into administration after their coaching or playing careers, they had a real affinity towards those types of sports, as opposed to something like water polo," Sharadin said. "So you're trying to develop relationships with these administrators so that they trust your judgment and what you're saying to them – so that they feel like you're not going to try to sell them on something that wasn't of value to them."

When Sharadin took the position of Director of Collegiate and Senior Programs, his primary objective was to save men's collegiate water polo. He succeeded, stabilizing the sponsorship of the sport.

He also oversaw the rapid expansion of women's collegiate water polo. From four varsity teams when he began, the women's collegiate varsity ranks comprised fifty-two teams when Sharadin's office was closed by United States Water Polo in 2002.

Both Sharadin and Hedlund viewed the office closure as a lost opportunity. Many schools that had been identified as prime candidates to add the sport slipped through the cracks with no official water polo entity to provide information and guidance.

With colleges adding women's water polo, girls' high school water polo naturally boomed in the late 1990s and early 2000s.

Kaia Hedlund saw first-hand the demand for girls' teams at two independent schools in Honolulu: Punahou and I'olani.

"Punahou had girls playing on the boys' team, who were going on to earn scholarships at major colleges," Hedlund said. But at both schools, many of the girls who played on the boys' teams ended up quitting. When it came time to explore adding a team specifically for girls in 1996, she remembers the remarkable response. "They had a meeting for any girls who were interested in playing water polo. They had 120 girls show up, and that year they had ninety girls or so out for water polo."

Coach Aaron Chaney at I'olani welcomed close to fifty girls in the first season, which was played on an experimental basis, with no official Interscholastic League of Honolulu championship.

"A lot of girls from different sports came out to try water polo," Chaney said. "We advertised it pretty heavily. I don't know if they wanted to try a different sport, or if they were trying to get out of PE. It was sort of a novelty at the beginning."

At the time, the University of Hawaii was looking to add a women's sport to its athletic department: water polo, rowing, and women's track were among the options under consideration. Water polo won out. Hedlund's rationale for pushing the sport was simple: the newness of women's water polo put UH on an even playing field nationally.

"My biggest point was, if we get in now, we can play and beat the 'big kids' like USC, UCLA, Cal, and Stanford," Hedlund said. "If we added track, we would never win championships and compete head-to-head with the 'big kids' as they were established and had an NCAA Championship for years."

"Then it was like, 'Oh, whoa.' All the moms are going, 'Oh, my daughter might get a scholarship to play water polo. Sure, I want her to have an opportunity.'"

In similar fashion to the addition of women's water polo at UH in 1996 fueling the local high schools to add girls' teams, female athletes around the country benefitted as collegiate water polo exploded.

In California, several sections of the California Interscholastic Federation (CIF) established girls' water polo as an official championship sport. The North Coast Section became official in 1995. The Sac-Joaquin Section was next in the fall of 1996, followed by the Central Coast Section which played its first girls' season in the spring of that year. The San Diego Section held its first championship in 1997, and finally, the Southern Section, largest in the CIF, officially sponsored girls' water polo in 1998.

Women's water polo was experiencing a glorious growth spurt. The increase in college teams gave rise to massive participation at the high school level, which in turn spurred the development of age group programs for girls. As a result, the girls' brackets at Junior Olympics exploded in number of participating teams and athletes in the late 1990s; in 1997, the Speedo Cup, now known as the Champions Cup, held its first girls' division.

The numbers demonstrate the impact of these opportunities for girls and women on USA Water Polo membership. Female registration in USA Water Polo increased from just under 2,000 athletes in 1994 to 13,935 in 2002.

The announcement of women's water polo in the Olympics came in the midst of this storm; while not the direct reason for growth at each level, the Olympics provided the most recognizable proof that women's water polo had arrived.

"It all sort of came together at the same time," said Kaia Hedlund.

According to Hedlund, the Women's Collegiate Committee was pushing hard to host the first Women's NCAA Championship in 2000.

"That's what we wanted," she said. "We wanted it to be in 2000, and we wanted it to be sixteen teams."

Although women's water polo hadn't been granted an NCAA championship by that time as hoped, the committee strategically placed the 2000 Collegiate Championships as close to the NCAA's Indianapolis headquarters as they could. The tournament's location at nearby Indiana University–Purdue University Indianapolis (IUPUI) was a bold move and provided much needed visibility for the sport.

"We had the banquet in the NCAA Hall," Hedlund said. "Sharon Cessna, who was going to be our sport's NCAA liaison, came to the banquet, and attended much of the tournament. We did all that, deliberately targeting the NCAA Championship."

When it didn't happen in 2000, the committee turned its attention to 2001. The 16-team format was an important piece to the committee's plan. In the end, 2001 was indeed a time to celebrate, as women's water polo held its first NCAA Championship – but the tournament included only four teams.

"We were sitting there with our diagrams of regional play-in, all of that," Hedlund recalled. "Then the NCAA came out and said, 'The men have four; you have four.' That was pretty much what we got the first year."

The inaugural field comprised Loyola Marymount University, Brown University, UCLA, and Stanford.

The now-Women's NCAA Committee – chaired by Hedlund – seized the opportunity: Anita deFrantz was the keynote speaker at the tournament banquet, and a major effort was made to bring Senior Woman Administrators, Athletic Directors, and conference commissioners to a VIP reception and to the pool to watch the tournament games. Female coaches from all over the country attended a coaching seminar. And a standing room only crowd packed Avery Stadium at Stanford University for the first-ever NCAA title match, won by UCLA over Stanford, 5-4.

Even with only four teams, women's water polo now had it all: age group and high school championships, the NCAA Championship, and the Olympic Games.

As women's water polo thrived, Nicolle Payne rode the wave of the sport's growth, competing for UCLA's inaugural varsity team and the first women's Olympic team.

"I tell people, if I was born a year earlier or a year later, it could have been a very different path for me," she said.

Payne refers to the perfect timing to explain how she got into water polo, how it became her passion, and the abundance of opportunities that opened up for female water polo players her age.

"It was almost like a gauntlet, and I kind of just walked through those doors as they opened. They opened at exactly the right time for me."

Raised by a single mom, Carol, Nicolle Payne grew up in Cerritos with her older brother Eddie.

"My mom was a nurse who worked nights, so it was just my brother and me a lot of the time," Payne said. "Just the two of us hanging out. We were really close."

The neighborhood was mostly boys, who were mostly Eddie's age. Payne spent most of her free time with Eddie's friends, playing outside after school and throughout the summers.

"I grew up playing sports with all these guys that were five years older than me," she said. "I just loved it. We played everything: football, basketball, ran around playing tag. All those kinds of things."

Payne describes growing up in her brother's shadow, following him around. Eddie's primary sport was soccer, so naturally Nicolle followed him onto the pitch. She even played goalie from the day she started soccer at age five, because that was his position. When Eddie joined a swim team, his younger sister was right behind him, taking the plunge, too.

At her first lesson, Payne screamed bloody murder and ran around the pool deck, petrified of the swim instructor.

"Eventually, I got in the water and loved it," she said. "When we were growing up, my next-door neighbors had a pool, so we spent a lot of time in there."

While Eddie only lasted on the swim team for about a month, opting to stick to soccer, Nicolle added swimming to her other athletic activities.

"I was juggling year-round swimming, soccer, and softball already at nine years old, ten years old," she recalled. "I loved being an athlete. That's what I did all the time anyway – it was just more organized."

Payne's first introduction to water polo came through her age group swim coach, Mark Johnson, and the Southern Pacific Association league during the fall.

"It was co-ed, obviously, and crazy," she remembers. "We would play like 20-on-20. Just Jungle Ball most days so that our coach could incorporate as many kids as wanted to play on that day. The other pool would be all the hard core swimmers."

Early in her water polo days, the regular goalie didn't show up one day, and Payne found herself between the posts.

"I got put in the goal in that crazy chaos," she recalled fondly.

A soccer goalie for almost five years at that point, Payne quickly excelled at the position in the water as well. So well, in fact, that the goal became her permanent home when she was a 10-and-under. A standout at that level, and into 12-and-under, Payne drew the attention of local coaches, who passed on her name to the Junior National Team head coach, Brent Bohlender, who contacted her mom about an upcoming tryout.

"I went to the Junior National Team tryout in Modesto when I was 12," said Payne. "I didn't make it, and I was super pissed. I remember thinking, 'Why would they invite me to this? What am I doing here?' I didn't get it – I didn't even know what it was."

Even though she was young, and unclear of the circumstances, or what was at stake, Payne understood competition. She credits that first Junior Team tryout for developing a sense of an underdog mentality that she carried with her.

"It's a theme that runs through my early water polo career – being completely out of my league at all times. Just trying to hang on, and being completely motivated by the experience of, 'Oh, my gosh, what am I doing here?'" Payne explained. "Just pushing myself … I think that was probably why I developed the way I did. I was put in situations where maybe I wasn't ready, and I just pushed my way through, and tried to prove that I was supposed to be there."

Payne returned home from Modesto confused, but not discouraged. And her love of water polo only grew when she was invited by Doug Drury to join his women's club in Long Beach, near her home in Cerritos. She continued to play on the 12-and-under team for Cerritos Aquatics, but came to love the all-female club, despite an age difference of nearly ten years with some of her teammates. When she was 13, Payne played on Long Beach's girls' teams at Junior Olympics and Junior Nationals.

Then, to her surprise, another phone call. This time, it was Sandy Nitta, who watched Payne play at Junior Olympics. The head coach of the National Team asked the 14-year-old Payne to attend Senior National Team practices.

"I was thinking, 'Okay, I didn't make the Junior Team at 12, I just started playing with girls that were 19 and under when I was 13 ... this is crazy,'" Payne said. "My mom would drive me to workouts. All the other girls on the team were in college; some of them had kids, who my mom would babysit on the side.

"I'd get in with women like Mo and Maggi, and they were all in their primes," she continued. "Amber was the young one on the team, and then there was me, significantly younger than that. It was crazy."

Payne played water polo throughout her years at Gahr High School, three on the varsity. She remembers opposing teams always being surprised to face a team with girls at all, not to mention a team with a female goalkeeper. Gahr didn't win many games; and on that team, Payne saw plenty of shots.

She continued to develop with the National Team, attending training sessions over holiday breaks. When Doug Drury moved from Long Beach, he established a new club in Pomona, The Outsiders. Carol Payne drove her daughter to practices as many as three times a week.

"I don't know how she did it because she was working nights most of the time, but we made it work," Payne said. "There weren't a lot of girls' teams then, so if someone needed a place to play, the club was always really welcoming."

When it came time to think about college, Payne had her mind set on following her passion for the beach into marine biology. She knew she could pursue her interests in both water polo and marine biology at UC San Diego and UC Santa Barbara. She also considered UC Santa Cruz and Humboldt State. After applying to those four schools, Payne received another life-changing phone call.

It was the head coach of the UCLA women's team, Guy Baker.

"He let me know that UCLA added women's water polo and that there would be a varsity team there," said Payne. "That kind of changed everything."

Payne had never been to the UCLA campus; she didn't consider the school at all, because it had neither women's water polo nor marine biology. She also had a narrow view of the real estate she wanted to inhabit during her college years.

"I wanted to go to school on the beach," she said. "LA wasn't on the beach, so I didn't really think about going there."

Once Baker extended a scholarship offer, though, there was no question of where Payne would enroll. Both she and Baker look back at what was surely the easiest recruitment of the modern era.

"It was the only scholarship I was offered," Payne said. "Paying for school was going to be challenging. I would hear about kids in other sports getting scholarships to play their sport. It was never an option for me to think about, getting a scholarship for water polo. You have no expectations of that, so when someone presents that to you, you're like, 'Awesome. Yes, please.'"

Payne told Baker she would attend UCLA. The coach made his first-ever recruiting home visit for the UCLA women's program to the Payne home in Cerritos.

"I really didn't understand why he needed to come over," Payne recalls. "We weren't familiar with that process at all. It's not like I had other peers to compare that experience with; it wasn't like people were asking, 'So who were your home visits this year?' People weren't talking about it in my sport. And I played with the guys, so it was different."

Baker arrived for the home visit with Nicolle and Carol Payne, where the prized recruit affirmed her commitment to become a Bruin.

"We didn't quite understand why he was here at my house," Nicolle said. "He popped in a video, and we watched it. It's not like my mom cooked dinner or anything. We didn't know what this was about. It wasn't on the radar, so it was pretty hilarious."

Baker left the visit thrilled with having the centerpiece of UCLA's first women's varsity team on board – and with a skewed impression of recruiting for the women's squad.

"I drove home thinking, 'This is really easy,'" Baker said.

Arriving at UCLA as a freshman, Payne was thrilled with her new surroundings, and the chance to be a part of a special team in its inaugural season.

"We were so excited about what we were creating," she said. "The fall was pretty challenging, I'm sure, for the club girls, and for me coming out of high school. I think the players who had played club before weren't used to that level of commitment; the time commitment and the training were challenging. Everyone that made it through the fall training was all in. We were excited about creating women's water polo at UCLA."

Along with that enthusiasm, Payne remembers the growing pains of being a new program at a university with such a strong athletics tradition. As women's water polo enjoyed its beginnings, sports such as men's swimming, a program that produced sixteen Olympians, forty-one individual national titles, and an NCAA team title in 1982; and both men's and women's gymnastics, were cut from the athletic department in 1994.

"It was challenging, because other sports weren't familiar with our program being added," she said. "There were some athletes there who were not so happy that we were added; their sport may have been cut. There was a little bit of being the new team on the block at such an established athletic university. Again, you could take that and get frustrated, or disappointed, or stressed out about it, or you could just go with excitement, and say, 'This is awesome that we get to be a part of it.'"

Baker educated the women's team on the history of UCLA athletics. The team saw Olympic track and field legend, and UCLA alumna, Jackie Joyner-Kersee training on the track. He made sure to cover the men's basketball dynasty created by legendary coach John Wooden. And they knew the men's water polo team owned a history of success.

When she grasped the responsibility of being an athlete at UCLA, Payne thought back to when she was a kid, playing sports with her brother, and older boys, in the street.

"I always had to prove myself so that my brother didn't look bad," she said. "At UCLA, there was a similar feeling. We have to rise to the occasion. We can't represent UCLA and not win championships, or at least be in contention."

It didn't take Payne and the Bruins long to live up to tradition of athletic excellence at UCLA. The team brought the school's first women's water polo national title to Westwood in 1996 – the first of three consecutive championships, cementing its own tradition of success.

Nicolle Payne trained with the Senior National Team beginning in 1990. In the summer after her freshman season at UCLA, she finally officially debuted on the Senior Team roster at the 1995 World Cup in Sydney. Her sights were never set on the Olympics, although she loved watching the 1984 Los Angeles Games on television. None of the sports she played – soccer, softball, and water polo – were played by women in the Olympics when she first competed at the Senior level.

"I remember the older players on the team talking about it and trying to push," said Payne. "I remember the Australians making their efforts, and the Dutch girls making their efforts. I listened to Mo talk about it.

"But again, I was so young, I wasn't maybe privy to all those conversations," she continued. "I wasn't disappointed that it wasn't an Olympic sport. I really wasn't. I didn't know that was an option. I didn't understand that they were fighting for that. Again, you have to have someone teach you these things. You don't just know them. Someone has to teach you the history, like when we arrived at UCLA, Guy had to teach us the history. Sandy and Vaune had to teach us the history, and other players had to teach us about what they had tried and their dreams. You just didn't know them until someone teaches you."

In her early years on the National Team, the results dipped, as the team struggled to keep pace with their longtime rivals, and the European nations new to the international scene. But Payne points to funding and resources, while making no apologies for the results the team earned during that era.

"I wouldn't take anything away from those teams and those experiences, given the resources that we had at that time," she said. "The amount of time that we were training together as a team was totally different. Looking back at it, I think it was great that we were on that world stage, in those games. It was hard not to have the finishes we wanted, but I think with what we were provided, resource-wise, it was pretty sweet."

Throughout her life as an athlete, beginning on the streets of Cerritos competing with her brother and his friends, Nicolle Payne found motivation in proving that she belonged. The 12-year-old at the Junior Team tryout, the 14-year-old at Senior National Team practice, the freshman competing for the first UCLA women's water polo team … and eventually a goalkeeper aspiring to be among the first women's water polo players in the Olympics.

"I'm pretty lucky," she stated. "I've had some time to think about it over the course of a lifetime, and it's certainly very cool how it all lined up for me, really. I did the work, for sure. There's a quote I like, '*Luck is what happens when preparation meets opportunity.*'

"That is the truth of my journey, for sure."

☺☺☺☺☺

The journey for Coralie Simmons took a similar path to that of her teammate Nicolle Payne: both had backgrounds in swimming and soccer. But Simmons picked up water polo much later than Payne, who is a year older. Simmons also joined The Outsiders club, but as a senior in high school – Payne graduated the year before, and was already at UCLA. When the two finally joined forces in Westwood, they led the Bruins to collegiate titles in 1996, 1997, and 1998.

Simmons was in the water at a young age, swimming competitively by age five. A native of Hemet, California, in the San Jacinto Valley between Riverside and Palm Springs, she swam in the San Gorgonio League. Swimming against clubs from San Dimas, Palm Springs, and Indio in her youth, Simmons moved on to USS meets. She quickly developed into a successful sprint freestyler and breaststroker, earning Junior Olympic, then "Q," then Junior National time standards.

"I actually kind of went for it in swimming when I was in high school, because my club was going to fly me out for the Western Zones competition, which was in Maui that year," Simmons recalled. "So I had a little carrot dangling there to try to become a fast swimmer."

Simmons did qualify for the 1994 Western Zones team, and her swimming career seemed to be taking off – so much so, that she broke her mom's heart by quitting the high school soccer team. Debbie Simmons wasn't simply an interested parent, who wanted to enjoy watching her daughter play soccer. She was the coach.

Debbie Simmons didn't have a background in sports; growing up in Utah, she was a cheerleader.

"There weren't many athletic options for her in Utah in the 1960s," Coralie said. "She got suckered into coaching my teams when I was young, then my club travel team. Then she became the high school coach."

Debbie went through soccer clinics to earn the required coaching licenses. In Coralie's freshman year, her mother was an assistant coach; daughter played for mom on the varsity team the next two years. Debbie coached the team one more year, after Coralie quit to focus on swimming.

At around the same time, in her junior year of high school, Simmons picked up water polo. She didn't have a fall sport, with soccer in the winter and swimming in the spring. So she joined the boys' water polo team, playing her final two years at Hemet High School.

In her senior year, a meeting with Doug Drury, who was the referee at one of Hemet's games, changed Simmons' path.

"Doug said, 'Hey, you should try girls' club water polo,'" she recalled, "which I didn't necessarily know existed."

Simmons jumped at the opportunity, joining Drury's club, The Outsiders, where she met future college teammates Amanda Gall and Nicolle Payne.

"I would drive an hour, hour and fifteen minutes to Claremont, depending on traffic, on Sundays," Simmons said. "We called ourselves The Outsiders, because no one was really from Pomona or Claremont. Everyone was from outside the area."

Drury was well connected with the women's Senior National Team – his daughter, Amber, retired from the team following the 1994 World Championships, and moved into the position of assistant coach the following year. Doug Drury encouraged Simmons to attend an open tryout and with just two seasons of water polo experience, she was selected to train with the Senior National Team.

When the Senior and Junior Team staffs sat down to discuss new players, Simmons stood out as a new find: a strong swimmer and possible elite water polo player. She was deemed a project, not quite ready for the Junior World Championships in the summer of 1995.

It wasn't long before the "project" label was removed. Continually impressing the Senior Team staff whenever she was training with the team, Simmons forced the staff to select her with her dynamic playmaking abilities.

She made her Senior Team debut, along with Payne, in October of 1995 at the World Cup in Sydney.

But before heading to Sydney with the National Team, Coralie Simmons started her freshman year at UCLA. Unlike teammate Nicolle Payne, Simmons held no scholarship offers. She hadn't been playing water polo long enough to be well-known to college coaches. Making the Senior National Team gave her a bump in visibility, but even so, her recruitment tale is one that would be foreign to a player of her caliber today.

Simmons was lightly recruited by a few schools, mostly for swimming.

"In my senior year, I was becoming less interested in swimming, and once I started club water polo and started to hear that you can play polo in college, I was looking for a means to not swim," Simmons said.

Loyola Marymount University and San Diego State were interested in Simmons participating in both swimming and water polo. UC San Diego was the first school to recruit her for water polo only.

"That obviously sounded a lot better," Simmons said.

"I really wasn't on anyone's radar until I went to the open tryout because coaches weren't recruiting much back then, unless you were playing club, which I wasn't until that time," she added.

Like in Northern California with the Pacific Coast Championships, women's college and club teams competed against each other in tournaments in Southern California. At a tournament in the spring of Simmons' senior year, her Outsiders team played UCLA. Simmons met Payne for the first time. Payne became the lead recruiter for Simmons' services.

"She talked to Guy and said, 'Hey, we need to bring this girl in.'"

A week later, Simmons was on an unofficial visit to UCLA, talking to Guy Baker about submitting her application. Once things were set for admission, it was an easy decision for Simmons, whose brother attended UCLA and played two seasons of water polo.

"I knew Amanda Gall from Outsiders was going to be in the class at UCLA," Simmons said. "Guy was naming off names – I knew Amanda, but I didn't know anyone else. 'Mandy McAloon is coming, Cat von Schwarz is coming.' He's reeling off all these names, which meant nothing to me, because I didn't know them, because I wasn't in the Junior system. But it was obviously a pretty hefty class to be able to go in with."

Even with Baker's reminders about the hallowed tradition of UCLA athletics, Simmons said she and her teammates didn't fully register the significance of their roles at ground zero of the explosion in college water polo.

"We understood we were in the beginning of something, but we didn't know how big that could get," she said. "For me, I was just pumped, like, 'Hey, I get to play water polo with women. This is really cool.' We were just happy to get the t-shirt.

"Even being on the National Team, it was a big deal, but we were still paying our way to go places," Simmons continued. "It didn't really hit until it became an Olympic sport, and then it was, *Hey, we're big*."

@@@@@@

Before becoming the head women's water polo coach at Stanford University, John Tanner was at the helm of the men's water polo and swimming and diving teams at the University of the Pacific from 1984 until 1997. While in Stockton, Tanner oversaw the move of UOP women's water polo from a club team, created in 1994, to varsity status in 1996.

Women's water polo's inclusion on the NCAA's Emerging Sport list was a key to UOP's plans to elevate the sport on its campus. Watching the number of programs climb toward the goal of forty, Tanner knew it was inevitable that women's water polo would receive championship status.

"As that took off, we were able to sell to Pacific with, 'Hey, this is going to happen,'" Tanner said.

UOP announced its women's varsity program in 1995 and hired Susan Ortwein as its head coach in the summer of that year.

"By then there were about twenty-five varsity programs," Tanner said. "Each year we seemed to add ten or fifteen schools."

Tanner pointed out the advantages in hiring and recruiting for programs that made the jump from club to varsity.

"The schools are able to hire a full-time coach and start recruiting in earnest," he explained. "The recruits became people who wanted to come as water polo players, rather than just having swimmers stick around after conference meets, which is what it was those first couple of years."

At the time, UOP's women's program had one tuition, not even a full scholarship, to be distributed as Ortwein saw fit. The change in status was crucial to the growth of women's water polo; but while the impact wasn't insignificant, it wasn't ground-shaking, either. The budget went from next to nothing to around $4000 to $5000 a year. Team travel took a step up, but would never be mistaken for luxury.

"We were able to use the Pacific vans but our coaches did all the driving anyway," Tanner continued. "Players didn't have to drive their own cars; they didn't have to sleep at a teammate's house."

The small bump in budget was only the beginning, in Tanner's mind. He saw the potential in the sport, beyond the necessary process of growth.

"The season was still done primarily with tournaments that club teams or varsity teams could compete in; Collegiate Nationals were the pinnacle of the season," Tanner said. "The exciting thing was not so much what was happening in '95, or that transition from club to varsity, but more the idea that pretty soon it was going to meet the emerging sports standard and become an NCAA sport. We knew at that point it would achieve viability long-term within the athletic department."

Stanford made the move to the varsity ranks in 1996, and after two seasons, Athletic Director Ted Leland launched a search for a head coach. His efforts brought Tanner back to his alma mater, where he was a member of three NCAA championship teams, and an NCAA All-American. The two had worked together in Stockton when Leland served as athletic director at Pacific. The fit was a good one for Tanner, who could see the growth of women's water polo on the horizon.

"It was clear that we had the momentum to have it become an NCAA Championship sport," he said. "Even though it hadn't yet met the standards, it was on the list, and it was clear that we were in very good company to have made that list. There were a lot of schools who had men's water polo that were adding women's. You saw a lot of coaches doubling up, and making sure that they had good practice times in terms of facility usage. It was becoming clear that this was going to happen, and would, sooner rather than later, become a championship sport."

Ted Leland didn't have to twist John Tanner's arm to land him as the women's water polo coach at Stanford; it was a time of impressive growth within the Athletic Department. Tanner was familiar with Leland and his leadership ability; when he met with Senior Associate Athletic Director Cheryl Levick, her message was clear.

"She said, 'We intend to win championships. We want to hire great coaches. We want to provide the resources they need from the point of view of scholarships and budgeting. We want to give them the premiere facilities, and then we intend to win championships,'" recalls Tanner. He was convinced to make the move from Stockton to Palo Alto and from men's collegiate to women's collegiate water polo.

Another factor was the growing positive outlook on women's water polo throughout the nation.

"It wasn't just the fact it was an emerging sport. The economy was exploding nationally," Tanner said. "People were adding a lot of sports. This whole women's emerging sport thing was a big, big deal."

Tanner coached double Olympic gold-medalist Brad Schumacher at UOP, and at the 1996 Olympic Games in swimming. He remembers an Olympic team training camp in Knoxville, Tennessee, prior to the Atlanta Games where there was talk about the Southeastern Conference's interest in women's water polo. Building pools and adding varsity programs seemed like a possibility, especially when names like the University of Tennessee, the University of Florida, and the University of Georgia were part of the speculation.

When the SEC plan didn't pan out for women's water polo, the sport missed out on the potentially explosive impact of having collegiate programs throughout the Southern United States. Another conference deep in discussion with Daniel Sharadin was the Pacific 10 – which potentially could have added teams at the University of Arizona, the University of Washington, the University of Oregon, and Oregon State University.

"From my point of view there was a sense that women's water polo, in participation, at the grassroots level, and at the collegiate level, was poised to become bigger than men's water polo," Tanner said. "And it is. Not maybe in raw participation numbers, but it's sponsored by 60-plus schools now versus forty or forty-five for the men. It really had the feel, at that point, that we might get to 100 or more schools sponsoring."

From Daniel Sharadin's point of view as Director of Collegiate and Senior Programs, the benefits of women's water polo reaching full championship sport status were substantial. Prior to the first NCAA Championship in 2001, teams had to pay their own way to the Collegiate Championship. The classification also helped Sharadin pitch the sport to both school and conference administrators.

John Tanner spoke about the vision for what an NCAA championship would do for women's water polo.

"First of all, the NCAA is 1200 schools, half a million student-athletes, billions and billions of dollars of scholarship and general resources poured toward those student athletes," he said. "It meant credibility campus-wide at these amazing research institutions. Going to NCAA status was, in most people's mind, a huge step forward."

On the Stanford campus, where construction and renovation of the old deGuerre Pool complex was about to begin, it seemed that the sky was the limit. The plans and possibilities were another reason for Tanner to be intrigued by the job at Stanford.

"We actually had it in mind starting back in '98, when we saw the construction timeline for the new pool, we're talking about the Belardi pool being indoor," Tanner said. Head women's swim coach Richard Quick and Tanner had conversations about what an indoor pool would do for aquatics at Stanford. The campus would become a destination for NCAA Swimming and Diving and other major championships, which are required to be held indoors.

"For the money that was being put up, there was the idea that we'd have an indoor pool, an outdoor pool, and the stadium pool," Tanner recalled. "They were talking about putting a temporary roof over this like they had at Georgia Tech for the 1996 Olympic swimming venue. There was just all this talk, a lot of excitement surrounding that."

With the progress in terms of official NCAA status came a reduction in teams competing in the post-season. The Women's Collegiate Championship was a 16-team tournament; the first NCAA Championship in 2001 featured four teams.

"I think other coaches initially were a little worried about it," Tanner said. "The fact that there was a process for all three major conferences to have an automatic, the 16-team championship was really just being pushed to a conference championship to get that AQ. Everyone could feel connected to that NCAA Championship at their conference tournament. Everyone felt they had a way in, and there was a sense that it was going to expand as we added more schools. After the first year, I don't think there was a strong sense that that wasn't going to happen."

The women's NCAA Championship tournament did expand; in 2005, the field was doubled from four to eight teams. In 2014, two play-in games were added, bringing the total number of teams to ten. These matches between at-large entries took place at home sites prior to the eight-team NCAA Championship.

Tanner pointed to the legitimacy the NCAA Championship brought to women's water polo – not only in the eyes of the public, but also behind the walls of the athletic department.

"Before the NCAA Championships, you didn't get the kind of crowds, or visibility, or acknowledgement within the athletic department," he said. "When it was Collegiate they were putting just enough resources into women's water polo to maybe satisfy Title IX, because it can count toward Title IX compliance. But I think most schools were one foot in, one foot out, in terms of pushing for the sport, until it became an NCAA championship sport. We knew the viability was huge."

Another factor John Tanner is quick to point out, in terms of the triumph of women's water polo as an emerging sport success story, is the professionalism and participation coaches are afforded as full-time employees at many of the country's top research institutions. He stresses the viability and visibility having an NCAA Championship gives women's water polo on every campus, and the benefits available to the staff. While a coach of an emerging or club sport may be on campus, a wide gap exists between that position and that of a full-time varsity coach.

"If you're not a coach within the athletic department – somebody who's competing for conference championships and NCAA Championships – you don't have the same access," he said. "At Pacific, our department was part of the Sport Sciences Department. We had professors in physiology, sport psych, and coaching as teaching, who were influential and available."

As the coach of varsity swimming and water polo, Tanner had access to these resources, as well as fellow coaching colleagues who were in Stockton at the time.

"When I was at Pacific, Jon Gruden was on the football staff," he said. "He was just there one year, but I could catch him in the hall and talk to him about how they were running their offense. Pete Carroll would come to campus regularly and talk, as an NFL coach."

Tanner had a professional relationship with former UOP football head coach Walt Harris, who left Stockton for the New York Jets, where he coached the quarterbacks.

"Walt came to UOP from the University of Tennessee, as the hottest offensive coordinator," Tanner said. "After he left UOP, I had regular correspondence with him while he was coaching Boomer Esiason on the Jets."

Another source of inspiration for Tanner on the Pacific campus was Glen Albaugh, a pioneer in sports psychology. Albaugh, a leader in his field, is widely known for his work with professional and amateur golfers.

"He was really tied in with a lot of other forward-thinking coaches, specifically Bill Walsh," Tanner said. "Because of his connection to Ted Leland, who's also a PhD in sport psych and a Pacific alum, there's a lot of this cross-pollination between Pacific, Stanford, and the world of sport psych. We would get access to these amazing minds, and cutting edge research."

Because of its small size, Tanner described Pacific, a Division I school, as having the intimacy and access of a Division III institution.

"So I think you can't underestimate the value to a coach, and a coach's development, and athlete development, even at the Division III level," he said.

Tanner continued, "I think some of the most innovative stuff in our sport has come from the D-III coaches. They're willing to take these crazy chances, and they run the most interesting timeout plays. They have some really great thoughts on offense, and they're willing to take chances."

Coaches such as Mike Sutton at Claremont-Mudd-Scripps, Tom Whittemore at Redlands, and Clint Dodd at Cal Tech employed underwater plays, and offensive sets that started in a large cluster before a choreographed dispersal. Sometimes the two concepts were combined, and a player who went under popped back up, unguarded.

"Many times in sports like football and basketball, it's those D-III coaches who lead the way in spread offense, in fast-paced, fast-break, basketball stuff," Tanner went on. "Now, the Warriors play it, but LMU did it back in the day. And as a water polo coach, to get access to those kinds of minds, and that kind of innovation, it runs through Division III, Division II, and Division I."

Access to NFL Hall of Fame coach Bill Walsh, among other professional football and basketball coaches who regularly stopped in to speak to the staff at Pacific, raised the bar for coaches throughout the department.

"These coaches would hang around and make themselves available," Tanner remembers. "Within our staff, we had some people who didn't stay long – Jon Gruden was there just one year, but he had very real impact on the conversations that were going on daily within our department."

Another example of the caliber of the coaching staff at Pacific during Tanner's years in Stockton is John Dunning, a mathematician by training, whose precise systematic approach to volleyball produced the first NCAA team titles in UOP's history. The women's team won back-to-back championships in 1985 and 1986, the second title earned on their home court in Stockton. Dunning took the reins from Terry Liskevych, who started the women's volleyball program at UOP, before departing to become the head coach of the United States Women's National Team, a position he held through three Olympic Games.

"Every school has stories like that," Tanner said. "In so many cases, you wouldn't get access to these types of people without the varsity status, without the NCAA stamp, NCAA sponsorship. Then flash forward to Stanford, and we have just so many people on the faculty who are doing amazing research that are interested in athletics because our student athletes are held in such high regard."

One highlight of Tanner's time as head coach at Stanford was spending one-on-one time with Bill Walsh while on athletic department speaking tours in Southern California.

"These were opportunities to ask him anything," Tanner said. "You take someone who is one of the foremost thinkers in teaching, in coaching, and in leadership – someone that these multi-billion dollar companies would have come in to speak with their executives about these matters. To have access to someone like that is incredible.

"To talk to Bill Walsh about the practice planning, the strategizing, every-thing, down to how you build a game prep week, that people from all the world want to come and be a part of. Football game-week preparation. How does all that unfold? That's incredibly valuable access, that not many people get. I don't think that can be underestimated, when it comes to the growth in women's water polo, and our ability to prepare people for success on the Olympic stage."

Courtney Johnson and Coralie Simmons

7

WINNIPEG WOES

1999 FINA World Cup   **Courtney Johnson**
1999 Pan American Games   **Heather Moody**
1999 Holiday Cup

The trip to Europe in the summer of 1998 left Guy Baker feeling the team was in a great position to qualify for the Olympics at the FINA World Cup in May of 1999. Despite not playing Canada at the Dutch Trophy, the team provided Baker encouragement by way of its results against Holland, Italy, Australia, and Hungary. And the United States wouldn't necessarily face Canada with the Olympics on the line – a higher finish than Canada in the tournament was the only requirement.

The fall saw the collegiate players return to school. Susan Ortwein ran practices during the week for those in Northern California, and they headed south for weekend training sessions twice a month. The team trained in Long Beach, and everyone was fighting weekday traffic to get there – Baker and the UCLA players drove from Westwood; another group carpooled from San Diego. During the week, the team practiced on Tuesday and Thursday nights. Weekend training took place Friday to Sunday.

With a full training schedule in the fall, the team needed games to complete the season and evaluate where it stood against its competition. At the same time, Baker's vision included making the United States a destination for international teams. His goal was for the United States to regain its importance in women's water polo, its status as an international power having gradually slipped since hosting the 1991 World Cup in Long Beach.

To that end, Baker and his staff created the Holiday Cup and invited Australia, Brazil, and Canada. The international guests arrived at the newly reopened pool at the Los Alamitos Joint Forces Training Base in December of 1998.

"This was our test at the end of the fall," Baker said. "We needed to find out where we were, whether we failed or whether we succeeded. You can't just train for twelve weeks and then, nothing."

Bringing in three teams, including visitors from two other continents, fit Baker's goals for the first Holiday Cup. He was surprised to find that the toughest part of putting together the small field was convincing North American neighbor Canada to take part.

When he took charge of the women's program, Baker saw an advantage in the close proximity of a world-class opponent such as Canada. Unlike the men's program, which sought to train with European teams or Australia because the Canadian men weren't an ideal competitive match at the time, Baker figured the women's programs could help each other. It made sense to him from a competitive and financial standpoint that a series of games with Canada would benefit both sides.

"My approach was, the FINA Cup is going to happen," Baker said. "One of us is going to make it, and one of us isn't, but we can still help each other. We both should make it when it's all said and done. I met a lot of resistance from Canada on that."

Baker credits United States Water Polo Executive Director Bruce Wigo with working behind the scenes to make it happen. Canada agreed to a week of training prior to the Holiday Cup, including three official games in the lead-up to the competition. Baker knew there was a historical rivalry between the neighboring nations but noted a particular intensity in their training and matchups. He attributed that to the compressed timeline of Olympic qualifying and the incredible opportunity to play in the first Olympic Games for women.

"In a normal quad, you have teams with different motivations in the first year, then you kick into gear in the second," Baker said. "Then the third year, you've got your team. In the Olympic year, you're ready to go. This situation was just, *We've got to get this done, right now.* Everyone had the feeling of, *You've got to go.*"

One team that was ready to go was Australia. The Olympic host benefitted from the luxury of not having to qualify, although carrying medal hopes for their country created pressure enough. The Aussies swept through the Holiday Cup, smashing the United States 11-4 in the round robin. Bouncing back with a win over Canada the next day, the United States earned a rematch with Australia in the final. A 4-3 lead early in the third quarter was promising, but the favored Aussies went on a four-goal run to grab control of the match and the inaugural Holiday Cup title.

The second-place finish gave coaches and players reason for optimism as year one of their Olympic pursuit came to an end.

As they left to take time off following a strenuous fall, neither the players nor the coach anticipated the lows that 1999 would bring.

@@@@@@

When the awards had been handed out, and the first Holiday Cup was in the books, spectators made their way to the exit. Then the foreign teams left, followed by the American players, saying their goodbyes before leaving for some well-deserved rest and family time.

The sun set; when the lights at the Los Alamitos pool were dimmed, darkness covered the deck.

Only two people remained, engaged in conversation well after the facility emptied. Guy Baker and Brenda Villa sat on the pool deck talking, Villa's future with the team the topic.

After being left off the Senior Team trip in the summer, Villa gained a Holiday Cup roster spot on the strength of her performance during the fall.

"We treated every Holiday Cup as if we were naming the team for the next major event, whatever it might be," Baker said. "At that point we were focused on who would be on the team for the Olympic qualifier. Brenda was part of the group."

But to remain part of the group, Villa had a huge decision to make. During the fall of 1998, the women's team received funding from the United States Olympic Committee to go into residential training.

"The USOC was big on full-time residential training as the way for national teams to be successful," Baker said. "They actually wanted us to move out to Colorado Springs to train there full-time. Fortunately, we had the pool at Los Al. It wasn't open yet, but it was going to be our training center."

The USOC started offering support, and the conversation got serious in the summer of 1998. Baker took a leave of absence from the women's team at UCLA to make it work. Full-time training meant the college players had to do the same. Several stopped out of school and missed the collegiate season. For most, it was a difficult decision, but one they were willing to make in order to pursue the Olympics.

By the time the Holiday Cup ended, all the collegiate players on the roster were squared away – except for Villa. A freshman at Stanford, she was torn. She didn't want to make the choice.

"I wanted someone to make it for me," she admitted. "But Guy couldn't tell me, *You're going to make the team*, and my parents weren't telling me, *Go for it*. J.T. wasn't too excited about it. No one was telling this 18-year-old what to do; I'm just bawling on the pool deck in front of Guy."

Villa's parents were concerned about her leaving Stanford and what would happen to her scholarship if she did. A handful of players from Commerce had gone on to four-year colleges such as Cal-State Los Angeles, but Villa was the first to leave "the Commerce bubble." She was the first member of her immediate family to go to college, the first student from Bell Gardens High School to attend Stanford, and the first woman from Commerce to earn a water polo scholarship. She hated the idea of postponing her college career before it even began and felt she was letting down her coach, John Tanner – and her Stanford teammates.

Her first set of college final exams was waiting for her in Palo Alto. Whether she would enroll for classes in the winter quarter was up in the air. Full-time training in preparation for an attempt to qualify for the Olympics would begin in three weeks, whether Villa chose to be there or not.

Her Olympic dream won out.

"Not having any assurance from Guy made it that much harder to take a leave of absence from Stanford," Villa said. "That was a huge leap of faith and determination from my end."

☺☺☺☺☺☺

At the end of the 1999 FINA World Cup in Winnipeg, half of the six-team Olympic field would be confirmed. The Australians, as the host nation, were automatic qualifiers. The results of this World Cup would determine the awarding of two more continental bids: one for the highest-finishing European team, another for the highest-placed team from the Americas. Vying for the European spot were Italy, Greece, Hungary, and Russia, all in Group A, and the Netherlands in Group B. The Americas prize would go to the best finish between the United States and Canada, both in Group B for the preliminary round.

Australia rounded out Group B, making it a bracket comprised of women's water polo's historical "Big Four": the nations which had paved the way for women's water polo for so many years.

The United States opened the tournament with a 4-4 result against Australia. Matching up favorably with Australia was important for the team's psyche after being drubbed by the same team just a month before at the Hunguest Cup in Sopron, Hungary. In that match, the United States found itself on the wrong end of a 9-5 decision.

Such a comprehensive drubbing demanded immediate attention, and at the game's final buzzer, Baker ordered the team to report directly to his hotel room for a video session – swimsuits still on.

"It wasn't even like the game's over," Baker recalls. "It was, 'You're in my room, now.'"

Baker gave the team five minutes to be at the hotel to watch video.

"It was a 10-minute walk up a hill," said Rachel Scott.

When they arrived at Baker's room, the video was already being projected onto the wall. The coach pressed play and the session began. First quarter, first play.

Heather Moody described the scene in the hotel room:

> Every possession would be played ten times; every time you made the mistake, it would be a different zinger right at you. You were just hoping the parts that you were watching were not you; then when you saw yourself on there, you're like, "Oh, my god. Here it comes, here it comes, here it comes." You try to mentally prepare for what was coming at you, and then it shocked you anyway, and then you'd hear someone else gasp in the background, like, "That was a really bad one." The gasping from your teammates as you're trying to look him in the face as you're just getting ripped – then it got to the point where it was so bad, people were crying.

In most cases, it wasn't even the player being criticized who was shedding the tears, Scott clarified. "There were people sobbing in the corners because some-one *else* was getting their ass chewed out."

By all accounts, the meeting went for at least two hours. And most are sure that Baker had covered just the first half of the game. Only an emergency situation put an end to the scathing critique.

"It was so bad, someone had to say, 'Guy, I actually have to go to the bath-room,'" Baker admitted. "Which means they probably were waiting. If I had said no, they probably would have…"

"Wet their pants," Brenda Villa finished the sentence, finding humor in the memory.

But that game in Hungary was in the past; in the present, the tourna-ment-opening tie against Australia was more than acceptable. Baker turned his attention immediately to continental rival Canada, the next opponent.

On the tournament's second day, the American and Canadian women hit the water, with bracket positioning at stake. After Canada was blown out by

Holland the day before, a United States win would banish Canada to a bottom-four finish, opening the door for the USA to qualify for Sydney simply by reaching the semifinals. That scenario would guarantee the United States a higher finish than Canada, and the results of the last two days of the tournament would be irrelevant to Olympic qualification.

The game was tight throughout. With the score tied late in the fourth, the United States found itself defending a Canadian power-play. After the defense came up with a critical stop, Courtney Johnson streaked down the pool for a breakaway goal. The United States posted a 6-5 win. In the standings, the team was tied with Australia, who defeated Holland, atop the Group B standings. The United States succeeded in putting Canada's Olympic hopes in jeopardy, as their northern neighbors were bound for the 5th through 8th place bracket. At the same time, their own semifinal hopes were alive.

The final day of group play offered the United States women a clear path to the Olympic Games. A win or tie against Holland would give the team no worse than second place in the group, a berth in the semifinals, and a spot in the Olympic Games.

The stakes were high for the Americans, but the Dutch faced even more immediate pressure. With Group A consisting entirely of European teams, two were guaranteed to advance to the semifinals. If Holland failed to reach the semifinals from Group B, the most decorated women's water polo nation in the world would be headed to the last-chance Olympic Qualification Tournament in Palermo, Italy – in April of 2000.

"It was a big game for them," Baker said. "If we tie or win, they're out. The Aussies were already in the Olympics. The World Cup was a free tournament for them. Whether they were first or last, they're still in the Olympics. But for Netherlands, if we even just tied that game, they were off to the qualifying tournament. For that day and age, that would be unheard of, that they would have to go through that process."

The Dutch took care of business at the expense of the United States, winning by three.

"They showed us, 'This is what you're supposed to do,'" said Baker, referring to the focus and calm professionalism of the Dutch team in a back-to-the-wall game.

Holland executed its game plan at a high level, creating separation early. Even when the United States tried to scratch its way back, things went awry. After an American goal, the defense miscommunicated its assignments on the restart, and a Dutch player swam unguarded straight to the goal, converting the easiest of opportunities.

"It was like we didn't know how to play water polo," Villa recalled. "That's just how shell-shocked we were in that situation – or not prepared to play at that level or under that pressure."

"We were not even close to ready for prime time," Baker added.

Needing just a tie to qualify for Sydney, the United States fell to Holland, 11-8.

The teams headed to different final round groups – the Netherlands to the semifinals, and the United States to the 5th-8th bracket – where both would keep a close eye on their continental foes. The next two days in Winnipeg would see history made by two of the five teams – Holland, Italy, Hungary, the United States, and Canada – still in contention to qualify for the Olympics.

A veteran of three Olympic Games and numerous World Championships as a head coach, Baker points to the ups and downs of performance in high-pressure situations that occur when tangible goals are within reach. "It's always a learning experience," he said. "We beat Canada in the group, and we play Netherlands the next day. You can't help but start to think about the Olympics. All of a sudden, an athlete's mind goes to, 'If I tie or win, I get to go to the Olympics.' That's what we've been talking about this whole time, and now it's sitting there right in front of you."

Heading into the World Cup, he felt the team was mentally prepared. To Baker, the increase in confidence level and overall play was impressive.

"At that point, it felt like we were right where we were supposed to be," he said. "We got a tie with Australia, which was good, and then we beat Canada in a tough game. Now we've got this opportunity against Holland. And you're just not ready."

Finding that out the hard way can leave a scar, and this lesson cut deep for the United States team.

"I'm sure that impacted us a little bit, because you feel like you're there," Baker said. "Human nature is human nature. You can't help but visualize it all the way through. I'm going to visualize at the end of this thing, we're going to the Olympics. You can't help getting that mindset, and what it's going to mean."

After a rest day for all the teams following the group stage, the schedule on May 28 featured Canada versus Russia, and the United States facing off against Greece. While the games were of monumental importance to the North American teams, they were meaningless to the Europeans, who were destined for the Olympic Qualification Tournament. Canada had the first chance to advance to the fifth-place game, and they made easy work of the Russians. The Canadian win put the United States on the edge – one game after having a chance to beat or tie Holland for the Olympic bid, a United States loss to Greece would hand the berth to Canada.

"It was a weird tournament when we didn't have to beat everyone," Baker said. "You had to finish higher. We wouldn't necessarily have even had to play Canada for the Olympic spot. They were in our group, but beyond that, either team could have qualified without beating the other."

Against the United States, the Greek team enjoyed the support of every Canadian in the natatorium, each hoping the Olympic suspense would end that night with a Greek win. But the United States played to keep their Olympic dream alive, and Greece had nothing riding on the outcome. The United States took care of its business; a North American showdown loomed. There would be no medal to play for but rather a unique reward of much greater magnitude. After a roller-coaster week for both teams, a head-to-head encounter seemed the only fitting way to settle the quest for the coveted continental bid.

Later that same night, the World Cup semifinals took place, with the European Olympic bid in play. Europe was guaranteed a finalist, as Group A winner Italy faced off with the Netherlands in the first semi. If Hungary also advanced over Australia, the gold medal match would not only crown the World Cup champion; it would offer a ticket to Sydney to the victor. The Dutch, hitting on all cylinders as they had in dismantling the United States to end group play, rolled into the finals with a comfortable win over Italy. Dutch players and coaching staff then settled into the spectator seating to watch Australia and Hungary battle for a championship berth.

For four quarters, the Dutch were the biggest Australian fans in the arena, urging the Olympic host to boost them to the Olympics. A loss by Hungary would ensure Holland the top position among the European teams, no matter the outcome of the final. The Australians powered to a drama-free victory, and the Dutch team celebrated in their seats fifty feet above the pool. The gold medal match the next day would be an Olympic preview between two traditional powerhouse teams safely qualified for the inaugural six-team field.

While the Dutch did their part with the semifinal win, the help from the Australians ruled out a head-to-head showdown for the European bid. Meanwhile, the Americas continental berth would be decided in a direct clash between decades-long rivals. The stakes were clear. Win and go to Sydney. Lose and take your chances against Europe – in Europe – to qualify.

The opportunity against the Netherlands earlier in the tournament was simply a missed chance. To Baker, the Netherlands game was part of the process. The Dutch were the giants of women's water polo at the time; while the Olympic prize was in sight with a win or tie, such a result would have been considered a major upset.

In the ensuing days, the pressure ramped up quickly as the bracket sorted itself out, and the continental showdown was confirmed. Those days felt more like a grind. The momentum built up in the early tournament successes seemed to wane; by the time they met Canada for fifth place, the United States had no answers, failing to capitalize on the presumed best path to Sydney. Canada triumphed, 6-4.

Fifth place at the FINA World Cup. There was no medal for fifth. Canada had qualified for the Olympics. Beating their rival head-to-head to earn the bid and having done it on home soil in Winnipeg were bonuses that sweetened the frenzied celebration in the middle of the pool. There had never been greater joy for a fifth-place finish.

At the other end of the course were silent stares and blank faces.

"We were dominating Canada during that time. I figured it would be a close, tight game," Baker said. "We had flipped the switch on Canada and were mostly beating them in that time period."

Maureen O'Toole put it more bluntly: "We could have played Canada ten times and beaten them ten times; all we needed to do was beat Canada to go to the Olympics. And we lost. And it was terrible."

While memories of the actual match are few – many players sense their minds have blocked out much of the Winnipeg World Cup experience – the image of the devastating aftermath stayed with every United States player and coach.

Brenda Villa recalls sitting on the bench long after the final whistle. "That image is ingrained in my head. Everyone's heads in their hands, sitting on the bench, just like, *We blew it.*"

The threat of not qualifying for Sydney suddenly became very real. The thought had not been part of the team's consciousness heading into the game, but now crept into the minds of the players while watching Canada celebrate.

To them, the scene was surreal. Despite the effort and focus of the past year they fell short of their goal, and a wave of disbelief overcame many of the team members.

"It was like one of those things in life that happen to you, and you think, *How did this happen?*" said Maureen O'Toole. "There was just no way that anybody had worked as hard as we had. There's just no way. And the one game we needed to win, we lost."

The team arrived in Winnipeg with high hopes, ready to show the world how far they had come. They were heading home crestfallen. No one let go of the Olympic dream, but the reality was sobering. Leading into the tournament, Baker considered allowing the collegiate players to go back to school, play the college season, then reconvene to train from May until the Olympics in September. That option was off the table by mid-tournament, when the United States melted down against the Netherlands.

Baker admitted surprise at the loss to Canada, having been certain that the team would qualify for the Olympics in Winnipeg. But in the big picture, his concern was rooted much deeper. The loss to Holland actually had the most effect on his long-term plan.

"It's one thing to lose, but the way that we lost, and that goal they scored? We're not even close to ready to compete," he said. "We're not going to show up to the Olympics just to say we're part of the Olympics. We're going to be there to do something, and at that time, we weren't ready to beat Netherlands or those top teams."

Whether they qualified or not in Winnipeg, Baker had decided 1999 would be another year of full-time training. The fact that they failed to qualify meant they would do it not knowing if they were going to go to the Olympics or not. Their backs were up against the wall.

At the final buzzer, the FINA World Cup ended for the United States, but their quest to qualify for the Olympics could not. In that moment, the long-term plan ending at the Sydney Games changed significantly for the United States. There would now be a stop in Palermo in April 2000 for the Olympic Qualification Tournament, a last chance to crash the global party in Sydney to which women's water polo had just recently been invited.

Looking back at the heartache of Winnipeg, Baker added a touch of perspective to the outcome. "It had a big effect on us," he said. "I think it's still good that we went through that process. Ultimately … I don't know where we would have ended up if we actually qualified there."

☺☺☺☺☺☺

Half of the first women's Olympic water polo field was in place. The Sydney Games would be well represented by women's water polo's pioneering nations: host Australia, European qualifier Holland, and the Americas qualifier Canada. Only one team from the original Big Four left Winnipeg with an uncertain Olympic future.

For Brenda Villa, the pain of the missed opportunity is still fresh in her memory. "I was sitting there on the bench after the game questioning everything. I've taken time off of school, and now I'll have to do it again," Villa said. "My parents were concerned about me taking time off from Stanford. Here it is, like, *Hey,*

Mom and Dad, I'm stopping out of school. This is all going to work out perfectly; and it's like, *Holy shit, it didn't.*"

After Winnipeg, Villa questioned her future once again. The answer came from within – she hated the feeling of failure. Ultra-competitive from the time she learned what winning was, Villa had to see this through. And she was finally playing better, as well. Refocusing attention on her game, Villa asked Baker in her one-on-one meeting after the World Cup what he needed from her in the water.

"I asked how I could help the team more," Villa said. "I wasn't getting a lot of minutes at the FINA Cup in '99, so there was a feeling of helplessness."

At the World Cup, Villa was primarily a six-on-five specialist to take advantage of her shooting prowess. She thought she knew the answer to her own question: improve on defense.

Baker's response came as a surprise. He wanted to see more from her at the offensive end.

"Brenda's moment for me was after Winnipeg; she was with the Junior Team, and they were at Los Al training for the Junior World Championships," Baker said. "With the Juniors, she was fantastic. With the Senior Team, she was a step behind defensively, but she also wasn't bringing enough offensively, so what are we actually getting?"

What Baker saw was Villa driving, moving, and being active with the Junior Team. He suspected that with the Senior National Team, she was getting bogged down in the system, feeling like those skills were being taken away.

The two talked after the workout ended.

"That was great," Baker told Villa. "Where has that been?"

Villa replied, "I can do that?"

"Yeah, you can do that. It would be great if you did that."

"I didn't know I could do that," Villa said.

The disconnect was suddenly clear to Baker.

"She was probably a little bit paralyzed that first year," he said. "She didn't want me to get upset with her, so she didn't know what to do; she felt it was safer not to do those things."

For his part, Baker admitted he had not watched Villa play with her club team or in high school. He had only seen her play in Perth at the World

Championships, then evaluated her in Senior Team training. His philosophy of evaluation included watching players in varied situations, then finding out if their skill at one level translated to the Senior level. He simply had not seen Villa using her entire palette of skill, playing at her best.

The initial difficulties caused a rocky start to their relationship, but Baker quickly came to respect Villa's deep understanding of the game and her determination to make the team.

"Brenda's not the type who just nodded her head or would come afterwards and ask questions or really try to establish that kind of relationship," he said. "Which is fine. She's always processing, *How does this work?* She has in her mind how she wants to play or how the game should be played."

Over the course of ten years and three Olympic Games together, the player and coach often had to get on the same page with one another.

"I think she's brilliant," Baker said. "She's a brilliant water polo mind. I enjoyed that process with her."

By the fall of 1999, Baker was pleased with the team's progress, and his rising sense of confidence was due in part to Villa's expanded role in the water.

"Brenda's legacy is going to be that she's the Wayne Gretzky of water polo," Baker said. "She physically does not test well, but she's exceptional – one of the best players that's ever played the game."

Looking back on the process, Baker was late to recognize Villa's full value to the team, but confident that the principles of evaluation were sound.

After a period of frustration and difficulty, Brenda Villa and Guy Baker found their fit. Fortunately for both, it happened in time for Sydney.

The one-on-one meeting between Brenda Villa and Guy Baker was one of fourteen that the coach held that day in June of 1999. The team took two weeks off after its failure to qualify for the Olympics, returning to Los Al to prepare for the Pan American Games in mid-July. Instead of starting the training on Friday evening as was customary, Baker scheduled the first workout for Saturday afternoon. Before they returned to the water, he wanted to meet with each player. Those meetings were scheduled for 8:00 a.m. until noon.

Baker had let the players know that these individual meetings were wide open; the intention was to get everything out, both from the players and the coach.

"It was, 'You can say to me whatever you want to say, but just understand, I get to do the same,'" Baker said. "I told them, 'There's nothing that will be held against you. Let's get it all out, but I have stuff I need to say also'. I wanted to hear their information; it didn't go the way that it should have gone in Winnipeg."

It quickly became clear the team meeting at noon was going to be delayed, and the team would get in the water in the evening; eventually it was all called off. Players brought Baker food. They showed up, hung out with teammates, left, came back. Baker didn't sense frustration caused by the delay.

By the time Baker emerged from the last meeting, it was dark at Los Al. The clock read 9:00 p.m.

"People leaving their meeting told others what we talked about," Baker said. "There wasn't any confidentiality. People coming in knew they could get stuff off their chest. People came ready to talk."

However the team and individuals interpreted the day, Baker considered it a good moment for himself as their coach. It gave him tons of information – insight into issues both personal and team-oriented ... that he had no idea were brewing under the surface.

"Obviously, they've got stuff to say," he said. "I had no clue. No clue they had stuff to say. Why? Because most of the time I was flying solo. My job was to run the practices."

The marathon meeting day served to establish a bond between Baker and the athletes, another key step toward team success.

"Those meetings established for the first time that we're going to have a coach and athlete relationship," he said. "It's one of the most critical things for success at any level. You've got to be on the same page when you get to big events; we weren't always, but that's the goal. That was the starting point for us."

Baker credited himself for one thing – being bold enough to start that day with a "we're going to go for it" mentality.

"I was honest with them; they gave just as good," he said. "It helped me coaching-wise, explaining things, slowing down, clarifying things communication-wise – all of which they had been saying to me."

For any Olympian, the road to the Games is a long one, with winding twists and unexpected turns. There are the rare few who joined their sport and had a clear path of development, aided by talent and resources, and surely luck. But for most, the story behind the road taken by each athlete is what makes American viewers fall in love with the Olympics. Hurdles are part of everyday life, and heroes turn hurdles into triumphs.

Of particular interest are underdogs. Outsiders. Those whose accomplishments are achieved against all odds.

Courtney Johnson was an outsider. Hailing from Salt Lake City, Johnson had a long road to the Olympics – one that started with one lap of the pool. The youngest of six children, Johnson was happiest when active, so her mom put her in everything – and anything – as a child, just to keep her going. Sitting on the pool deck at age four while her siblings swam, she was eager to be in the water with them. At four-and-a-half, the swim coach relented, making a deal with the precocious youngster.

"Basically, she said as soon as I could swim a lap, I could join the team," Johnson said. It took roughly a week of her coach getting in the water to monitor her attempts. At the end of the week, the determined little sister earned her spot alongside her siblings. She was thrown into swim practices immediately and loved it.

Johnson was always eager to try new things, especially if her friends were there too. She took up gymnastics, dance, volleyball, and soccer.

She followed her brother, Jared, into water polo, but the sport didn't call to her right away. "At first I was like, 'Yeah, I don't think I want to do water polo,'" she said. "I liked swimming more."

That changed in ninth grade, when Johnson tried water polo again on the boys' team at Skyline High School. Giving water polo another chance, she fell in love with the sport by the time she left her first practice. Just like when she got promoted to the swim team after a week in the water, Johnson was moved up to the varsity team at the end of her first week of high school water polo. Her experience in soccer and volleyball gave her the athletic intelligence that many of the other players lacked.

Being fast-tracked to the varsity was exciting for Johnson, but it left her without a key skill. She couldn't eggbeater.

"After that first week, they threw me on the varsity and everybody on the varsity knew how to eggbeater," she said.

It was a secret she kept to herself for a decade, through all of her success as she rose through the ranks.

"I knew it, and it was frustrating," she remembers. "I was embarrassed, and was not about to tell anybody that I didn't know how to eggbeater. I tried to adapt."

Johnson adapted, and covered her deficiency well enough with her strengths to start making an impact. Her first major tryout was during her freshman year of high school, when her coach, Steve Marsing, a regional coach for the Olympic Festival, encouraged her to attend the team auditions. While she was too young and inexperienced to be selected, she had the water polo bug. Johnson's next opportunity came the next year, at a regional Junior National Team tryout in New Mexico. Her prospects looked dim, especially after the first day of drills.

"I didn't have the skills," she admitted. "They were going to pick three players and I was 13th or 14th after the first day because I hadn't been playing long enough to really pick up a lot of the basics. Then the next day was mostly scrimmages. I knew it was a chance to show my speed and game sense."

Johnson put those attributes on display, and by the end of the tryout, she had edged her way into the third position – and a spot on the Junior National "B" team. With no team from Utah competing at Junior Olympics, she joined the Junior "B" coach, Jim McMaster, and his Newberg, Oregon, based club for the tournament. When the Junior Olympics ended, the Junior "B" Team departed for Brazil. The excitement and travel was enough to impel Johnson, who was still playing competitive travel soccer, to make a permanent switch to water polo.

When it came time to look at colleges, there were no water polo scholarships, and most schools were sponsoring club teams, not varsity. So Junior National-level athletes like Johnson looked for the opportunity to swim in college while continuing their water polo careers.

"I was an okay swimmer, but not a premier recruit or anything," she said. A Junior Nationals qualifier in the sprint freestyle events, she was looking at Brown and Harvard, plus Redlands, where her brother Jared was playing. Johnson committed to Brown, and had already put in her tuition deposit, when the phone rang. It was Sandy Nitta, head coach of the Senior National Team.

"Out of the blue, I got a call from the national coach and she said, 'I've heard that you're going to Brown. I'm a little bit worried – if water polo is the way you want to go – if that's the right place for you,'" Johnson remembers. "They had a reasonable club team, and I could swim there."

Knowing that Johnson wouldn't consider a school unless it was academically on par with Brown, Nitta suggested she consider Cal. Senior National Team member Lynn Wittstock got in touch with Golden Bears swim coach Karen Moe-Thornton, and soon Johnson's phone rang again. "Karen called me and said, 'Obviously we don't have enough for a scholarship with your times, but absolutely, we'll have you as a recruited walk-on.'"

It was April of her senior year. Johnson had been to Berkeley once for a tournament, and found the urban environment intimidating.

"It was a little scary, especially coming from Utah," she said.

But Johnson was committed to reaching her potential in water polo, so she reneged on her enrolment at Brown and headed west to California.

Once she arrived in Berkeley, Johnson enjoyed school and swimming. But her love was water polo.

"Lynn Wittstock and Jocelyn Wilkie trained with the Cal club team," she said. "I remember walking into my first practice and knowing who they were from the National Team. They invited me over to pass with them. They took me under their wing, and I was training with them on the Cal club team both in-season and out of season."

Because of the club status, as opposed to varsity, the Cal players could benefit from playing alongside experienced players such as Wittstock and Wilkie. Throughout her career in Berkeley, Johnson gained appreciation for that unexpected phone call from Nitta, and the advice she offered. Her game continued to develop and as a senior she was named Mountain Pacific Sports Federation Player of the Year, and a first-team collegiate All-American.

Johnson was on the Senior "B" Team, and tried out for the Senior Team for the World Championships in 1994. She just missed that roster, but when several players retired after Rome, Johnson was prepared to step into their shoes. She debuted on the Senior National Team in 1995 at the World Cup in Sydney, and became a mainstay on the United States roster.

Johnson described the experience in her early days as a "part-time National Team."

"We basically were expected to train on our own," she said. "There was some funding that allowed us to do weekends. In the off-season, we tried to get together once a month for a weekend, and put in as much water polo as we could. We didn't have hotels, and we didn't have funding, so we would stay at people's houses, and squeeze as many girls as we could in a house, and squeeze as many girls as we could in a van, or a car."

For a post-graduate athlete like Johnson, training to remain a world-class athlete was a challenge. Married in 1995, while at Cal, Johnson and husband Darren moved to Pittsburgh in 1996 to pursue their graduate degrees in law at Duquesne, and business at Carnegie Mellon. With one year of athletic eligibility remaining, Courtney was on scholarship at Duquesne as a swimmer. After one year in Pittsburgh, she took a leave from law school and returned to Salt Lake City to prepare for the 1998 World Championships. The move allowed her to live at home, train full-time, and be closer to California.

"You were kind of on your own, as far as training," she said. "You were isolated. You didn't really have a coach or a season. We'd come together for two or three weeks before a tournament, but that was all. It was really a transient team."

Johnson puts the results of the Senior National Team during that era in perspective, considering the resources available at the time.

"We had a lot of players retire, and other teams were starting to get funding," she said, referring to the mass retirement after the 1994 World Championships. "We were kind of consistently outside of medal contention from '95 to '98. When I describe it, I feel like we had the talent. If you look at our team at that time, there wasn't a lot of turnover from 1995 to 2000. We had the talent, but we underperformed, because we didn't have the training and we weren't in the type of shape we needed to be in, because we didn't have the time together, and we didn't develop the team chemistry."

Johnson transferred to Santa Clara University, earning her law degree while serving as volunteer assistant coach at Stanford. The position gave Johnson a place to train consistently up to the time that Guy Baker took over the National Team, and the pursuit of Olympic qualifying began.

When women's water polo became an Olympic event, the program's budget ballooned from $100,000 in 1997 to over $400,000 in 1999. Other benefits for the athletes included USOC Athlete Support, insurance, and access to the Olympic Job Opportunity Program.

"That made a huge difference," she said. "All of a sudden, we had a lot more training together; we had funding, so we were together more often, and we went to more tournaments. That changed the whole culture of the National Team."

Baker's arrival to the Senior National Team brought one more change for Johnson. She learned to eggbeater.

"Over all the years, I hid it well enough, that coaches just thought I wasn't good at eggbeater," Johnson said, laughing. "The first coach to figure it out, or to actually recognize that I didn't know how to eggbeater, was Guy. On the National Team. A year before the Olympics."

Sitting on the edge of the deck with Robin Beauregard after finishing leg training, Johnson noticed Baker staring at her.

"I'm like, 'Yeah?' she recalled. "And Guy asked, 'Why are you so bad at eggbeater?'"

Johnson, embarrassed, was speechless. So Beauregard jumped in.

"She never learned how."

Baker's response was a relief to Johnson, whose long-held secret was now out in the open.

"He said, 'That's awesome! We can fix that,'" she laughed. "So I started remedial eggbeater lessons with Chris Duplanty. We started on the deck, learning the right motions for my feet."

Armed with collegiate and National Team experience, a law degree, and now a complete set of water polo skills, Courtney Johnson – once an outsider from Utah – was ready to pursue her Olympic dream.

At the Red Cross swim lessons in Albuquerque, New Mexico, there was a girl hanging on the laneline in the middle of the pool, screaming. And screaming, and screaming. One day, she would become an Olympic water polo player, but at age six, swimming wasn't her choice, and she was choosing to scream.

"We had just moved to Albuquerque from Rock Springs, Wyoming," recalls Heather Moody, a two-time Olympic athlete and two-time Olympic coach. "It was our first summer and my older sister and I got to pick a summer activity. I picked tennis. I thought that would be really cool to do. I was actually pretty good at tennis. We had tennis first, and then we would walk across the parking lot and there was swimming. That's what my sister chose. She wanted to learn how to swim. She loved the water. I hated it. I don't think I ever passed swim lessons, to be completely honest with you," she admitted.

While her older sister Kim breezed through the week of swim lessons, Heather stubbornly refused. The next week, Kim was promoted, moving a couple of lanes over. Heather was left with the beginners, miserable, with no desire to learn to swim. But, as often happens with siblings and summer activities, Heather couldn't escape from her older sister's success.

"Because Kim did such a great job, the coach of the local swim team that practiced in the same pool noticed her and suggested to my parents that she join the swim team," Heather said. "Of course they thought that was a good idea, an activity for us to be healthy, and with other kids, so we joined the swim team."

Being three years younger, Heather was forced to follow suit; now a member of the team, the screaming continued.

"My parents were very much the types that said, 'You sign up, you participate. If this is what you're choosing to do, and this is what we're paying for, you're going to participate,'" Moody said. "Not that I was choosing to do it. I would swim to the middle of the pool, because then I knew my parents couldn't reach me, and hang on the lane line and do nothing. I didn't quite think about the fact that at some point I had to get out of the pool. It was a learning process."

Eventually, after some long talks with her mom and dad, Moody started swimming productively. She was a natural swimmer, who improved quickly once she agreed to embrace the activity. Her swimming skills blossomed, and soon Moody considered herself a die-hard swimmer. So die-hard, that when her Duke City Aquatics coaches Reed Barnitz and Tim Wild introduced afternoon water polo as a break from summer double workouts, Moody reverted to her six-year-old self, and refused.

"Reed and Tim thought it was instrumental to have a little break here and there instead of just chasing the black line all year," Moody said. "Our mornings would be swimming and then on certain afternoons, there would be water polo to mix it up. I absolutely refused. I wanted to swim."

That first year, Barnitz relented and wrote swim workouts for Moody to complete while her teammates played water polo. She swam in the far lane, all by herself, while the entire swim team was engaged in learning a new sport. And, she said, "I was perfectly okay with that."

The next year, Barnitz insisted upon the importance of Moody taking a physical and mental break from her swimming regimen. Moody made the leap into water polo and soon after headed off to her first tournament.

"We were the only club that played polo in Albuquerque, so we would travel to play games," she said. "I remember going to Arizona for my first tournament. It was back when offensive fouls counted as a major. I got put in the game, and I was probably in the pool for less than a minute and a half, and I had three majors. I was back on the bench. I remember my dad getting in the car and going, 'I didn't drive all the way here to watch you play a minute and a half of water polo. You need to figure this out.'"

Bit by bit, Moody figured it out. Playing water polo exclusively in the summer months, she pointed to her first tryout with the Junior National Team while in high school as a turning point. Barnitz was an assistant under Brent Bohlender on the Junior Team, and he made sure Moody attended a tryout held in her hometown of Albuquerque.

"I remember Brent being very honest in his assessment of my abilities," Moody said. "I was fast. I swam really well. Ball handling: not so good. So he said he wanted to bring me along on the B team. The B team didn't really do anything at that point."

When Moody got to high school, Bohlender was happy with the progress she was making. But being in Albuquerque was not ideal for getting games and experience, even in the summer. So he extended an invitation to play with his club, Modesto-Stanislaus, during the summer after her freshman year.

Moody jumped at the opportunity. To make it work for her family financially, she lived in the Bohlender household, and was the nanny for his children. The first year, she took care of the Bohlender's first child, Megan, to pay for her room and board and club dues.

"It was a way for my parents to teach me the importance of, 'If this is truly what you want to do, you have to work at it," Moody recalls. "It was hard. I remember calling home, and just crying, wanting to come home, because I was homesick; this isn't what I wanted to do. My parents, they used this opportunity to drill into me that life lesson of, 'This is your choice. Next summer you can make the choice again if you want to do this, but this summer you've made this choice. You've made the commitment to the team. You made the commitment to the Bohlenders, to watch Megan during the summer. You're not coming home.'

"It sucked."

Moody made it through that first summer – and all the summers of high school after that. When she returned after her junior year, the Bohlender family had grown with the addition of Brian.

"It was just a process of growing," she said. "It's just one of those growing up moments of, 'Okay, this is what I want to do,' and spending summers in Turlock allowed me to develop as a water polo player."

Moody went on to UC Santa Barbara as a varsity swimmer on a small scholarship. She played club water polo, because the sport wasn't varsity. In two years at UCSB, she struggled in school and took two years off. For her last year of eligibility, Moody played at San Diego State.

As a member of the Junior National Team, the Senior Team was a goal for Moody, but there were always hurdles that had to be cleared.

"Honestly it was the day in and day out struggles of not being in a real water polo environment," she said. "To be from a place without the option of playing club or high school water polo year round, and overcoming that. I remember meeting Rachel [Scott] and Courtney [Johnson]. There was always a group of us that were from outside of California, and we always gravitated toward each other on our Junior Team trip, because we didn't know anybody else. You had all the California kids that seemed to know everybody. So we stuck together."

Heather Moody and Rachel Scott became college teammates at San Diego State, and formed a lifelong friendship through water polo. Their first trip together with the Senior National Team was in 1997, to the World Cup in Nancy, France. After the United States' seventh-place finish, Moody and Scott hopped on a train and headed to Rome for a vacation.

"We went backpacking, on a budget," Moody said.

"Before the trip, we got a credit card for food, and we decided we'd have one meal a day on the credit card, because we couldn't afford more," Scott explained. "We'd walk around town, looking for the biggest meal that we could eat."

When they met their teammates to fly back home, Scott figures she had lost five to eight pounds. Moody estimates she lost closer to twenty.

Moody and Scott took the train from France to Italy, and walked everywhere once they got there.

"At the tournament, they had little water bottles that you could take," Moody said. "I'm like, 'Let's just hoard these.' I'm hoarding little water bottles for our trip."

Scott was on board with the idea as a way to save money. But there was one problem.

"Water is heavy," said Scott.

"So heavy," Moody agreed. "I'm getting off the train, with all these waters in my backpack, and I'm wobbling, wobbling, wobbling … and I fell."

Scott nearly fell out, too. "I'm holding up my backpack that's so heavy with water. I'm hanging onto the handle, laughing my ass off, because she's laying there on the ground, like a turtle."

They got rid of half of the bottles, purely so they wouldn't have to lug them around Italy. What they did keep, they drank in a day.

And that wasn't the end of their water woes on this adventure.

"We had a certain amount of cash for souvenirs," Scott began. "You couldn't just use credit everywhere at that time. Heather drinks so much water, that we stop one day at a small store, and I'm waiting outside. She comes out with two big bottles of water, and she tells me it cost almost all of our money. I'm like, 'What! How much did you give them?'"

Scott went inside, speaking Spanish to the Italians inside the store.

"They're blowing me off," she said. "They finally gave me a little bit of money, because they knew that they ripped her off. She must have paid twenty, thirty bucks for two bottles of water. So we carry them all over Rome, and we get lost."

The pair wandered around Rome, carrying their water, lost, for about nine hours.

"We're walking around Rome, trying to get back to our hostel," Scott continued. The teammates finally found the McDonald's right around the corner from their lodging, and sat down. Moody went to the counter to order food.

"I'm carrying the waters," Scott said. "And I'm carrying both backpacks, because when Heather is this way, she will fall over and die. She's quit on me three times that day already; I'm dragging her through the streets of Rome. We're fighting about how to read the freaking map. We're angry; we're not talking to each other."

Sitting down, parched, Scott opened one of the bottles she had lugged around for hours.

"It's fizzy water," she said, flatly.

"It explodes all over me, all over anybody within the room. Everybody's yelling at me in Italian. I just carried these waters through town, and Heather's standing at the cash register, looking at me like, *Oh, my God; what have I done?* To top it all off, she won't drink fizzy water."

Scott walked the bottles to the garbage, and pitched them in. She grabbed a handful of napkins, and started wiping everyone down.

Leading up to the 1998 World Championships, which were held in January, Heather Moody and Rachel Scott relocated to Scott's home in Bainbridge Island, Washington. They lived with her mom from late August to November, returning to California when the National Team got together to train. Scott's high school coach, Steve Killpack, helped them with training while they were in Washington. During the day, Scott worked with a neighbor, laying tile; Moody waitressed at a local coffee shop.

"We spent almost half of our time training Heather to run, because there was a time trial that she had to pass," Scott recalled. The requirement for the Senior National Team was running two miles in under twenty minutes.

"Not only is she not a runner, but she has to be laying down to have a resting heart rate," Scott continued. "When she's upright, she overheats, and she ... "

"I die," Moody said.

Scott, a versatile athlete, who could easily run the mandatory time, put Moody through wind sprints – and more – all so that her friend could stay on the Senior Team.

Moody recalls the efforts, with no fondness. "Running on the treadmill, running outside, running in the stadium, doing all kinds of stuff, and I thought I was going to die the whole time," she said. "It was terrible."

The two National Team members played water polo with the Bainbridge Island High School team, and attended the University of Washington's workouts, most of which took place at 10:00 at night. Moody routinely got sick on the ferry boat.

"It was a rough go in Washington for me," she admitted.

After the 1998 World Championships in Perth, Australia, Moody and Scott went through the transition to the new coaching staff, led by Guy Baker. When Moody first received word that Baker would be leading the team, the first thing she said to Scott was, "I don't think I'm going to make it."

"With him as the coach, with his philosophy, and his connections with LA, and us being the outside crew from Washington and New Mexico, and Courtney from Utah – how are you going to break into that? How do you do that? I remember my fear of not making it," Moody said.

Moody liked the structured way Baker approached the team. While she perceived a challenge ahead, she felt good about the chance to prove herself to the new coach. The first training weekend with Baker began with a swim set; Moody nailed it.

"We started that weekend, finished the meeting, and were in the pool doing a long swim set," she recalled. "No problem, swimming is easy for me. Looking around, there are teammates falling off, not making the set, so I'm feeling, *All right, I'm one step up, I'm moving up*."

Where Moody faced the biggest challenge was in her lack of game experience.

"Coming from New Mexico, where you don't play a lot, that's where I struggled," she said. "That was the theme of my meeting with Guy afterwards. He told me I had to step up and start using my size and my strength in the pool, polo-wise, or I wasn't going to make it."

She appreciated the straightforward feedback, something she has carried over into her coaching philosophy.

"That's one of the things I respected the most," Moody said. "The fact is, you have to be honest with your athletes. That honesty is what's going to drive them to be successful. It hurt to hear, 'Someone smaller than you is pushing you around, and you need to step up.' But the bottom line is, if I didn't hear that, then I would feel that I'd done what I was supposed to be doing, and there's nowhere to improve. I walked away from that weekend of training knowing, here it is, this is what I need to do to make this team."

✇✇✇✇✇✇

Although they hadn't made history by qualifying for the Olympics as they had hoped, the United States women took part in a historic first to end the summer of 1999. In a step toward gender equity, the Pan American Games, a multi-sport Olympic-style competition, added women's water polo to its program. Men's water polo had been part of the Pan Am Games since its inception in 1951.

While their inclusion was cause to celebrate, one detail put a damper on the team and staff's enthusiasm – the location of the Games. In the cruelest possible twist, Guy Baker and the United States women's water polo team headed back to Winnipeg less than two months after their nightmare result at the World Cup.

"You talk about brutal," Baker said. "We had to go right back to the scene of the crime."

Back to the same pool, although with a different team. The rosters for the women's competition at the Pan Ams featured eleven players, to mirror the format of the Olympic tournament. The staff shuffled the squad, scrambling for bodies as some players took care of summer classes; those young enough went to the Junior World Championships. Preparation for Junior Worlds overlapped with the

Pam Am schedule, prohibiting players from competing at both. The United States arrived in Winnipeg with a roster of only ten players. In the absence of Nicolle Payne and Jackie Frank, goalkeeper Bernice Orwig joined the team, fresh off leading USC to the Collegiate National Championship.

One experience the team looked forward to was the opening ceremony. Captain Julie Swail asked Baker if the team could attend. But Baker was intent on redemption after the previous disaster in Winnipeg; he told Swail that avoiding fatigue and distraction were reasons to avoid the ceremony.

"This was our first Games experience, so I had no idea what I was talking about when we discussed it," said Swail. "But it just seemed like it would be so exciting."

The water polo team watched in dismay as athletes from the United States delegation donned their opening ceremony outfits and prepared to leave the athlete village. Instead of joining them, the team headed to the pool for a practice.

"We got extra pool time because, guess what, no one else wanted it that night," said Swail.

The team swam a hard set and completed a full workout with the promise of a team dinner afterwards.

"We went to Applebee's," Swail said. "It took forever to get all of us fed, and the food wasn't good. We got back to the village at the same time as the athletes returning from the opening ceremonies. I think Guy realized we looked like a bunch of wet puppies. Everyone was moping around."

The team malaise carried over to the competition. After breezing past Puerto Rico in a perfunctory performance, the United States fell to Brazil on the second day of the tournament. The loss was noteworthy: it was the first-ever defeat at the hands of Brazil in women's program history. The mastermind of the upset was none other than Sandy Nitta, longtime United States head coach and National Team pioneer. Things went from bad to worse the next day as the United States fell to Canada.

Next up for the United States was Cuba. The game took place on July 26, the Cuban holiday *Día de la Rebeldía Nacional,* commemorating the beginning of the Fidel Castro-led insurrection against Fulgencio Batista in 1953.

"It was the most amazingly violent game of all time," said Baker. "The Cuban players were just crazy."

While the scoreboard showed a comfortable United States win, it was anything but. A scheduled bye served Baker and the team well as they cooled their heads and prepared for a semifinal matchup with Brazil. The United States avoided a second loss to their South American foe, escaping with an overtime victory.

The stage was set for yet another showdown between the United States and Canada in Winnipeg. With the wounds of the World Cup still fresh, the United States was unable to turn the tables, falling once again to its rival. Despite breaking ground as the first women to compete in water polo at the Pan Am Games, the silver medals around their necks provided little solace for the defeated United States team.

The mountain ahead of them seemed to loom even larger as they once again departed Winnipeg for home.

Baker summed up the experience tersely: "I'll never go to that city again."

⊘⊘⊘⊘⊘⊘

The day after the Pan American Games final, the FINA Junior World Championships got underway in Messina, a city of a quarter million people in the northeast corner of Sicily. Bronze medalists at the first two Junior World Championships, coach Brent Bohlender and his squad arrived in the Italian city with high hopes. A loss to Hungary on the tournament's opening day preceded four straight wins, including victories over the host nation Italy and Russia to finish group play.

But the United States ended up on the short end of a three-way tie atop its bracket. The unfortunate tie-breaker meant the Americans crossed over against Australia, second-place finisher in its group, in the quarterfinals. A furious fourth quarter rally erased an early deficit, but it wasn't enough. The United States fell in overtime, hopes of a bringing home a medal dashed.

Baker was in Brazil with the UCLA men at the time; upon hearing the news via phone, he simply hung up and took off on a run, as Chris Duplanty had following the World Cup loss to Canada. As Baker ran to clear his mind, one phrase kept polluting it: *You've got to be kidding me.*

⊚⊚⊚⊚⊚⊚

Many members of the 1999 Women's National Team subconsciously blocked out the games, the results, or the training. Some blocked it all out – for good reason.

"That year was brutal," said Brenda Villa.

It was the year in between. Between the new start with Guy Baker and the 2000 Olympic Games. It was the year so much changed within the team. But outsiders saw nothing change in the results column. It was a year in which so much was at stake, yet nothing was won.

But it was the year in which the heart of the team was forged. The fall brought a return to their home pool at the Los Alamitos Joint Forces Training Base – and the coining of the motto that would carry the team through hard times along their journey: *Los Al Style.*

Following the World Cup in Winnipeg, the team started a book club. Some book discussions took place at players' apartments; others happened in locales around the world as the team traveled together.

"After the World Cup, we decided as a group that we needed to be the best possible teammates because that was the way we were going to win," said Maureen O'Toole. "I learned so much about my teammates by doing the book club. It really made us come together as a team."

The group became unified in their pursuit more than ever. And it would need to be.

The fall training schedule tested their endurance and desire. College players went back to school for the quarter or semester; full-time training would begin again in January. Everyone swam and lifted weights and sent progress reports to the staff.

A week of training consisted of lifting weights three times, running twice, swim conditioning twice, shooting practice twice and two nights together for water polo workouts. Up north, the players from Stanford and Cal were driving to practices two nights a week and recording their swim data.

And everyone got together for three weekends in October and November. With the Northern California group flying down on Fridays after classes, practice regularly ran from 7:00-10:00 p.m. Saturday consisted of two practices; Sunday featured two more. The team finished late in the afternoon on Sunday before dispersing to start the demanding routine again on Monday morning.

"The foundation was built during that time," Baker said. "It was hard. There was a lot of pressure on them all the time. Ultimately, it's going to come down to *Do I really want to do this?* The opponent is going to do that to you. To me, it has to get tested during the training. For them, it was a little bit brand new. It wasn't something that they'd gone through up to that time."

December brought an end to the monotony of training, but competition provided no relief from the pressure of playing catch-up with Australia and Canada. Assistant coach Chris Duplanty took the team to Montreal for the Canada Cup at the beginning of the month while Baker finished the men's season at UCLA. Winning the NCAA title over Stanford provided the highlight of his water polo year. Meanwhile, the women finished third in Montreal. Wins over Australia and Russia in the last two games were cause for optimism heading into the Holiday Cup at Los Alamitos the following week.

The United States returned to its home pool, and the Holiday Cup started swimmingly. The team followed up a tournament-opening win over Russia by beating World Cup champion Holland. Home pool advantage helped, but it wasn't the only edge in favor of the United States – food poisoning struck several members of the Dutch team. For Baker and the team, a win over the Netherlands under any conditions was a welcome result. But as at the Hunguest Cup and the World Cup, the United States couldn't overcome Australia. A slim one-goal loss at the Holiday Cup provided small consolation.

Despite the results of the first three days, Baker felt the team wasn't playing up to its capabilities. The next game exposed the team as performing below Olympic standard. The Saturday night crowd at the Holiday Cup was the biggest of the tournament, turning out despite the frigid December temperature to watch the

United States take on rival Canada. But fans who arrived early to catch Australia take on Holland found an empty Los Al pool – the game was cancelled due to Dutch illness.

In the morning session, Canada had cancelled its match against Australia due to food poisoning – and Canadian officials told Baker they were unable to play the United States that evening.

"They didn't want to play," Baker said. "They were sick. We were being accused of deliberately food poisoning people. They didn't want to play the game."

It was an unacceptable proposition to Baker, who insisted the game take place.

"It's Saturday night – people are showing up," he said. "We can't cancel the featured game of our own tournament on a Saturday night."

So Canada played. And won.

"They came in with barely enough players, everyone else has food poisoning, and they beat us," Baker

lamented. "We couldn't get out of our own way."

Baker pointed to the rivalry between the two nations, and where both teams stood at the time, as having impacted the result that night.

"It's just sports," he commented. "They had the total upper hand on us. They had qualified for the Olympics. We're struggling. That loss in Winnipeg when we didn't qualify, it really did a number on us. We were still working through that."

Beating Russia for third place on Sunday barely raised the spirits of the women and staff. Once again, the United States finished behind two of the teams already in the Olympic field. They placed ahead of world number one Holland – who played two games with food poisoning and forfeited another. It was time to leave Los Al – time to take a break. At last, 1999 came to a merciful end.

But 1999 mattered. Baker found persistence, and an uncommon perseverance, on everybody's part.

"The fall was really, really hard," Baker said. "What we had just been through at the Holiday Cup, on top of not qualifying, on top of the double-whammy of going back to Winnipeg – it was a lot. But we were still not playing well. We're still putting in all this time. They're killing themselves, three times a week, some players coming down south almost every weekend, and we're still falling flat. We're still not doing what we need to do."

Baker created the Holiday Cup as a progress report, marking the team's standing after toiling together throughout the fall.

"We set up the Holiday Cup to create pressure," Baker said. "We had to do well at the Holiday Cup because it's our event. It was another mechanism to put pressure on our team. It wasn't like we were just having fun hosting this tournament. It's our tournament, and we always set out to win our tournament. It took us a while to do that, but that was always the intent from the start."

January was only a few days away, and with it would come the Olympic year.

"We had put in so much that year," Baker began. "We were at a point there was just still something missing."

It was time to cast 1999 behind. The team would start fresh in 2000. The turning of the calendar would bring change, but time was running short.

2000 Olympic Qualifying Tournament – Palermo

8

TURNING POINT

2000 Olympic Qualification Tournament   **Heather Petri**

The turning of the calendar brought a new year and new faces to the Women's National Team. The arrival of Heather Petri and Ericka Lorenz at Los Al wrapped up a frenetic few months for the pair of Cal athletes.

Two weeks before, the duo played on the United States B team at the Holiday Cup. Despite taking their lumps against the international competition, the B team, coached by Jamey Wright, competed with enthusiasm, excited for the opportunity. Their games served as undercards each day of the tournament – training matches for the visiting teams and the United States' Olympic hopefuls. But one person watched the B games intently and with a purpose. Guy Baker had already decided to bring new blood to the Senior Team when training resumed in January.

Following their final exams at Cal, Petri and Lorenz drove down from Berkeley to Los Al for the Holiday Cup. On the last day of the tournament, Lorenz' truck was all packed up, and the teammates were set to drive back to Cal after their last game. When the B team's final group meeting ended, the players dispersed, but Baker approached Petri, Lorenz, Margie Dingeldein, and Amber Stachowski. He wanted to meet with them individually before they left.

Petri vividly remembers sitting at the base of the palm tree outside the pool fence, waiting her turn to be called into Baker's office. Her heart raced – not from anticipation, but out of fear.

"You've got to know, we were terrified of Guy," she said, laughing. "He was this very scary, intense man. He was the National Team coach, and he held all of our dreams in his hands."

She didn't see Lorenz exit, but Baker came around the corner and summoned her.

Petri, still sitting under the palm tree, looked up at him. "My mind was just going *Oh, my God*," she said. "I was freaking out."

Taking the seat across from Baker's desk, Petri wrung her hands nervously in her lap, her palms beginning to perspire.

Baker began. *I saw you play. I have this plan for the next phase of our training as we head into the Olympic Games. We really have to change things up, and I'd like to see if you'd want to come down and train with us starting January 1.*

Petri's heart nearly stopped. *Is he serious?* Immediately, before he could rescind the offer, Petri said yes. "Of course, one hundred percent," she said. "I wanted this chance, whatever it meant."

An accomplished collegiate player herself, Petri viewed the National Team athletes as heroes. She knew a handful personally, but for the most part she had admired their abilities from afar. She pictured helping the team get to the Olympics; the idea that she could help the team get to the Olympics blew her mind. She barely heard Baker as he thanked her, promised to send along more details, and said he would see her in January. *What does this even mean?* she asked herself, dizzy with shock.

Walking out on shaky legs, she found Lorenz outside the fence. Both women unsure of what the other just heard, they looked at each other, quickly communicating with their eyes, *Did that just really happen?*

"We started screaming and jumping up and down," Petri said. They crumpled back to the ground underneath the palm tree. Their lives had just been tossed up in the air like confetti. "We're not going back to school next semester. We're not playing for Cal that season," Petri said. "We get a chance to be with these girls and play this game we love."

The 400-mile drive back to Berkeley seemed to last mere minutes as they rode the emotional high, talking, singing, laughing, and imagining what the change to their lives would bring.

The Olympic year upon him, Baker wondered the exact same thing.

@@@@@@

Orinda, California, and the surrounding area of Lafayette, Moraga, and Walnut Creek is a hotbed of competitive aquatics. Swimming, water polo, and synchronized swimming have deep roots in the community, and almost every child growing up in the Lamorinda boundaries is a water baby.

Heather Petri was no exception.

"In the summer, it was swim, swim, swim," she said. But during the rest of the year, Petri left the pool behind to pursue a host of other interests ranging from basketball and horseback riding to sewing. For a period of time when she was a child, she sewed her own clothes.

"I just wanted to try everything," she said. "My parents listened to me and allowed me to have experiences in different sports and activities. It really bolstered my culture for trying new things."

Heather and her brother Brandon selected their activities, but one family rule was always enforced. The Petri kids had to be committed, never missing a practice or class, and they had to finish the season or year before reevaluating future participation.

"At the end, they'd ask us, 'How did you like it? Do you want to do it again?'" she said. "I didn't realize it then – I just thought it was my parents' weird rule that you never miss anything – but at the end of the season they were allowing us to put that responsibility for our future paths in our own hands. They were asking me to choose. They weren't telling me, *You have to play polo*, or whatever else. They were giving me that opportunity to decide for myself."

Spending time following all sorts of interests kept Petri happy and busy. And eventually, through her own choice, she made her way back to swimming, and ultimately she found water polo.

"I kept gravitating back to the pool," she recalled. "I liked softball; I liked volleyball, but they didn't give me that same passion, and so I kept telling my parents, 'Okay, I really want to do swimming.' It was during that period that my brother Brandon was playing water polo, so they suggested that might be something I would enjoy."

Petri tagged along with her parents to watch Brandon's high school games at Miramonte, but what really got her attention was Jungle Ball – a loose take on water polo with very few rules, especially when it comes to dunking opponents. Brandon coached Heather's summer swim group, and Fridays were special because everyone looked forward to Jungle Ball. It wasn't real water polo, but Heather loved the contact and the competitive game aspect.

As she got closer to high school, water polo was on Petri's radar, but it wasn't an option – there was no girls' water polo team at Miramonte, or any of the high schools in the area at the time. So she participated on the swim team as a freshman. During the summer before her sophomore year, inspiration came from an unexpected source.

Ronda Lathrop, mother of James, one of Petri's high school swimming teammates, approached her at the Orinda-Moraga Championship Swim Meet and asked, "Hey, Heather, why don't you play water polo with James and the boys?"

Petri laughed at the idea. James added his two cents.

"Mom, leave her alone."

Ronda persisted. She promised Petri the boys would take care of her, pointing out that she swam fast enough to keep up with them.

"We were joking at the time, but the idea kind of stuck with me," Petri said. "I knew these guys – James, Dave Parker, Sean Joy – were awesome. They were in my class and ultimately went on to play at Cal, UCLA, and Stanford. All of them were incredible athletes."

Although it started off as a far-fetched idea and simple pool deck banter, Petri started to mull over the idea of playing water polo at Miramonte. She ran the possibility by two of her swimming teammates, Chris Lane and Ali Riddell. Both liked the idea. They kept talking about it and got up the nerve to approach the boys coach, Bill Brown.

The girls knew enough to know they were approaching a legend. Brown had paced the deck at Miramonte since 1966, when a group of swimmers asked him to start a water polo team. Originally hired to coach football and basketball, Brown found a home at the Miramonte pool – having never played water polo himself. Three of his athletes – Peter Schnugg, Jon Svendsen, and Drew McDonald – were named to the 1980 Olympic team. Svendsen and McDonald went on to win silver in the 1984 Olympics. Miramonte grad Kirk Everist played in the 1992 Games before being joined by high school teammate Rick McNair on the 1996 Olympic team.

Little did Brown know, the interaction with the nervous 10th grade Heather Petri would mark the beginnings of another Miramonte Olympian.

Petri remembers the day clearly. "We went and talked to Bill, and he was so cute that day," she said. "We asked, 'Would it be okay if we played?' I don't know what he really thought about us coming there, but right away he said yes. He was 100 percent behind us."

Brown sent the girls to talk to Leo Hanley, the JV coach, and they started that day.

"Because of Bill's attitude in terms of the way he approached us, these girls being on the team, the way he embraced it, all of the boys were in line with him," Petri recalled. "If he had wavered even a bit, or if they had seen him be wishy-washy about it, I know for a fact that that first year playing with boys would have been hell, and I never would have continued."

Petri still gets emotional speaking about the impact of feeling included and being a respected member of the Miramonte boys' team. Over the years, she has thanked her male teammates and Bill Brown for giving her the one moment that would define her pursuits for nearly two decades in the pool.

"Everybody has the a-ha moment," Petri said. "You don't know when it will come, but it's this time when you realize, *This is my thing. I want to do this.* Bill Brown gave it to us. I am forever grateful for that experience that year."

While she and her friends loved playing on the boys team, at the end of the next summer, there was a swell of interest in girls' water polo in the Lamorinda area. Word spread among the local moms that girls had played on the boys' team, and soon Petri and her female teammates were in front of the school board, petitioning to form a team for girls. They went to board meetings and agreed to ask their swimming friends and their schools – Northgate, Campolindo, San Ramon, and Las Lomas – to agree to play water polo in the fall of 1995.

The effort drummed up enough interest, and the school district gave the go-ahead to start a girls' league on an introductory basis – provided each school kept a minimum number of athletes who had signed the petition. Miramonte was required to keep fifty girls, while the other schools were obliged to have fifteen. Girls' water polo was on its way to inclusion in the Foothill Athletic League. Fittingly, Brown assisted in bringing the girls' program to Miramonte nearly thirty years after he did the same for the boys.

Miramonte had no problem with the mandate – close to seventy girls showed up for the first season.

With such a huge turnout of girls and competing for pool time in the same season as the boys, the girls' coaches had to get creative with teaching time. Miramonte's Bill Brown Aquatic Center, dedicated in the coach's honor in 2002 before he retired in 2005 after thirty-nine years guiding the Mats, now boasts a 40-meter by 25-yard pool. At the time, however, there was a narrow six-lane, shallow-deep 25-yard pool and a small diving tank. The first girls' coach, Donnie Heidary, who coached swimming at Miramonte, addressed both the problem of pool space and the issue of teaching so many girls how to play water polo with one simple solution.

He used most of the practice time teaching the girls on land. Heidary took the girls to the adjacent field for an hour each day, focusing on setting up the front court offense, walking through how to drive, and how to defend.

"Every single one of us was new, so we had no idea what we were doing," Petri said. "So it was a cool way to learn. The idea of it was to get it in our brain so when we jumped in the water we could make use of the little time we had."

Heidary coached the girls during Petri's junior year. In her senior season, Peter Asch, a member of the bronze medal-winning 1972 Olympic team, took over the head coaching duties. Without realizing it, Petri was surrounded by Olympic pedigree at Miramonte. The humble Asch never brought up his own accomplishments, and Everist, an assistant on the boys' team at the time, was generous with his coaching, even to Petri.

"It blows my mind thinking back to it because I was so grateful that they all were there for me, but I don't think I understood the level of what they were giving to me," Petri said. "As Olympians, they were so knowledgeable, and it may have planted a seed. I never thought I'd be an Olympian, I was just inspired by these great people that were around us. I think back now, and I'm like, *Damn, that was cool.*"

After stumbling upon water polo in high school, Petri cherished the activity and loved the camaraderie of the team, but she had no long-term goals to seriously pursue the highest levels of the sport. Her career was all about timing – forming a team of girls in high school, followed by the explosion of collegiate programs transitioning to varsity status, and on top of it all, the addition of women's water polo to the Olympic Games. All of it happened while Petri could take advantage of each opportunity, and her love of working hard, learning, and achieving led her onward.

"There were doors opening for us due to Title IX and the wonderfulness of ladies that had come before us," Petri said. "As the doors opened, I really feel like I was just running through them. I had no idea how they were opening in front of me until recently. I was blessed. This moment in time was very unique."

With her girls' team recently assembled at Miramonte, a chance meeting between Petri and Maureen O'Toole, the coach at Cal at the time, got her thinking about the possibility of playing water polo in college. Petri and a handful of female teammates attended the Camp of Champions at Long Beach State in the summer of 1995. She recalls being one of seven girls among nearly 200 boys and enjoying every moment. For the scrimmages at the end of the camp, the girls were put together on one team, coached by O'Toole.

The girls notched only a couple of wins amongst a slew of losses, but Petri was unfazed by the results. When the games ended, O'Toole encouraged the girls to think about playing water polo in college. Petri had no idea college water polo existed, let alone ten miles from Miramonte at Cal.

Petri tucked away the new knowledge but focused her college search on swimming, with water polo a side option if the school had a team. When many of the coaches she contacted suggested that she should choose either swimming or water polo, Petri was disappointed. If she had to choose, swimming would be the way to go. Until another twist of fate pushed her toward water polo.

A knee injury and surgery before her senior swim season kept Petri out of the water for most of the season. A team captain, she cheered on her teammates every day at practice and meets, but her recruitment dried up. Coaches were wary of her injury, and contacts became more and more infrequent. Petri remembered the seed planted by O'Toole at the summer camp in Long Beach. She picked up the phone and called O'Toole about playing water polo at Cal. O'Toole offered a walk-on spot, which Petri quickly accepted.

It didn't take long for Petri to know that things had fallen perfectly into place.

Her knee strong enough to play with a brace, Petri joined the team for summer practices after graduation. She immediately experienced a physical and mental transformation, gaining speed and fitness while soaking up a sea of water polo instruction from the Cal coaches. At the end of the fall, with the season around the corner, O'Toole delivered shocking news to the unheralded freshman – Petri had made the roster.

"I was like, *Excuse me?*" Petri said. "And I think most of my teammates were like, *Who the hell is this kid?*"

Thrust into action as a freshman, Petri thrived.

"That first year at Cal gave me everything I needed," she recalled. "It was such an incredible foundation – to be able to understand the game at such a higher speed and be pushed in ways that I never thought possible. I was just like a sponge. It was insane."

Playing alongside Alisa von Hartitzsch and her sister Melanie, members of the Senior and Junior National Teams, intrigued Petri, who had no knowledge of water polo outside of her own experiences. Always curious, Petri learned more about the National Team from her coach, Maureen O'Toole. With the announcement of the Olympics, and O'Toole's return to action, Petri's high school coach, Peter Asch, joined the Cal coaching staff. Petri enjoyed hearing stories of training and travel from O'Toole and Golden Bear teammates such as the von Hartitzsch sisters.

Her own ambitions remained squarely focused on Cal and her steep learning curve. But O'Toole encouraged Petri to attend National Team tryouts whenever the staff was in Northern California. She went, and quickly found out the college players were primarily there to be practice dummies. And she loved it.

"We just got our butts kicked, which is awesome," she said. "Those were the best experiences for me because I was playing against a new level of player. I remember clearly Heather Kohler and Mo and all these women doing things that made me think *Wait a minute. How do they do that?* Even when I was expecting what they were doing to me, it happened over and over again."

In the fall of 1999, Petri was asked to train with the Northern California National Team members. From that group, Baker gave the non-National Team players the option to travel to weekend practices with the entire National Team, and Petri snapped up every opportunity to do so.

"By going down there on weekends, Guy got to see us more, and I think he appreciated the effort we were putting in," Petri said. "After all those weekends, he selected a B team from all of us that had been participating during those fall months."

Petri was wide-eyed and eager when she arrived at the Holiday Cup as a member of the United States B team. Less than a month later, she was headed back to Los Al to join the Senior Team in its pursuit of the Sydney Olympics. In her mind, she was pretty sure she was there to be a practice dummy. If she was, she had no objection whatsoever.

Before meeting with Heather Petri and Ericka Lorenz at the end of the 1999 Holiday Cup, Guy Baker had spoken to Peter Asch, their coach at Cal. Baker grabbed Asch, who was at Los Al watching his players compete, and shared his thoughts about infusing the two into the mix in January. Asch was immediately supportive. When Petri approached him about the plan, he assured her that everything would work out.

Not everyone Baker asked accepted the invitation. Margie Dingeldein, a sophomore at Stanford, opted to stay in Palo Alto. The logistics of training full-time with the National Team were too difficult for high school junior Amber Stachowski. (In 2004, both Dingeldein and Stachowski helped the United States win a bronze medal at the Athens Olympics.)

On New Year's Day, Petri packed her car to the brim and hit the road, full of anxiety about the adventure ahead. From what she had been told, she would be living with the "Irvs Crew," the part of the team housed together in apartments in Irvine.

Driving down Interstate 5, Petri got instructions from Baker. "He told me to drive to Irvine and find my apartment," she said. "I thought, *Okay*. Then he told me I was going to be staying in a house with Ellen, and my heart sank. Immediately, I'm thinking, *Oh, my God. I'm in so much trouble. This is going to be terrible*."

Petri and Ellen Estes' only personal encounters to that point had taken place in the pool, mostly in front of the goal. Estes, a center at Stanford, and Petri, a defender at Cal, had tussled fiercely in the past but never met in more friendly circumstances.

"The only thing I know about Ellen is playing against her," Petri said. "We would get into the most crazy water polo battles. So at this time what I thought about Ellen was that she hated my guts – that she just couldn't stand me. I didn't know how sweet a person she was."

The last meeting between the two, the semifinals at the 1999 Collegiate Nationals at USC, resulted in an Estes elbow dislocating Petri's jaw. Driving to her new home in Irvine, Petri called Lorenz, distraught that they were assigned to separate apartments.

Arriving at the front door, Petri took a deep breath and knocked. "The door opened, and Ellen and Courtney Johnson were so excited to see me," she recalled. "They said *Welcome! Yay!* and it immediately melted my heart. It meant so much that they were ready and excited for me to be there."

Instantly, Petri felt she had a family in the Irvs Crew. The six athletes – Petri, Estes, and Johnson in one apartment, and Lorenz, Coralie Simmons, and Nicolle Payne in the other – drove in brutal traffic back and forth to practice together every day. The time spent on the road was a great way to get to know each other.

But the support through a time of great uncertainty was the lasting impact of the Irvs Crew on Petri.

"They saw you when you got home and crashed on the couch, and you wanted to cry," she said. "They sat next to you and helped talk you through it. We were allowed to do that for each other. This happened in later Olympic teams, too, but this was very different. I think it's because we were all in this new situation, this new world where nobody knew what was going on."

◎◎◎◎◎◎

Meanwhile, another crew of five athletes lived together in a two-story four-bedroom house in Cerritos, less than ten miles from the Los Al pool. Heather Moody, Rachel Scott, Robin Beauregard, and Bernice Orwig each had their own room and shared the cooking duties. With the two apartments in Irvine full, and Brenda Villa still in need of housing, Guy Baker and Michelle Pickering approached the Cerritos Crew about adding one more body to the house. Naturally, the group agreed.

"It was a process taking in one of the youngest members of the team," recalled Moody, who volunteered to share her room with Villa. "Our routine was that everyone cooked one night a week, so Brenda was now in the mix. Brenda didn't know how to cook. Brenda didn't know how to drive. So it was kind of a growing up phase for her in this environment with older teammates."

Moody and Scott recalled a Friday night dinner out when the Cerritos Crew took advantage of Villa's age to have a designated driver. "We didn't have practice Saturday, so we were hanging out and all of us older players had drinks," Scott said. "When we left, it was *All right, B, you're driving us home. We can't drive, so it's all you.* She was absolutely furious with us, but it was a way that she was forced to practice driving."

Villa recalls learning to drive in a black Cadillac that Scott won in a lottery as part of General Motors' "Support the Team" initiative.

"I never had a car, so I never really wanted to learn to drive," Villa said. "I was 19, and they were encouraging me to learn. There were times when Bernie or somebody would have to go to the grocery store, a couple blocks away, so I would drive. It was definitely a household effort to make me learn to drive. When I finally got my driver's license, it was a big moment."

As for her weekly turn to cook, Villa would sometimes return from weekend visits home with a meal cooked by her mom. Other times, she grilled carne asada or chicken. But her housemates remember Villa branching out in her culinary pursuits, working up to pasta dishes. There were no complaints from the famished calorie-seeking post-workout crew about Villa's dinner offerings.

The roommate pair of Moody and Villa turned out to be a classic Odd Couple combination.

Moody, the super neat-freak, needed everything to be organized just so. She marveled at her younger roommate, who was her polar opposite.

"Brenda had this little single bed that was in the corner, and absolutely everything she owned was on that bed," Moody said. "It was a complete disaster zone. She would crawl into bed with everything still on it and go to sleep. Then she'd wake up and just roll over everything, pull some stuff on, and then go to practice. It was like, *I don't understand. I don't understand. There's a dresser for you.*

"It was this little itty-bitty pig pen," Moody continued, smiling at the memory. "The thing that blew me away is that she would sleep in it, and nothing would ever fall. She would just lay there, and she'd wake up and everything would be right where it was, and she'd just be, *All right; I'm ready to go.*"

©/© ©/© ©/© ©/© ©/©

For Maureen O'Toole, residential training was an entirely different experience than that of her teammates. In January of 2000, her daughter Kelly was almost eight years old. O'Toole herself was about to turn 39 and had a full nine years in age over her next oldest teammate. Mother and daughter moved in with

O'Toole's brother, Mike, in Long Beach for the full-time training that would hopefully result in qualifying for the Sydney Olympics.

On a normal day, O'Toole would get Kelly ready in the morning and take her across the street from the house to elementary school. Often, Kelly would be picked up by Guy Baker, whose daughters Sam and Chris were in the same school. Baker would bring all three girls to the pool at Los Al, where they would spend the afternoon while the National Team practiced. O'Toole and Kelly would head home together and repeat the process every day of the week.

But the toughest times for O'Toole were the weekends. The team had its final workout of the week on Saturday morning – a scrimmage at high intensity, intended to challenge each individual and the team to perform through fatigue. When practice was over, O'Toole's teammates headed straight home to eat and recover throughout the rest of Saturday and all day Sunday.

"I would go home and be a mom," O'Toole said. "I wasn't sitting around on the couch all weekend. The weekends were totally exhausting."

Between five and eight years old, Kelly had soccer games, swim meets, and other activities on the weekends. O'Toole, training harder than ever in her career, fell asleep almost every night reading to her daughter or helping her study and complete her homework.

"I didn't get any rest, so it was really difficult in that way being a mom," O'Toole said. "I really felt like I wasn't as good a mom as I could have been to Kelly because I was training full-time. During school I would get her there, and in the summer when we were training, she would be doing junior lifeguards and all kinds of other stuff that I missed."

In the summer of 2000, Maureen and Kelly moved in with Janice O'Toole, Maureen's mom. Janice took Kelly to junior lifeguards in the morning and often brought her to the Los Al pool in the afternoons where she would play with Sam and Chris Baker.

Without a doubt, the grande dame of the team had a different situation than her younger teammates. Many of the women she played with in the 1970s and 1980s were raising families, long since retired from playing competitive water polo. Even those she teamed with in the 1990s were mostly long gone. Maggi Kelly and Lynn Wittstock left in 1998. O'Toole was the last survivor from the pioneer days of women's water polo. Five of her current teammates weren't yet born when O'Toole made her National Team debut. At 39, she was twenty years older than Ericka Lorenz, the youngest player in the group.

More than anyone else, O'Toole needed to rest her body on the weekend. But the duties of motherhood didn't slow down for the pursuit of history. O'Toole was carrying the banner for an entire generation of past National Team players while paving the way for future generations of women's water polo players, including her daughter Kelly, who would play for the Junior and Senior National Teams and win an NCAA championship.

For Maureen O'Toole there wasn't time to rest – she had too much to play for.

◎◎◎◎◎◎

The countdown to Olympic qualifying in Italy flew by in the winter of 2000. The work remained the same as the year before, but the dynamic was different. The addition of Heather Petri and Ericka Lorenz brought a fresh outlook to the group. Integrating them into the team proved easier than anticipated, and the feeling was that having two people going through the grind for the first time was simpler than the previous years, when everyone went through the learning process all at once.

Baker's vision was coming together. For the first time, the team was playing at a high level on a consistent basis. He found himself feeling, *Whoa, that was a good practice*, and the next day, *Whoa, that was a good practice*, and over and over again. It had taken more than a year to reach this point, and now the Olympic qualifier was a couple of months away. Baker was confident the team's timeline was on target.

One month before the do-or-die qualification attempt, Heather Petri found herself in Baker's office once again. Despite being new to the group, she was not immune from taking her lumps from Baker in practice. She had a lot to learn, beginning in the weight room, where she had no experience upon arriving at Los Al. Fellow defender Robin Beauregard mentored her during drills and gave reassuring pep talks when her mistakes drew Baker's ire. The tips were like gold to Petri, who focused her role on gaining experience and learning everything she could from the players she held in such high regard..

This meeting with Baker was brief. He was naming the team for the Olympic Qualification Tournament.

"Hey, you're on the roster," he told her.

"It blew my mind," Petri said. "Honestly, I didn't think I would ever be on the team until Guy told me that I was going to be playing on the squad that went to Palermo. I didn't really understand what I was doing there until that day. I have a thick head – I don't see that I'm there until you shake me."

Petri's water polo career had taken a rocket's trajectory since the days of Jungle Ball at summer swim practice. Ericka Lorenz, on the same rocket as Petri, would be by her side in Palermo, also earning a spot on the most important roster in United States women's water polo history.

Baker's new additions were fully on board. One year after the failed attempt in Winnipeg, the team set out to make the most if its last chance.

@@@@@@

In April, the United States Women's National Team departed for Italy with the intention of returning as the first United States Women's Olympic Team. The roster included thirteen athletes who had put their lives – school, family, career – on hold to achieve a common goal. But if the team qualified for the Olympics, roster changes were not only possible; they were guaranteed. The deal from the day women's water polo was added to the Olympics included six teams with a roster size of eleven players each. At the moment, it didn't matter to any of the athletes or the staff. To a person, they were focused on the task at hand – qualifying as a team.

Three spots remained available for the field in Sydney, and they would be awarded at the Olympic Qualification Tournament in Palermo on the island of Sicily. But the bids weren't automatically reserved for the top three finishers. In a final exemption for continental qualification, the top-placed team from Asia would earn an Olympic berth – provided it placed eighth or better. So the safe play for the Americans was to reach and win the tournament semifinal, guaranteeing a top-two finish.

United States captain Julie Swail went a step further. "My theory was simple," she said. "If we win the tournament, we go to the Olympics. Our goal was always to win the tournament. It made no sense to play the numbers. We wanted to put fate in our own hands."

The first stop in Europe was Athens, Greece, for the eight-team Thetis Cup. Six Olympic hopefuls – the United States, Spain, Hungary, Italy, Russia, and Greece – were joined by Australia and Canada in preparation for the qualifier in Palermo.

Played over only three days, the United States swept its group on Friday and Saturday to reach the tournament final. Especially satisfying was a solid victory over Hungary. Wins over Russia and Greece were important in Baker's mind, as well – the ability to beat European teams in Palermo would be the key to qualifying for the Olympics.

On Sunday, the bus was late picking up the United States and Australia at the hotel. The final day game schedule was condensed, as often is the case in European tournaments, to allow teams to catch a flight and be home that evening. The result was a lack of warm-up time for the two finalists, and when the game started, both teams took a few minutes to get up to speed.

Baker didn't mind, because as he had seen throughout the tournament, the team competed physically and mentally from the opening whistle. The consistency which had eluded the group in 1999 appeared to be found; Baker saw it from the start of the game until the end. Another positive against Australia was the strength of the United States' defense. The defense was unified, transitioning smoothly, and showing that it had the ability to prevent a team from scoring for long periods of time. Australia edged the United States, 2-1.

"Our mentality to compete was very good," Baker said of the Thetis Cup. "It was the first tournament that we finished where we felt good about how we were playing. It had been a long time, and it was important we played good water polo at that point."

Everyone in the United States contingent left Athens feeling positive about the performance. Confidence was on the rise at just the right time.

But the team's mentality would be tested during its next stop: training with the Italians in Rome. The 13-team qualification tournament was set up such that it wasn't possible for the two teams to face each other with an Olympic bid on the line, making them perfect training partners in the final week of preparation.

The training facility at the Giulio Onesti dell'Acqua Acetosa in Rome left much to be desired, however. On top of cold and rainy weather, the dorm rooms had miserable beds, and the first trip to the cafeteria found the famished athletes living a famous Seinfeld episode.

"We go into the cafeteria, and the Soup Nazi is there," Heather Moody explained. "The head chef would only give us one roll each. When we asked for more, we got shot down with *One roll only!* along with a look of total disapproval."

Cereal was also at a premium each morning. Training several hours a day, the team arrived at each meal in search of calories to refuel their bodies. International relations in the cafeteria did not improve when team manager Michelle Pickering solved the problem by making a market run for cereal and extra bread for the team.

"He got really mad; it was not allowed," Moody recalled. "*Why are these Americans eating so much food?* He should have taken it as a compliment."

◎◎◎◎◎◎

With the food situation under control, the team focused on final preparations for Palermo. Training with Italy served its purpose for both teams. The play was physical, but civil – not necessarily a given for common training of this type. The training camp ended with an official game before the two teams headed to Sicily.

With plenty of time to kill before the pre-game team meeting in the late afternoon, captain Julie Swail and Maureen O'Toole boarded the train at the station near their accommodations. It was a routine outing for the two veteran players. O'Toole needed to stop at a post office; Swail's penchant for gelato was well known. Enjoying the time away from the training center, Swail and O'Toole responsibly caught the return train with plenty of time to spare.

Except they boarded the wrong one.

Swail and O'Toole unknowingly boarded a local express; to their horror, their intended station was a blur as the train zoomed right past. Frantic, they disembarked at the next stop. Explaining their situation to some locals, they asked if hailing a taxi would save time.

"They told us no, our best option was to wait for the next train because the street traffic would be worse," Swail said.

The two National Team veterans waited for what seemed like an eternity.

"It was probably ten to fifteen minutes, but it seemed to take forever," Swail continued. "We're sweating on the train. Not because it was hot, but because we're thinking *Oh, my gosh; we are so busted.* When we finally got off at our stop, we ran faster than I've ever run before, but by that point, we were about fifteen to twenty minutes late. If we could have been scared into playing great, we would have been superstars that night."

In the meeting room, Baker stewed in silence as the minutes ticked by. The pair arrived, panting and perspiring after their sprint from the train station. Each person cringed inside, bracing for the reaction of their coach.

Baker handled it simply. The team punishment for being late was clear: carrying the balls and caps. He treated the infraction without fanfare, and the team meeting commenced. But as scared as Swail and O'Toole were, there were no superstars that night; Baker would unleash on the pair before the evening was over.

The contest against Italy took place at the 50-meter indoor pool at Foro Italico. The vast sports complex was once known as Foro Mussolini, for the Fascist dictator, the visionary behind the art and architecture on the grounds. The venue for the match, which the players refer to as "the marble pool," resembles an ancient Roman bath. (Author Nancy Greenleese describes the art: *"Mosaics of seahorses and lobsters cover the deck, and the walls explode with blue prancing horses and tanned runners."*)

In this historic setting, the Italian and American teams faced off in their final tune-up. The conditions were not ideal.

"It was absolutely freezing," said Heather Moody. "It's cold in the building; it's cold in the water. There's no warmth anywhere."

The narrow pool also provided an advantage to the home team, especially on defense, where their zone scheme benefitted from shorter gaps for their swarming defenders on the perimeter.

The combination of factors added up to a sub-par outing for the United States.

"We didn't play well," Moody said bluntly. "We really, truly didn't play well. It was our last game before going to the qualifying tournament. As a coach, I understand looking at that and getting anxious. As a player, though, who cares? Let's just get off this pool deck; it's freezing. Yeah, you're disappointed. You wanted to play well. You wanted to have a good showing, but the bottom line is you look around the room, and you have confidence in what we've done on our journey to get to this point. I felt like we were in an okay place."

The head coach disagreed.

"We got pulled out and sat on the freezing cold marble deck," Moody said. "We're just cold. Guy just went through his process of *This is wrong. You didn't show up. This, and this, and this.* It was probably a good 20-minute lecture."

Baker directed a healthy portion of his message at the veteran players whose tardiness held up the pre-game routine. Finally, Baker released the players, who scurried to the warmth of the locker room and hot showers.

O'Toole, who along with captain Swail had endured the brunt of Baker's ire in the postgame lashing, stood under the hot water, warming her cold and aching body, eyes fixed on the ground.

"Getting yelled at, I can take it," she said. "It didn't really bother me that much. The only thing that was scary was that I might get cut. That was always in my mind."

The arrival of a crying Brenda Villa snapped O'Toole out of her daze, and she sought to console her young teammate.

"What's wrong, Brenda?" O'Toole asked.

In between sobs, Villa responded, "He's just so mean to you. He just screams and yells at you."

The veteran tried to put Villa, nearly twenty years her younger, at ease. "I'm all right, Brenda," she assured. "It's okay. I can handle it, I've been here before."

The exchange stuck with O'Toole over the years. "It was so cute because she was really, truly upset," she said.

The collection of wildly diverse individuals had grown together for a full two years. They had seen each other's frayed edges and provided support through the toughest of times. Their next destination was Palermo. If they didn't succeed in this mission, it would be their last.

The team was scheduled to depart Rome the next afternoon. Baker declared the next morning free time. He himself needed the time – a buffer to settle his mind and his mood. Despite the successful Thetis Cup, he sensed the team wasn't capitalizing on the momentum. Maintaining rhythm proved difficult following the tournament in Athens. The first game in Palermo wouldn't take place until thirteen days after the Thetis Cup ended, and the lack of comfort and amenities in Rome made the bridge between the two tournaments shaky.

The team and the coach needed a reset.

"The last thing he told us after the game in the marble pool was, *Once we get back to the training facility, I don't want to see you. I don't want to hear from you until we meet tomorrow*," Moody said. With a morning meeting time set, the players and coach parted ways.

Upon reflection that evening, Baker was able to put things into perspective. Playing Italy in their country with Italian referees – winning the game was a long shot at best. The team didn't play well; he was aggravated with the players who were late to the meeting. And everyone's vulnerabilities were beginning to show.

"We were all kind of nervous," Baker said. "I'm sure they were nervous about whether I was going to keep it together. And from my part, do I trust them? Are they actually going to pull through? That dynamic was going on with us."

Baker and Michelle Pickering left the complex for dinner; they agreed the group couldn't leave Rome for Palermo weighed down by the final performance, Baker's hammering of the team, and the rising anxiety within the group.

The morning meeting contained a positive tone.

"It's a little bit of getting on them, but more a reflection on the team's success at the Thetis Cup; all the work they had done, and letting them know they were ready," Baker said.

Then he dropped a final inspirational message on the team.

If you don't want to do this, this is your opportunity to go. Some of you are going to get on the bus, and we're going to go to Palermo. If you don't, Michelle will get you a taxi, and you can go home. I don't care how many people go. As long as we have seven, that's all we need. We need a goalkeeper and six field players. If that's all it is, then that's all it is.

"I got a little fired up there at the end," he said. "We were going to get our stuff and charge; I fully expected to go out to a waiting bus and everybody would get on board together."

The symbolism of taking the next step of the journey as one went south quickly as the team stepped outside the building. There was no bus.

Players, luggage, and travel gear waited at the curb. The staff had encouraged the athletes to bring whatever they needed for comfort on the six-week trip; packing light had been discouraged. *Los Al Style* was the rally cry for the long march through Europe – the more it felt like home, the better. Dry-land equipment, video equipment, medical supplies, a massage table – all waited to be loaded onto the yet-to-appear bus.

While team members lounged in the sun and chatted in small groups, Baker, visibly agitated, paced by himself off to the side.

As was her knack, Robin Beauregard brought a touch of levity to the situation.

Sitting next to Heather Moody, Beauregard asked, "Should we say something? Who's going to go qualify for the Olympics?"

Moody replied sarcastically, "Yeah, go tell him that and see what happens."

Sidling up to Baker, Beauregard casually remarked, "Kinda hard to get on the bus right now."

As the team waited, Michelle Pickering tried to reach the Italian Federation, who took care of the transportation reservations for its guests, as was customary in international travel. Unsurprising for a Sunday morning, her calls went unanswered. The initial anxiety of whether the bus was coming, and when it might show up, escalated to the realization that there was no bus.

Pickering began to improvise. Hailing first one taxi, then another, and another, she started the process of getting players and gear loaded up.

"Those little Italian taxis hold maybe two normal-sized humans and maybe a bag in the back," Moody said. "It took a huge line of them to take all of us and all our stuff. It was insane."

Players squeezed in together, bags stacked on their laps. Passengers in the front seat hugged luggage, blocking the view out the front windshield. The fleet of taxis set off for the airport, and the team was on its way. The Americans were off to conquer Palermo. But instead of arriving in force on a destroyer, it swarmed the airport in a host of tiny ships.

At the airport, the orderly group check-in process the team was accustomed to gave way to near-chaos; Pickering urged players to get their boarding passes and head to the gate individually instead of waiting for the entire team. With scant minutes to spare, everyone was accounted for and buckled in. Unfazed by the hubbub of the morning, the athletes knew they wouldn't be tripped up by such an inconvenience.

"We were just sitting back, chuckling, and thinking, *Whatever, just another hurdle to overcome*," said Moody.

Founded by the Phoenicians in the 8th century B.C.E. under the name Ziz, the modern city of Palermo sits on the northwest coast of Sicily on the Tyrrhenian Sea. The city changed hands repeatedly throughout ancient times, from the Carthaginians, to the Romans, to the Greeks. From the 9th to 11th centuries, it was under Arab rule as the Saracens renamed the city Balharm and made it the capital of Arabian Sicily. During Norman rule, architecture flourished, and many structures from this time period still stand.

To the women's team, the architectural beauty combined with the idyllic seaside scenery made Palermo a perfect coastal haven after the previous stops in the bustling and loud cities of Athens and Rome.

After the dorms of the training center in Rome, the hotel with its panoramic views of the sea was luxurious. The athletes stayed two to a room instead of four, and the relaxed environment gave everyone the necessary space to focus on the task ahead. Knowing the importance of accommodations getting nicer as a long trip continued, rather than the other way around, Baker and Pickering had scouted the particular location and property in Palermo far in advance. Life in Palermo promised to be comfortable.

The near fiasco with transportation earlier in the day in Rome was far behind them. Heather Moody thought of it as a "breaking of the ice," a bit of humor and a much-needed tension-reducer.

Moody understood Baker's anxiety after the game in the marble pool. "With our performance being so hot and cold leading to that point, I think he thought, *Oh, my gosh; they're getting cold*," she said. "We always had a good game and then a dip down. Palermo was our turning point as a team as far as developing a consistent approach."

For more than a year, Baker and the team had been developing an established group approach to training and competition that also allowed for individuals to prepare themselves as necessary. At the World Cup in Winnipeg, pre-game nerves, fed and fueled by the magnitude of the games, overwhelmed more than a few players.

"When you go into games, and you're super nervous, it's difficult to play well," said Robin Beauregard. "If you put too much on each game, your performance falters, and every mistake you make becomes magnified. Winnipeg was a good testing ground to figure out how to make it just a game."

Baker had begun to create a standard routine early in 1999, but the mindset hadn't fully set in by the time the team arrived at the World Cup. "He started it a little bit before Winnipeg," Beauregard said. "We wanted to prepare for every practice, every game, the same way – a routine, so one game wasn't that big a deal. It didn't really fully make sense until after Winnipeg."

By the time the team got to Palermo, the players had the routine wired. The nerves that struck them down at the most important moments in Winnipeg were a thing of the past. There wouldn't be a situation too big for any of them – not after what they had been through and knowing what they were primed to achieve.

They reminded each other of their mantra: *Los Al Style*. The team believed strongly that the work they did on a daily basis would carry them through the Olympic Qualifying Tournament.

"It reminded us that although so much was riding on this one tournament, we had to keep things how we did them every single day," said Bernice Orwig. "Guy and the staff did a great job of always bringing it back to our routine, our lifestyle. Wherever we were in the world, it came back to what we did every day at Los Al."

Baker wanted the team to approach each game with the confidence that they were doing something they had done hundreds of times before.

"It was the scattered version of things in Winnipeg that caused that," Beauregard said. "Like a lot of teams, we had our mix tape we listened to pregame, with everybody contributing a song. But we didn't have a set routine. After Winnipeg is when we first started it, and I think that's what got our ragtag-ness to come together and be able to mesh enough to get us over the top."

In the days leading up to the qualifying tournament, there was no fear amongst the team as they relaxed in the hotel or strolled along the nearby shore. Within the team, the mindset was unified. Palermo would be the end of this trip, but not their journey. They intended to finish in Sydney.

When recalling the trip as a whole, Guy Baker remembers a sense of start and stop throughout. The results at the Thetis Cup gave rise to optimism. He felt the team was ready to perform, but then had a letdown during the training in Rome. At the conclusion of that stage, the qualifying tournament was still more than a week away, and it was nearly two weeks until Baker expected to face an opponent that would pose a real challenge. Having arrived in Palermo six days before the opener, everyone was antsy for the action to begin.

Even once the games commenced, the United States' schedule was choppy. An expected victory over Kazakhstan was followed with a bye on Easter Sunday. To the delight of the team, Michelle Pickering set up an Easter egg hunt, and the athletes scrambled around the hotel, looking for the golden egg. After returning to the pool to easily dispatch the Czech Republic, the United States had another day off before overpowering Germany.

Two opponents remained in group play, Greece and Italy. Losing both would eliminate the United States from Olympic contention. A win over Greece would assure a semifinal berth and the opportunity to play for a spot in Sydney. Armed with confidence gained in a solid win over Greece at the Thetis Cup, the United States stormed to a dominating 6-1 victory. The stifling defense shut out Greece for the final three quarters, while five American players scored goals, led by captain Julie Swail's pair.

As the last day of group play began, four teams–Hungary, Russia, Italy, and the United States–had already secured the four semifinal spots. That last day, though, featured two games which would decide the pairings in those semifinals. The first pitted Hungary against Russia, followed by Italy and the United States. Despite an upward trend in results leading into the tournament, the United States was considered a clear underdog to the reigning world champion. Anticipating an Italian victory, the Hungarians and Russians battled desperately for the top spot in their group in order to avoid the home team in the crucial semifinal. Few in the know would bet against Italy taking one of the Olympic bids.

Meanwhile, both Kazakhstan and Japan had reached the top eight, guaranteeing an Asian nation in Sydney. Third place in this tournament would be for naught. Only the top two would leave Palermo in joy.

Trailing by a goal midway through the final quarter, Hungary rallied past Russia behind two goals by Noemi Toth. The two teams awaited the final result of the evening, and knowledge of who would stand in their way of the Olympic Games.

As it had throughout the entire tournament, The Village People's "Macho Man" blared over the speakers as the teams from Italy and the United States marched out for introductions. The home crowd enjoyed an early lead for their team, but each goal was matched by the Americans. Midway through the second quarter, two goals by Robin Beauregard and one from the arm of Brenda Villa pushed the United States ahead, 5-3. But the world champions rallied back behind their raucous crowd, and, despite a pair of fourth quarter goals by Coralie Simmons, Italy sealed a 10-8 victory.

The United States had given Italy all they could handle. The semifinals loomed, and the only consequence of the loss was a matchup with Hungary, the winner to qualify for the Olympics. The game with Italy required Baker to balance his options.

"I thought we could have won. I backed off a little," Baker admitted. "The semifinal the next day was the game that mattered. We could have fully invested in the Italy game with no guarantee of winning. I had to gauge what the cost would be for the next day. Even if we won, what would be the cost. I decided to focus on being ready for the semifinal game."

The team had found its rhythm. The result against Italy barely mattered. The United States women controlled their own Olympic destiny – and only Hungary stood in their way.

While the semifinals on April 29 would determine two Olympic berths, there was a third spot in Sydney up for grabs that evening. Japan and Kazakhstan advanced to the top eight and faced off in a 5th-8th semifinal to determine the

Asian qualifier for Sydney. Japan surprised many by reaching the top eight with a tie against France and a solid win over Spain, but favored Kazakhstan took control of the game early, and their celebration began as the final horn sounded.

The Olympic field was now four. Two spots in Sydney remained. The next hours would see the final two teams advance, and two historically strong water polo nations miss out on the first Olympic Games for women.

After all the difficulties of the past two years – a transition in coaching, residential training, losses when it was all on the line – the United States women boarded the bus to the biggest game of their lives full of confidence, ready to enjoy the experience. On the way to the pool, the bus radio blared Kenny Chesney's "She Thinks My Tractor's Sexy" – Bernice Orwig's selection for the team CD.

That bus ride remains one of the best memories among the group. Guy Baker called it one of his favorite in his coaching career. Looking up and down the bus, feeling the energy, he thought to himself *Yeah, we got this.* "The feeling was totally confident, totally an attack mentality, totally ready to go," he said.

Baker remembers Orwig dancing on the bus to "some song about a tractor," and having the sense that the mood was serious, focused, and loose all at the same time.

The Hungarian team was emotionally charged, too. Olympic success was an expectation for Hungarian water polo, whose men earned a medal at twelve consecutive Games between 1928 and 1980, a streak snapped by the Soviet-led boycott of the 1984 Games in Los Angeles. Winners of a record six Olympic titles, the Hungarian men fell from the pedestal upon their return to the Games, finishing fifth in Seoul before sliding to an all-time worst sixth place in Barcelona. With expectations of rekindling Olympic glory in 1996, a disappointing fourth-place finish in Atlanta extended the medal drought. Favorites for gold heading into Sydney, the Hungarian men aimed to return to the Olympic podium after a 20-year absence. The women, too, were eager to take their shot at gold in Australia.

Once the game began, the United States found itself trailing almost immediately, conceding a goal less than 30 seconds after the first sprint. But the defense, which took pride in shutting down opponents for long stretches, held for the rest of the quarter. Midway through the opening frame, Robin Beauregard pulled the United States even. Shortly after, Coralie Simmons and Heather Petri tacked on to the count, and the United States opened up a 3-1 lead at the quarter break. Gubba Sheehy added a goal to start the second quarter, and the lead ballooned to 4-1. Hungary's Mercédesz Stieber broke through to stem the tide, but Maureen O'Toole quickly reasserted the United States' three-goal cushion. The halftime lead was two after another Stieber strike a minute before the second quarter came to a close.

The third quarter belonged to Stieber. One of the premier shooters in the world and a gold medalist at the 1994 World Championships, she also played professionally for Gifa Palermo in the Italian league. Local fans of the club were thrilled when Stieber scored a pair of third quarter goals to pull Hungary even. One seven-minute quarter remained, the score deadlocked at 5-5.

As the teams lined up for the fourth quarter sprint, O'Toole leaned back against the goal line and stared at the ceiling, breathing deep. *This can't be my last international game. This won't be my last international game.* She took another slow, long breath and prepared to fight one final round for her Olympic dream.

The United States won the fourth quarter sprint, and took the first opportunity to attack. O'Toole found herself posted up in front of the goal, pinning Hungary's Edit Sipos as she had done to countless defenders over the course of her career. When the ball arrived, she churned her legs to counteract the weight of Sipos' lunging body – earning the exclusion and a precious power-play for the United States just 24 seconds into the quarter.

Energized after the intermission, the Americans passed with precision, strong legs supporting bodies rising high to attack the Hungarian defense. With no left-hander on the team, Brenda Villa occupied the right side of the power-play formation. As the ball moved to her left, her eyes scanned to the right, spotting an opening next to a misplaced defender. Below the surface of the water, she set her legs and readied her body. By the time the ball touched her hand, her arm was in motion. Lunging in vain, the Hungarian defender saw the ball fly by, undoubtedly hoping to hear the sound of contact with the goalkeeper. Instead, she heard the referee's whistle, signaling that Villa's quick release netted the United States the lead.

With nearly a whole quarter left to play, the trademark defense that Baker espoused and the team embraced smothered the Hungarian attack as precious seconds ticked off the game clock. Twice, the United States earned power-plays and the chance to extend the lead, but Hungary's defense rose to the occasion, leaving the American defense no margin for error. As the clock neared four minutes, O'Toole was called for an exclusion, but the defense stood its ground. As desperation and fatigue descended on the Hungarian players, the United States' Simmons fouled out with a minute and a half left, giving the Europeans hope of drawing even. Again the defense and goalkeeper Bernice Orwig were under assault. Again the team protected its narrow lead.

The superior conditioning Baker demanded, instilled by Coach Jim Lowell in Indio during his own playing days, was punishing Hungary, whose attacks, while increasing in desperation, became sloppy and ineffective as the American strength and speed took its toll on weary Hungarian bodies.

Yet Hungary's defense, drained but not defeated, refused to yield an insurance goal that would surely clinch victory for the United States. When another American possession came up empty, Hungarian coach Gyula Toth called time-out with 36 ticks remaining. His exhausted players gathered at his feet – there was little doubt whose hand the ball would be in. Armed with one of the world's most deceptive deliveries and the confidence to knock down any shot under pressure, Stieber loaded her nation's Olympic hopes on her shoulders.

In the American huddle, Baker assigned defensive matchups. The quick and mobile Courtney Johnson drew the assignment of shadowing the Hungarian sharpshooter. As expected, Stieber settled into her preferred spot on the outside right – uncommon for right-handed scorers. Orwig was aware of her presence, and Johnson pressed the Hungarian star tightly. Supremely patient with the ball, even under duress, Stieber watched intently as her teammates ran a pick to her left. Out of the corner of her eye, Orwig spotted Rita Dravucz pop open five meters out and then Stieber's pass arriving on her hand. Dravucz' shot was a bullet, screaming towards Orwig's left. With an explosive burst, the goalkeeper propelled herself out of the water. With a loud smack, the ball ricocheted off

Orwig's shoulder before landing on the water near Johnson. Arms spinning, Johnson pounced. Swarmed by desperate Hungarians, she deftly flicked the ball to Villa, who turned to open water and swam toward the sideline.

Players and coaches on the American bench rose as one. The last seconds seemed a lifetime before the final buzzer confirmed the United States' triumph. All of a sudden, the nightmare of Winnipeg felt far, far away. And Sydney wasn't merely a dream – it was a reality.

The celebration in the pool was short-lived – the second set of semifinalists, the Russians and Italians, watched intently, attempting to keep their own anxieties in balance. The night would yield one – and only one – more berth to the Olympics.

Those of the American players whose parents were in Palermo shared joyous hugs and tears outside the pool. No one had a mobile phone – there were no texts or Tweets or Facebook posts to share the historic news. There was a pay phone. And it was no easy feat to make international calls.

The players without family at the tournament waited in line as one after another connected with loved ones at home, retelling the dramatic finish and squealing with delight at the thought of the Olympics.

Brenda Villa made that call to her dad, Ines. Years later, she found out what happened when she hung up. Asking her mother, Rosario, to name the most memorable moment from the four Olympic Games she attended – Sydney, Athens, Beijing, and London – Brenda was shocked at the answer.

"I remember your goal in Palermo," was Rosario's response.

"I'm like, *What?*" said Brenda.

While her daughter and the American team were more than 6,500 miles away, battling to the last second to achieve their dreams, Rosario was at work in Commerce, a nervous wreck. All day, she was anxious, avoiding interactions with her co-workers. A seamstress at Warnaco, she was sewing away when she heard her name announced over the loudspeaker. There was a phone call for her.

Walking to the office, she knew there were two possible outcomes. *Either they won, they qualified, and they're going to the Olympics, or my daughter's dreams are shattered.* She was nearly too nervous to pick up the phone. When she did, she heard her husband repeating, "Do you hear me? Do you hear me?"

"Did they win?"

"Do you hear me?" she heard her husband say again.

Confused, Rosario repeated urgently, "Did they win?"

Ines had said nothing else.

"Can't you hear that I'm crying?" he finally managed to say. "Your daughter scored the winning goal. Come home, already. We need to celebrate."

The story made Brenda smile wide. "My mom had to finish working the rest of the day," she said. "My parents celebrated, and my mom couldn't wait for me to come home so we could talk about it. She says this is the one goal that she never saw, but has always visualized."

2000 Olympic Qualifying Tournament silver medalists

United States and Australian teams at Australia Zoo with Steve Irwin and
23-month-old daughter Bindi – June 2000

9

THE ROAD TO SYDNEY

2000 Holiday Cup   **Robin Beauregard**

Although their achievement was monumental, a muted celebration took place at the team hotel. The United States shared the hotel with the team from Kazakhstan, who partied loud and late into the night. They also shared the hotel with the Italian team. Reigning world champion and ranked fourth in the world following the 1999 World Cup, the Italians failed to reach the finals of the Olympic Qualification Tournament. And that meant they were not going to Sydney.

To the dismay of the raucous home crowd, it was Russia who prevailed in the second semifinal, leaving the Italians stunned. The teams waged an epic back-and-forth battle, deadlocked at every quarter break. Neither team could grab more than a one-goal advantage, and the lead changed hands four times. With two minutes left, Russia gained the upper hand. When Italy's leading scorer, center Giusi Malato, fouled out soon after, things looked bleak for the home team. But Alexandra Araujo, Malato's backup, pulled Italy even with just over one minute remaining. Russia wasted no time, quickly earning an exclusion after the restart of play. A goal by Joulia Petrova with 41 seconds on the clock booked the final spot in the Olympics for Russia.

Underdogs ruled the night. The first Olympic field was set.

Back at the hotel, the United States team, still high on adrenaline, was eating dinner when the devastated Italians returned. As ecstatic as they were, the Americans refrained from an over-the-top celebration in front of a team who had fallen short. They knew first hand what it felt like.

"We were just in their position a year ago," Guy Baker said, "hurting like crazy."

Although the purpose of the tournament – Olympic qualification – was complete, there was still one more day of games to be played. The third-place game, rendered meaningless by Kazakhstan finishing sixth to qualify for the Olympics, was a moribund affair. Hungary's Mercédesz Stieber rattled off three consecutive goals in the second quarter to break open the game, and a downtrodden Italy put up little resistance. Hungary won by the score of 8-4.

Still floating on air after the thrill of the night before, Russia and the United States met for the tournament championship. When the game started, Russia fell into form quickly, while the United States worked its way back into rhythm. Each time the Americans pulled even, Russia answered to regain their lead. Brenda Villa hit the net with two and a half minutes to play, tying the score 5-5, but Russia scored the game-winner inside of a minute remaining. The United States fell short, 6-5, in the least-important championship game possible at this level.

Even so, the result didn't sit well with Baker – the team's goal was to win every time out – but there would be no lecture or video critique after this loss. There would be ample time to pick apart the performance when they returned home.

Mission accomplished: the United States women left Palermo as Olympians.

More often than not, the National Team takes a break after a major tournament. After the championship game in Palermo, the group parted ways in the early hours of the morning. Arriving at the airport together, some left for home via Rome, while others departed for Milan and some well-deserved vacation days.

With two weeks until the team reconvened, Baker and the staff set upon the task of Olympic preparation. Up to Palermo, the focus was solely on qualifying for the Olympic Games. Assistant coach Chris Duplanty, a three-time Olympian, offered insights into the myriad obligations athletes juggle during the event. His most recent experience in 1996 was compounded by playing on home soil in Atlanta. Duplanty described the difficulties for players trying to focus on their performance while fielding calls from friends and family in need of tickets and other requests for access.

Baker, Duplanty, and Michelle Pickering sat down to draw up their organizational plan. The theme was eliminating distractions. The solution was a designated "Friends and Family" contact who would manage all requests. Pickering would handle all media.

"All of a sudden, people were calling us," Baker said. "You get all these random requests because it's the Olympics. If you're a basketball or even soccer player, you're doing this all the time. Water polo, you don't do this. It's totally foreign."

The final piece of staffing to fall into place was the team doctor, Larry Drum. After serving the team for two years, Drum was informed that he wasn't certified through the USOC. The team would be assigned a new, USOC-certified, doctor for Sydney. When the staff's objections failed to change the policy, they added Drum to the team as the Friends and Family liaison. The staff was prepared to handle the chaos of the Olympics, allowing the athletes to focus on competing at their best.

"We broke it all down, starting with training and competition plans between qualifying and the Olympics," Baker said. "Second was coach and athlete relationships. We just went through a whole year of getting my relationship with the athletes on the same page. The organizational plan focused on eliminating distractions was third, and international relations was our fourth priority. That was our relationship with FINA and maintaining international success. Coming off qualifying, we felt like we had pretty decent respect based on our performance."

Pleased with the progress the staff achieved during the two-week break, Baker turned his attention to the return of the athletes and the next phase of training and competition. Prior to Palermo, Baker promised the Australian federation he would bring the team to Australia, whether the United States qualified or not.

"If we didn't qualify, I'm not sure who we would have taken on that trip, but that's where our budget ended," Baker said. "The Australians wanted plans well in advance because they were automatically qualified, and we assured them that we would bring a team over to help them prepare."

The two weeks off did wonders for a majority of the players, who returned to Los Al refreshed and excited to be past the anxiety of qualifying for the Olympics. But not everyone reported back in good health.

Working with the goalies at her alma mater, USC, Bernice Orwig traveled to Indianapolis for the Collegiate Nationals. After the Women of Troy advanced to the second round, she changed in the locker room to do her water workout. Walking out, Orwig slipped and fell backwards, using her right hand to break her fall. Bouncing right back up as if nothing happened, she heard one of the girls say jokingly, *Bye, bye, Olympics.* Thinking nothing was wrong, Orwig jumped in the water; she quickly realized she could not stroke with her right arm. A day later, the elbow was black and blue. Upon returning to Los Al, Orwig was unable to swim and had no range of motion. X-rays showed a fracture of the radial head near the right elbow. Because two weeks had already passed, Orwig was spared a cast; but she was forbidden from blocking shots for another four weeks.

The team got back into its routine gradually. Soccer, basketball, and ultimate frisbee on the field next to the Los Al pool complemented the daily swimming and weightlifting regimen. The water polo work was limited and low-key. Baker would pick up the workload once the team arrived in Australia.

Already down one goalkeeper, the squad took another hit during its first weekend back. Heather Moody joined Orwig on the injured list, another casualty of misadventures on land. Having never played basketball in her youth, Moody got frustrated with the team's cross-training on the courts at 24 Hour Fitness. Seeking advice to improve her jump shot, she called on housemates and former hoopsters, Orwig and Rachel Scott.

"Heather was terrible," Scott flatly stated. "We had Saturday off, so we walked to the local park in Cerritos and taught her how to shoot. By the time we left, she was draining it."

Returning home, the teammates shared in the weekend cleaning chores. Finishing her vacuuming duty, Moody spent the remainder of her Saturday relaxing on the couch. Anxious to build on her newfound basketball skill, Moody talked Scott into returning to the park to shoot hoops on Sunday.

"She went up for the first shot with perfect form," Scott said, "and promptly hit the deck."

With a tweaked back, Moody walked home half-bent over.

"We think it was the vacuuming from the day before," Scott surmised.

Whatever the cause, playing water polo wasn't possible. And there was good reason for Moody to be concerned about that.

The entire squad of fourteen athletes was slated to go on the trip to Australia. But the elephant in the room remained – to reach the Olympic roster size, the team had to be cut from thirteen players to eleven. In Palermo, a roster of thirteen competed while the alternate, Rachel Scott, filmed the games for the staff. They had qualified as a team of thirteen. When the Olympic Team was officially announced, two of them would not hear their names called.

In the movie *Miracle*, Herb Brooks, head coach of the 1980 United States Olympic hockey team, searches for the right combination of players as the Lake Placid Games loom. Brooks surprises and disappoints the training squad by adding University of Minnesota star Tim Harrer to the mix weeks before the Olympics. When team leadership, including captain Mike Eruzione, pleads with Brooks to preserve the chemistry of the "family" the team has become, he sends Harrer home, knowing he has the right squad.

The women's water polo team felt the same anxiety at the beginning of 2000, when Heather Petri and Ericka Lorenz showed up at Los Al – not that Baker hadn't informed them when they left the 1999 Holiday Cup that changes were coming.

"When Guy brought Petie and Ericka in, it was last second," said Courtney Johnson. "All of a sudden, a week before, we found out, not only are these girls coming – we're living with them. We had to come to terms with the fact that nobody's spot was safe."

Unlike the situation of the 1980 Olympic hockey team, the newcomers to the squad were welcomed – even mentored – by the veterans. It may have been the difference between men's and women's teams, or the fact that the hockey team was on the verge of competing at the Olympic Games, while the water polo team still sought to qualify – in any case, Petri and Lorenz quickly became part of the group. As Baker intended, the additions changed the dynamic of the team.

"It's kind of an interesting part of the story, where with team sports, you're trying to build this chemistry, but at the same time you're fighting for spots," Johnson continued.

Baker expected a group of fifteen athletes in the full-time program beginning on January 1, 2000. When that day came, Alisa von Hartitzsch informed him she would not be continuing with the team, leaving the squad size at fourteen.

The Olympic roster size had no impact on the team before Palermo – at that point, they weren't going to Sydney. Their single goal was to qualify, a feat that required the faith and teamwork of all thirteen players who made that team.

"I didn't even think about it; none of us did – until we qualified," Johnson said.

The reality of the situation brought new nerves. *Would the Olympic roster include one or two goalkeepers? What positions would be valued most? What two players are not going to make this team?*

"We didn't talk about it as a team, but now it was definitely on everybody's mind," Johnson said. "At practices, it was easy to overthink everything. If you had a bad practice that was stressful because does that mean your spot is up for grabs? It was a lot of stress for sure when we knew it was only eleven."

The fight to get women's water polo added to the Olympic program hinged on gender equity – yet when the event was added to the Sydney Games, the terms were far from equitable. At twelve teams of thirteen players, the men's tournament included 156 participants, compared to the sixty-six slated for the women's competition.

Shortly after qualifying in Palermo, Guy Baker met with Chris Duplanty and Michelle Pickering to discuss the unthinkable but inevitable – cutting two of the players who helped the United States earn an Olympic berth.

"We sat down, and we knew this is a huge deal," Baker recalled.

The staff had discussion and debate about carrying one or two goalkeepers. Baker felt it was a close competition between Bernice Orwig and Nicolle Payne – close enough that his mind wasn't settled on only one or the other. At the qualification tournament, Baker was playing primarily nine field players, with Ericka

Lorenz and Ellen Estes receiving the least minutes. But their youth represented the future – and if the future was now, where did that put the older players, including the longest-tenured player in international women's water polo history, 39-year-old Maureen O'Toole?

Despite being the youngest on the team, Lorenz was a player Baker decided to use a roster spot on. At only nineteen years old and blessed with uncommon speed and pure athleticism, Lorenz was a long-term project, in Baker's mind. The plan for Sydney was to give Lorenz as much experience as possible – Baker projected her ceiling to be phenomenally high at the international level.

When the Olympic field was complete, Baker categorized the competition in three groups. At the top were Holland and Australia. For the time being, Baker put these foes on a different level than the United States. At the bottom as Kazakhstan, the Asian qualifier. In the middle, he placed Canada, Russia, and the United States. Two of these teams were likely to join Holland and Australia in the semifinals. The third he projected to face Kazakhstan for fifth place at the end of the round-robin portion of the competition.

Baker's primary concern was getting the United States to the medal round. With that goal in mind, he decided the benefits of Lorenz being on the 11-player team outweighed her lack of international experience. The payoff of playing in Sydney would be reaped in future World Championships, World Cups, and Olympic Games.

"Our first focus was Russia and Canada," he said. "We've got to beat one of those teams. Once you get to the medal round, you're playing for a medal, and that's all that matters. Ericka was the future – she had to be there and play. It wasn't like we were going to go win a medal necessarily; we just wanted to get as many games as we could and not play for fifth."

When the team began training after Palermo, Baker enjoyed the process, engaged by the next challenge of preparing for the Olympics. But the eventual trimming of the roster lurked in the background.

"With the team, I'd be talking about what we're going to do as far as schedule, training, everything's planned and organized, but the one thing I didn't talk to the team about is we're going to go from thirteen to eleven. It's the elephant in the room, because everybody knows we're going to have to get down to eleven players."

With the entire group slated to travel to Australia, tensions about the roster cuts hadn't erupted, but they surely bubbled just beneath the surface. On the Monday before departure, the team was playing soccer on the grass next to the pool at Los Al. As he often did, Baker joined in. Taking his turn to sub out, he reached the sideline just as Michelle Pickering emerged from her office, approaching him.

"Bruce is on the phone," she said. "He wants to talk to you."

Baker refused to leave the team to take the call from United States Water Polo Executive Director, Bruce Wigo.

"Tell Bruce to call back," he said tersely. "I'm in practice."

He quickly added, "I know it looks like soccer, but we're practicing."

"No, you need to talk to Bruce," Pickering calmly replied.

Baker was starting to get irritated. "I don't need to, I'm practicing. I don't talk during practice."

The action on the soccer field ceased as attention turned to the coach and manager, facing off, an argument apparently brewing.

Sensing the lost focus on the field, Baker ended the discussion. "I'm not coming in."

Pickering didn't budge. "You need to come talk to Bruce."

"Then she gave me a look like, *You **really** have to talk to Bruce*," Baker said. "I'm thinking, *Oh, man*. Well, first of all, it's not good. He knows what time we practice and wouldn't interrupt. Michelle's coming out in the middle of practice so, what the hell, this is not good."

Leaving the team on the field, Baker ducked into the office. He listened to Wigo say he had news.

"Then he says they've decided to have thirteen players per team in Sydney," Baker said, understanding Pickering's urgency in getting him to the phone. The two shared a laugh of both joy and relief.

Emerging from the office, Baker and Pickering found a minority of the team half-heartedly kicking the soccer ball around, the remainder lingering near the sideline.

"Michelle comes out and says I have to talk to Bruce, that's usually never a good thing, so everybody's wondering what's going on," Baker said. "I pulled everybody over and let them know that now it's going to be thirteen players. And they just go nuts."

For water polo players, who usually celebrate victories together in the pool, this was breaking new ground. The team went crazy, hugging and falling into a huge dog pile. Some ran around on the grass. Several cried.

"They just went absolutely, absolutely nuts," Baker repeated. "You think you know your team, like, *Oh, maybe we don't need to address this, or we can talk about this later*. They didn't show it, but it was definitely on everybody's mind at that point in time."

After enduring difficult times and overcoming the challenges of the past two years, things were coming together quickly for the United States team. Guy Baker pointed to a strengthened mentality across the boards, born from the entire qualification process.

"Coming back with all the coaches' experience and the team's experience, there was a really good connection between us all," he said. "We just had something tremendously special."

Arriving in Sydney at the beginning of June, the team was immediately immersed in the Olympic experience. The first official game was played at the Ryde Aquatic Leisure Centre, host of the preliminary round of women's and men's water polo when the world arrived in September. Olympic organizers used the match as a full dress rehearsal for the venue – including volunteers, team staging, warm-ups, introductions, announcers, clocks, and scoreboard.

"The chance to test everything out at Ryde eliminated some of the mystique of the venue," said Robin Beauregard. "That was probably one of the best experiences that we could have as a team, because it took away some of that Winnipeg stuff where you're in this big setting wondering, *Oh, my God, what's going to happen?*"

Nearly 4,000 spectators created an electric atmosphere worthy of the Olympic Games themselves.

The United States was promptly stomped.

The environment that pumped up the American team sent the Australians into orbit. Backed by the rocking home crowd, Australia executed in all phases of the game en route to an 11-3 victory.

To the team's surprise, Baker was fine with it.

"That probably shocked them," he said. "I told them it didn't matter. That whole setup was great practice for us."

The United States had yet to fully return to water polo training after the qualification tournament. And Australia had been amped up for the chance to play at Ryde, against the United States, in front of a crowd. The Australians had been training hard while the Americans were in Europe for qualifying. For both teams, the taste of the Olympic atmosphere was every bit as exciting as it was in their dreams.

Despite the lopsided score, Baker saw something from the team that let him know the work of the past two years would pay off. He sensed the shift in the attitude of both team and individuals. The process was on target. The team was ready to take aim at the heavyweights of women's water polo.

"In those circumstances, they should have blown us out. If they didn't, that would be a real problem," Baker said. "That set the tone for the trip."

While in Australia, the team got back to water polo business, as Baker ramped up the intensity.

"They saw us training," he said. "They were not training like we were training."

Gubba Sheehy felt no team was working harder than the United States. She recalled a training session on the Australia trip that Baker called "unacceptable."

"The Aussie team, they're over there getting their protein shakes, stretching out and stuff, and we had to hop back in and do twenty 100s or something crazy like that," Sheehy said. "And we hopped in, and we did it. The Aussie girls were looking at us like, *Oh, my gosh. They have to swim more?* We just got in and did it. That was that."

The United States team played soccer for an hour and a half to two hours, then jumped in the pool and trained for two hours.

After a week in Sydney, consisting of joint-training and scrimmaging, the teams headed up the coast about 500 miles to Burleigh Heads on the Sunshine Coast in Queensland. Famous for its great surf beaches, Burleigh seemed like paradise to the American team.

"It was absolutely beautiful," Baker said. "Nicolle, Ericka, and I would wake up early in the morning and go surfing at Surfers Paradise. It was just beautiful, and we're having the time of our lives. We were in Australia; the weather was great, and we're getting back into training. The Australians had more going on at that time."

Specifically, coach Istvan Gorgenyi was using the training camp to select Australia's Olympic team. The Australians were spared the stress of the qualification process by virtue of being the host nation. But by the same token, the stakes for individual team members were high, as each dreamed of playing in the Olympics in front of her friends and family in Sydney.

Team USA at Kawana Waters – June 2000

The final stop of the Australian tour took the teams another 100 miles up the Queensland coast to Kawana Waters, where they continued common training and had a game scheduled to conclude the trip.

On the day of the last official game in Kawana Waters, the American and Australian teams took part in a parade as part of the Olympic torch relay. Under a constant drizzle, local residents lined the streets, waiting to see the iconic symbol of the Games make its way through the community. The Australian women loaded into the open beds of a classic Australian make and model – Holden Utes. For the United States, organizers had a surprise in store. A fleet of beautiful all-American machines – Harley-Davidson motorcycles – awaited the athletes and staff. The parade route took the two teams straight to the pool.

Robin Beauregard approached her Harley and planted her left leg on the wet pavement, putting all her weight on it. As she started to lift her right, she felt something go very wrong.

"Out goes the kneecap," she said. "I knew it immediately."

Now a Doctor of Physical Therapy, Beauregard describes her injury: It's more genetic than anything. Basically, my kneecaps sit a little high. My foot was turned out. In order to get on a Harley you've got to put all your weight on there. The ground's a little slippery. With all the weight and then the position of my foot, it just basically pulled my kneecap out. Once your kneecap gets pulled out, your knee buckles because your quad is attached to your kneecap, and that's what determines if you get to still be standing up. I was kind of still standing up.

Knowing she either had to get on the Harley or be left behind, Beauregard hobbled around to the other side of the bike and got on the back.

"People are waving at you, and you're trying really hard to smile, but man, does it hurt a lot," she said. "I was waving and smiling. It's a really long route, and it's cold."

While mustering a smile for the parade-goers lining the route, Beauregard's mind reeled. *Well, that's awesome. I am so not going to the Olympics now.*

"At this point, I was a starting defender, playing all the games," she said. "Then all of a sudden all those Olympic hopes are crashing down around you. I was thinking, *This may be it for my Olympic experience, riding behind a torch*, and also *Why the hell can't we be on the back of a Ute like the Australians?*"

Before the parade ended, Beauregard settled down enough to convince herself to stay positive. But her knee, huge and swollen, did its part to fill her with concern.

Arriving at the pool, Beauregard subtly got Rachel Scott's attention and informed her that she couldn't walk. Scott responded in surprise: "What do you mean you can't walk?" After explaining her situation, Beauregard said simply, "I need your help."

Beauregard delivered the news to Baker, then watched her teammates tie Australia in the final match of the trip. With no other option, Baker told

Beauregard they would evaluate her situation when they found out more after arriving back home.

"Guy's not one to kick you when you're down if it's not because of water polo," Beauregard said. "If it's something you don't necessarily have control over, he's pretty understanding."

Because of the pre-travel injuries to Bernice Orwig and Heather Moody, the United States team in Australia included Catharine von Schwarz, a member of the Pan American Games team in 1999, and Amber Stachowski, who herself fell victim to injury on the trip. The team was the walking wounded, and now Beauregard, in a wheelchair for the remainder of the time in Australia, was among the infirmed. The final roster wasn't picked yet, and Baker was clearly open to giving an opportunity to any players who could help the team.

Determined to remain optimistic, a fleeting thought bounced around Robin Beauregard's mind: *After all this time, I'm not going to be on the Olympic Team.*

The last game drew a decent crowd despite pouring rain. Guy Baker was pleased with the training sessions the United States was having both on their own and with the Australians.

"We would be working our asses off, and they're showing up just for the joint-training," he said. "We're doing stuff before and after. That last game, it's raining, and they're not sure if they want to play the game. I'm like, *There's a bunch of people, just play the game. Who cares?*

With the injured reserve piling up big names such as Beauregard, Moody, and Orwig, the United States matched up evenly with Australia. In the driving rain, the two teams battled to a draw. The result infused confidence into the American team.

The timing of the trip was perfect, and the production exceeded everyone's expectations, including Baker's. After the opening-night rout at Ryde, the United States more than acquitted itself over the course of the training. And they left Australia sensing a tide was turning – the Americans felt they possessed an edge in toughness over their opponent.

"I don't know if we'd ever quite felt that way with Australia," Baker said. "We always felt if we did well, it's okay, maybe fortunate. At the end of that trip, we were feeling, *We should beat these guys.*"

@@@@@@

Bumps and bruises are no big deal to Robin Beauregard. The knee injury that almost derailed her Olympic aspirations was one in a long line of physical mishaps she overcame. A car accident with her grandfather even delayed the beginning of her water polo career by one year. Beauregard lost a front tooth and had symptoms of concussion – so her parents pushed back her water polo debut until she was nine.

As a child, she participated in plenty of athletic activities – basketball, volleyball, junior lifeguards, track, and even softball, which she hated.

"Softball back then was like water polo when it first came around for women," she said. "There weren't enough players to have teams of all the same age. So it was 12-and-under, and I was five, playing with 12-year-olds. You know how fast a 12-year-old throws – and a five-year-old is like, "What happened?" There was one other five-year-old on the team, and the coach could never keep us straight. I was the five-year-old that caught the ball, but I'd have to run because she thought that I was the other one. So softball just wasn't for me."

One other softball tradition never jibed with Beauregard's personality.

"There was too much cheering," she said. "I'm not a big rah-rah person, so it was annoying."

Seeing her brother, Mike, swimming and playing water polo, Robin naturally wanted to follow him into the pool. Waiting eagerly for the day she was old enough to join the swim team, she got her wish the day she turned four.

Once she was old enough for water polo, she again followed in her brother's footsteps. Part of swim team in the fall included participating in the Southern Pacific Association water polo league. Boys and girls finished swim practice early and piled into carpools to head off to water polo, with maybe a run to the McDonald's drive-thru en route.

From her first days in water polo, Beauregard played co-ed, so competing with boys was never an issue. There weren't many girls' teams around Orange County and Los Angeles, so boys and mixed games were the norm. Early in their careers, Beauregard and Brenda Villa both played goalie for their co-ed teams, Golden West and Commerce.

"Back then it wasn't uncommon to play seven or eight games in a weekend, because you had your different teams," Beauregard said. "If you were a really good 10-and-under, you played on the 12-and-under team, plus you had the girls' team. Next thing you knew, you're like, *I can't see because my eyes are burning so much.*"

When Beauregard arrived at Marina High School as a freshman in 1993, almost twenty years after Maureen O'Toole entered high school, girls' water polo still didn't exist in the CIF Southern Section. She played on the freshman team but was called up to the varsity at times. From her sophomore year on, Beauregard was a standout on the Marina varsity. In 1995, the Mariners defeated Servite in the CIF semifinals before falling to Costa Mesa in the championship game. Beauregard drew her fair share of defensive assignments against the top boys' players, many of whom went on to great collegiate careers.

She acknowledged the value playing with boys added to her game, particularly how it forced her to take initiative and speed up her decision-making.

"With boys, there is a certain amount of 'I'm going to score, I'm going to win this game,'" she said. "It's not necessarily ego, but confidence about your offensive skills. It's something you don't always get when playing with girls. The confidence isn't always there. With the boys, they always have that confidence. If you don't take your shot, they're not going to throw it back to you."

On the boys' team, Beauregard learned to make the most of her opportunities – and to do so without remorse.

"If you think you're open, you better shoot it," she said. "If you miss, they'll probably yell at you. That's okay; you can yell at them when they miss, too, and they don't care."

After the CIF run with the boys in the fall of her junior year, Beauregard joined the newly formed Marina girls' team, leading the Mariners to first place at the Southern California Championships. Though girls' water polo was not yet sanctioned as an official CIF sport, the end-of-season tournament was considered the premier event of the season for the rapidly growing number of girls' high school teams in Orange County, the Ventura coast, and San Diego. The following year, the first full-fledged girls' CIF season in the Southern Section was slated for the winter season. A handful of girls, including Beauregard and Villa, who had played with the boys, were granted the ability to choose playing either the boys' season in the fall or the girls' season in the winter. Beauregard chose the boys', during which she would captain the team as a senior.

But after Marina's first tournament, the injury bug struck once again. Playing tennis with a couple of friends, Beauregard dislocated her right kneecap, an injury which would likely end her season. Marina's athletic director made an appeal to CIF to allow her to play the girls' season. The request was denied.

"They said it would be unfair for me to play with the girls because of my ability level," she said.

Beauregard sat out most of her senior season, returning to the water for one game in the CIF playoffs – as the goalie.

"Our goalie got a detached retina, so I had to bring back the goalie skills of age group and my freshman year," she said.

Her last season playing on a boys' team amounted to all of four games. Once she moved on to college and the National Team, Beauregard missed playing with the guys in some ways.

"It's a different type of physical," she explained. "Guys are physical; girls are dirty. The guys will kick and they'll push and they'll hold, but they don't do it for no reason. Girls are more likely to just sit there and hold onto your suit for absolutely no reason whatsoever, giving them no advantage. I was like, *Really? What's going on? This isn't actually helping either one of us right now; we're just both getting really tired.*"

Continuing to describe the difference in play, Beauregard said, "Guys will leave it in the pool, and it's done. Girls remember from four years ago when you kicked them in this one game, and it really hurt, and then they'll bring it back and attack you for no reason. There is a different psychosocial portion of playing with guys versus girls."

In the summers, she remembers bouncing back and forth between boys' and girls' teams. "Once you got used to it you became good at changing gears," she said. "You've got club with girls but boys' high school summer league at the same time. The dynamic was always different. Like when you see girls hanging out, it's very different from a group of guys. The girls are chatty and playful. Being with the guys centers around food. I definitely learned how to eat super fast from playing with guys – if you weren't done with your food by the time the guy that was always really hungry was done, he was going to eat all your food."

Many of Robin Beauregard's teammates on the National Team got a late start in water polo and the pipeline of the Youth and Junior National Teams. When she went to her first National Team tryout, it was for a 17-and-under team that was scheduled to train and compete in Jamaica. Beauregard made the team and was the youngest player selected. She was twelve.

"I was a goalie on that trip," she said. "It was my first time traveling internationally, and that's when I decided that swimming was not going to be my focus."

While she narrowed her athletic focus to water polo, the opportunities in front of her grew. There were no Olympics to aspire to, but Beauregard participated on the Junior National Team and set her sights on a future career on the Senior Team.

"Initially, when I was a freshman going into high school, the only option for playing beyond high school was collegiate club or National Team stuff," she said. "While I was in high school, lots of colleges became varsity, and scholarships became more widespread. I was thinking, *Now it's a varsity sport. This is going to change the ballgame.*"

By her sophomore year of high school, Beauregard knew she would play water polo in college. A self-described nerd, she was deep into honors and AP classes when she received her first invitation to a Senior National Team tryout in 1996. But the tryout included practices all day long, and Beauregard was in school. Sights set on becoming a surgeon, she made the decision to skip portions of the tryout, attending her classes instead.

"Other high school players were on a break from school, but it didn't work out that way for me," she said. "My approach was, I'm going to go to my class, and I'll be here for the next practices. I know I won't make the team, but I'll still be present and play. That's where my route and Brenda's kind of diverged."

Brenda Villa was selected at the end of that tryout, beginning her long National Team career. Beauregard was at peace with her decision to stay focused on her own personal long-term goals.

"It wasn't like it was for the Olympics at that time," she said. "The National Team wasn't a career. You were still fundraising to travel, paying your own way. I loved water polo, but I didn't love it enough to discard my dreams of my future career just to travel and play water polo."

Part of the first wave of high school players recruited heavily by college coaches, Beauregard took visits to Stanford, USC, and UCLA before signing with coach Guy Baker and the Bruins. In the fall of her first year on campus, women's water polo was added to the Sydney Olympic program, and in the spring of that year, she was in the water at Baker's first tryout as head coach of the National Team. Shortly after, Beauregard found herself in Yugoslavia with the team.

For someone whose career had always moved quickly – except when injuries got in the way – the path to the Olympics seemed to be opening up in front of her. After Palermo, it seemed a sure thing. Until she tried to get on a Harley in Australia.

@@@@@@

The American team returned home from Sydney in mid-June, and it wasn't long before they locked horns with the Australians again. The entire Olympic field was scheduled to be at Los Alamitos for a historic Holiday Cup. With the commencement of the summer of 2000, Olympic fever was spreading throughout the water polo community. The tournament opener was slated for the Fourth of July against rival Canada, with a fireworks show to cap off the night. As the reality of women's water polo making its Olympic debut set in, excitement throughout the Southern California region reached a crescendo.

The Dutch team had actually arrived a week earlier, before the fanfare surrounding the Holiday Cup, to train with Baker's squad. The two teams worked out at Los Al, then played a game at Commerce before the start of the tournament.

"We crushed them," Baker said. "We won by four or five goals. Then everybody was just kind of, *Hmmm*. It felt easy. Things are kind of clicking, and for a lot of people, just to beat the Netherlands – it didn't matter where – just to beat them was a big change."

The teams had last trained together in February in Holland, a trip Baker described as "pretty bad."

"They kicked the crap out of us," Baker said. "Ellen and I lost it on each other, and we were falling apart still in February of 2000."

Ellen Estes remembers the day well. "He officially kicked me off the team."

"He probably doesn't remember it exactly like that," Estes conceded, before continuing. "Guy had been riding us really hard the entire week. On those training trips, after three or four days, you start to get pretty exhausted. I remember he was screaming at me. I screwed up something defensively, and he's yelling at me. I just couldn't take anymore, and I splashed the water.

"Well, *that* set him off even more, because he said, 'That's it. Get out. You're done. Go back to Stanford,'" Estes recalled. "So I'm thinking, 'Okay. This is awesome. I just took two quarters off, and now I've been fired from this experience. Now I need to go back to Stanford.'"

"Well, I don't even know *how* to get home," Estes went on. "I'm in the Netherlands. I literally thought I had to go home. When he's mad, you think, 'Okay.' He was pretty clear, I was done. I don't quite know how I'm going to get home to California from the Netherlands, but I guess I've got to go figure it out."

Estes went to the locker room, got changed, and, with no cell phone at the time, looked for a payphone. Finding one outside the pool, she called her college coach, John Tanner.

"I left a message on JT's voicemail at Stanford," she said. "I said, 'Well, I think I can probably still get back in Stanford. I don't know if I can still enroll, but maybe I can play this season. Guy just kicked me off the National Team.'"

Estes returned to the locker room, where Robin Beauregard, Julie Swail, and Maureen O'Toole found her crying.

"They're trying to calm me down, saying, 'Ellen, trust us, he'll get over it. Don't worry: he didn't really kick you off the team,'" Estes said. "I'm like, 'No, I think that was pretty clear. I'm done.'"

When the team went to the restaurant at the hotel to eat dinner, Beauregard, Swail, and O'Toole approached Baker, telling him, "Guy, you need to go tell Ellen that you weren't serious, because she's called and she's trying to figure out how to get on a flight home because you told her to go back to Stanford. She's literally following your directions."

"He called me over to his table after dinner, and told me, 'No, I don't really want you to go home. I was just frustrated,'" Estes added. "He would never really apologize, but it was an apology. 'Let's just start again tomorrow.' I'm like, 'Okay, I guess we're starting over, whatever that means.'"

Estes laughed at the memory.

"If it wasn't for Robin and Julie and Mo, the next day, Guy probably would have been like, 'Where's Ellen?'"

Four months later, the transformation of the United States team was complete and fully evident. The Americans were dominant in the training sessions with Holland at Los Al. Baker and his staff considered the possibility that the Dutch were viewing the trip to California as vacation, just cruising along in training. But deep down, Baker knew what he was seeing.

"I thought they were actually out of shape," he said. "I don't think they ever got back in shape."

When the Holiday Cup began on the Fourth of July, the celebration of the women's Olympic Team truly began, not only for American water polo fans, but for the team itself. In a decision that would become tradition during his tenure as head coach, Baker named the Olympic roster prior to the Holiday Cup.

"With the Olympics being in the fall, we still had time," Baker said. "Initially, we thought it might be post-Holiday Cup. We named it before so they could play together. It was going to be the last time we got to play before the Olympics, so we decided let's let them play the Holiday Cup as the Olympic Team."

The longest-tenured member of any team naturally sees the most teammates retire. Maureen O'Toole had seen so many friends come and go during her first run with the National Team from 1977 to 1994. She herself hung up her cap after the 1994 World Championships, a team on which Julie Swail and Gubba Sheehy were youngsters. They were veterans when O'Toole returned in late 1997 to pursue the Olympics. In her comeback, O'Toole was reunited with veteran teammates Lynn Wittstock and Maggi Kelly. Like O'Toole, Kelly also came out of retirement, in her early 30s, with an eye on Sydney.

It was no secret to O'Toole that Guy Baker wanted to take younger players to the Olympics – he had been clear about his opinion of her age in their first meeting as player and coach two years before.

"When I came out of retirement, I had a lot of what you would call my friends on the team, and it dwindled down as we went," O'Toole said. "A lot of older players started and slowly got cut or decided to quit. As far as playing with younger players, it wasn't a problem for me at all. I loved it."

A superstar of the women's game over the course of three decades, O'Toole found fitting her skills into Baker's system – which was more strict than any she had played in before – to be her toughest task.

"I definitely had to change my game," she said. "It was very, very different. I always had freedom to do what I wanted to do and as a player, I never really ... thought: I just reacted to the situation. With Guy it was different, because he had a very strict system. He really didn't want us to play outside the box of the system."

For example, O'Toole was ambidextrous, comfortable with both hands in the water. A natural left-hander who played the perimeter right-handed, she was able to use whichever hand was available when in front of the goal as the center.

"He really didn't like me using my left hand," she said. "At set, I really didn't know the difference. So it caused me to really have to think, which was hard, because that is not the way I ever played."

Despite having to adjust her game, the veteran athlete and coach appreciated the results the system produced.

"I will say that the way Guy taught us and had us play in that strict system is a big reason for our success," she said. "There was never one person scoring all the goals. It was always spread out, and that was part of his system."

The system, unreliant on superstars, allowed every player to step up at the right moments, as evidenced by the Olympic-clinching victory over Hungary in Palermo. The United States' six goals were spread out among six different scorers, while Hungary's Mercedesz Stieber netted four of her team's five. A big goal-scorer throughout her career, she felt that – with this group especially – she fit in well as a distributor making assists and by drawing exclusions when she was at center.

"The way we played, not everyone had to have a good game on certain days," she said. "Sometimes you're off, and you can't hit the goal, or you hit every part of the bar that there is. Because of they way he did it, that was never really a problem, because everybody was a scorer in that system. It's harder to scout us, because if a team wanted to shut down Mo, well, there's Brenda, and there's Coralie, and there's everybody else. As hard as it was for me, he was still a huge reason why we did so well."

But from the first day at San Jose, the relationship between O'Toole and Baker wasn't one to write home about.

"Guy and I didn't not get along," O'Toole said. "It was just that, in my personal opinion, he wasn't going to make me a better player. I was going to give the team experience. I mean, I was thirty-nine years old. Are you really going to get better at thirty-nine, or are you going to give the team experience? Maybe because we were so close in age, I feel like that was hard."

For Baker's part, he was never going to give O'Toole a break because of her previous status or her age. O'Toole was motivated by the challenge and her perception that Baker didn't think she could handle the strain of the training. Worried about getting cut from day one, O'Toole is sure that without the news of the Olympic roster being expanded to thirteen players, she would not have made it to Sydney.

"I honestly believe that with only eleven players, I wouldn't have made it," she said. "I really believe that, because he didn't think I could do it. He didn't think I could do it physically."

O'Toole would never let the strain of training get the best of her. She amazed her younger teammates with her speed and stamina and work in the weight room. And she believed that her value existed in her ability to draw exclusions, especially late in games at the center position.

At the end of 1999, it was brought to Baker's attention that O'Toole could use more rest. Not by O'Toole herself, but rather a nutritionist at the USOC. In Colorado Springs for his annual meetings and program review, Baker addressed the topic of training. The coach firmly believed that given the choice between overtraining and undertraining before a tournament, he would always opt for the former.

"If we're overtrained, we can back off, and we can get rested and be ready to go," he said. "If we come into the tournament undertrained, there's nothing I can do about it. If I'm going to make an error, it's going to be on the side of overtraining."

At that point, the conversation with a nutritionist from the USOC turned to O'Toole.

"The nutritionist said a number of times how physically tired Mo was, and that I should take into consideration her age and the fact that she was trying to make the team; it might be time that she needs to take some practices off," Baker said. "I just subtly agreed with her that Mo could take off as many practices as she would like."

The nutritionist bit. "Oh, she can really take some time off during training? That's great. Does she know that? Have you told her?"

Baker pounced.

"Yeah. In fact, she can stop training right now," he said. "And when she stops training, then she can go on with the rest of her life. I was very clear from the very first day. Mo can take as much time off as she wants. She won't be part of our team. She's not going to miss training. If she's sick or hurt? That's different. But she's not resting."

When she heard about the exchange, O'Toole immediately thought, *Yeah, I can rest all I want as soon as I quit.*

She knew special treatment was not on the table; her age wasn't going to get her sympathy. Still, O'Toole was quick to let Baker know that she hadn't asked the nutritionist to go to bat for her.

Although unwilling to bend on the issue of training, Baker did appreciate what O'Toole was accomplishing.

"Mo is incredibly tough," he said. "The training was hard for everybody. Mo is a phenomenal athlete and was probably one of our most gifted athletes. Even the great athletes slow down, hit a wall, and it goes downhill. But with her, there wasn't a lot of slowdown. She was thirty-nine years old and still playing really good water polo – playing at a high level and helping us. Was she as good as when she was younger? Probably not. If she had been in our training when she was younger, training like this? It's incredible what would have happened to her and what she would have done."

From the first day, Baker let O'Toole know she had to compete for a spot on the team. Her heralded past scored her no bonus consideration.

"Before she even touched the water with us, she was fighting for a spot on the team just like everybody else was," Baker said. "She was no different than anybody else."

For Maureen O'Toole, the anxiety over making the team was always present. In 2000, before Baker announced the team, she was living with her mom in Long Beach.

"I never knew if I was going to make that team," she said. "I really, truly didn't. I would go home and tell my mom, *I don't think I'm going to make it. I think he's going to cut me.* And my mom would say, *No way, you're not going to get cut.*

"And I'm like, *No, I mean, I'm scared.* And I was."

O'Toole recounted the moment she finally learned her pursuit was a success.

"We were all standing there in a line, holding hands," she said. "He named the team, and I was like, *Oh, my God, I can't believe it.* My hands were sweating. It was crazy."

Every Olympic athlete represents their country. They also all represent a specific place – Brenda Villa from Commerce, Courtney Johnson from Utah, Heather Moody from Wyoming and New Mexico.

Maureen O'Toole represented a time – the entire era of international women's water polo. She played in the first FINA World Cup in 1979, both World Championship exhibitions in 1978 and 1982, and the first official World Championship in 1986, where she was selected flag bearer for the entire United States delegation.

Over more than two decades, the women who played international water polo could not earn the distinction of playing in the Olympic Games. Carrying the torch for all the pioneers of international women's water polo, Maureen O'Toole was now among the first women to earn the title of Olympian.

@@@@@@

The first-ever United States Women's Olympic Team kicked off the Holiday Cup against Canada in front of a standing room only crowd at Los Alamitos. The festive Fourth of July atmosphere included a flyover before the first game, between Kazakhstan and the Netherlands, and a fireworks show after the nightcap.

The spectators were treated to a United States victory over Canada, the team that had sent the team on its quest to qualify for the Olympics a long year ago. The crowds returned day after day, and the United States didn't disappoint. Following the Fourth of July win, the team reeled off victories over Australia, Russia, Kazakhstan, and the Netherlands to sweep its way into the tournament finals, where Canada awaited.

When he took over the team in March of 1998, the immediate task for Guy Baker and the team was to place higher than Canada at the 1999 World Cup. A huge amount of energy was spent on beating Canada during the first year of Baker's tenure. As devastating as the loss in Winnipeg was, Baker and most of the team feel that it was a blessing in disguise. Every player had to make the decision to fully commit to the ensuing process without knowing the outcome. Every day together was a small step toward reaching their collective promise.

From Baker's point of view, the biggest change was the wider view of the team's world-wide competition after putting so much focus on Canada from the time of his hiring to the 1999 World Cup.

"What really helped us, program-wise, was a more global approach," Baker said. "This was no longer about beating Canada. Once we got the draw for qualifying, we knew who we'd have to go through to get to the Olympic Games. It could be Greece, Italy, Hungary, Russia, whatever. We had to become more global."

Baker pointed to common training in the Netherlands and Australia, and Holland and Russia working with the United States before and after the 2000 Holiday Cup, as factors leading to increased acceptance internationally. It was also evidence that the program had moved past its reliance on Canada.

"What the Holiday Cup became, with teams coming over and us being a major player in international water polo, all happened during that time," Baker said. "When I first started, we were regional. It was us and Canada and whatever is happening over in Europe. We took a much more global approach to everything."

The United States had hosted the entire inaugural Olympic field at the Holiday Cup, six teams from four continents. After five days of competition, the championship game featured the classic matchup of North American rivals. Only seven months after the 1999 Holiday Cup debacle against a Canadian team crippled with food poisoning, the United States powered to its sixth win in six days, achieving its long-stated goal of winning its home tournament.

"That was consistent, we played good water polo all the way through," Baker said. "It felt like all the teams were serious about it. Holland was the only team that did poorly. Australia seemed to be feeling it a little bit, pressure-wise. We gained a tremendous amount of confidence and left the Holiday Cup in a really good position."

Members of the team remember the Holiday Cup as the event that really brought home what the Olympics meant to the American supporters they were going to represent in Sydney.

"The Holiday Cup was where you got the sense that this was bigger than yourself," Baker said. "We'd been so isolated at Los Al for the whole year leading up to the qualifying tournament. It was the fourteen athletes and the coaches, and Michelle, the manager. That was it. Our doctor, Larry Drum, would occasionally bring some comic relief. When he came to the pool, everybody went to Larry because he was a new face on deck. It was like, *I haven't seen anybody else for the last five weeks.* We were so isolated, so relentless in the pursuit to try to qualify, and no one thought we were going to succeed, so we were just left alone."

Seeing the Olympic spirit in Australia at the venue in Ryde and the parade in Kawana gave the team a sense of what was to come. But they were still blown away by the response they received on home soil.

"Coming back to our place and the Holiday Cup, it's packed and people are going nuts," Baker said. "There's people setting up autograph tables. We never did things like that. There was so much energy surrounding us qualifying for the Olympic Games. It was a brand new experience for everybody."

Julie Swail signing autographs – Sendoff to Sydney, July 2000

10

DOG DAYS AND DIAZ

Sendoff to Sydney   **Rachel Scott**

The naming of the Olympic Team before the Holiday Cup put thirteen athletes in the history books. The fourteenth player, Rachel Scott, became the first woman to occupy the unenviable position of Olympic alternate. The left-handed sharp-shooter from Bainbridge Island, Washington, overcame numerous hurdles to reach the National Team. In the end, her lack of experience caught up with her.

Scott started playing water polo in eighth grade and continued through college. She didn't lack experience in the sport itself. She lacked experience playing in the field. A goalkeeper until her senior season of college, she debuted on the National Team in the goal at the 1997 World Cup. Scott played sparingly at the 1998 World Championships in Perth, then left the cage for the field during the 1998 collegiate season at San Diego State.

Just one year later, Scott was in Winnipeg as a field player when the United States attempted to qualify for the Olympics.

Her earliest experiences in the field came in pick-up games during high school.

"I remember thinking I was literally going to drown," she said. "You just can't stop, or you're going to go under. It was ugly."

On her first team, she wasn't needed in the field. In fact, she had been recruited by her swimmer friends to be their goalie. When they first asked Steve Killpack, the boys' water polo coach at Bainbridge Island High School, to start a girls' team, they had only six players. Scott and a basketball teammate with a swimming background made the group eight, and the team began playing. With no high school girls' teams to play in Washington, four-hour drives to Newberg, Oregon, for games were common.

"Our team didn't play against boys too often, but I loved the sport, so I'd go to as many boys' tournaments as I could," Scott said. "Other teams would pick me up to play goalie for them. I'd just play absolutely as much as I could."

By the time Scott was a senior, high school girls' water polo had grown in Washington. Eight teams, four from each of two divisions, competed for the first state championship at the King County Aquatic Center in the spring of 1994. A three-sport athlete in high school, Scott lettered in soccer, basketball, and water polo. When it came time to make a college decision, water polo won out over basketball.

"I happened to get more scholarship money for water polo," she said. "I got some money from San Diego State, and I had to take that in order to get to college."

Scott feels fortunate for the timing of her entry into college at the same time many schools were gaining varsity status and offering scholarships to women's water polo players.

"Without the scholarship money, I would not have continued," she said. "I was offered a place at a couple of local junior colleges for basketball, which would have been a fine fit. Water polo was the avenue for school. I was very up-front with my college coaches about that. They didn't always appreciate that, I suppose. I knew that because of water polo, I was going to get the best education I could."

Scott credits Killpack with getting her the exposure she needed to attract the attention of college coaches. In the summer after her sophomore year, Killpack borrowed a van from a Bainbridge Island water polo family and hit the road with a carload of players to attend a Youth Team Tryout in Pomona, California.

"It was really just a fundraiser for the Senior National Team," Scott said. "But I was fortunate to be one of only two goalies in the tryout, and the other had knee problems and couldn't even practice the whole week. So I made the team, which was awesome."

Scott traveled to Canada with the Youth Team and began to meet girls from other states who would become future teammates on the Senior Team. Through the Junior National Team, she met Nicolle Payne, a goalkeeper in the same high school class. When news of Payne signing to play at UCLA reached Scott, she knew there were only a few other options for herself.

Killpack helped pay for a flight to San Diego for Scott's recruiting weekend on campus, and she signed with the Aztecs upon returning to Bainbridge. Scott played nearly three years in the goal at San Diego State, earning numerous honors for her play, before she was abruptly pulled from the position two weeks before the Collegiate National Championships.

"My coach didn't think I was trying," she said matter-of-factly. "We were at a tournament, and he decided I wasn't trying in there anymore, so he pulled me out two weeks from the end of the season. He put me in the field, and I had two weeks to figure out how to get conditioned enough to play at the championships."

As soon as the college season ended, it was back to the goal for Scott, who made her National Team debut that very summer at the 1997 World Cup in Nancy, France. Because of the Southern Hemisphere location of 1998 World Championships, they were held in January, before the next college season began. After an uninspiring experience that put her confidence to the test at the World Championships in Perth, Scott decided her goalkeeping days were done. She returned to the Aztecs for her final season determined to become the best field player she could be.

Armed with the experience of watching the game from the goal, the ability to throw the ball hard, and the advantage of being left-handed, Scott was nearly ready for the move to the field. But one glaring problem existed: she hated swimming.

"I couldn't swim. I was pathetic at best," she said. "When I got to college, I could not do a flip turn."

As a youth, Scott put in a brief stint on the local swim team, during which she did her best to resist actual swimming. The 10-year-old hid in the locker room every day to avoid practice.

"It was hard, and I didn't want to do anything hard," she explained. "Ultimately, had I swum more and paid more attention to it, it probably could have yielded me more successes later."

While in college, Scott described herself as a game-time player who loafed through practice. She didn't necessarily mind working hard, but was always on the lookout for an easy way out. What she found with swimming, though, was that there was no easy way out.

When Guy Baker took the helm of the National Team, the members of the Perth World Championship team were invited to the first training session. Although she was goalie in Perth, Scott had just finished the collegiate season as a field player, earning Second-Team All-American honors. From coaching against San Diego State, Baker knew Scott's abilities well enough. After the two training camps and only four months removed from representing the United States as a goalkeeper, Baker selected Scott for the European tour in the summer of 1998.

She immediately knew there was no room for loafing through practice or seeking easy ways out. Training harder than she ever had in her life, Scott came to regret the lost years of swimming that would provide the perfect addition to her game as she competed against her teammates for a spot on every roster leading up to the naming of the Olympic Team.

Covering up her deficiency in swimming caused Scott ongoing angst.

"I worked really hard at it," she said. "But when we were training, I cried every night at dinner. Every night at dinner, I cried, knowing that I'd cry during the swim set the next day, then come home and cry at dinner. It was a vicious cycle."

After traveling with the National Team in 1998, Scott was on the team for the World Cup, Pan American Games, and Holiday Cup in 1999. But she was the player most directly impacted by the additions of Heather Petri and Ericka Lorenz as the Olympic year got underway. She was named alternate for the Olympic Qualification Tournament in Palermo. And on the day Baker named the 13-player Olympic team, Rachel Scott drew the most unlucky number of all: #14.

The tingling sensation created by the hugely successful Holiday Cup was still in the air when the teams from Australia, Canada, Holland, and Kazakhstan departed. The next assembly of these nations would take place in Sydney in two months' time. The Russian team remained in Southern California to train with the United States, playing one more exhibition game at Los Al before the two squads headed 400 miles north to Palo Alto. The final match prior to the Olympic Games – dubbed "Sendoff to Sydney" – was scheduled for July 14 at Stanford University.

The day before the game, the teams trained separately at Menlo College in Atherton. As part of the post-practice autograph session, girls from the Stanford Water Polo Club introduced each player individually.

"I remember the detail of my intro was really impressive," said Bernice Orwig. "And this was pre-Google. My high school coach got a call from one of the club girls asking for stories about me."

Before the days of social media, face-to-face interactions were the only way young players and fans could gain exposure to the Olympic athletes.

"Having the Stanford club girls know so much about each one of us was really neat," Orwig said. "It was another piece of tangible proof that the Olympics was special to the water polo community; we got so much great support from people who wanted to share in the Olympic experience."

Brenda Villa agreed; the Holiday Cup demonstrated the effect the Olympic team had on a huge crowd – the Sendoff to Sydney brought it to a more personalized level.

"That was the first time I realized that we were people's role models," Villa said. "Someone did all this research on me; they're so excited to meet us. It was the first time we all realized the opportunity that we had, and what an impact we had as Olympians."

Two hours before game time, hundreds of spectators formed a line on the south side of the Avery Aquatic Center, stretching the length of the facility and wrapping around toward Stanford Stadium. Begun in May of 1999, the expansion of Stanford's deGuerre Pools was still in progress. Because the renovations to the

Avery Stadium Pool were yet to be finished, the Sendoff to Sydney game took place in the newly completed Belardi Pool.

The demand for an appearance by the Olympic Team in Northern California was clearly apparent as the crowd poured through the gate, quickly overwhelming the grassy slope on the south side of Belardi. Unlike fans in Southern California, who had six chances to catch a game at the Holiday Cup, plus the exhibition after the tournament, residents of the Bay Area had only this one opportunity to get a taste of Olympic water polo. People who arrived near game time found the event completely sold-out; they watched the game free of charge from outside the fence.

For Ellen Estes and Brenda Villa, the Sendoff to Sydney was a homecoming, although the two Stanford students had widely different experiences on The Farm up to that point. Estes played two seasons for the Cardinal before stopping out to pursue the Olympics. She had already scored 142 goals for Stanford, including a school-record 93 as a sophomore in 1998. Originally a member of the Class of 2000, Estes was training at Los Alamitos when her classmates graduated that June in Palo Alto. Villa had spent all of two fall quarters on campus, meeting new friends then leaving abruptly twice. Although she trained with her Stanford team-mates in the fall, she had yet to make her collegiate water polo debut. The Sendoff to Sydney was Villa's first competitive game on campus.

The Cardinal duo didn't disappoint the crowd of more than 1,800; Villa assisted on a goal by Estes in the second quarter of the United States' 7-5 victory over Russia.

Just like the Holiday Cup, the United States team met a tidal wave of energy and enthusiasm from their supporters at the Sendoff to Sydney that made the magnitude of their status and responsibility as Olympians hit home. The buzz of excitement was still fresh in their bones as the players settled in their seats on the flight back to Orange County.

It was a tremendously exciting time.

The next time they were scheduled to board a plane together, the destination would be Sydney, Australia.

United States Olympic Team – Sendoff to Sydney, July 2000

@/@/@/@/@/@/

Before Sydney, however, came the dog days of summer at Los Alamitos.

"There was so much work and training put into qualifying for the Olympics," said Guy Baker. "That post-qualifying time period was a whirlwind – a couple weeks of rest for the players, two weeks of pretty light practices at Los Al, a couple weeks in Australia where we're training and we're enjoying ourselves, then coming back and getting right into the Holiday Cup – we hadn't grinded away at training in quite a while. It was a nice break."

The crowds and energy, combined with the great results earned by the team, put Baker and the entire squad in a good spot. But once Russia went home, and everyone reconvened after a few days off, it was time to get down to serious work as the final phase of training began. And it was nothing short of a grind.

"If I have any skin cancer or anything like that, it is from July and August of 2000 being at Los Al," Baker said, referring to the reflective oven the white pool deck became when the sun rose high in the sky. "There is not a more horrific, hot, sun-beating-down-on-you place that I have found in the world than Los Al in July and August."

The team got back to work; the theme of the final phase was counterattack. Baker began introducing a new counterattack concept through cross-training prior to the trip to Australia. Three-on-two basketball and soccer demonstrated the structure, balance, and organization of the first line of the counterattack that he sought.

"We were just pushing, pushing, pushing the first line," he said. "At the qualifying tournament, we were open all over the place."

Studying the tapes from Palermo, Baker saw players open everywhere, but inefficient structures for finishing the counterattack and then transitioning into the front court offense.

"There were times we ended up two, two, two, all bracketed at the end," Baker said. "When it was time for us to set up our offense, it's taking us five, six, seven seconds to get into an offense. The whole focus was to get right into our offense when the counterattack was over."

Practices were long and filled with swimming, as Baker demanded repetition of the counterattack drills; up and back, over and over again. Players slathered themselves in sunblock before each practice and dragged their fried bodies from the water at the conclusion of each torturous session. The huge crowds and adoring fans from the Holiday Cup and Sendoff to Sydney faded from memory as the players slogged through the necessary routine, preparing for the biggest tournament of their lives.

After the rash of injuries endured in May and June, the team had nearly returned to full strength by the summer. Bernice Orwig and Heather Moody were back in the lineup by the Holiday Cup. Only Robin Beauregard remained on injured reserve.

Throughout the summer, Beauregard faced a different type of grind than her teammates.

"I was still out every practice, and I had a lovely little rubber tubing wrapped around my waist, swimming in one spot in the middle of the pool," she said. "I would periodically get beaned with balls. Every once in awhile they would loosen the reins a little bit and let me sit on a ball to pass. I basically went to therapy, went to practice, went back to therapy, and went back to practice."

When she was able to see a doctor upon her return from Australia in June, Beauregard was told she was probably going to need surgery.

"I'm like, 'I know, but I'm not doing it before the Olympics,'" she recalled. "I wasn't positive I was going to make the team."

When Beauregard was named to the Olympic Team she was still on crutches.

While she wasn't in the thick of the practices, Beauregard remained engaged when it came to the tactics Baker was installing at the time.

"We trained hard, and got everything organized," Baker said. "We got our plays down during this time. There had been that nice little 'everybody's happy' period after returning from Stanford; and then it was right back to me being an asshole; they don't know what the hell they're doing. We got back into our regular rhythm of what we do."

Baker sensed rapidly growing confidence from the team as they cranked out promising training sessions. Beginning with the training trip to Holland in February, the team was hitting a rhythm. As players committed to meeting the high standards laid out for them, their receptiveness increased. Baker found the team moved much quicker through his objectives.

"We were just way dialed in, but still pushing really hard," he said. "We were crazy. The fitness level of the team was off the charts."

When the men's Olympic team arrived on deck at Los Al, they regularly encountered the women's athletes in the midst of a 14-station fitness circuit. Women were running up the bleachers, jumping rope, doing sit-ups, tossing heavy balls, sprinting … all with an attitude of, *I don't care who's watching.*

As the Olympics neared, Baker realized another important piece was falling into place for the players and the team. When their schedule allowed, the women watched the men's team in their pre-Olympic contests.

"Before, sitting and watching games with the players, they would be mostly in awe of the men's physical abilities," Baker said. "Eventually, they became critical of how the men's teams were actually playing, making comments like, *What are they doing? This is stupid.* They became wonderful players. They became students of the game. They all knew how the game should look and how they should play."

The dog days dragged on, but one incident broke up the monotony, to the delight of the Women's Olympic Team.

"It's Friday afternoon, mid-August, hotter than hell," Guy Baker said. "And they come into practice kind of giddy. This is unusual."

The team always took Saturday and Sunday off, so Fridays were generally business-like. Players and coaches aimed to finish off the week on a high note before the precious time off on the weekend. The level of enthusiasm raised Baker's suspicions that something was afoot.

"The practice was awful. Just bad," he said. "It's a bad practice, and I'm losing it on them."

Even the most reliable attention spans seemed to wander; wishful eyes repeatedly found their way to the pool gate. Of all the improvements the team had made, the lingering bad habit of ending the week with a poor effort incensed Baker. His pleas and threats fell on deaf ears.

"So I get to the point of, *Screw it, we're done, practice is over*," Baker said. "*You guys have a good weekend.* I don't even know if I said good weekend. Anyhow, we're done."

But contrary to every other Friday, the team moved slowly upon its dismissal.

"Fridays were always like, let's get the hell out of here, clean up, boom, out, done, no showers, just out and go," Baker explained. "But they're hanging around; things are moving slow."

As much as he wanted to high-tail it out, Baker's daughter, Chris, was in the pool, finishing up her swim practice. Stewing in his office, Baker was caught by surprise when a couple of players popped in, sat down, and initiated small talk.

"They're like, *Hey, Guy, what are you doing this weekend?*" he said. "I'm thinking, *What are you guys doing?* No one ever comes in and asks me what I'm doing on the weekend, and no one ever comes in after a bad practice and just wants to hang out."

As the awkward exchange continued, and more and more players entered the room, Baker's suspicions that something was up were confirmed: into his office walked actress Cameron Diaz.

The joke that led up to the appearance began when Nicolle Payne and her roommates lived near Diaz' parents the year before and occasionally saw her around when she visited. Asked what he would do if Cameron Diaz ever came to Los Al, Baker replied, *If Cameron Diaz ever shows up to practice, we'll cancel. We'll be done.* The story took on a life of its own during the team's travels around the world.

"Cameron Diaz would show up in Hungary and Holland," Baker said. "There'd be a photo of her from a magazine, like, *Guy, I'm sorry I missed you, I hope to see you soon.* She would pop up at different times on our trips, but I'd always just missed her." The running joke kept things light when the team was on the road.

Larry Drum, the team doctor, engineered Diaz' actual appearance at Los Al. Drum was the family doctor for Diaz' parents, who helped get their daughter in on the prank. The plan was in place, and all the players were positive practice would be cancelled. But Diaz got delayed in Los Angeles.

"She was supposed to show up before we started – ergo the bad practice," Baker said. "She was going to come save the day, but she didn't show up. In their minds, they came in giddy; they were never planning on getting in the pool. And then they're in the pool, and it's a Friday, and I'm going to wrap up the whole week. I'm ready to go; they're just like, *Where the hell is she? I was never going to practice today.* That's why they kept looking at the gate; they were just like, *Please rescue me.*"

Baker laughed as he continued, "I'm losing it on them, and they're thinking, *This is like the worst thing ever.*"

As soon as practice ended, the players reached Dr. Drum, who assured them that Diaz was near. By the time she arrived, nearly the entire team filled Baker's office; his rising concern about what they had cooked up for him was assuaged, replaced by shock.

Cameron Diaz entered the room and walked straight up to Baker.

"Hi, coach. How are you? I've been wanting to meet you. I've been looking for you all over the world, and I've finally found you."

The days until departure dwindled quickly. Before leaving for Sydney, the team went through Olympic Team Processing – an experience that tangibly drives home the feeling of being an Olympian. At Processing, every member of the United States delegation gets outfitted. Pushing a shopping cart through a warehouse, athletes receive shirts, shorts, warm-ups, jackets, footwear, headwear, and even luggage. They also get fitted for their opening and closing ceremony outfits. Lastly, their haul includes an item that every Olympian hopes to use, but not all get the chance to – the medal ceremony attire.

Processing took place in San Diego, so the team drove the 100 miles from Los Al. Loaded with Olympic loot, the team proceeded to briefings covering topics such as security, media, and information about Australian culture and customs.

Guy Baker went through Olympic Processing with the United States men in 1992. Knowing what to expect, he allowed the players to enjoy the Olympic treatment. Practice could wait until the next morning.

Still abuzz with excitement, the team arrived for a workout at the local Bud Kearns Pool. Having trained before in all types of weather and all conditions, the players found a new challenge when they jumped into the tank.

"The water was hot," said Heather Moody. "Not warm. It's like, Jacuzzi hot."

Baker immediately knew the water temperature was enough to affect the practice, but his plan didn't include swimming or counterattacking. Time out plays were on the day's agenda.

"What are we actually going to get done? It's too hot," he said. "But the way I look at things, what happens if we show up at the Olympics and the pool is too hot? We're not going to play? It's a hot August day, so it's not like it's cold outside; we're going to practice."

Not even Cameron Diaz could save the team. Two days from departing for Sydney, the timeout plays had to be nailed down. After quickly mastering a timeout six-on-five play to Baker's satisfaction, they moved on to one designed for a late-game six-on-six situation. The team did a run-through with no defense and talked about the available options. The first attempt with defense went pretty well. The players felt prepared; if they had a vote, practice would be over.

"We could have got out at that point; we did it right," Baker said, "but the key is going to be after the defense knows what you're doing. They're going to figure what you're trying to do. Plan A isn't always going to work."

So they did it again. The defense made a stop. And another. Baker credits the players who weren't on the timeout play for buckling down, competing hard, and playing good defense.

"They could have just let it work every time and we're out," he said. "But we're doing it legit – playing it live. Game on. They can't get it right and we keep repeating it."

Do it again. Do it again. Do it again.

"Sometimes we would get close and start to get it," Baker continued. "But in my mind, once you get it, then you have to keep doing it so that it's instinctive. It took us forever."

Baker was satisfied. In his mind, they finally had the plays nailed down.

With every reason to simply go through the motions – Olympic Processing, miserably hot water, and the impending departure – every player stayed mentally strong. The preparation was done. Each individual knew her role; the United States women were ready for Sydney.

Ericka Lorenz, Heather Petri, Gubba Sheehy, Nicolle Payne, Brenda Villa, and Chris Duplanty – Opening ceremony, September 15, 2000

11

TRAILBLAZERS

2000 Olympic Games
USA versus Netherlands

Bernice Orwig
Ericka Lorenz

After fifteen hours of flight, the team arrived in Sydney, home of the Games of the XXVII Olympiad. A record-total 10,651 athletes descended on the Southern Hemisphere city on the east coast of Australia. While that number represented a roughly three percent increase over the previous high at the 1996 Atlanta Games, the number of female participants topped 4,000 for the first time – an increase of nearly 14 percent over Atlanta, and nearly double the number of female athletes in Seoul in 1988.

Gubba Sheehy felt an array of emotions during the flight – a mixture of nervousness and excitement at the same time. She spent time imagining the Olympic Village. Thinking about spending the next month with her teammates, experiencing this adventure, blew her mind.

The Olympic Village did nothing to disappoint. Located in Newington, two kilometers east of the Homebush Bay athletic complex, the construction included nearly 900 townhouses and 700 apartments. At the urging of the Olympic Committee, environmental sustainability featured heavily in the planning of the community that would host over 15,000 athletes and team officials. Solar panels on every home made the Olympic Village the largest solar-powered suburb in the world at the time of its construction. Immediately overwhelmed by its size, Sheehy and the team made a brief stop at their house before setting out to explore, like children set free at Disneyland.

Cruising around the Village, seeing the Olympic rings everywhere, as well as athletes from all over the world dressed in their national colors, Sheehy felt as if she were in a dream.

"I was thinking, *Wow, we made it to the show*," she said. "All these athletes were in one village, trying to accomplish the same thing I was hoping to do – medal at the Olympics."

When she walked into the Olympic Village, Courtney Johnson also had the feeling of, *We've made it.*

"All of a sudden, it validated women's water polo," she said. "I felt a sense of validation, not as a person, but as a sport. All of a sudden, we were a legitimate sport, whereas before, we were always on that cusp of being seen as equals. To feel that camaraderie throughout the whole United States team, and the pride for your country, was really unbelievable."

Arriving a few days before the opening ceremonies, the team had daily training sessions and team meetings, but plenty of spare time to relax and enjoy the amenities of the Olympic Village. Among the highlights for the women were a movie theater, an arcade, internet cafes, and, of course, the dining hall.

Open 24 hours, the cafeteria featured cuisine from all over the world to help Olympic athletes from every continent feel at home while at the Games. The team quickly realized that the dining hall at the Olympic Games is one of the world's greatest people-watching venues. Athletes of all heights, weights, and builds streamed through the cavernous cafeteria. Almost comically, teams travelled in packs – groups of female gymnasts in the five-foot range could be seen walking past a men's volleyball team, towering a foot-and-a-half above their diminutive peers. Boxing and wrestling teams boasted a range of physiques, from the fly-weights to the heavyweights. Heads were commonly seen craning to get a glimpse of an athlete's identification badge hanging from their neck – *Where is she from? What sport does he play?* Languages from every corner of the world could be heard among the din of a room feeding every nation's greatest athletes.

"That's probably the place to be at an Olympics," said Brenda Villa. "You walk in, and you hear so many different languages being spoken. You see all these cool uniforms, and you're walking around like a chicken with its head cut off, just trying to take it all in. You would think it'd be intimidating, but it's not. It's just a world of wonder and excitement, where you just kind of wish you knew everyone; that you had the time to talk to everyone in there. But everyone is so focused on their job there; to compete. It's a rare scene."

While the United States women saw many famous athletes in the dining hall, the faces they were most familiar with were those of their competition. When they came across another women's water polo team, the Americans headed in a different direction.

"We wouldn't sit near them," Villa said. "Because if you're having fun and laughing, you don't want the opponents to think that you're not taking it seriously. So we'd always find our own area away from them."

Even in her dreams of being at the show, Gubba Sheehy never imagined the impact the Olympic Village would have on her.

"I was just so proud to be there," she said. "It was truly amazing."

❀❀❀❀❀

Bernice Orwig dreamed of being an Olympian since she was a young girl.

As a seven-year-old, she was inspired by the 1984 Olympics, held in her backyard. The pageantry and international flair intrigued her, setting her on a path to not only pursue sport, but to become world-class.

"I was so into the LA Olympics," she said. "I thought, *How cool is it that these people get to go to this huge party and play their game?*"

Women's water polo wasn't on the 1984 Olympic program, which didn't matter because Orwig was years away from learning about the sport that would ultimately fulfill her dreams. Her sport of choice at the moment wasn't on the program either, but that didn't discourage the determined girl.

"At the time, jump roping was my big thing," Orwig said. "I asked my mom if she thought they would ever put jump roping in the Olympics."

Orwig declared confidently that if it were, she could win gold.

Supporting her daughter's dreams, her mother, also named Bernice, responded, "I don't know if it will ever be in the Olympics or not. Why don't you keep practicing?"

If not for finding and falling in love with water polo, Orwig may still be waiting for jump rope's debut in the Olympic Games. But in the meantime, between the height of her jump-roping prowess and her introduction to water polo, Orwig took up basketball, playing at the Y and on her junior high school team. She set equally high goals in this new endeavor, vowing to become the first female player in the NBA.

While sports were her love, Orwig hated school – so much so, she tried to flunk herself out of fifth grade. That year, she transferred schools to join her brother, and quickly brewed up a plan to get kicked out.

"I would throw my homework away as soon as I got on campus," she said. "I would do it at home and then throw it away so I wouldn't have it to turn in. When my mom would get phone calls she would say, *She did her homework. She sat at the table and did it.* And the school would tell her, *Well, she's not turning it in.*"

When the adults got to the bottom of what was going on, Orwig remembers the response.

"It finally came out what I was doing," she said. "They sent me to a psychiatrist because something was wrong with me. They paid how much money just to be like, *She just isn't happy. She doesn't want to be there.*"

Orwig missed her friends from her old school, but that wasn't the whole picture. Being taller than everyone led to getting picked on; she found it hard to make friends. Without the comfort of friends from the neighborhood, her church, or the YMCA, she was looking for a way to get put back in her old school.

By the time she reached high school, Orwig was turning in her homework, but was looking for a ticket out of Phys Ed. One option was to join a fall sport. Despite her height, she wasn't interested in volleyball, and cross country wasn't an attractive option. A suggestion from her mother got her in the pool, despite a complete lack of experience.

Savanna High School offered a 6th period swim conditioning class. When Orwig showed up the first day, the water polo coach rounded up all the freshmen and made a pitch to them to try out the sport.

"He said if you like it, stay. If you don't, you can go back to your 6th period swim class," Orwig recalled. Looking around, she found two other girls in the group. "One of the girls and I agreed: I'll stay if you stay. Neither of us had any experience in swimming or water polo, but we gave it a try."

At her first water polo practice, the team was told to get in and swim a 200. Orwig was the first to pipe up, with, "What's a 200?"

Despite being a fish out of water on her first day, Orwig enjoyed the practice – and she made a lifelong friend, Suzanne Hughes. The pair played together throughout high school and for a season at Cypress College. Hughes went on to play at San Jose State on a water polo scholarship; the two remain best friends.

Her sophomore year, Orwig was moved into the goal; she was the only girl on the varsity team. When a majority of the team graduated after that season, six girls from the JV joined her on the next year's varsity squad. In her junior season, Savanna's varsity was made up of seven girls and seven boys.

"We didn't win very many games, but we had fun," she said. "We showed up to practice every day and had a great time. We had an amazing coach."

That coach was Patty Smith, whom Orwig credits for opening her eyes to the possibilities that water polo held for her. Smith received a letter from Junior National Team coach Brent Bohlender about tryouts; she encouraged Orwig to go.

"I remember thinking, *Why should I do this?*" Orwig said. The tryouts were in Merced, a 300-mile drive from Anaheim; even her mother wanted a better understanding before committing to the trip. She called Smith to learn more.

"My mom never called a coach, never questioned anything any coach said," Orwig said. "I found out years later; she called Patty and asked, *Should I take my daughter to this?*"

Smith was firm in her response. "Yes. Get her to that tryout."

"That changed everything," Orwig mused.

Heading along Highway 99 to Merced, Orwig had no idea that water polo existed competitively for girls. Co-ed water polo was all she knew; she assumed that at the higher levels, men prevailed because of strength.

"I was really sheltered because I didn't know what was beyond," she said. "When I went to the Junior National Team tryout in Merced, I didn't know that girls played against girls."

In fact, earlier during that year, the high school junior had written a paper about her future. No longer striving for a future in jump roping, water polo was her new passion.

"I was going to be the first woman on the men's Olympic water polo team," she said. "In the gold medal game, there's a penalty called. I'd block the penalty, and we'd win gold. Everything was always about the Olympics for me. I wrote that in the fall; the Junior National Team tryout was in the spring. My mom kept that paper."

The tryout was a whole new world for Orwig. She quickly realized that many of the younger athletes played on girls' clubs, and many were shocked to hear that she had only played with boys. At the end of the weekend, Orwig found herself selected for the Junior National Team; she was headed to England and the Netherlands with the team in the summer. But that didn't mean her confidence was at a new high.

"I knew I was doing well, but these girls play all the time, and I only play a couple of months out of the year, during high school season," she said. "I was pretty surprised when they told me I made it. At first I thought it was just because of my size; I was taller than everyone."

While her height was definitely an asset, Bohlender saw much more in the unknown goalie who had showed up at the tryout. He also knew that Orwig would benefit from playing more water polo. Bohlender talked to Doug Drury, coach of The Outsiders, about reaching out to Orwig. Drury was happy to have her join the team.

"I didn't know anything about club water polo," Orwig said. "I guess Golden West had a club, which would have been a lot closer for me, but Doug got me first; so we made the drive out to Pomona."

Before she got her driver's license, Orwig's mother would take her to Pomona, sometimes a two-hour trip in traffic. In her senior year, she was able to carpool with a friend. She loved the experience, but found some unexpected challenges playing against girls. In fact, in many ways, she found playing against boys easier.

"It was a different approach to shooting," she said. "With boys it was just pure brute strength. A guy's shot is always easier to block than a woman's shot; a woman is going to look to see where to shoot for the highest probability, whereas a guy is just going to shoot it. At least that was the case in high school.

"I would average about fifteen saves a game in high school," Orwig continued. "The boys would just try to shoot the ball harder. The harder they shot, the easier it was to block. With women, though, sometimes they would shoot it hard. Sometimes they would put a little off speed on it. I had to start thinking more. I was exhausted after club practices because it took more from a mental standpoint as well."

By her senior year of high school, Orwig was lightly recruited for athletics in college – but not for water polo. Joining the basketball team in her junior year, she started to attract some attention from colleges, until she tore her ACL. After that, the phone stopped ringing.

By then, however, water polo was her passion; her only focus was to play as much as possible. Choosing water polo over basketball affected the treatment of Orwig's knee: instead of replacement surgery, her doctor advised cleaning up the meniscus and strengthening the leg.

Minor discomfort and swelling were the challenges – nothing ibuprofen and ice couldn't mitigate. Orwig experienced no pain around 90 percent of the time, and relied on a strict regimen of exercises to keep the muscles strong.

Unrecruited in water polo out of high school, Orwig went on to play for the men's team at Cypress College, earning Second-Team All-Conference honors. But the new connections she made playing with The Outsiders made the biggest impact on her career. Orwig's club played in tournaments against college teams, just as the clubs in Northern California did at the time.

Playing in a tournament at UC San Diego in the spring of 1996, Orwig ran into a former Outsiders teammate who was playing for USC. The next thing she knew, her pregame warm-up was interrupted by the USC head coach, Jovan Vavic.

"I shook his hand, and he told me he was going to watch my game," Orwig said. "After the game, he had to leave right away, but he told me he would call on Monday and that he had scholarship money for me. And that was pretty much it."

Orwig knew about athletes from her high school receiving athletic scholarships for sports such as football and wrestling, but she had no idea there was athletic aid for women's water polo. In fact, she would become one of the first at USC to receive a scholarship for the sport. Vavic, who was also coaching the USC men's team, was eager to make Orwig the centerpiece of the newly funded women's program.

"In the recruiting process, he told me that by my senior year, we would win a national championship," Orwig said. "He said that with the scholarship money, he would get the right players to build the team around me."

Of all her athletic aspirations, being a Trojan was simply a dream come true.

"It was always in the back of my mind, being a USC fan," she said. "I had USC sweatshirts and t-shirts that I loved to wear. But I never ever thought I'd be able to go there, because of how expensive it was. I went home and told my mom Jovan was going to call me. She said, *Who's Jovan?*"

Things fell in place for Orwig, Vavic and the Women of Troy; their national finishes went from seventh to fifth in Orwig's first two years, to a national title in her senior season.

While the direction of her collegiate career skyrocketed, culminating in Collegiate Player of the Year honors in 1999, her National Team career was an up-and-down experience. After the surprise of her selection to the Junior National Team and the trip to Europe, she was passed up at the next year's tryouts. Undaunted, she resolved to work harder; she got back to work with Outsiders and the men's team at Cypress College. But at the next tryout for the Senior National Team, she was cut again.

"Vaune told me I played too much like a men's goalie," said Orwig, referring to Senior Team head coach Vaune Kadlubek. "I was only playing a couple nights a week with all girls; the rest of the time I was playing with men. Against women, I would get burned on lob shots, or anything off-speed. I had to make a mental adjustment."

Again, Orwig got back to work, determined to show that she had the ability to play at the National Team level. The next time she tried out, a coaching change had occurred; Sandy Nitta was back at the reins. A compliment from Nitta was good for Orwig's spirit, but left her unsure of her style.

Nitta told Orwig that playing goalkeeper like a man was beneficial, because many international women shoot like men. She specifically pointed out Mercedesz Stieber of Hungary. But at the end of the training camp with Nitta, Orwig found herself cut again – and confused.

Ultimately, the consistent coaching she received at USC was the key to her development. Orwig flourished with consistent play against women; she made the physical and mental adjustments necessary to unlock her potential. For the first time in her career, she was given specific goalkeeper training. Assistant coach Sasha Bucur focused on body position for the variety of shots she saw regularly. The USC team had a full spectrum of talent, from world-class international players to teammates who played collegiate club before the transition to varsity status. The wide range of shot selections helped Orwig's intellectual approach to the position.

The work paid off. In the spring of 1998, when Guy Baker became coach of the Senior National Team, he invited Orwig to try out and selected her for the European trip that summer. She played with the Senior Team throughout the summer and in the Holiday Cup in December. With her star on the rise and the chance to qualify for the Olympics at the 1999 World Cup just months away, Orwig made a tough decision. She dropped her Olympic pursuit to play her senior season at USC – and equally as important, to finish her degree.

While it was a crucial decision in terms of its impact on her future with the national team, she was committed to her choice.

Bernice Orwig -- Sendoff to Sydney, July 2000

"The scholarship was the most important factor," Orwig said. "I would not have been able to afford to go back to USC without scholarship money to finish my degree. I thought if I stopped out of school, I would end up dragging my feet to get it done. The big picture was this: yes, it would be great to play on the National Team and try to qualify for the Olympics; however, that's not going to get me a job. I felt I needed my degree to make sure to set up stepping stones for my future."

The option came with risk. There was no guarantee her position would be available after the school year, and Jackie Frank, a goalkeeper from Seal Beach and a freshman at Stanford, had accepted an invitation to join the Senior National Team's full-time training for 1999.

Orwig's parents provided a sound voice of support. Yes, water polo would be there after she graduated. Yes, she would have to work harder, but she would also have her degree. Happy to have the backing of her family, Orwig then turned her attention to informing Guy Baker of her decision. It wasn't a conversation she looked forward to.

"I didn't know his standpoint, but for me, I was nervous because I was afraid," she said. "Even though he brought me on the team and very much coached me, I had the USC-UCLA thing in the back of my mind. He's UCLA, I'm USC – he didn't go down that road, though. He always kept it about what's the best for the sport. He told me I would not be out of the National Team program, and I should finish my degree."

For the young girl who had so loved to jump rope, the Olympics was always a goal. In an athletic career that hinged on being in the right place, with the right coaches who set her on her path, the one thing she knew that existed was the Olympics. She didn't know what a 200 was, didn't know about the Junior National Team or club water polo, or college scholarships. But Bernice Orwig knew that she was drawn to the highest level of international competition, even if the sport she came to love wasn't yet a part of it.

"For all those years, the Olympics were always there in my mind," she said.

@@@@@@

After the unilateral decision by Guy Baker to skip the opening ceremonies at the 1999 Pan American Games in Winnipeg, the coach consulted the team captain, Julie Swail, about the Sydney plan once the team was qualified. When Baker mentioned that he was thinking about making the opening ceremonies available, Swail jumped on the offer. "I told him that's the best decision he could make," she said.

It wasn't a decision that came easily to Baker, who valued keeping a tight grip on circumstances when it came to competition and preparation. But the decision was a function of preparation. When he and the team staff sat down after Palermo to plan for Sydney, they left no stone unturned. When it came to the Olympics, the staff made as many decisions as they could prior to arriving in Australia; they were fully dialed in.

Just like at the Pan Ams the year before, the competition began the day after opening ceremonies. The women's tournament would debut the next afternoon at 1:00 p.m. with Australia and Kazakhstan meeting in the historic first game. The Australian team would not be at the opening ceremony; nor would Canada, who played Russia at 6:00 p.m. the next day. The United States drew the nightcap, a 7:15 p.m. start against the Netherlands.

Baker was not without his concerns; the game against Holland was of course at the forefront. Additionally, he knew the opening ceremonies would make for a long night, and the team had training in the morning. So a deal was in place for the United States women.

"It's not like training training, but it's preparation to get ready for the game," Baker said. "The deal was, go to the opening ceremonies; take it as easy as possible, don't go crazy. Don't go running across the fields and jump over people to get photos. Act like you've been there before; enjoy the hell out of it, and then you've got to get back to the Village. You can't hang around."

Like teenagers given a longer leash by their parents, the team pledged to hold up their end of the bargain.

☺☺☺☺☺☺

The Opening Ceremonies are a special moment in the journey of an Olympic athlete. It is a time when athletes from around the world have an opportunity to come together and celebrate the pure joy of sport and live the ideals of Olympism. Competition has not started; no one has won or lost; at that moment, there is just excitement (and maybe a few nerves) for what is to come.

Heather Petri's words summed up a feeling that every member of the team experienced for the first time, at the same time, on the day of the Sydney Olympics opening ceremony. There were no Olympic veterans on the team, as there would be in Athens, Beijing, and London. No one could say what it was like last time. This was the first time.

If receiving all of their Olympic gear at Processing in San Diego gave the women a good sense of being Olympians, preparing for the opening ceremonies made them know that their dreams had become reality. Getting dressed in the United States outfit – long skirt, sweater, blazer, scarf, and hat – together in the house, the team emerged to find a swarm of fellow American athletes filling the streets in the United States section of the Village.

"We stepped onto our front porch, and into the street, where we joined more than 500 of our fellow Americans," said Heather Petri. "It was in this moment that the magnitude of the opportunity ahead of us sank in. This was special, and women's water polo was now a part of it."

From mingling in the front yard, taking pictures with famous athletes; to sitting in the gymnastics venue, the holding area for all the nations waiting to march; to hearing "The United States of America" announced as Team USA emerged from the tunnel and into the belly of Stadium Australia with its cacophony and color, emotions were sky-high.

"It was a full-body experience, assaulting all of our senses," Petri continued. "The heat from the lights, sound vibrations, and people screaming, flashes of cameras, movement of people whizzing by you, faces plastered with smiles, the waving of flags - all while on the inside we were full of adrenaline, hearts bursting with pride to be able to represent our country on this stage."

Petri kept asking herself, *Is this really happening?* The experience was beyond her imagination.

Meanwhile, at the Olympic Village, Guy Baker and Robin Beauregard watched the festivities on the closed-circuit television in the women's water polo house. Beauregard, still nursing her knee from the Harley incident up the Australian coast months before, couldn't risk standing for hours at the opening ceremony. So Baker skipped the event – a tradition he continued in Athens and Beijing.

The quiet time while the majority of the Village residents were at Stadium Australia for the festivities suited Baker perfectly. The coach got his head clear, focusing on what would go into the next day's game, and any last-minute preparation he felt was necessary.

Not a fan of big crowds, or waiting in long lines, Baker cherished the time to relax.

"The team would have a much better time without my tension around them," he said.

As Australian track star Cathy Freeman lit the Olympic flame, the United States women's water polo team began jockeying for position to be the first out of the stadium.

"We were running to the bus, which probably wasn't in Guy's plan," said captain Julie Swail. "But we said we'd be the first ones back. We ditched our heels in some trash can on the way. We're thinking, *We had better beat Holland tomorrow.* If we don't, there will never be a team that's allowed to go to the opening ceremonies ever again, in the whole history of the Olympics. We were very motivated."

Baker appreciated the team's seriousness about getting back to the Village quickly. Once at the house, the team told stories of cutting people off in the dash to get on the first bus, ate some food, and shared favorite moments of the night.

Swail, who had asked Baker to allow the team to go to the opening ceremonies at the Pan American Games, summed up what the experience did for the team.

"You feed off the excitement," she said. "I think physiologists would probably say, *That's going to take a lot of emotional energy. That's going to take physical energy.* But you cannot put a value on the emotional energy that you receive from being in an environment like the opening ceremonies of the Olympics."

The Games of the New Millennium had begun. The event of the new millennium – women's water polo – was set to make its grand debut.

✇✇✇✇✇✇

Dominance. The record of Dutch women's water polo in the international game embodied the word. Prior to the Sydney Olympics, nineteen FINA events for women had been contested, including the exhibitions at the 1978 and 1982 World Championships. The Netherlands collected medals nineteen times – including twelve trips to the top of the podium. The Dutch trophy case housed twelve gold, six silver, and one bronze medal. By comparison, Australia's twelve total medals and the United States' ten were the closest historical totals. Australia was second to Holland in titles, having struck gold at the 1984 World Cup, the 1986 World Championships, and the 1995 World Cup. The United States, Canada, Hungary, and Italy claimed the title of world's best team once each.

Adding European Championship hardware to the count, Holland's legendary medal haul increased; the Netherlands appeared on the podium at all eight editions of its continental championship prior to the Sydney Olympics. The Dutch won the first three titles awarded upon the tournament's inception, and four golds in all.

From 1988 to 1993, the Dutch won gold at an unprecedented five consecutive FINA events. After slipping to silver at the 1994 World Championships and the 1995 World Cup, they righted the ship and won three of the next four tournaments leading up to the first Olympic competition.

The Dutch women arrived in Sydney with one thing on their minds: adding a chapter of Olympic glory to their illustrious history.

The United States team had plenty of time to think about opening their Olympic campaign against this juggernaut. In head-to-head action in FINA events since 1978, the United States managed a record of one win, 15 losses, and two ties. The ties were each more than two decades old: one at the 1978 World Championships, the other a key factor in the United States winning the gold medal at the 1979 World Cup in Merced. The United States recorded its lone victory at the 1984 World Cup, played at Irvine's Woollett Aquatics Center, known at the time as Heritage Park.

Since joining the National Team in 1993, Gubba Sheehy experienced an 0-6 record against Holland in major competitions, with an average margin of loss slightly over three goals. But the United States scored two wins over the Dutch in 2000, one in February in Holland, the other at the Holiday Cup in July. Whether Holland played possum or not at Los Al, Sheehy's confidence against the powerful Dutch was at an all-time high.

"In the past, we always had to watch out for their counterattack because they were so fast," she said. "In 2000 our thinking kind of flipped. We're just as fast as them; we're just as strong as them. We can counterattack on them, beat them at their own game. Instead of us being afraid of their counterattack, I think they were afraid of ours."

The United States backed up Sheehy's bold declaration, storming out of the gate in the Olympic opener. Heather Moody made history as the first woman to score a goal in the Olympic Games for the United States when Coralie Simmons found her on the post for a six-on-five tally just over a minute into the game. After a defensive stop, the hours of tedious counterattack work throughout the dog days of summer at Los Al paid off; with Dutch defenders overcommitted to the hard-charging first line, Ericka Lorenz, open up top, slid forward, faked goalkeeper Karla Plugge into submission, and drilled the net. When the horn signaled the end of the first quarter, the United States held a 2-0 lead.

"The counterattack made all the difference in the world," Baker said. "We crushed them on the transition. Our counterattack was night-and-day different from the qualification tournament."

The second quarter was a swim meet for more than four minutes until Brenda Villa got on the board from long range, assisted by Maureen O'Toole. In a breakdown less egregious than the disaster in Winnipeg, the American defense miscommunicated on the Dutch after-goal play; the United States' lead was cut to 3-1 at halftime.

Holland shifted its counterattack into top gear in the third quarter. The sleeping giant awoke, twice scoring with breakaway speed down the right side. Danielle de Bruijn's second goal of the match pulled the Dutch even for the first time. But the United States answered minutes later; O'Toole took an entry pass from Swail, spun to her right, leaving her defender no options, and clinically finished past Plugge to the far post. The veteran O'Toole was officially in the scorebook; among the countless goals in her storied career, she had now scored one in the Olympic Games. The quarter ended with the United States possessing a 4-3 lead.

Built to wear down its opponent, the United States kept the pressure on as the fourth quarter began. When the team won possession on the sprint, Baker called timeout immediately to take advantage of a Dutch exclusion at the end of the third quarter. Although the power play elapsed, O'Toole earned another as Holland came to full strength; Lorenz rifled in her second goal of the game to push the lead back to two. Dominating time of possession through tip-outs and earned exclusions, the United States iced its Olympic debut when Robin Beauregard netted a power-play goal for a 6-3 advantage. A meaningless Dutch tally with six seconds remaining accounted for the final score of 6-4. The United States toppled its long-time nemesis to begin its Olympic journey.

"We set the whole tone with our attack, right from the first quarter," Baker said. "We controlled the whole game; we were stronger, faster, quicker, and more mentally prepared."

Fans of the Dutch machine surely waited, patiently at first, then later with more urgency, for their team to gain the upper hand over the Americans. Surely, the result would end in their favor. But the United States defense never allowed the Dutch to ignite a rally. And yet, like every team in the tournament, Holland was very much alive despite the setback; they only needed to put themselves in the top four to remain on track for a medal. Veterans filled the Dutch roster; their experience would pave the way over the coming days.

Meanwhile, the United States women sent a message to the field – they believed they would reach the podium.

"We showed the world that we had arrived," Villa said, "and we were ready to compete."

❧❧❧❧❧

Not only had the United States women arrived; the youngest player in the first women's Olympic tournament made an emphatic statement in the team's opening win over Holland, as well.

At 19 years, 210 days old, the United States' Ericka Lorenz was the only player under 20 years old in Sydney. Yet to play a college game at Cal, Lorenz had been on the Senior National Team since the beginning of the year – a grand total of of eight and a half months. Maureen O'Toole was almost exactly twenty years older than Lorenz; she debuted on the National Team *fourteen years before Lorenz was born.* Acknowledging her inexperience and youth, Guy Baker thrust Lorenz into the fray for one reason – her staggering athleticism represented the future of women's water polo in the United States.

Placed in the starting lineup for the Olympic opener against the Netherlands, Lorenz responded by sparking the team with two laser goals from the perimeter – the second of which put an end to a Dutch rally, giving the United States the lead for good.

Most of the Americans on the Sydney Olympic team swam as kids before turning their full attention to water polo. A handful played soccer; a couple spent time on the basketball court.

Lorenz – nicknamed "Monkey" by her teammates because of her penchant for climbing – lettered in five sports at Patrick Henry High School in San Diego. As a freshman, she made the boys' varsity water polo team in the fall before playing varsity basketball in the winter. That led into the spring, and her primary sport: softball.

Girls' water polo became an official sport in the CIF-San Diego section in Lorenz' sophomore year, freeing up her fall. A friend from the softball team suggested she join her on the volleyball team. Despite never playing volleyball before, Lorenz earned First-Team All-CIF honors twice in three seasons. Naturally, water polo honors rolled in as well; Lorenz was a two-time CIF Most Valuable Player and three-time All-American.

Lorenz' fifth varsity letter came in swimming, which conflicted with softball season in the spring. Without training, she participated in meets to qualify for the CIF Championships. As a senior, Lorenz helped Patrick Henry win the CIF team championship, swimming on two first-place relays; individually, she was a finalist in the sprint freestyle races.

On the softball field, Lorenz terrorized opponents' pitchers, named to the CIF First-Team three times, while capturing her school's Offensive MVP honors all four years of high school. Lorenz was the only girl who could hit the ball over the fence at Patrick Henry.

"I liked scoring points," Lorenz said. "That carried over in all my sports. I was very offensive-minded."

A little more than a year after graduating from Patrick Henry, Lorenz was playing in the Olympic Games in Sydney. And she brought her offense with her.

The baby of the family, Ericka Lorenz grew up with her older sister, Rhena, and her brother, Nathan. Closer in age to Nathan, the two hung out a lot.

"He beat the crap out of me," Lorenz said. "He's a big reason why I'm so tough and kind of stubborn. And very patient – a cat doesn't like to play with a dead mouse; I learned that very quickly."

Lorenz looked up to her parents – her dad a Navy officer, her mom a registered nurse – as great examples of good work ethic. The family was always active, spending plenty of time at the beach and on the water both water skiing and sailing. In a family of athletic individuals, the youngest Lorenz picked up skills such as skiing and riding a bike from watching.

"I've always been a big watch-and-learn person, so being around my family I had a lot of great examples of how to do things physically," she said. "I was a quiet kid; I would just sit back and watch and observe. I'd be like, *I could do that*, and then have a go at it."

Lorenz started playing organized sports when she was five and a half. Softball was her first love; for a long time, she assumed it would be her primary sport beyond high school. When Lorenz' mom put her brother in the summer swim league, Ericka followed him into the pool with her typical "I can do that" attitude. She also enjoyed basketball; its popularity and visibility excited her, especially the United States Dream Team at the 1992 Olympics.

Two-a-day swim workouts in seventh grade led to burnout; Lorenz gave up swimming at fourteen.

"I was really hardcore about swimming, but I wasn't so fast anymore," she said. "I kind of lost interest. Also, when you turn fourteen … teenagers are just weird. I just wasn't into it anymore."

Lorenz focused on softball. But something else piqued her interest. Her brother started playing water polo.

"Again, that was like, *Yeah, what's that? I could do that*," she said.

Lorenz immediately found a marriage between her swimming ability, hand-eye coordination, and throwing ability.

"Those skills made me a decent water polo player," she said. "I didn't know much about the game. I didn't really understand all the whistles. I would be offended when they blew the whistle for a foul. In basketball, getting a foul is kind of a big deal, so it was part of my learning process."

In her freshman year with the Patrick Henry boys, Lorenz' philosophy was: Swim fast, throw hard, and it'll get you through. Keep your head up and stay driven so you can figure out what's going on.

She made the varsity team, and was hooked. Water polo was the perfect combination of sports, one that catered to and promised to highlight Lorenz' abilities.

Before she played in the first women's Olympics, Ericka Lorenz played in the first sanctioned CIF Girls' Water Polo Championship in the San Diego Section. Patrick Henry competed that first season with only seven girls on its varsity.

"We would usually bring up some of the JV girls to be on the bench in case somebody got injured," she said. "But most of time, we played full iron-woman style. We played every minute of every game."

The Patriots' iron women navigated their way through the first CIF playoffs, meeting Coronado in the finals. Tied at the end of regulation, the teams still couldn't decide a champion in the two overtime periods. Double-teamed throughout the entire game, Lorenz won the sprint to begin the second period of sudden death.

"I was kind of at half tank and I was open," she said. "It was one of the first times during the whole game that I was that open."

Screaming for the ball at half pool, Lorenz received a pass and let a shot rip.

"It went in, and we won," she said. "That was the first shining moment in my water polo career – the biggest highlight up to that point."

While Lorenz and her Patrick Henry teams couldn't recreate that championship magic again, her water polo career was moving forward quickly. Encouraged by Brad Kreutzkamp, her first water polo coach, Lorenz went to Colorado Springs after her sophomore year to try out for the Youth National Team. Despite her accomplishments, she felt intimidated by girls with more playing experience. Kreutzkamp convinced her to take the next step.

"My junior high was grades seven through nine, but if you were in ninth grade, you got to participate in the high school sports," Lorenz said. "We would do morning weights for water polo before school at the high school, and then I would need to get driven to my junior high. Brad lived a quarter mile from my parents, so he would drive me to my junior high after weights, and we would talk. Actually, he would do most of the talking because I barely spoke when I was that age. He became a really cool mentor for me."

Lorenz took Kreutzkamp's advice; she earned a spot on the Youth National Team at Colorado Springs at age sixteen, and quickly made the move to the Junior National Team with Brent Bohlender the following year. During her senior year, Guy Baker invited Lorenz to train with the Senior Team during the week in the fall. She would hop into the carpool with Heather Moody, Rachel Scott, and Gubba Sheehy, and head to Los Al, where some Junior Team athletes filled out the Senior practice.

"Again, super intimidated," Lorenz admitted. "I'm playing against these girls that are on their athletic department's brochures. I'm like, *Wow, that's Coralie. Wow, that's Mo*. All these players that I'm aspiring to be like and I can model myself after. I'd show up to these practices and just be silent."

Lorenz continued to use the formula that worked since she started playing water polo against boys: Get

in, swim fast, throw hard. That'll be good.

"That experience was really valuable," she said. "It pushed me to be better. Just being at the Holiday Cup with the B Team getting to play against some international teams was awesome."

Lorenz recalled the meeting with Baker at the end of the 1999 Holiday Cup; the meeting that changed her water polo career. And her life.

"With Guy, every meeting that I sat in, it was always terrifying," she said. "Even if it was something good, something about being there with him was terrifying. Then he's asking me about moving down, putting school on hold, training to qualify, and then possibly going to the Olympics."

As if afraid Baker might take back the offer if she hesitated, Lorenz accepted immediately.

"It was like, *Let me think about it for a second – heck, yeah*," she said.

Water polo was all Lorenz wanted to do at the time; school was simply something that was allowing her to play. "School was great, but at the moment, my head and my heart were into playing water polo," she said. "It was a total no-brainer."

Lorenz was numb, unable to process what the opportunity meant or what it could turn into. Her coach at Cal, Peter Asch, was at Los Al for the Holiday Cup. Asch, an Olympic bronze-medalist, was one of the first people Lorenz shared the news with.

"He was really supportive," she said. "He told me, *You can't say no to that.*"

Lorenz was also grateful for the support she received from her parents.

"They have always been so supporting of whatever I choose to do," she said. "I'm so lucky for that. I'm sure there might have been some hesitation in their minds, especially my mom. She's always been really all for school and education. But I don't think I ever saw that at all, if there was any reservation about me moving down and leaving school."

Moving in with Coralie Simmons and Nicolle Payne as part of the Irvine crew, Lorenz was living her dream. With four years of water polo, and no college experience under her belt, Lorenz knew her learning curve needed to be steep.

"I never felt confident, like I had a spot on the team in the bag," she said. "I never ever felt that way, even later into my career. There's a tone that I set; that's how it was for me. It was day-to-day. Get through this practice. Get through the next practice. I was on a fast track, because in water polo, I relied heavily on my athletic ability and just working hard."

Lorenz knew she could rely on her teammates for support, and could bounce her thoughts off of them. She focused on controlling what she could control.

"It was about working hard, and showing up, and just trying to keep my eyes and ears open, soaking everything up because I had a lot to learn about water polo in general," Lorenz said. "It was pretty terrifying."

Having her Cal teammate, Heather Petri, going through the same experience was critical for Lorenz' well-being in the first weeks and months of training at Los Al. Petri was the sounding board Lorenz needed; she provided positive feedback that fostered feelings of confidence.

"With Guy, it's a lot of negative feedback and not a lot of praise," Lorenz said. "That's fine; I don't really need that. But it's nice to hear positives from a friend when you're going through a tough time."

Baker believes the addition of Lorenz and Petri also worked because of the support they received from the rest of the team, who had been through the full-time training routine the year before. A big part of the difficulty in 1999 was the fact that everyone was going through the experience for the first time – there were no veterans. In 2000, the team took the two newcomers under its collective wing, having been through it together the previous year.

By the time April and the Olympic Qualification Tournament rolled around, the four months at Los Al felt like a year to Lorenz.

"Time passes more slowly when you're younger anyway," she said. "I think it was such a big deal, and every day was a struggle. Every day it was like, 'God, I'm going to get yelled at. What am I going to do wrong?' I was stressed out every day. It was so gnarly. I was so new to all of it; so new to the sport and new to that type of schedule of training, that intensity."

Looking back at her teenage self, Lorenz recognizes that she was quiet, and not a great communicator.

"It was difficult," she said. "Everything was just through expression of movement. I just remember it being a really difficult time. It was a growing period."

While Lorenz didn't see much playing time at the Olympic Qualifying Tournament in Palermo, she was – as she had been since a child – observant. She marveled at how she was at the right place at the right time: a combination of hard work and opportunity.

"Up until that point, I hadn't really failed at anything," she said. "It's kind of weird to say, but I never played on a JV team. All I knew how to do was work hard, and I'd had the same results through my hard work. I figured, *Hey, if I do what I've always done, and I just work my ass off, things will happen for me*. That's just how my life had been. It wasn't until I was a little older, where life throws things at you, and you have to deal with different things, like getting cut or just failing at something. It was tough when I went back to school. It was like, *Wow, this new feeling, that's just life. I'm getting older and having more things to deal with*."

In Sydney, she was a 19-year-old. She worked hard, and she saw results. She was the new breed of American women's water polo player.

Swim fast. Throw hard.

That was more than enough for her opponents to deal with.

Maureen O'Toole and family – Sydney, September 2000

12

REVERSAL OF FORTUNES

2000 Olympic Games
USA versus Canada

Entering the Sydney Olympics, the goal of the United States women's water polo team was to reach the medal round. In the six-team, round-robin preliminary round, that meant winning two games would put the team in good position. While filled with experienced players, several of whom competed for Russia in the past, Kazakhstan ranked well below the rest of the field; they were expected to be in the playoff for fifth place, out of medal contention. In the eyes of many experts, there were five teams battling for four spots in the semifinals. The opening day victory over Holland wasn't just groundbreaking because of its rarity – the last United States triumph over the Netherlands was in 1984 – it was also a huge boost to the team's medal round mission.

In plotting a path to the top four places in the standings, Baker made the assumption that the team couldn't afford losses to both Canada and Russia;

it needed to collect points against one or the other, at a minimum. Beating the Netherlands put the United States ahead of schedule.

"That Netherlands game was the first we played in that whole time period I was with the team, whether at the Olympic Games or before, that we played phenomenal water polo," Baker said.

Next up in the gauntlet was Canada. In the time period from 1998 through the Sydney Olympics, no team had inflicted as much pain on the United States as their continental rival. Canada opened the tournament the previous day with a tie against Russia; a win at the United States' expense would be a pleasing result for head coach Daniel Berthelette and his squad. Canada led 6-5 at halftime, arousing no concerns from the United States' staff. But by the end of the third quarter, Canada was firmly in control of the match, ahead 8-5. Baker's objective at that point was clear.

"Going into that last quarter, to be honest, my thoughts were on goal difference," he said, referring to the potential tie-breaking criterion. "We've got to get this down; we cannot lose by three. We needed to get this closer."

The team had to win the quarter; falling further behind Canada would put the United States at a huge disadvantage should they find themselves needing a tiebreaker. And the bracket promised to be tight. A small voice in Baker's head reminded him that they had the two points from the win over Holland, but his major concern at the moment was closing the gap over the next seven minutes.

Still within striking distance, Baker wasn't upset at the quarter break. Up to that point, Canadian goalkeeper Josee Marsolais dazzled with a number of stellar saves; the United States was struggling to score. And the chippiness between the two teams was rising.

"It was a big lesson for us over the years as far as just play water polo," Baker said. "We always had a hard time playing water polo against them. We didn't have that problem against anybody else. We were always a completely different team against Canada. I guess you've got to give them credit, because they were the one team that could get us off our game."

The fourth quarter began; precious seconds, then minutes, disappeared with no progress made in slicing the deficit. With the defense holding tight, Heather

Moody finally broke through on the power-play with 1:50 on the clock to draw the United States to 8-6. Canada called timeout.

When the team gathered in the huddle, optimism abounded. They had been in this position plenty of times before.

Sometimes, it was in games against actual competition; far more frequently, the United States team played out this situation in front of zero spectators, just the fourteen American players, training at Los Al, on freezing winter days, or under the punishing summer sun, wracked with fatigue. They had practiced this scenario at full speed and full intensity enough times to know that a positive outcome was possible if they executed from this point through the final buzzer.

"We practiced the situation so often: down two with two minutes to go in the game," Baker said. "And we got it. Now this is Los Al; we were right back to Los Al. When we practiced situations, we practiced like it was a game. Now we're feeling pretty good about it."

On the ensuing Canadian possession, the United States got a defensive stop, and took control of the ball as the clock showed 1:30 remaining.

At the offensive end: Brenda Villa drew an exclusion in transition and passed to Robin Beauregard, who shot and scored immediately.

Down 8-7, 1:18 on the clock.

With 35-second possessions, Baker expected one more opportunity with the ball. The team lined up to play after-goal defense; needing a steal, the United States got one. Coralie Simmons crashing onto a post entry deflected the exit pass, and the ball changed hands as the game clock crossed the one minute mark. In what would surely be the United States' final full offensive possession, Maureen O'Toole secured position at center. Robin Beauregard delivered a long entry pass, and O'Toole turned and fired. Her shot sailed just wide of the right post with 43 seconds to go.

Before the ball was put into play, the referee's double whistle signaled an exclusion against Coralie Simmons. Canada was on the power-play, but opted to milk the clock rather than attack. They could use the entire shot clock and leave the United States only eight seconds with the ball.

When the game clock reached 23, Simmons re-entered from the penalty box. Canada passed the ball around the left side, between Cora Campbell at the wing, Marie Claude Deslieres out wide, and Waneek Horn-Miller at the point. With eight seconds remaining on the shot clock, Horn-Miller delivered to Deslieres. O'Toole swam to her briefly, but with six seconds on the shot clock, turned and swam toward the offensive end. Beauregard was also headed that direction, shadowed by Horn-Miller.

Deslieres, in possession of the ball, turned and looked twice at O'Toole swimming away. But instead of passing the ball and covering O'Toole, the Canadian took one dribble forward, and picked up the ball.

Then, a surprise.

Deslieres launched a lob shot toward the United States' goal with two seconds on the shot clock, 11 remaining in the game. The ball, taking a majestic arc, eluded the outstretched fingers of goalkeeper Nicolle Payne before solidly ricocheting off the crossbar as the game clock dipped to single digits.

The rebound landed right in front of Brenda Villa, who, from her defensive position, had watched O'Toole take off unguarded. Without hesitation, Villa scooped up the ball, spun, and fired a rope down-pool. The pass arrived in-stroke to the streaking O'Toole, four meters from the goal. Four seconds remained.

"I had the ball, wide open, one-on-nobody," said O'Toole. She remembers exactly what went through her mind in that moment.

Oh, my gosh, I want to take the screw shot.

The screw shot had been one of O'Toole's favorite weapons since Bob Gruniesson taught it to her on the JV team at Long Beach Wilson. When executed fluidly, a screw shot gave the goalkeeper no time to react, the ball seeming to leap off the water as the shooter swam. O'Toole was sure it would work.

"That was the bread and butter shot of my entire career," she continued. "But I can't take the screw shot because Guy doesn't like the screw shot."

What if I take the screw shot and I miss it? He's going to kill me.

"I never, ever thought like that as a player, but because Guy didn't like the screw shot, it made me think a little bit," O'Toole admitted. Her intelligence for the game, in addition to her athletic gifts, separated her from her peers since she first touched a water polo ball. The speed at which her mind raced through this shot selection debate – the considerations, the calculations – made time slow to a crawl. She looked to her right, at Beauregard, swimming even with her to the far post.

If I swim over closer to Robin, it'll give me a better angle. I can actually pick the ball up and slide left, slide across the goal, make the goalie move.

If O'Toole got there in time, the finish would be simple – a shot she had made thousands of times before. But the crafty O'Toole kept her options open. And she had always loved assisting her teammates as much as scoring goals.

"My hope was that Robin's defender left her," O'Toole said. "The goalie would be set on me; Robin would be wide open."

A quick check confirmed O'Toole's wish – Horn-Miller was stuck between the two Americans, therefore defending neither.

O'Toole picked up the ball. Josee Marsolais, the Canadian goalkeeper, rose up to prepare for her shot. But instead, O'Toole lofted a pass over Horn-Miller. Three seconds.

The right-handed Beauregard pulled her hips underneath her body, setting her legs to catch the spinning yellow sphere arriving from her left, across the front of her body.

Please don't drop it. Don't drop the ball.

Those words were flashing across Beauregard's brain, like a Broadway marquee, as she felt contact on her fingers. It was an action she repeated every day in practice, when passing with a partner, or in any mundane counterattack drill. But this was the Olympics. In front of 4,000 spectators. Time was running out. Two seconds.

Catch. One second.

Shoot. Goal. Buzzer. Zero point four.

The scoreboard showed the tie score. And 0.4 seconds remaining in the game.

The rally complete, the United States picked up a point when it seemed another loss to their rival was inevitable. Canada remained undefeated in Olympic play. But their first Olympic victory slipped through their fingers in agonizing fashion.

At the 1999 World Cup in Winnipeg, losses to the Netherlands and Canada set the direction of the United States program for the next sixteen months. While it was mostly the same individuals who experienced the success of the first two days of the Olympics, it was a different team.

"The physical and mental toughness still resonates with me," Baker said. "It took us over five minutes to score in the fourth quarter. We totally dominated and controlled the fourth quarter at both ends. There was no quit in the team."

Two days into the Olympic Games, the United States sat in second place in the standings, trailing the host Australians, the only team with a pair of wins. The ball was rolling; Russia was next.

☙☙☙☙☙☙

From the day Guy Baker was appointed head coach of the Women's National Team, he was adamant about one thing: there would be no token roster spot for six-time World MVP Maureen O'Toole.

Before the team assembled for the first time in May of 1998, an article ran in *USA Today*, profiling women's water polo as the newest women's Olympic team sport hoping to follow in the golden footsteps of softball, soccer, and ice hockey.

"It was essentially announcing our first training camp and that we were now an Olympic sport," Baker said of the article.

The only athlete quoted in the story was O'Toole. And one comment from the veteran and de facto team spokesperson pushed Baker's buttons.

> *O'Toole says her "best guess" is about six of the 13 players on the Perth roster could turn into Olympians.*

"In my meeting with her that first weekend, I agreed with her about that," Baker said. "But she was leading the pack of not being on the team. I told her, *Now that you've opened the door, let's talk about you.*"

Baker proceeded to launch into a stunned Maureen O'Toole: *You're too old. You're going to be 39 years old in the Olympics. You're past your prime. You're not going to be able to physically hang in there. You don't ever say something like that to the media, so you're off to a bad start with me. You don't ever speak on behalf of the team or say who's going to be on the team.*

Baker wasn't done. The message was clear: O'Toole wasn't going to be gifted a position.

Baker continued to drive home his point, telling O'Toole, "If you can make the team, you can be on the team. But you don't have a position, nor does anybody. We'll talk about that as a group when we come together. But you have to make the team."

Before O'Toole could get the first words of a response out of her mouth, Baker interrupted: "You can go. We're not having a discussion."

Maureen O'Toole's personal fan club in Sydney was seven strong; her mom, her brother and sister, her sister's husband and two kids, and her own eight-year-old daughter, Kelly. Janice O'Toole, Maureen's mother, found a house through a friend of a friend of a friend, nearly an hour and a half away from the Ryde venue by train.

Maureen's sister Colleen described to her the morning routine at the house as the clan prepared for each long day in Sydney. Getting Kelly's hair brushed against her will was an ordeal, followed by a predictable debate between grandmother and granddaughter about young Kelly's outfit.

Each day was a marathon, beginning with the train ride to the city. The United States women played several games late at night, resulting in returning to the house in the wee hours, before waking up early to repeat the routine the next day.

Staying so far away, the group would be in Sydney for the entire day upon their arrival each morning. In between games and tourist activities, they enjoyed a home base at the AT&T hospitality center for American athletes and their families and friends. Located at Darling Harbour, near the city center, the building was a wonderland to eight-year-old Kelly.

"As a child, the building was massive; four stories high of just *food*," she recalled. "It was a different flavor on every floor and at the top … dessert. Imagine how great that is for a kid. We'd go there every day and chow down."

Kelly remembers attending beach volleyball, watching Misty May-Treanor and Holly McPeak win a match on the sand.

"It was pretty cool to go to a different sport and see the difference between fans and players," she said.

The enthusiasm fans displayed for their countries stuck with Kelly at the time. Her favorite memory is of a Russian water polo fan, face painted like a clown in red, white, and blue.

One non-water polo-related highlight for the family occurred courtesy of O'Toole's luck. She won two tickets to the opening ceremony in a lottery amongst American athletes. Janice and Kelly got the initial nods to attend, but the group decided Kelly was too young and likely to fall asleep, so O'Toole's brother Mike took her place.

While her family had a blast during the Olympics, there was precious little time to visit with their hero who was doing her thing in the Games.

"I didn't get to really spend any time with them at all," O'Toole said. "After almost every game, I got drug tested, or was asked to do an interview."

Now that she was in Sydney with the Olympic team, O'Toole had the green light to speak to the media; she took the responsibility seriously. "I always wanted to do the interviews because I felt like it was really great for water polo," she said. "But that was pretty much our only family time, after each game."

The only mother on the team, O'Toole wished she could be with Kelly more often during the Olympics.

Mother and daughter did get to spend one afternoon together in the Olympic Village. Kelly loved seeing all the flags and the athletes dressed in their colorful outfits. But her favorite feature of the Village was the "magic token" her mom showed her. When using the special coin in any vending machine in the Village, the user received their beverage of choice, and the coin returned, for unlimited use.

"I remember showing that to Kelly, and she was like, 'Whoa, can I keep this? For when we get home?'" O'Toole laughed. "I told her I didn't think it was going to work that way. She was just enamored by that – she was walking all through the Olympic Village getting drinks."

After each game, even the briefest of hugs and hellos with Kelly and her family fan club energized the 39-year-old O'Toole.

As recently as a month before the team's departure for Sydney, energy was something she was in serious need of.

In the months leading up to the 2000 Olympics, Maureen O'Toole was more tired than she ever imagined possible. The physical and mental exertion she experienced over the two years in pursuit of her dream were taking their toll; in O'Toole's mind, it was going to be a struggle to the finish line.

"I remember thinking if there were two more months, I couldn't do this," she said. "I was at the end physically. Just completely depleted."

At night, she woke up nearly every hour, needing to go to the bathroom – a sign that her kidneys were working overtime due to the effects of her training. From the physical nature of play at the center position, and O'Toole's style of creating contact, the constant elbows to the chest caused chronic soreness in her left breast.

Living with her mom, Janice, during the summer before Sydney, O'Toole had serious doubts that she would have made it without the support she received.

"I came home every night from practice, and my mom would be out in the front of the house," O'Toole said. "She lived on the water. I'd tell her I was going upstairs to just rest; I'd never come down. She would wake me up and bring dinner to me. I wouldn't have eaten; I couldn't. I was too tired."

The household had a typical morning routine as well. Every morning, O'Toole arrived in the downstairs kitchen, "looking like death warmed over."

"Every morning, I would come down those stairs and make myself a smoothie," she said. "And it was hilarious, the interaction every day with my mom. She'd say, *You know, Maureen, you are just really tired. You should not go to practice today.* I'm like, *Mom, if I don't go to practice, I will not be on the team.*"

The conversation always continued, "Oh, he's not going to cut you."

"Mom, you have no idea," O'Toole would respond.

"Every morning, that was how it went," she said. "*You really shouldn't go to practice; you really need to rest.* Followed by, *Mom, I can't do that.*"

Feeling nauseated and sore every morning, and completely exhausted at all times, O'Toole held a secret fear to herself.

"I don't know if there's very many people in this world that have gone through what I went through at 39, as a high-level athlete; I was so exhausted that I felt sick every morning when I woke up," she said. "I was convinced I had cancer. I have breast cancer; I convinced myself. But I wasn't going to go to the doctor until the Olympics were over, because I was not going to miss the Olympics. I completely talked myself into believing I was dying of cancer, but I would go to the Olympics first."

O'Toole never told anybody how wrecked she felt. Her brother, Mike, knew because she lived with him in 1999; her mom pleaded with her every day to get rest.

"I can't even tell you how it felt, but it was really, really, bad," she said.

When O'Toole told her story and did motivational speeches after the Olympics, two questions most frequently arose.

Are you going to do the next Olympics?

"Okay, you really don't get it. Absolutely not. It's impossible."

How hard was it?

"It was like running a marathon, going home for two or three hours, and running another marathon, six days a week for three years. That's what it was like. I ran a marathon before, and honestly, I think that would've been easier than what we did."

Mental toughness was a necessity, helping O'Toole will herself to the Olympic Games. In the pool, she proved her worth on a consistent basis. Survival instincts kept her going.

"I was really strong mentally," she said, stating the obvious. "If I didn't have that, I wouldn't have made it, because physically, it was everything I could do to get through it – to constantly be proving to Guy that I was worthy of making that team. I could never cruise through a workout. I'd give it 110 percent every single practice because I'm thinking if I don't, it's going to give him a reason to cut me; that alone almost killed me, because I had to work so hard."

O'Toole acknowledged she could have worked smarter, not worked to that extreme, and felt a lot better at the age of 39.

"But I would've been sitting on the couch watching the Olympics on TV," she said. "I wouldn't have been there and been a part of it. It all works out; you figure it out. It's the ultimate mental task, that's for sure."

Playing in the Olympics fulfilled a dream for Maureen O'Toole. The nightmare of getting to Sydney was over, and it wasn't something she would ever repeat.

"I wouldn't wish it upon anybody to do that at 39 years old. It's not fun. There's no fun in that."

Day three of the Olympic tournament began with Holland asserting its strength, rallying past Australia in the fourth quarter to claim a 5-4 victory. Later in the evening, the United States became the only unbeaten team in the competition, downing Russia, 7-5.

With five points, the United States sat atop the standings with two games remaining in the preliminary round. In the matches against Canada and Russia – deemed by Guy Baker to be crucial to the team's chances of advancing to the medal round – it collected three points. With the United States favored to defeat Kazakhstan on the final day of bracket play, Baker felt optimistic about his team's chances of advancing.

Russia did not trigger the emotional reaction in the American team that Canada did; nor did they intimidate through a dominating head-to-head record, like the Dutch. Still, the United States needed no extra incentive against their opponent. The last time the teams met in a FINA event, each had just qualified for the Olympics. Russia handed the United States a 6-5 loss in the championship game of the Olympic Qualification Tournament in Palermo.

When the teams met at the Olympics, the Russians were responsible for the hot topic around town. The media, most of which found water polo a once-every-four-years curiosity, vigorously latched onto the happenings of the day before, when Australia downed Russia, 6-3. Despite the score, the Australians' win came at a cost – Russian defenders destroyed ten heavy-duty water polo suits that were promised by the manufacturer to be tear-proof. The Australian team was annoyed at the maulings it endured – the suits had a price tag of $100 apiece, and they had a limited supply for the entire Olympic tournament – but happy to record the victory. Newspaper and television reports were filled with references to exposure and images of the swimsuit carnage.

Against Russia, the United States played with good rhythm throughout; Baker felt the team was in control from start to finish in a well-played game. Maureen O'Toole notched her first multiple-goal game of the Olympics, netting a pair. The first came on the power-play, after O'Toole drew an exclusion at center. That goal put the United States ahead for good midway through the third quarter.

For good measure, she tacked on an insurance goal in the fourth quarter. Sprinting through the Russian defense on the counterattack, she spun to receive the ball from Coralie Simmons and swiveled back toward the goal; like a sniper, O'Toole picked out the perfect spot in the upper right corner.

After all the work it took to reach Sydney, O'Toole was making the Olympics her playground.

"I'll never forget what I had to do to get here. But now that I finally am here, it all seems worthwhile," she told reporters after the win over Russia.

A starter for the National Team for nearly two decades, O'Toole began the Olympics playing the role of substitute. The veteran warmed to the idea when she entered the games and found her opponents already fatigued. Baker discussed the strategy behind the decision to leave O'Toole out of the starting lineup.

"Coming off the bench didn't matter," said Baker. "The key was to make sure she was going to be there with us in the fourth quarter; she always played the fourth quarter. It was to keep her as strong as possible for the end of the game."

Baker acknowledged the impact O'Toole had on the team's successful start in Sydney.

"Mo played her best water polo during our whole time together at the Olympic Games," he said. "She was good on defense and great on the counterattack. She did a great job at the center position. Her awareness was fantastic. Mo was consistently very, very strong throughout."

Australia and the United States met at the Ryde Aquatic Leisure Centre once before. In June, the Americans were blown out of the water by their hosts. On the fourth day of the Olympics, with the United States atop the tournament standings, one point ahead of Australia, that result was long in the past.

Chants of *Aussie! Aussie! Aussie! Oi! Oi! Oi!* reverberated throughout the venue, as the crowd of 5,000 strong reveled in the matchup of historical rivals. Both sides could guarantee themselves a spot in the medal round with a victory. Confident in his team's ability to collect two points against Kazakhstan the next day, Guy Baker wasn't overly concerned with whom the United States might face in the semifinals, should they indeed qualify.

"When you look at who you're going to end up playing in the semis, it doesn't matter," he said. "There's no easy way out of this. Win or lose against Australia, win the group or don't win the group, it doesn't matter."

The coaching staff didn't worry about overly preparing the team tactically; the message was to just play a straight, basic game.

"We held everything," Baker said, referring to plays and tactics that the team would have used if its fate were on the line. "We had things that were set up and ready. There were things we did against them in June; I wanted to see if they would work against Australia, and when they did, we saved those things. We practiced all that stuff, but in this first game against Australia at the Olympics, no."

Since the day the schedule for Sydney was released, Baker prepared for a scenario in which the United States might have to beat Australia in Australia to advance to the medal round, or to win a medal.

"It might have been all hands on deck, so we prepared for that," he said. "But I felt good that we were in a position that we could just go out and play and see where we were against Australia."

Without talking to the team about it, Baker had already moved on to preparation for the semifinals the moment the Russia win ended. The United States played toe-to-toe with Australia, leading at halftime, 3-2. The home team blitzed the American net with three goals in the first 1:19 of the third quarter; Australia took a one-goal lead into the final seven minutes.

The opening minutes of the fourth quarter were scoreless, but the United States tied things at 6 when a steal by Maureen O'Toole led to a Brenda Villa goal at the midway point of the final quarter. The Australian crowd whipped itself into a frenzy when captain Bridgette Gusterson struck for the game winner on the ensuing possession.

"It wasn't a scrimmage – it's the Olympic Games," Baker said. "But we're already getting ready for the semifinals. We don't know who we're going to play, but physically, mentally, and preparation-wise, we're going to be in a good spot on that day. We're coming back the next day to play Kazakhstan, then we've got a day off to get stuff together. As soon as the Russia game was over, it was all about that semifinal game – just making sure everything's right when we get to that."

Riding the wave of enthusiasm their home crowd provided, the Australians moved to the top of the standings, securing their spot in the medal round.

Despite its first Olympic loss, the United States' level of intensity and will to compete had Guy Baker feeling pretty good. He left Ryde that afternoon thinking, "I can't wait to see them again."

On September 20, the United States did defeat Kazakhstan as expected. The surprise of the day happened just prior to their match, when Russia toppled Holland, 6-3. Combined with the first result of the day, which saw Australia topple Canada, Russia claimed the last spot in the semifinals. With its 9-6 victory over Kazakhstan, the United States claimed second place behind Australia, with Holland and Russia rounding out the medal hopefuls.

While not overly concerned about the outcome of the match with Kazakhstan, Courtney Johnson still dreaded facing the Asian continental qualifier. The pit in her stomach wasn't caused by fear of losing; it was the fear of losing her suit and potentially a layer or two of skin.

"To call Kazakhstan fierce would be an understatement," Johnson said.

She would find out first-hand.

Swimming on the counterattack, doing her best to elude the grasp of her defender, Johnson was late to see an opponent slow down in front of her, lying in wait. She saw a coiled up leg, then a foot aimed at her face. Johnson turned to preserve her nose; the blow landed squarely on her jaw.

Hearing a pop and feeling liquid draining through her ear, Johnson knew she had a busted ear drum. At the next stoppage, she signaled for a sub.

"Courtney was concussed, back before there were concussions," Guy Baker said facetiously. "She was wobbling, walking toward me."

At the time, FINA allowed three team officials on the bench; teams routinely allotted these spaces for a head coach and two assistants. Team doctors weren't given a place on the pool deck – the United States doctor sat in the spectator seating.

"She had to come down out of the stands; she's making her way through the crowd," Baker said. "Meanwhile, Courtney's wobbling, and I had to hold her."

The medical staff confirmed Johnson suffered a perforated eardrum and a separated jaw. She watched the rest of the game on closed circuit television from a hot tub behind the bleachers, away from the fray that continued all the way until the final buzzer.

After the game, Baker went through the post-game ritual of speaking to the media. He remembered this particular session because of the questions he faced regarding the physicality of the game, and of the sport.

"This was the first game where there's actually a lot of media," Baker said. "They're asking about suits ripping, and Courtney coming out woozy. They're asking, *What is this? This is brutal. Should women play this game?* You get a lot of random media people who show up at the Olympics. It wasn't a good presentation of water polo."

The 2000 Olympics were the only Games in the women's era in which the women's and men's tournaments were played separately – in each edition since Sydney, game days alternated by gender. The same format is used at the World Championships. But in Sydney, the women's tournament was played in the first week of the Olympics – the men opened play at Ryde on the day of the women's medal games, played at the Sydney International Aquatic Centre.

The spotlight was squarely on women's water polo during that week. Interest on the part of the media increased as the race to the medal round sorted itself out. The success of the Australian team captured the attention of the local and national media; the United States establishing itself as a medal threat gave all the more reason for coverage of women's water polo to spike.

Baker was disappointed that the largest media contingent to date witnessed an overabundance of physicality, rather than the fast-paced, flowing, skillful style that many of the women's matches displayed. He wondered if they would be coming back.

"Please come back in two days," was his plea.

The preliminary round complete, the United States accomplished its first goal – reaching the medal round.

Its reward for the achievement?

A rematch with Holland.

Ines, Rosario, and Brenda Villa – September 2000

13

BACK TO THE BEGINNING

2000 Olympic Games
USA versus Netherlands
Semifinal

Rosario Villa was nervous.

Not for her daughter, Brenda – or for the United States Women's Olympic Team. She and her husband Ines had never traveled so far from home. The discomfort of such travel wore off after a couple of days, replaced by excitement and pride as the spirit of the Sydney Games soaked into their bones.

Rosario and Ines had seen Brenda represent the United States many times in games in Southern California, near their home in Commerce. But Sydney was a first: the first time they traveled overseas to watch their daughter and her teammates take on the world.

Seeing Brenda perform filled Rosario with pride. She saw Brenda score goals. She saw the attention the women's team received. She saw people from all over the world admiring her daughter.

"She got the feeling of, my daughter is doing great things," Brenda said. "I think that kind of put it in her head what I was doing, and how good I was, finally. She'd always kind of known, but when other people start saying your daughter is doing so well … she understood, *Oh, she is*."

Brenda remembers vividly the image of her parents, natives of Mexico, waving the American flag at her games in Sydney. The vision struck her, having grown up watching soccer, always cheering for Mexico with her mother and father. For Rosario and Ines, seeing Brenda represent the United States was perfectly natural.

"My mom said it was never a thought to them," Brenda said. "She said, 'This is where you were born, this is what you're doing.' To me, that was interesting because in my head it was a bigger deal to me to see them wave the American flag. To them it was, *Of course, that's what our kids are*."

Representing the United States at the Olympic Games, Brenda Villa felt blessed to grow up in Commerce, learning the game she loved, supported by a community that loved her. Rosario and Ines made sure their children grew up in such a community. While other families came and went, moving on to find work or better opportunities, Rosario was adamant about staying in place.

"They wanted us to grow up in one neighborhood, put our roots somewhere," Brenda said.

Rosario would tell her daughter, "I'm glad that it ended up being in Commerce because maybe I knew all along this is where you needed to be."

The Villas are still there. The pool where Brenda began playing water polo is still there. Young girls still learn to love the sport there. Only its name is different.

It is now the Brenda Villa Aquatic Center.

෧෧෧෧෧෧

At the Ryde Aquatic Leisure Centre, it was back to the beginning for the United States and the Netherlands: a rematch of their Olympic opener six days before. Despite the United States' 6-4 win and its place above Holland in the preliminary round standings, history favored the Dutch.

Experience was on their side. Holland entered the Sydney Olympics with an average age of over twenty-eight – two full years older than the next teams,

Kazakhstan and Australia. The Americans averaged just under twenty-five years of age.

The World Cup title holders brought a streak of nineteen straight medals at FINA events, counting the two World Championship exhibitions in 1978 and 1982. The Dutch had never finished off the podium. A victory over the United States in the semifinal would extend the run to an even twenty events, and add Olympic hardware to the coffers.

But since falling victim to the enormousness of the moment at the World Cup in 1999, the United States had begun to push back against its longtime nemesis. A training camp in Holland in February of 2000 gave Guy Baker reason for optimism. Common training prior to the Holiday Cup produced positive results; then the United States defeated the Dutch in the Holiday Cup, and again to start its Olympic campaign.

If the pendulum had indeed swung, it was incredible timing for the United States and the worst possible scenario for Holland.

The United States' confidence swelled throughout the preliminary round. Even its one loss, a narrow defeat to Australia, provided a measure of hope. At the same time, the normally rock-steady Dutch began and ended the group stage with multi-goal losses, including a 6-3 loss to Russia to close out the preliminaries. Holland wasn't completely devoid of its dominant form – a victory over Australia tagged the host with its only loss of the opening round.

Still, every player on the United States team had experienced a career full of futility against the Dutch. Questions crept into some of their minds.

Heather Moody knew the team was prepared, but still wondered, *We beat them once; do we have it in us to do it again?*

The United States and Holland met in the second semifinal; the host nation awaited the winner in the first-ever women's gold medal match. At mid-day, the Australians rallied from a two-goal deficit with under five minutes to play to defeat Russia in the semifinals. The game-winning goal by captain Bridgette Gusterson hit the net with 40 seconds remaining, setting off an emotional celebration in the pool and in the spectator seats.

With a 7:15 p.m. opening sprint, the United States team had a morning loosen-up, then spent the day in the Olympic Village. Guy Baker watched the action of the first semi on the Olympic feed in the house in the Village. Unconcerned about the result, the athletes relaxed, took naps, and focused on their impending matchup with the Goliath of women's water polo.

The air was electric as the teams entered for introductions. Tension rose as the athletes hit the water, some spinning their arms to steady their nerves, others spending an extra long moment under the surface to clear their heads. The newest of the United States' starting lineup was the oldest of the squad. After serving as a substitute for the first four games of the tournament, Maureen O'Toole made her first start of the Olympics two days before against Kazakhstan. She would remain in the starting seven for the remainder of the tournament. There was no more strategy to saving the 39-year-old's energy – O'Toole was playing great water polo at the Olympic Games; the next two days would put an exclamation point on her unparalleled career.

When the first whistle sounded, it took only 22 seconds for O'Toole to make her presence known. Coralie Simmons won the sprint; two passes later, she delivered an entry pass to O'Toole posted up in front of the goal. O'Toole took a moment to collect the ball, shrugged off a brief grab of her head as she turned to face the net, and fired past Dutch goalkeeper Karla Plugge.

The United States was on the board.

Bernice Orwig easily collected the first Dutch shot, and the United States counterattack, the focus of countless hours of attention under the searing sun at Los Al in the summer, exploded down the pool. Orwig's outlet found Simmons, who led Robin Beauregard into the heart of the defense. As Dutch defenders collapsed toward Beauregard, she returned the favor from the end of the Canada game, setting up O'Toole. The legend cashed in, converting past the helpless Plugge.

The United States had come charging out of its corner and landed the first critical blows against the giant; after 55 seconds, the lead was 2-0.

"We came out great," Baker said. "If there was any thinking in their mind that they got the good matchup in the semis or they're happy with the matchup and this is going to be like it's always been, that was erased quickly."

But it didn't take long for Holland to respond. A bullet from the top off the arm of Danielle de Bruijn brought Dutch fans relief as it eluded Orwig's outstretched hand.

The explosive pace of the match continued. With three minutes left in the first quarter, Coralie Simmons struck for the United States. Simmons pump-faked twice from the right side, her shot rattling the far post before finding the goal. The Americans at Ryde rose as one, flags waving, chants raining down on the pool.

Karin Kuipers capitalized on a Brenda Villa exclusion 30 seconds before the quarter's end, powering in a shot to the lower left. The goal came at a crucial time; the quarter break served to settle the Dutch. Having weathered the United States' early flurry, the veteran squad sought to seize the momentum.

Holland broke the huddle and unleashed a furious second quarter; passing crisply, swarming on defense, and executing in the front court and on the power-play. De Bruijn pulled the Dutch even, and Marjan Op den Velde set off orange celebrations in the crowd when she vaulted the Netherlands to a two-goal lead with a pair of second quarter goals. The clinical effort turned the 3-1 first quarter deficit into a 5-3 advantage with just over a minute left in the period. The machine was rolling, primed to steamroll its way past the upstart United States, into the expected matchup with Australia for Olympic gold.

But the United States wouldn't submit. Simmons stopped the onslaught, scoring her second goal of the game with 57 seconds left in the half. When the horn sounded, the Dutch held a one-goal lead. After producing only one tally in the first half of their opening clash, Holland's offense was hitting on all cylinders in the semifinal, peppering the United States' net with five goals.

"Holland gave it to us in the second quarter," Baker said. "They established themselves."

As the teams lined up for the third quarter sprint, Bernice Orwig submerged herself beneath the water's surface. The American goalkeeper adjusted the red cap on her head.

She vowed to herself: *No more.*

Bernice Orwig was tested in the opening seconds of the third quarter; Karin Kuipers whipped off a backhand from the left side, but Orwig, rising confidently out of the water, smothered the attempt. A minute later, she received help from Heather Moody, who swatted away a power-play attempt from Kuipers.

The pace picked up; the United States counterattack produced a frenzy of whitewater. The payoff was an exclusion, drawn on the counterattack, converted quickly by Robin Beauregard from the right side for a 5-5 tie with four minutes left in the third frame. Held scoreless for over six minutes, the Dutch drew an exclusion in the final minute of the quarter. Their attack moved the American defense out of position; Carla Quint was open on the post. Receiving the pass from her right, Quint hesitated as Ellen Estes lunged to her body. Orwig started to rise, anticipating a shot; during Quint's brief delay, Orwig's legs churned to stop her downward momentum. Regaining balance, the American goalkeeper got her right arm into the ball's path just as it arrived – causing a deflection into the crossbar with 20 ticks remaining, preserving the tie.

When the team arrived at the huddle before the fourth quarter, the mantra was, "We've been here before."

And they had.

Their current situation mirrored the most critical win in program history, over Hungary at the Olympic Qualification Tournament almost six months before. That game went to the fourth quarter with the score exactly the same – a 5-5 tie.

"We're good," Baker said. "We have two timeouts; we've got our six players. If needed, they can go a full quarter. Timeouts or no timeouts, the team is in great shape."

The parallel to Palermo went off script briefly, as the United States lost the sprint to begin fourth quarter action; but as they did against Hungary to qualify for the Olympics, the team scored in its first opportunity. A long entry pass from Julie Swail to Maureen O'Toole in the post was deflected by the Dutch defender. An opportunistic Heather Moody, who beat her defender on a drive, picked up the loose ball and deposited it in the lower left-hand corner of the net.

Just like in Palermo, the go-ahead goal came early in the final frame. The United States was confident in its ability to play defense down the stretch – though keeping the ball out of Holland's possession entirely was the ultimate strategy. In the middle of the quarter, the Americans managed to do just that.

Following a Dutch exclusion, a second infraction was whistled as the first power-play ended. When Brenda Villa collected the rebound of a shot by Coralie Simmons, the United States bled more clock. In all, the American offense held the ball for 90 seconds of game time; with a stoppage to tie a cap and a United States timeout included, the Dutch went nearly four minutes of actual time without the ball. When they finally gained possession, less than four minutes remained in the contest.

Holland squandered its next offensive opportunity. In the transition to offense, Moody raced down the pool – like hitting a brick wall, she was stunned by a Dutch elbow. Subtle and swift, the elbow met its target. Moody spun around, away from the culprit, her face throbbing. Drifting backwards, creating space around her, she saw the ball arriving from teammate Swail. The referee's eyes were drawn to the blood, and play was halted. Floating on the ball, Moody made her way to the side of the pool with the assistance of Swail; all the while, referee Patrick Clémençon of France insistently signaled for Baker to make a substitution.

Courtney Johnson replaced Moody, and the action recommenced. Taken far behind the bench for medical attention, Moody heard the whistle restart play.

"All I wanted to do was watch the end," she said. "The doctor was trying to get something to stop the bleeding and mend the cut across my nose; I kept asking to be left alone so I could see the game."

In a compromise, Moody was moved to an angle with a view; the doctor continued her care.

Despite the deficit, the experienced Dutch were patient at the offensive end. But the long possessions came up empty, and the clock continued to wind down, to the United States' favor. With her team defending their slim lead and just over minute to play, Brenda Villa saw an opportunity. Leaving her player, she swam laterally to blindside Ingrid Leijendekker, making an apparent steal. A desperate Danielle de Bruijn won the ball back and fed Leijendekker streaking down the right side, open. Julie Swail sprinted after Leijendekker, making a critical spin to cut off her angle to the goal.

The near steal by Villa caught Beauregard and Johnson leaning toward the offensive counter. The split second of misguided momentum was costly. Maureen O'Toole found herself in a dire position, the single defender of two of Holland's most powerful shooters – six-time FINA gold medalist Karin Kuipers to her right out wide, and four-time gold medal winner Carla Quint to her left, dead center, four meters out. Leijendekker, the crafty Dutch playmaker, had her choice of targets after being fouled by Swail. O'Toole hedged, staying between the two. Beauregard charged at Quint as the ball was in the air.

It was too late.

Leijendekker's perfect delivery settled on Quint's right hand. Without hesitation, the veteran fired to her left as the clock showed one minute exactly.

Positioning herself perfectly after the foul to Leijendekker, Bernice Orwig locked her eyes on Quint. Before it was released, she uncoiled and lunged, legs thrusting her body with explosive force toward the yellow sphere. Right arm fully extended, Orwig knocked the ball harmlessly to the water. She had vowed to allow nothing into her net in the second half. She and her teammates would have to thwart one more Dutch attack to make good on that promise.

With chants of *U-S-A! U-S-A!* echoing throughout the building, the United States swam to offense, protecting against an all-out press. The Dutch tactic worked; a steal with 27 seconds left and a timeout brought Holland into the attacking zone one last time. In its final attempt, the Dutch looked to feed Kuipers in the post, while precious seconds drained off the clock. On a second entry to Kuipers, O'Toole crashed back, swiping the ball away; the final buzzer sounded with the ball in O'Toole's possession, her right fist raised high in the air in celebration.

Maureen O'Toole and the United States women's water polo team had just won an Olympic medal.

Guy Baker has a way of looking at water polo, and the difference between winning and losing.

"A great thing about our sport – if you win by a goal, you have kicked the other team's ass," he said. "We won by the smallest of margins, but we were better than them in every aspect because of that one goal. That's the way it goes."

The team that celebrated its trip to the Olympic gold medal game that night was seasoned – veterans of the heartbreak of Winnipeg and the intensity of Palermo. The road to Sydney was full of pain, disappointment, fatigue – and sometimes doubt. But Baker marveled at the team's ability to remain in the moment, taking experience from past games or training, and performing their best at the most important times.

When asked why the team was so good at execution under stress, Baker didn't hesitate.

"Because we had to be," he said. "I don't think we were the most talented team. I don't think we were more talented than Australia, or more talented than Holland – physically talented, ability-wise. I hate that word, talent. I'm old school – talent is the most overrated thing at that level because everybody's good.

"Ability-wise, the Netherlands – they're big, fast, can shoot – all of it. Who do you guard? How do you match up? They're active, posting up. They had the best counterattack during that time. They were loaded."

The flow of the game demonstrated the growth of the team from the beginning of its Olympic pursuit to its crashing of the medal round in Sydney.

"We had to have a good start," Baker said. "We were in that frame of mind, and we did have a good start. The third quarter was key, because they kicked our ass in the second quarter. They might have thought it was going to start moving that way, and we've done the best we could – we gave a good show, thank you for coming. But it wasn't like Winnipeg where we were already way behind, so we came back."

The comeback wouldn't be possible without the team's deep-rooted identity – defense. The United States held the Netherlands scoreless over the final fifteen minutes of play; Bernice Orwig recorded the second-half shutout she pledged to herself.

"We spent months, years, so many hours on defense. Just defense," Baker said. "That second half is what we were and who we were."

They were Olympic medalists.

Almost a quarter-century before, in the summer of 1976, the United States and Australia faced off against one another for the first time.

On September 23, 2000, they would clash again; this time with Olympic gold on the line, in the most important match in women's water polo history.

Sydney Olympics gold medal game – September 23, 2000

14

STRENGTH OF THE CIRCLE

2000 Olympic Games
USA versus Australia
Gold medal game

At fifteen years old, less than a year after picking up a water polo ball for the first time, Simone Hankin made her debut with the Australian Women's National Team at the 1989 World Cup. Growing up with three brothers in Sydney, she played sports in the street in the afternoons – always throwing and kicking a ball with the boys. And like a majority of Australian children, Hankin loved to swim.

"I always wanted to play a sport at a high level, but I was really young when I went on that tour," she said. "I was fifteen; the next girl was twenty-one. It was a really big generation gap."

A typical week for Hankin at that age included going from age group trainings to girls' club trainings, then topping that off with the men's first grade training at her club, Cronulla. The men's sessions featured multiple Olympians, including current representatives of the Australian National Team. Clearly able to hold her own, she was invited back more and more.

Playing against the bigger and more physical men proved perfect for Hankin's development as a center and center defender. Herself a big and strong athlete at age fifteen, Hankin often overpowered female opponents, including those older than she.

"Certainly training alongside the men allowed me to maintain that size and capacity in the water," she said. "That was a really critical part of my training, because of the decentralized nature of our sport at the time. It was really important to my preparation for any national selection."

A wide-eyed rookie at her first World Cup in Eindhoven, Holland, Hankin recalled her first matchup with Maureen O'Toole and the United States team.

"Maureen was the player, and we had the other player, Debbie Watson," she said. "Maureen was a bit scary to me when I was fifteen, even though I was probably up to fifteen kilos heavier and a little bit taller than her. Her capability was huge at that time, and through the 90s. She was the player to be wary about and worried about and she had an impact in every single game we played against the U.S. There were some pretty big clashes there."

None with the ramifications of the clash that would occur on that late-September evening in Sydney.

By the time the matchup was set, both the United States and Australian women's teams had been through the labyrinth that is the Olympic experience. For one team, the pressure to qualify; for the other, the pressure to perform at home. The emotions of being part of the spectacle, and the responsibility of being the first to represent women's water polo. The competition, the spotlight, the desperation of trailing in the semifinals, and the ecstasy of advancing to the ultimate moment in their sport.

It was the dream matchup.

"All of a sudden it became like we've been world beaters for the whole time," said Guy Baker. "This is what everybody wanted. This is definitely what NBC wanted, for us to play Australia for gold."

As for the players – they knew each other; they were friends with each other.

"I like all those girls," said Gubba Sheehy. "When we were training with them, that was our favorite team to play against because I felt like they weren't dirty. They just played hard just like we did."

Hankin felt the same way about the United States team.

"They were an awesome group of girls," she said. "The whole way through my career, from the late 80s to 2000, we always had a heap of fun. What I really respected was, as soon as we hit the water we had some really, if you could call it, positive aggression. We never really disliked each other as competitors either. We'd certainly had some very physical battles all the time. There were some teams, some people that you got a real distaste for. It was typically because they were rough or they used bad sportsmanship as part of their play. I never felt like that against the Yanks. We never ever felt that way."

Hankin spoke of a mutual relationship the teams developed: a healthy respect that allowed for social interaction.

"We'd come across them in the same hotel at tournaments and really enjoy that out of the water thing," she said. "The rivalry in the water was certainly really fantastic. We'd developed some really strong relationships outside of the water, and we'd had some great times celebrating their success and our success in the lead up.

"I always felt that we were going to have a really big battle against the Americans," she continued. "That's probably down to the day that we played them in that game."

The journey to the Olympic gold medal game held similarities for the two programs, long before the world arrived in Sydney.

Things changed for Australian women's water polo on the day it gained inclusion in the Olympic Games. Funding increases included a six-month centralized training program in Kawana Waters on the Sunshine Coast in the summer of 2000. The team was happy to be far from the cold weather of Canberra, site of the Australian Institute of Sport, with all the other Australian sport teams.

"They were all down there, and we were up on the Sunshine Coast in Queensland," said Hankin, reasserting how pleased the team was with its coastal locale. "But we went through some pretty tough times from a team-building perspective up there."

The athletes were accustomed to spending weeks on tour together; living together for six months proved to be an entirely different experience. Liz Weekes, a goalkeeper on the Australian team, commented on the change from a decentralized program to a residential setup – a change similar to what the United States team experienced post-Olympics announcement.

"It's like going to work," she said. "When we went into full camp in Queensland in the summer, we had no family, nothing. No one had anyone around us. To be honest, that part wasn't really enjoyable. Now when I look back at it, I wish it was."

Many of the Australian players agree that the Olympic Team selection was the toughest time in Kawana Waters. Just weeks before moving out of Kawana and down to the Olympic Village, coach Istvan Gorgenyi announced the final roster of thirteen athletes to be the first Australian women's water polo Olympians. One thing the players appreciated was having a say in how Gorgenyi broke the news.

"Typically, water polo cuts were announced through the media," said Hankin. "Or the coach would stand up and say, 'It's you, you, you and you on this tour. The rest of you, thanks for coming along, but you're out.' It could be a really awkward situation. Sometimes, your absolute best friend in the team was not getting selected, and you have been, so you want to be really excited, but you also want to lend support. There's a certain amount of sympathy and empathy, and it's hard to split those two things and then combine as the final group who was selected."

The players made a request to Gorgenyi. They would all be in their apartments, where they had lived throughout the final training camp. While roommates might receive opposite news, the proposal aimed to preserve privacy, avoiding an announcement to the larger group. Each player received an envelope under the door with their name on it.

After suffering a severe wrist injury, Hankin's roommate departed Kawana Waters, leaving her Olympic dream behind.

"My mom came up and stayed with me for that period, so she was with me when I received my envelope," said Hankin. "My envelope arrived under the door, and she and I pondered on who would open it and who would read it."

Simone Hankin read the letter.

"We sat next to each other," she said. "We read it and had a bit of a tear and a hug."

Thrilled and relieved for her own journey to continue to Sydney, Hankin didn't know which teammates would be joining her. The letter instructed her to attend a meeting of the Australian Olympic water polo team.

"Part of what we requested was for the non-selected athletes to have a chance to meet with Istvan and the coaches, if they chose," she said. "They could schedule a time that was appropriate for them, when they felt they could face him and talk to him."

The process was designed to ensure that there were no awkward feelings when the team met for the first time.

"It was about a celebration," Hankin recalled. "Thankfully, the first people I saw were the nucleus of us, who had been together for about seven years. That top-end group had been together for all of that journey, all of that fight. That was really nice just to see them. Deb Watson's face, and a few of the others; it was really great."

Almost exactly a month later, the Australian team stormed through the preliminary round of the Olympic tournament, finishing atop the standings while losing only to the powerhouse Dutch. Urged on by their adoring fans in green and yellow wigs, the team dug deep to rally past Russia in the semifinals, fulfilling its mission of reaching the gold medal game.

As they did in Honolulu twenty-four years before, the women's water polo teams from Australia and the United States were poised to make history.

@@@@@@

When Maureen O'Toole snatched the ball from Karin Kuipers, and the final buzzer sounded on the semifinal match, the United States celebration began both in the water and on the pool deck. Eventually, the team surrounded Heather Moody, whose broken nose hurt less and less as joy swept over her body.

The United States women were going to leave Sydney with hardware – the color of which was yet to be determined.

"It's crazy at that moment, knowing you've won a medal," said Guy Baker. "The whole focus was just to leave with something. That was going to be the ultimate; now we're leaving with something automatically."

The final matchup was set; the post-game press conference overflowed with media interested in the United States team. NBC people grabbed Baker, expressing their enthusiasm for the made-for-TV event. Baker sensed the energy in their voices, a sign that momentum and interest was peaking.

As always, the team met back at the Olympic Village to talk about the game and preview their next day.

"We said the rest of the world might be shocked at what's going to happen the next night, but I don't think anyone in the room was going to be shocked at what was going to happen. We were fully confident going in – fully confident by that point in time. We were definitely looking forward to it."

With the swimming competition concluding in a finals-only morning session, the pool at the Sydney International Aquatics Centre in Homebush Bay was converted for the women's water polo medal games in the evening. In the early afternoon, the United States team bused to the new venue for its hour-long practice time.

The practice itself was just a warm-up, just to get a feel for the water. Both athletes and coaches felt fortunate to have the opportunity at Homebush. Compared to the cozy confines of Ryde, the swim stadium felt cavernous; even the difference between the eight-lane wide Ryde pool and the ten-lane Sydney International Swim Centre presented a visual difference. With the pool to themselves, players shot at both ends, and familiarized themselves with the clocks and the sightlines.

"That pool time was a chance to get everybody focused back on us," Baker said. "It's about us. It's Los Al and Los Al Style. It's water. Let's get back to what our work is. Visually, take it all in, so that when you come back tonight, you've been there, done that."

The staff also used the return to Homebush to complete an exercise that commenced before the Olympic tournament began. At their venue in Ryde, assistant coach Chris Duplanty gathered everyone in a circle.

"Dup said a lot of powerful things to us in the circle, and it was the strength of the circle that got adopted," said Baker. The tradition of joining in a circle before the start of each Olympic Games carried on through London 2012.

"Nothing is stronger than your circle; that started at the Sydney Olympics."

When the United States team arrived at Homebush for practice before the final, the circle was complete. The emotion of the triumph the night before was put in the past; the circle brought everyone back together in the moment. The players splashed around in the water where they would fulfill a dream later that night. It was their last practice together as the first Women's Olympic Team.

"It's the best practice because all that's left is playing for the gold medal," Baker said. "It's an honor to be in that practice."

For the first week of the Olympic Games, the Sydney International Aquatic Centre was the epicenter of Australian nationalism, even as the world's largest sporting event was taking place in venues spread all across the Eastern city. The first night alone nearly blew the lid off of the joint: hometown hero Ian Thorpe opened the action by crushing his own world record in the 400-meter freestyle, leaving the entire field in his wake. By the end of the night, the in-pool rivalry between Australia and the United States erupted. Motivated by Gary Hall, Jr.'s comment a month earlier that the United States would "smash [the Australians] like guitars," the team of Michael Klim, Chris Fydler, Ashley Callus, and Thorpe set out to strip the United States of the Olympic title in the race it dominated more than any other in Olympic history – the 4x100 freestyle relay.

Klim set the tone, dropping a world record 48.18 leadoff split. The United States' Neil Walker briefly took the lead as he and Fydler headed home, but Fydler touched first at 1:36.66; ahead of world record pace by 1.77 seconds. Again, the Americans edged ahead, as Jason Lezak held a slim advantage over Callus; but by the time they reached the end of their leg, it was Callus who turned over a slim edge to Thorpe.

Thorpe and Hall, Jr. hit the water nearly simultaneously; quickly it was the American pulling ahead. Hall, Jr. still led at the turn, and was the clear leader when the two emerged for the final lap; but Thorpe's long strokes and legendary propulsion generated by his fin-sized feet mesmerized the crowd, whose deafening roar rose to one howling boom. In the last fifteen meters, Thorpe made his move, racing past his opponent. When Thorpe hit the wall, time briefly froze, as if every person paused to double-check their eyes – Australia, gold; United States, silver. The Australians lowered the world record by nearly a second-and-a-half, handing the Americans their first-ever loss in the race at an Olympic Games. Celebrating on deck in response to Hall, Jr.'s pre-Olympic quip, the Australian quartet played air guitar much to the delight of their screaming countrymen and women.

On the day of the women's water polo final, the swimming competition at Homebush wrapped up with the final four events of the meet. Australian and American swimmers won three gold medals and eight medals overall during the session. The hometown crowd was treated to a 1-2 finish by distance legends Grant Hackett and Kieren Perkins in the men's 1500. American Chris Thompson won bronze. In the women's 50 freestyle, Dutch sprint star Inge de Bruijn captured gold, with the United States' Dara Torres finishing third.

The United States set new world records en route to gold in the afternoon's two team races, the men's and women's 400 medley relays. Australia captured silver in both.

The podium at Homebush saw a parade of American and Australian medal winners during the day. At night, the United States and Australia would grace the gold and silver platforms – who stood higher would be the ending to a long-running drama, waiting to unfold.

While the Netherlands and Russia battled for the bronze, Guy Baker drank coffee with Chris Duplanty in a coaches' lounge at deck level. Watching the game on a nearby monitor, Baker figured he'd go out and see the environment for himself. He couldn't get all the way to the pool deck, but he got close enough to be stunned at what he saw.

"I think it was good I did that. It was massive," he said.

The seating behind him was primarily for media and officials – across from where he stood sat a majority of the 17,000 spectators, all on one side, seats rising up so high that darkness enveloped the furthest reaches.

Baker retreated back into the lounge, catching the final moments of Russia's victory over Holland on a television monitor. The Dutch, having never finished off the podium at a FINA event in nineteen attempts, were leaving Sydney empty-handed. Russia and the United States, both unlikely participants, overcoming the odds at the Olympic Qualification Tournament only months before, would share the spotlight at the medal ceremony.

Maureen O'Toole watched on a big screen as the team stretched near the warm-up pool.

"I remember thinking how it was pretty amazing that Holland lost to Russia, not even getting a medal after all of their successes," she said.

As she prepared herself mentally, O'Toole mulled over the matchup Baker assigned her. Earlier in the day, when the team met in the driveway of their house at the Olympic Village, there was only one matchup O'Toole dreaded – Simone Hankin.

"She was super fast and big and strong, and my whole M.O. was, I'm going to wear you down, and then in the fourth quarter I'm going to beat you. She wasn't one of those people I could do that with," O'Toole said. "I'm thinking, 'Please don't give me Simone. Anybody but her.' And then Guy says I'm matched up with Simone."

In her head, O'Toole thought, *Ugh, great.*

Hankin had the ability to post up, and did so often. O'Toole knew that she would be both defending and playing center throughout the evening. Her final game in a USA cap promised to be both physically and emotionally challenging.

When warm-ups came to an end, officials escorted the athletes back to the locker room, then hustled them into a waiting room. With not much more than an aisle-width of separation, each player sat in a chair across from her opponent of the same cap number. Seated shoulder-to-shoulder with teammates, the teams stared at each other. Emotions in the tiny room were wide-ranging: intensity, excitement, nervousness, anxiety, and pride all mixed together as the minutes slowly passed. The relationship between the two teams allowed for familiarity to take a small edge off the mood.

"We were friends with the Aussies, so it was awesome," said O'Toole. "We couldn't have picked a better team to be playing against in the gold medal game. They appreciated what they had; we appreciated what we had, and we were both just like, 'Is this amazing? We're in the gold medal game of the first Olympics ever.'"

The memory of the waiting room in Sydney is still fresh to Brenda Villa, who eventually played in three Olympic finals.

"Sitting there, it was pretty quiet," she said. "You almost wish that there could have been some sort of organic moment where we all just acknowledged how cool that was, the first Olympic final. But we were just so into our own game plans, our own things, that it wouldn't have come to mind."

When a woman brought a sign announcing a five-minute countdown, the anticipation heightened; the players laughed nervously with each other.

"That was really cool, because it would've been such a different experience if we were playing Holland or Russia, because we were friends with the Aussies," O'Toole said.

In Simone Hankin's mind, the teams were evenly matched; the only advantage she gave to her side was the mental aspect of playing at home. In the call room, her green robe on, across from the United States' Coralie Simmons, Hankin felt tense. She flicked her hands out of nervousness, attempting to slow the adrenaline that coursed through her body, practically dripping out of her fingertips. She flicked Bronwyn Mayer, her teammate to the left; Mayer nudged Hankin back, as she tried to simultaneously release energy and nerves.

"There was this push and pull all the way along the line," Hankin said. "It started off this funny little push and pull by each player."

To settle it down, Hankin shouted: *Come on! Our place, our home, our house. No one beats us here!*

"We all took a deep breath and became quite robotic, which was unusual for us because we're quite an emotional group," Hankin said.

The pleasantries were over. Friends or not, the time to crown an Olympic champion was near.

"From the time we put our caps on, from the time we put our cossies on, we were real opponents," Hankin said.

And then it was time.

From the moment they arrived at the venue as the bronze medal match took place, the athletes from Australia and the United States had been escorted around the competition pool – from the locker room to the warm-up pool, back to the locker room, and on to the call room. They heard the noise; but they hadn't yet had a full look at the crowd.

The athletes exited from a hallway underneath the media side of the arena onto the pool deck, Australia first, followed by the United States. As each woman stepped out of the shadows and into the brightly lit venue, the view opened up in front of her.

"All the fans were on that other side, and it was like, 'Oh, my God,'" said Maureen O'Toole. "It was incredible, the sea of people."

O'Toole marched behind Coralie Simmons, who often provided just the right amount of chat or humor before the most tense games. As they walked around the perimeter of the competition pool to get to the spectator side for presentations, O'Toole joked to Simmons, "This would be incredible if I saw Kelly."

O'Toole laughed at the absurdity; the scene in the seats was chaotic. Australian fans in yellow and green afro wigs screamed; green flags emblazoned with the boxing kangaroo waved, and in one area, too far to see faces, were American flags and a smattering of red, white, and blue.

But when they reached the corner of the pool and made a left turn to step onto the referees' walk for introductions, O'Toole's saw her eight-year-old daughter. American flags painted on her cheeks, and red and blue ribbons in her hair, Kelly Mendoza was draped over the railing, waving to her mom. NBC producers had brought O'Toole's family to the front row.

O'Toole's heart leapt with joy. She told Simmons, "Look, Kelly's right there."

"I was dying. That was just so cool." O'Toole said.

A huge smile on her face, O'Toole thought to herself, *I don't even need to play this game.*

Brenda Villa searched for her parents as she walked toward the sea of spectators. The chants of *Aussies! Aussies!* grew louder as the home team approached the referee platform, completely drowning out the music on the public address system. Walking toward the overwhelming noise, Villa failed in her search for her family. But she did see one familiar face: Stan Sprague's.

The man who coached the first National Team game, against Australia, in Honolulu in 1976. The National Team coach at the Commerce Internationals in

1977, and the World Championships in Berlin in 1978. More than two decades later, Sprague was in attendance to see the United States and Australia face off for Olympic gold.

By 2000, Sprague and his wife, Mary, were known by hundreds of families and players who competed in the Southern Pacific Association age group fall league. Started in the 1970s, it began with swim teams fielding water polo programs in the fall months.

Sprague ran the league with a hands-on mindset. He knew all the coaches – he watched players begin as 10-and-unders, move on to the 12-and-under division, and eventually play high school water polo. Countless players from the SPA league starred in college. And a select few, many of whom showed uncommon talent as youths, reached the Olympic Games.

From the first time he saw Villa play, Sprague knew she was special. Not only as a player, but as a young person full of personality.

"We had a great relationship from the very first time I met Brenda," Sprague said. "I would give her a hard time, and this little 10-year-old would give it right back to me."

Villa remembers those days, and the friendly banter the two shared.

"He was always there and always so nice to me," she said. "He's someone that I've always had a soft spot for."

As she continued to walk behind Ericka Lorenz onto the raised platform, Villa drank in the sight of what is still the largest women's water polo crowd of all time.

"I always look in the stands," she said. "It's not like I'm not focused, but it's the last time you're really going to focus on who's in the stands and where they are. Because once the whistle blows, you're just all about water polo. So I like to take those moments just to look around and see, do I see anybody I know. It was crazy. 17,000 people, and I find Stan Sprague in the stands."

Including Villa, seven Americans and four Australians who lined up for introductions weren't yet born when the two teams met for the first time in Honolulu. Maureen O'Toole didn't play in that game, but her first clash with Australia took place twenty-three years prior. At the time, she couldn't have imagined the long journey ahead or the historic setting that would mark her final test against a longtime rival.

Pat Jones, the woman who arranged the inaugural tour for the Australian National Team, and who put the fight for recognition of women's water polo in front of the media at every opportunity, was one of the 17,000 that night. So were Americans Rich Foster and Bruce Wigo, who together championed the women's game, developing the video, "Now is the Time," urging those in power to include women's water polo in the Olympic Games. Leanne Barnes was there – the woman who twenty years earlier had to explain that there was no decision to be made regarding a boycott of the Moscow Olympics because there was no women's water polo in the Games. Barnes sat next to John Howard, the Australian Prime Minister, with a basket of roses sprayed gold tucked neatly under her seat.

Standing in line for introductions, Simone Hankin bounced her shoulders up and down. To her left, Yvette Higgins and Liz Weekes clenched hands. Across from the referees – Renato Dani of Italy and Vladimir Prikhodko from Kazakhstan – the American captain, Julie Swail smiled broadly. Ericka Lorenz stood motionless, eyes facing down, while Maureen O'Toole twitched her shoulders and grinned with joy. At the far end of the American lineup, Gubba Sheehy gave taps to Nicolle Payne to her right and Courtney Johnson to her left.

The crowd cheered and clapped in rhythm to the announcement of each player's name; when introductions were complete, the teams walked to their respective bench areas, huddling for final words of inspiration. The crowd roared as the thirteen Australian women stood at the pool's edge. It erupted when they dove into the pool in unison. At the other end, the United States team circled up in the water for a cheer, after which the starting seven remained to warm up in the water. The continuous buzz of the crowd spiked when the announcer gave a one-minute warning. The teams lined up, and the Italian referee stood at center pool, ready to signal the opening of the match.

Guy Baker remembers the noise, but also the way the United States team overcame any communication issues simply through the connections they had build over their time together.

"The cool thing about sports is you can be in an environment you've never been ever in your life, with that many people, but how connected you can be to everybody in your circle," he said. "I never felt communication was an issue – never felt like we wouldn't be heard, or we wouldn't talk. The team did a good job of talking."

The chants of *Aussie! Aussie! Aussie! Oi! Oi! Oi!* boomed throughout the arena. Baker had a saying that the players knew well: *Listen for the silence.* Its message was aimed at playing a road game, in front of loud and enthusiastic hometown supporters. *Play our game, fulfill your role, and silence the home crowd.*

"I think it would have been impossible to silence the crowd," Baker said. "But it would have been nice to try."

When the whistle sounded, the crowd screamed as one as Coralie Simmons and Melissa Mills streaked down the center of the pool. As the sprinters approached, the donut disappeared, leaving the ball floating for Mills to cleanly snare. The arena erupted. Every Australian in the building, whether they had ever seen a water polo game or not, knew that it was good. The first attack belonged to Australia.

Within seconds of the opening sprint, the matchup between Maureen O'Toole and Simone Hankin commenced. Hankin immediately posted up at the center position, O'Toole pushing against the wide shoulders of her adversary. Working the ball around the perimeter, Hankin's teammates couldn't find the right angle for an entry pass. Taryn Woods launched the first shot of the game; the crowd gasped as it sailed to the left of Bernice Orwig and out of play. The United States' counterattack raced down the pool.

From the backcourt, the savvy O'Toole gained an advantage over Hankin; crossing mid-pool, the American opened up a full body-length lead, making a beeline for the left post. Coralie Simmons drew a foul on the perimeter and immediately found O'Toole, on her back, wide open, three meters out. O'Toole received the pass cleanly, spun, and fired to her right. The fully-extended left hand of Liz Weekes deflected the ball out of bounds. It was the first sign of the focus Weekes would bring to the final.

O'Toole remembers the shot, and the advice from assistant coach Chris Duplanty that prompted her to put it there.

"Right before the game, Chris had said to go right," O'Toole said. "Not a donut, but between her head and her shoulders; she was really vulnerable there. I did that and she blocked it. Normally, I would've skipped it, or shot it right over her head."

O'Toole placed no blame on the last-minute shooting tip; but thinking back on the impact the attempt could have had, she regrets the decision to stray from her instincts.

"It was our first shot of the game, and I really believe if I would've scored that goal, the whole game would've been different," she said.

But the match remained scoreless. The initial fast pace gave way to more deliberate offensive attack. Both Orwig and Weekes were sharp, denying the opening attempts at both ends. As the halfway mark of the first quarter approached, the buzz of the crowd turned into a slow, rhythmic chant: *Au-ssies. Au-ssies.*

As the Australians worked the ball around to the left side, Bridgette Gusterson separated from Robin Beauregard at the center position. Bronwyn Mayer delivered a perfect pass over the top of Beauregard, which was neatly tucked into the net by Gusterson. The Australian chant burst into screams and applause – a celebration that lasted well after the teams began countering in the other direction: the apparent goal was actually an offensive foul.

Gusterson, and all the other players in the pool, knew from the referee's whistle that possession would be going the other way before the ball even arrived on her hand; she turned and swam dutifully to defense without complaint. Thousands of spectators new to water polo would turn to ask each other why there was no evidence of a goal on the scoreboard, and what did all the whistles mean?

While the spectators simmered down, the Americans used the turnover to quickly get into the offensive end, where the battle between O'Toole and Hankin raged on. The ageless veteran drew first blood in the matchup, earning an exclusion against Hankin at the center. The first power-play of the game belonged to the United States.

The Americans attacked both sides; first the left with Villa, then the right with Simmons. Julie Swail brought the ball center and dished to Beauregard on her right. As the pass was in the air, and Australian eyes shifted to Beauregard, two strokes forward put Villa in an open space. Beauregard knew to expect the movement. The play was one the team ran with success against Australia during its visit earlier in the year. Convinced it would work, Baker tucked it away, saving it for just this moment. Beauregard's pass was on the hand of her teammate, and without hesitation, Villa fired at the goal. Weekes was only a moment too late to her right – the ball hit her right hand, but deflected upward, hitting the inside of the top netting.

Villa turned to the patch of Americans fans in the sea of yellow and gold and thrust her fist in the air. 1-0, USA.

On the ensuing possession, a shot by Melissa Mills boomed off the crossbar, retrieved by Gusterson to extend the attack. An exclusion against Courtney Johnson handed Australia its first power-play of the night. After Gusterson drew American defenders center, she passed to Mayer on the left. Mayer's shot, headed to the upper left corner, was swatted away emphatically by a lunging Orwig. While Johnson remained in the penalty box, Australia shifted its attack to the right, where Mills slid into open water, nearly mimicking Villa's successful move – Mills' skip shot eluded Orwig's dive to the post, and, to the delight of nearly every spectator in the stadium, the score was knotted at one-all at the two-minute mark.

After the teams traded offensive fouls, O'Toole, holding nothing back in her final game, again put the United States on the power-play. Errant passing stalled the American attack, and Simmons' shot was blocked by Australia's grande dame, Debbie Watson.

In the final seconds of the first quarter, Gusterson launched a long-range missile – knocked aside with two hands by Orwig. The buzzer sounded; the din rose. The 17,000 in attendance were enjoying an epic effort for a first-time prize.

Baker was pleased with the way the game began.

"The times we struggled with Australia were when they got off to a good start on us," he said. "Even when I continued to coach later, I felt that the first quarter was critical with them. They can be lights out in the first quarter, so we wanted to get off to a good, strong start. I felt we controlled the first quarter."

As evenly as the teams played and as well as the defenses performed in the opening frame, things were about to get even tighter.

Another sprint won by Melissa Mills thrilled the crowd at the Sydney International Aquatic Centre. In the early minutes of the second quarter, tight interior defense forced both the United States and Australia to shoot from long distance, posing little threat to either goalkeeper. Australia's Bridgette Gusterson had the first true chance three minutes in; her backhand from center hit a rising Bernice Orwig just above the right elbow and bounced harmlessly off the crossbar.

As the clock neared three minutes, Gubba Sheehy battled Simone Hankin at center. Initially overwhelmed by Hankin's power and leg strength, Sheehy fought back, muscling her way back to the middle of the goal. An entry pass from Brenda Villa paid off; Sheehy drew Hankin's second exclusion of the game. It didn't take the United States long to cash in. Ericka Lorenz was left open at seven meters, center cage. Walking the ball forward, she used a shoulder fake to the left before rising up on her legs. Lorenz heard Coralie Simmons to her right yell, "Shoot that!"

"I thought, yeah, I should probably shoot it," Lorenz recalled.

Head and body leaning left, she delivered a dart to the right. The ball hit the net. 2-1, USA.

Both teams then squandered power-play opportunities – Australia hitting first the left post, and on their next chance, the right post. Heather Petri's power-play shot from the top hit the left post and was collected by Liz Weekes. A powerful backhand from center with 18 seconds left in the half was thwarted by Weekes, who kept Australia's deficit at one, midway through the gold medal game.

☺☺☺☺☺

It was only fitting that Maureen O'Toole, an international icon in women's water polo, reached the Sydney Olympic Games. A true pioneer, she played in the first World Championships (exhibition), the first FINA World Cup, the first World Championships (official), and she earned her place in Sydney for the first Olympics.

Guy Baker challenged her on his first day as head coach in 1998, told her he didn't think she would be there when the Olympics rolled around. But she made it. For herself. And for so many of her National Team friends from decades of competing together, who never had the chance to be Olympians.

"I felt I was carrying the weight of the world on me, for all my teammates that didn't get to go," O'Toole said. "I remember every team meeting, I thought, 'We have to do this for all these people that got us here.' I was the only one left out of everybody that got us there, and so a lot of me was playing for them."

Her teammates from the 1970s and 1980s especially felt that she definitely represented them in Sydney.

"When it was finally going to be in the Olympics, and Mo got back on the team, she was our hope," said Dion Gray. "She was the one that was going to represent us in the Olympics. I felt like that was our Olympic moment, when she played."

Emotions filled Gray as she watched O'Toole and the United States team on television.

"I was crying watching introductions, and thinking, that's us," she said. "When Mo scored, I was jumping up and down; I felt like I was there with her. She knew that she was representing us. I really think that she felt that."

While she consciously felt the burden of carrying the torch for other American water polo pioneers, O'Toole focused her concentration on resting her body as much as she could, and being mentally prepared to perform. Although pushed to her physical limits by Baker over the past two years, O'Toole appreciated the extent to which he simplified the Olympics for the team.

"Guy was really and truly our leader, and we just needed to follow his lead, which made it a lot more simple for us," she said. "Personally, I needed to take care of myself and have the most energy I could, but competitively, Guy broke it down really incredibly."

Written on the wall for all to see every day at Los Al were the team's three goals: get to the semifinals, win the semifinals, win the gold medal game.

"It was broken down very simply, and that was our focus," O'Toole said. "It was one game at a time. I never remember being afraid, and I give a lot of credit for that to Guy because he really had us ready. We really were the best-conditioned team in the world. You could never be afraid that the person you were playing against was in better shape than you. No way. That gives you confidence. We just had to do what Guy asked us to do, which took the pressure off individually."

After enjoying the opening ceremony, O'Toole and the team went into tournament mode. The world may have looked at the United States as underdogs, but winning the Holiday Cup in July was no fluke. The team knew its three goals were attainable.

"It was a matter of putting it together for every game of the Olympics, and we did," said O'Toole. "The semifinal game against Holland was the biggest for me."

O'Toole remembers the team meeting in the driveway of the house in the Olympic Village as if it were yesterday. Sitting with her head between her knees, she thought to herself, *All of my friends at home are thinking, "They have to play Holland again."*

"And probably not very confidently thinking that," she added. "To beat Holland and have them out of it, and we reach the gold medal game, that was huge. Huge. First-ever Olympics, and we're in the gold medal game, and Holland is not. It was amazing."

She was playing great water polo throughout the Olympics, putting on a display reminiscent of her younger days – passing, scoring, swimming, and facilitating. In the final, O'Toole was reaching deep to finish with a flourish.

"I was super tired in that gold medal game," she said. "That was a hard game. I think I could have done better if I was more rested, honestly. Physically, I was thirty-nine years old. I don't care what you say, you don't recover like you do when you're twenty-one. But who knows."

It took a full year before O'Toole felt recovered from the physical ordeal she put her body through to achieve her Olympic dream.

She had the respect of so many – past and present teammates, and even her opponents at the moment.

"Watching her at the Sydney Olympics, I think she always caused that stir in you no matter what her age was," said Simone Hankin, O'Toole's defensive assignment in the gold medal game. "I have the highest admiration and the greatest respect for someone like her."

⊚⊚⊚⊚⊚

Although Melissa Mills won the third quarter sprint, it looked as though the United States defense would continue to be impenetrable. But a late entry pass to Gusterson saw Robin Beauregard sent to the penalty box for the second time. The Australian power-play moved into positions, and when Bronwyn Mayer arrived at the near post, the left-handed Mills quickly delivered. Before Heather Moody could respond, Mayer's shot ricocheted off Orwig's left arm and into the net. The crowd stood and roared, honking horns, and once again chanting with pride. Less than a minute into the third quarter, the teams were locked at two.

Defense continued to rule as the quarter ticked away. Shots by Brenda Villa and Julie Swail hit the bar; attempts by Australians Taryn Woods and Jo Fox missed their mark. With just under two minutes remaining in the third, Villa took an outlet pass from Orwig and spotted Simmons breaking out of a cutoff move against Mills at mid-pool. Villa's long pass reached Simmons dry; a quick cut to the inside caught Mills taking a bad angle. Simmons faced Weekes one-on-one, just outside the left post. Rising high, Weekes cut off the angle and forced Simmons to squeeze the ball to the near side. Weekes got just enough of the ball to send it to the post before it skittered away harmlessly.

The score remained tied.

The last good look of the quarter went to Naomi Castle on the power-play, but her cross-cage shot hit the post.

Both teams swam to their huddles with one quarter to play. It was now a seven-minute game for the Olympic gold medal.

Bronwyn Mayer won the fourth quarter sprint; Australia attacked first, but the stalemate continued. Shots were fired at both ends, meeting only the goalkeepers and not the nets. Minutes flew off the clock, with neither team taking control. The audience, enjoying the action but yearning for release, increased the tempo and volume of its chants.

Let's go, Aus-sies! Let's go, Aus-sies!

A couple of seconds past the halfway point of the fourth quarter, the counter-attack the United States hammered throughout the dog days of the summer at Los Al bore fruit. Heather Moody raced toward the Australian goal, cutting off captain Bridgette Gusterson; Gusterson – whom the referee promptly excluded – swam off to the penalty box. The first power-play opportunity of the fourth quarter went to the visitors.

With two pump-fakes, Robin Beauregard shot from seven meters, center cage. Taryn Woods' right hand stopped the ball, which landed safely in front of Liz Weekes.

Back-and-forth, the teams continued, with no edge gained by either side. As the clock neared two minutes, an entry pass to Gusterson at center led to an exclusion against Moody. Australian players swam to their primary shooting positions; leading scorer Gusterson positioned herself at center-cage, with Naomi Castle to her left. Maureen O'Toole split the difference, stunting between the two. O'Toole made a lunge at Gusterson, who fed Castle. After one fake to steady her legs, Castle fired to the right post, through the United States' shot blockers and past Orwig. The swish of the ball in the side netting ignited a roar of approval; the crowd rose to its feet, jumping, waving arms, and screaming with full force. 3-2, Australia.

The clock showed 1:50.

While the Australian team celebrated in the water and on the bench, the United States lined up to restart.

"It was just like practice again," said Baker, who had two timeouts at his disposal. "We're going to get this opportunity and then possibly one or two more. So we're in good shape as far as that goes."

On the ensuing attack, a shot by Brenda Villa sailed high and wide at 1:26. The United States defense faced a must-stop situation.

Playing its possession conservatively, Australia backed up early against the United States press. As Woods swam backwards to retrieve an overpass, the game's final minute was announced. American players headed to offense as the shot clock wound down; Woods dumped the ball with 52 seconds remaining.

Surveying the pool, Guy Baker saw nothing worth immediately exploiting.

He called timeout with 47 precious ticks remaining.

United States calls timeout in the fourth quarter – September 23, 2000

Long-time rivals met for the first Olympic gold – September 23, 2000

15

ONE OLYMPIC MINUTE

2000 Olympic Games
USA versus Australia
Gold medal game

Instead of feeling overwhelmed by the 17,000 screaming Olympic spectators as they swam to the sideline, the United States women found themselves transported back to their training. Not to their home at the Los Alamitos Joint Forces Training Base, however. This situation took them back to Bud Kearns Pool in San Diego, where the team survived overheated water and

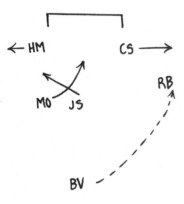

its coach's relentless demands for mastery of a timeout play designed for just this moment.

Taking his whiteboard from Chris Duplanty, Guy Baker strode to mid-pool. The crowd on its feet, chants of *Aus-sies!* rained down from high above the American huddle. The noise made it difficult to hear his words as Baker drew the play. It didn't matter. The team knew what they were doing.

Maureen O'Toole heard Baker say, "San Diego," and she knew what the play was.

The horn sounded, and the United States broke its huddle. Heather Moody and Coralie Simmons took places on the posts; Robin Beauregard positioned herself wide right at five meters. O'Toole and Julie Swail set up next to each other, nine meters out. Brenda Villa prepared to put the ball in play at half-tank.

On the referee's whistle, Beauregard and Simmons broke to the right; Villa delivered the ball to Beauregard, who turned and sent the ball deep to Simmons. That was the signal for Swail to set a pick with O'Toole as Moody cleared out to the left. Fouled by Debbie Watson, Simmons looked for O'Toole to flash ball-side.

42 seconds.

But the Australian defenders switched as O'Toole came over Swail's pick; Taryn Woods forced O'Toole away from Simmons.

Not to be denied, O'Toole spun into Woods at four-and-a-half meters. Legs churning furiously, she motored Woods backwards until the pair sat on the two-meter line. Without a clear entry lane, the patient Simmons sent the ball back to center pool, where Villa was being cautiously pressed.

36 seconds.

While Villa absorbed a foul, the battle at center raged. O'Toole spun and was dunked. Woods showed her left arm briefly, then plunged O'Toole with her right.

"She had one arm around my waist and the other arm around my neck, and I have pretty good position," O'Toole said. "The girl is freakin' drowning me, and I'm thinking, *Get the ball in! I need air!*"

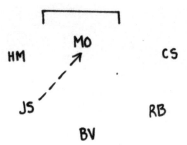

Certain the referees would reward an entry pass, O'Toole continued to surge against the pressure of Woods. Villa passed cleanly to Swail to her left, who took a foul from her defender. O'Toole disappeared again at the hands of Woods; Baker pleaded to the referee for a call, to no avail.

32 seconds.

Swail's free throw got to Villa, who took one fake before returning the ball to the team captain. Without hesitation, Swail rose up on her legs and sent an entry pass toward the center. Three Australian defenders swam back to crash, but the distance to cover made their efforts futile. Knowing the help wouldn't get there in time, Woods conceded. With both hands, she plunged O'Toole, leaving no possibility of the legend tying the game in that moment. The whistle blew. O'Toole had won the battle; Woods turned to swim to the penalty box, having done her job.

"If they would've waited much longer, I think I would have drowned," O'Toole said. "There was no way I was going to score."

26 seconds.

Timeout, United States.

As the teams met separately at poolside, the noise inside the Sydney International Aquatic Centre reached a new level. Layered over the constant buzz of 17,000 fans, ecstatic to see the home nation compete for Olympic gold, was the repeated chant, *Let's go, Aus-sies, let's go!*

Sans whiteboard, Baker leaned toward the athletes in the water, gesturing with his hands. Brenda Villa nodded, perhaps reading Baker's lips more than hearing his words. The call was the same power-play that resulted in Villa scoring the first goal of the Olympic final, nearly an hour earlier. The United States broke its huddle first, as Istvan Gorgenyi gave final instructions to his defense.

"Even at that point, we were calm," said Villa. "That was such an amazing feeling. There was never a sense of panic. We just had to find a way to score."

The referee delivered the ball to Bernice Orwig; the whistle blew, and the teams dug in for the final seconds of the game. The United States got straight to work, as Orwig fed Robin Beauregard at the top of the formation to start the attack. To her right was Julie Swail; to her left, at five meters, Brenda Villa. As Beauregard received the ball, Heather Moody began to slide out from the right post area. At the same time, but more subtly, Maureen O'Toole did the same to Moody's left.

Swail took a pass from Beauregard; the movement of Moody drew the attention of the defender nearest to Swail. O'Toole popped slightly out of the water, freezing her post defender, who took a quick look to the right to find Villa. Swail returned the ball to Beauregard in the center; both top row defenders moved toward the ball. Beauregard took two quick fakes, then tossed the ball back to Swail.

20 seconds.

At that moment, Villa made her move.

With O'Toole open in the middle, the Australian post defender moved out to her while the ball was on Swail's hand. Villa capitalized, first sliding forward, then taking one stroke with her right arm. Swail's pass was already in the air. Liz Weekes, the Australian goalkeeper, began moving to her right. Following the flight of the ball, she squared her hips. But when the ball landed perfectly on Villa's outstretched hand, Weekes was still at center cage with both hands in the water. Villa's eyes grew big as they saw half the goal open in front of her.

Simultaneously, Villa fired, and Weekes lunged. The sound of the shot hitting the bar was no match for the rumble of the crowd; the contact with the crossbar sent the ball straight down. It landed in front of Weekes just as her right arm splashed back into the water. A combination of the spin on the ball and the wave created by Weekes' arm ushered the ball to her left.

Immediately looking to the goal judge, Villa saw the signal. The ball had crossed the goal line before Weekes swiped it out with her left hand. The whistle from the referee confirmed the decision, as Villa desperately (and, in hindsight, unnecessarily) pointed to the goal judge.

"I was pointing out, 'He saw it; it's in,'" she said.

13.1 seconds.

"And then I'm thinking, *We're going to overtime.*"

As she swam to half pool for the restart, Maureen O'Toole's mind raced.

We're going to overtime, and we're going to friggin' win this thing because there's nobody that's in better shape than us in the world. This is amazing.

In the Australian net, Liz Weekes was alone with her thoughts. Although she was irked at the failure of the defense to deny Brenda Villa a shot from exactly that spot, Weekes was calm. She thought to herself, *This is going to go into extra time, and we're going to win it.*

Guy Baker was confident his defense could survive long stretches without conceding a goal. In his mind, overtime favored the United States.

"The longer the game, the better. Brenda scored the goal, tie game, thirteen seconds. I think we're going to overtime," he said. "I don't *think* we're going to overtime … they're out of timeouts. As they come off the lineup, there's not a lot going on. So it had that feeling like it's just going to overtime."

To a person, the 17,000 spectators probably agreed with Baker on that point. The pure intensity of this contest provided an exhilarating experience. Overtime seemed like the most fitting – perhaps only – way for the week-long celebration of women's water polo to end.

When Brenda Villa tied the score at 3-3 with thirteen seconds to go, Simone Hankin and Yvette Higgins sat on the bench next to Australian coach Istvan Gorgenyi. Hankin spent most of the game sitting in front of the team physiotherapist, who worked on her

left shoulder, dislocated the night before in the semifinals against Russia.

Higgins and Hankin were a bit of an odd couple on the Australian team – totally different in numerous ways. But during centralized training in Kawana earlier in the year, the pair found they shared a similar work ethic. While they weren't roommates, they often rode bikes or drove together to training.

"Yvette and I have really similar approaches to a number of life stresses," Hankin said. "Throughout that period of centralized life, we found that we actually coped with things quite similarly."

It was common for Higgins and Hankin to stay in the water long after practice was over, feeding each other pass after pass, practicing their shots, and at the same time building a bond.

Protecting the lead in the final minutes of the Olympic gold medal game, Gorgenyi had his defensive unit in the pool. Higgins looked to her coach the moment Villa brought the game level.

"In my head I thought, 'Well, if we're not going to get in the water, we've lost,'" she said, referring to herself and Hankin. "Well, not lost, but going to extra time. I was thinking that if he didn't put us in, then no one's going to pull this out."

Gorgenyi motioned for Higgins to get in. He looked at Hankin, her left arm covered with tape. The big, strong veteran was swaying forward and back, gripped by the pain in her shoulder.

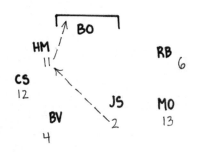

"Istvan's face is very demonstrative," Hankin said. "He looked down the bench and said, 'Hank, I don't know what you're going to do, but get in.'"

At mid-pool for the restart, waiting for the whistle to resume play, Hankin's mind raced. *My arms aren't working … I'm in immense pain … there's no way … we're going into extra time … let's just keep the ball … what do we do?*

As she had in the ready room seemingly hours before, Hankin yelled, "This is our house, our place. *Let's go!*"

13 seconds.

On the referee's signal, Naomi Castle dribbled the ball three strokes forward before passing to Jo Fox to her left.

Nine.

Bridgette Gusterson swam to the center, defended by Heather Moody. Fox returned the ball to Castle, who was quickly pressed by Brenda Villa.

Seven.

After setting up on the right post, Simone Hankin was being pushed out wide by Robin Beauregard. The ball swung from Castle to the right, into the left hand of Yvette Higgins.

Five.

Julie Swail pressed Higgins just outside of seven meters. Lunging toward her, Swail committed a foul.

Three.

Taking a quick look behind, Swail turned her attention back to Higgins, who held the ball high. Gusterson cleared out to the left, vacating the space in front of the goal. Swail put her right arm straight into the air and rose up on her legs. A double whistle blast rang out from the referee platform, excluding Swail for interference.

Two.

The ball left Higgins' hand, bound for Gusterson; it reached its target as more double whistles rang out. Moody didn't contest the pass; Bernice Orwig didn't contest Gusterson's shot.

A roar rocked the arena when the ball hit the left bar and ended up in the back of the goal.

The clock showed 1.3 seconds.

The thunderous noise continued, as Australian players celebrated. But instead of signaling a goal, the referees pointed to Higgins. The ball needed to return to Higgins to be properly put into play. Word of what was happening spread through the crowd; the joyous cheers turned to boos as Hankin swam past Orwig, into the goal, to retrieve the ball.

Hankin returned to the two-meter line, picked up the ball, and delivered it back to Higgins and the spot of the foul. The left-hander caught the pass, cocked her arm back, and fired toward the left post. Robin Beauregard, defending Hankin, reached for the ball with her right hand, but it was well out of her reach. Coralie Simmons plunged Jo Fox with her left hand, thrusting her right hand across her body, to her left. Orwig's eyes locked onto the flight of the ball, her body starting a lunge to her right.

The deflection off Simmons' fingers was just enough; the change in trajectory, miniscule as it was, affected Orwig's perception. Instead of hitting her palm, as her brain told her the ball should, it deflected off her fingers, into the upper corner of the net.

Zero.

Pandemonium.

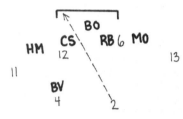

The Sydney International Aquatic Centre exploded. Australian players mobbed Higgins. Guy Baker pointed to the seven-meter line and held his hands out to the referees, Renato Dani and Vladimir Prikhodko, asking for an explanation. He didn't get one, and when it was clear by the referees' actions that the goal counted, the crowd nearly blew the roof off.

While the official scoresheet shows the game's last action as Higgins' goal, a fraction of a second showed on the scoreboard. Prikhodko whistled a restart. The long-distance shot fell short, setting off the celebration in the pool for real.

Ian Thorpe and the Australian swimmers held the country enthralled throughout the first week of the Olympics. The Australian women's water polo team closed the action at Homebush with a 4-3 victory and Olympic gold for the host nation.

Yvette Higgins instantly became Australia's newest Olympic star, joining the likes of fellow aquatic athletes Ian Thorpe, Michael Klim, and Susie O'Neill. Her shot may have surprised many at Homebush, but not her teammates.

Every member of the gold medal-winning team shared a common experience: waiting on the bus for Higgins.

"We'd be on tour or at training camps and it was, 'Where's Yvette?'" said Liz Weekes. "She was in the water, sitting in that spot, practicing that shot. And that was the shot that put it away for us. It was always going to be her. She was always putting in that little extra."

Higgins often asked Weekes to stay; Simone Hankin was a common buddy who helped her hone her shooting.

With 1.3 seconds remaining in the gold medal game, Hankin threw the pass she had delivered to her teammate hundreds of times before.

"I glanced out, and Yvie's sitting there, no one near her," Hankin recalled. "It's funny that it ended up being a pass off the two for me and her shot. Her eyes were saying to me, 'Give me the ball.' Her whole face said it."

Higgins acknowledges some people might consider the goal lucky. She and her teammates know the truth.

"That was a shot I had practiced for years," Higgins told an Australian Broadcasting Corporation radio audience in 2010 as the 10-year anniversary of the Sydney Olympics approached. "I visualized that goal when I was fourteen. It was something I had prepared myself for and practiced hours on end."

The final minute of the greatest women's water polo game had nothing to do with luck. The United States executed flawlessly on two plays in a 30-second span – Maureen O'Toole drawing the exclusion, and Brenda Villa cashing in to tie the score. Simone Hankin and Yvette Higgins hooked up for the game winner through a connection forged over years of being there for each other, pushing each other to improve.

Players on both teams were prepared for the greatest game of their lives.

"Never in a million years would I have thought we wouldn't get to overtime," Villa said. "I was like, fine, we'll finish it in overtime. And we never got to overtime."

The words "controversial" and "confusing" are used to describe the end of the gold medal game by many who were in attendance, whether they were seeing water polo for the first time, or if they lived a lifetime full of the sport. As much in question as whether the final shot should have counted is why the penultimate one did not.

Sitting across from the crowd, Phillip Bower, an Australian referee working the Sydney Olympics, was with a handful of his officiating peers from around the world. They unanimously agreed that Bridgette Gusterson's shot should have counted. They also expected Yvette Higgins' goal to be overturned.

"We thought they were going to bring it back because no one knew what was going on," Bower said, referring to the two men who had the power to overturn the call – the officials on the game.

In the moment after Higgins' goal, Guy Baker looked to Vladimir Prikhodko for clarification. Prikhodko held out his hands and shrugged his shoulders.

"It can be weird in the international game," Baker said. "There's the Kazakhstan referee, shrugging his shoulders to me. I'm thinking, 'Well, if you don't know, I don't know … shouldn't we do something about that?'"

Brenda Villa remembers looking to Baker to try to understand what was happening. She could see he wasn't making headway in getting an explanation.

"I didn't realize there was an ejection," she said. "It was kind of slow motion, the shot going in."

Even then, Villa wondered if the referees were going to pull the ball and explain what was going on.

"And then, no, the game was just over," she said. "At the time, I wondered why we didn't make more of a stink of it. But the moment was just too big for something like that."

As the Australian team celebrated its victory, the United States women gathered at the wall.

"People are throwing their caps, and everybody's mad," recalled Maureen O'Toole, who was sure the referees made a mistake. O'Toole told her teammates, "You guys, get it together. That goal is not going to count, we're going to go to overtime. There's no way that goal is going to count."

O'Toole's disbelief stemmed from the referees allowing Higgins a direct shot, "Unless you want to say that the ball could go from A to B to C to D, into the goal, to the two-meter line, and back to her, and the seven meter rule is still in effect."

The United States didn't file a protest. Baker's conversation with Gianni Lonzi, chairman of the FINA Technical Water Polo Committee, on the pool deck following the game centered around whether Yvette Higgins was fouled outside of seven meters or not. Lonzi issued a statement confirming that she was, and was thus entitled to "an instant shot." Questions surrounding the directness of Higgins' shot went unaddressed.

Baker called Higgins' first pass to Gusterson "definitely legit."

And Higgins' game winner?

"When she caught the ball, she shot it directly," he said. "So it's good."

Reflecting back, Villa put the moment, and the result, in perspective.

"Where we were at that point, the first time women's water polo is ever in the Olympics," she said. "Making a controversy out of the ending could have jeopardized what the future held for women's water polo. In hindsight, it worked out the way it worked out."

When Maureen O'Toole finally exited the pool for the last time, a spectacular international career came to a close. She joined the team in a final circle, as Guy Baker impressed upon the group the impact their journey would have on women's water polo in the United States. Part of the journey from the beginning, O'Toole was ready to pass the torch to the next generation of athletes.

Her head was spinning as the circle broke and she began to walk toward the locker room.

"It's over," she thought.

The scene seemed surreal to the fatigued O'Toole – then it became even more so when she spotted her daughter, Kelly, from a distance, on the pool deck.

"My immediate thought is, 'What is she doing down there?' O'Toole said. "Nobody can get down on the pool deck. What is she doing down there?"

NBC television, the folks who put Kelly in the front row for her mom to see as she marched in for introductions, brought the eight-year-old to the deck for the cameras and O'Toole's post-game interview.

"I knew I was done playing; I was really upset that we had just lost," O'Toole said. "Kelly is being handed to me in my arms, and she sees that I'm upset, so she starts crying, and I'm like, 'I can't deal with this right now.'"

So many thoughts raced through the legend's mind.

I'm done playing water polo ... I finally have Kelly back ... this is amazing, but we just lost the gold medal game of the Olympics ...

"And no sooner than that, they come," she said.

The NBC camera and crew were upon her. The interview began, with Kelly in her arms, and the first question was delivered: *I cannot think of a tougher way to lose a gold medal match – what happened in those final seconds?*

"I'm just going, wow," O'Toole recalled. "Luckily, I had done enough interviews and knew enough to not be negative, but that is a really hard question."

O'Toole closed her eyes. She thought, *What is this all about? How do I answer this question? How do I answer this question truthfully?*

Fifteen years after the gold medal game, O'Toole reflected on what she wished she could have said at that moment.

"'*The simple truth is, it sucks,*'" she might have told the NBC reporter, if she hadn't taken a moment to compose herself. "'*It sucks, and I don't want to talk to you.*' That's the simple truth. I feel like in that moment that I thought about how to answer the question, I learned so much about life."

With a camera aimed at her, and a microphone in front of her face, O'Toole took a deep breath, held her daughter Kelly close, and slowly began. She recalls saying that the United States was confused about the officiating in the frenetic finish to the game. O'Toole remembers continuing:

> It's been an incredibly great experience – everything went our way until that last one second. It's not about the last one second in the gold medal game. It's about the whole journey. It's about getting women's water polo to the Olympics. It's about getting to make the team to come to the first-ever Olympics, getting to walk through the opening ceremonies of the Olympics, and ultimately playing in the gold medal

game of the Olympics with my teammates. That's what it's all about. It's the journey.

In her motivational speeches since the Sydney Olympics, O'Toole talks about the silver lining at the heart of her experience.

"Had we won the gold medal, it would be unbelievable, a fairy tale," she tells corporate audiences. "But we didn't, and that's so much of life. At the end of the day, we didn't get what we wanted, but how do you deal with that? I feel like I'm a better person because I've had to think about it more because we lost. It was more thought-provoking to lose."

O'Toole's story goes back as far as international women's water polo itself. Competing for the final time, in the Olympics, in the gold medal game, was better than she ever imagined possible.

"It was an amazing experience," she said. "It really was."

"I wouldn't change it for anything."

Olympic silver medalists – September 23, 2000

16

SILVER LININGS

Guy Baker gathered the United States women's water polo team, and the team staff, into a circle on the pool deck of the Sydney International Aquatic Centre. There was no protest of the result. He thanked them for the journey, which had come to its end.

And within moments of the breaking of the circle, the athletes, for so long united on a path together, strayed apart. They looked for familiar faces in the darkness above, in the spectator seats. American flags caught their attention – they were easy to spot amid the sea of the Australian colors of yellow and green.

In minutes, everyone was being shooed off the deck, hustled to the change room. The American players pulled out their medal ceremony outfits – distributed to every United States athlete at Processing, but officially worn only by those who reached the Olympic podium. Donning the outfit was an honor – a reward in itself.

Beneath the media side of the arena, the three teams assembled, ready to march back out onto the pool deck. The medal ceremony soundtrack commenced, and the Russian team, dressed in blue, emerged from the tunnel. The spectators clapped politely for the bronze medalists, then burst into roars of joy at the sight of Melissa Mills leading the Australian team out of the shadows. Each athlete, dressed in a yellow jacket and green pants, carried a yellow stuffed boxing kangaroo. The players smiled broadly as they looked across the pool, and up into the audience. Many turned to receive congratulations from countrymen and women on the desk side – those who had helped run the competition, as well as volunteers, and VIPs.

As the Russians made their way off the referees' walk, Bernice Orwig led the United States team on to it at the other end. Clad in their white medal ceremony outfits, the Americans still wore stunned looks on their faces, many looking straight forward as they marched. The feeling was starkly different from the electricity of walking in for game introductions less than two hours before. The team poured every effort of its last two years together into the Olympic final; for some, adrenaline still coursed through their bodies, ready for the overtime that was snatched away in the last second.

The three teams stood behind their respective gold, silver, and bronze platforms, waiting for the medal ceremony to begin. With the announcement of the Olympic champion, Australia, a thunderous roar filled the arena. The team stepped onto the podium to receive its medals from none other than IOC Member and President of FINA, Mustapha Larfaoui, the man Liz Weeks, Yvette Higgins, and other female athletes hounded at the airport, and at a downtown meeting three years prior, to lobby for the inclusion of women's water polo in the Sydney Olympics.

Following the awarding of the gold medals, the United States was announced as Olympic silver medalist. Stepping onto the podium holding hands, team members raised their arms to the cheering crowd. Each player bowed her head to receive her medal from Larfaoui; many examined the precious award as he continued down the line. Feelings of disappointment gave way to pride and accomplishment; several players waved, and smiles spread across the faces of the American players.

After the Russians received their bronze medals, the first notes of the Australian national anthem began, sparking a rousing sing-along of "Advance Australia Fair." Of the nearly 17,000 singing the tune, none were louder, or more joyful, than the thirteen women on the podium.

The United States captured silver at the first women's Olympic
tournament – September 23, 2000

The United States team posed together on the podium as camera flashes
popped. From there, they began the walk around the pool. Marching towards the
spectators, they paused again for group photos, this time holding the American
flag proudly in front. Trailing behind the Australians, the American team was
slowed several times as the gold medalists stopped to acknowledge their friends,
family, and thousands of excited Australians, who had just witnessed history
at Homebush.

Australian captain, Bridgette Gusterson, spotted Pat Jones at the railing –
with a shooter's aim, she tossed her victory bouquet to the woman whose tireless
efforts played a major role making this moment possible.

Finally, athletes from every team dispersed as the victory lap ended. When
Bernice Orwig left the pool deck, she sought refuge in the first private space she
came upon; she broke down, sobbing uncontrollably. But her duties weren't done
– the media requested she attend the postgame press conference. Team manager
Michelle Pickering found Orwig crying in the locker room.

"Michelle was literally shouting at me, *You have to get it together*," Orwig
recalled. "She did what she had to do to get me to snap out of it."

Post-game press conference: Bernice Orwig, Brenda Villa, Maureen O'Toole,
Istvan Gorgenyi, and Debbie Watson – September 23, 2000

Orwig made it to the press conference, but keeping her emotions together was nearly impossible. Each time she managed to control her sobbing, another reporter's question directed at her caused her to break down again.

Unlike press conferences at many major competitions, which bring in the participants from the winning and losing teams separately, the Olympic press conference featured players and coaches from the gold and silver medalists at the same time.

The format of the press conference, plus the pure spectacle of the gold medal game, caught the attention of veteran *Boston Globe* sportswriter and columnist Bob Ryan. In his column the next morning, Ryan noted the night of firsts – both for women's water polo, and for his sports writing career.

> It was the first gold medal game in women's water polo and it set
> a standard that will be difficult for future teams to match. ... But
> the truly extraordinary moment came about 45 minutes later

during a peculiar press conference featuring representatives from both the victors and the vanquished. I've been to a lot of press conferences in a lot of sports at a lot of levels, but this one produced something I've never before experienced.

In his book, *Scribe: My Life in Sports*, Ryan included a chapter about the Olympics. He singled out his memory of the women's water polo final at the Sydney Olympics – the first water polo match he ever watched.

Sydney also provided me with a unique story in a sport about which I had close to zero knowledge. Nothing in my sports upbringing had prepared me to cover a women's gold medal match in water polo. About all I knew of this sport was that the 1956 men's match between the Soviet Union and Hungary had left plenty of blood in the pool.

There was no blood involved in Australia's 4-3 victory over the Americans, but there were buckets of tears shed by both side. The ending was beyond stunning. American Brenda Villa had scored with 13.1 seconds remaining to tie the match at 3. But with 1.3 seconds separating the USA from overtime, team captain Julie Swail was called for an "exclusion," the water polo term for a penalty. Amid what could only be described as complete confusion on the part of the Americans, Australia's Yvette Higgins fired a shot past USA goalkeeper Bernice Orwig with no time left. In the history of simultaneous Agony vs. Ecstasy, this has to rank near the top of any list.

The postgame press conference was unlike any I have ever attended. Everybody was crying, and this was forty-five minutes after the conclusion of the match! American coach Guy Baker hugged Australian coach Istvan Gorgenyi. The Australians clapped heartily for American grande dame Maureen O'Toole, who had come out of a three-year retirement at age thirty-nine the instant she heard women's water polo would be included in the Sydney Olympics. Anyone who had not seen the match would have had a hard time figuring out who had won and who had lost. And anyone who had questioned the feasibility of putting this sport, and these people, in the 2000 Olympics needed question it no longer. "All I know is that somewhere up there in that Big IOC In The Sky, good ol' Baron de Coubertin is telling people it sure was a good idea to let these folks into his little soiree," I wrote in my water polo column. It turned out to be the right place at the right time, and that's what you pray for at an Olympics.

The sport, the two teams, and the atmosphere at the historic event, made an impression on Bob Ryan, and thousands of others who were in attendance. But so few – no one outside of the inner circle of the American team – knew the story of how the United States women achieved their dream of competing in the Olympics. And while the American public and media gradually joined the bandwagon as the team stormed through the week of competition in Sydney, no one but Guy Baker was in a position to assess the effort that took the United States women to the Olympic podium.

"You compete, and then it's over, and you look back," he said. "It's truly about doing the best that you can do. And that group did the best that they could do. It would have been awesome to win, but as far as what would we have done differently, there's nothing. There wasn't anything else for them to give. There wasn't. They gave everything."

The Sydney team achieved what may have seemed impossible – at the least, improbable – at a time that was critical to the growth of an entire sport in the United States.

"Taking down Holland was a huge turning point," Baker said. "If we had walked out with the bronze medal during that time we would've been stoked. Some things would have still happened – becoming an NCAA sport, more women and girls playing, more opportunity, working together on all those things."

But Baker asserts that women's water polo in America rode the wave created by the work put in by the Sydney team.

"That moment doesn't happen if you don't qualify; if you finish fifth in the group at the Olympics and you're not playing for a medal," he said. "It's all of those things. If you don't play in that gold medal game, and you don't have the momentum that comes with it, then what's happening? Because just two years ago, that team was eighth, and then they didn't qualify in 1999.

"As a U.S. team, that was our only opportunity to be the underdog," he continued. "We got to enjoy that, and we emerged through that, and from that came everything else that happened. There's no denying that."

Baker expounded on the impact of the silver medal in Sydney on women's water polo in the United States.

"It was crazy. It changed so many things. Brenda became the next generational player after Mo. Where it shifted, that moment, that process, that journey – the Sydney team did that. It became what it is now."

Where is American women's water polo now?

Dominant.

Full of tradition. One of three nations to participate in the first four women's Olympic tournaments. The only nation to win a medal in Sydney, Athens, Beijing, and London.

The silver lining of Sydney is clear – the United States women's program established itself among the world's elite, a position it has only strengthened since 2000. And women's water polo at all levels across the country exploded in the wake of the greatest game ever played.

"The Sydney team made that happen," Baker said. "They set the standard. They set the culture. The younger generation may not fully understand. Why would they?

"This group had to start it. They started it, under the toughest of circumstances."

Athletes, families, and staff celebrate the end of the Sydney Olympic
journey – September 23, 2000

17

ALL GOLD EVERYTHING

The United States women's team qualified for the 2000 Olympics in April of that year. Since that time, beginning with the Sydney Games, FINA has sponsored thirty-eight tournaments at the Senior, Junior, and Youth levels. The United States has medaled in a staggering thirty of those thirty-eight. Australia checks in at second place in the medal count in the same time period, with twenty-one.

Starting with the Sydney Olympics, Guy Baker put a premium on reaching the medal round of major tournaments. In the fifteen years since qualifying for the first Olympic tournament, the United States women have played for a medal thirty-four times in thirty-eight events.

The thirty medals earned by American women's teams include twenty-one gold – sixteen at the Senior level, four at the Junior World Championships, and one at the Youth World Championships. Two nations are tied for next-most gold medals from 2000 through 2015: Australia and Greece both boast three.

A major factor in the sustained success of the United States women's water polo program was the hiring of a full time Technical Director. In 2001, Baker took on the title, on top of his role as head coach of the Women's National Team. Baker resigned as coach of the UCLA men's team after the 2000 season, turning his full attention to the Women's National Team, and the National Team pipeline.

"My perspective was that all the National Team coaches that I was competing against were just coaching their National Teams," said Baker. "There had been discussions at USA Water Polo about hiring full-time coaches; those thoughts really ramped up post-Sydney."

As the 2000 Olympics neared, the focus was squarely on Sydney, and talks of a full-time position were shelved. Baker suspects the USOC and United States Water Polo were also waiting to see what kind of result the women produced at the Olympic Games. In 2001, the USOC funded full-time positions for both the men's and women's National Teams. Baker became the Women's Technical Director; three-time Olympic gold medal-winning coach Ratko Rudic took on the same role for the men's program. The two became the first full-time National Team coaches for USA Water Polo.

"At that time, the USOC put an emphasis on long-term high performance plans, as well as athlete pipelines," Baker said. "There was no focus at all on the pipeline back when we first started."

The Women's National Team had a long tradition of identifying athletes from all corners of the United States, particularly under the leadership of Sandy Nitta at the Senior level and Brent Bohlender at the Junior level. And while the regional zones had long run local tryouts and selection camps to funnel players to National Team tryouts, the coaching was done by volunteers, given no direction or mandates, in terms of what to teach.

As Technical Director, Baker put together an official manual, outlining the program philosophy, standardizing terminology, and laying out a specific system of play, to be taught to coaches and athletes involved in what would eventually become known as the Olympic Development Program (ODP).

The pipeline – identifying athletes, educating coaches, and creating a vertical system in which players could move up to the Senior National Team and contribute immediately – had one aim in mind.

"The focus became to be the best in the world, all the time."

The 2001 World Championships in Fukuoka, Japan, produced results that were not surprising, as women's water polo began its first true Olympic quadrennium. Italy and Hungary, the two teams that narrowly missed out on Sydney at the Olympic Qualification Tournament, reached the World Championship final; Italy defended its 1998 world title. Canada, the fifth-place team in Sydney, won bronze. The Olympic medalists occupied the next three spots in the final ranking: the United States, Australia, and Russia finished fourth, fifth, and sixth, respectively.

But the impact of the vertical integration of Baker's system of play became apparent at the end of 2001, at the Junior World Championships in Perth, Australia.

"That started really showing the possibilities of what could happen, pipe-line-wise," Baker said.

In the fall of 2001, Baker and assistant coach Kyle Kopp spent more time with the Junior Team than they did the Senior Team. With a majority of the Junior World Championships roster, including head coach John Wright, living in Southern California, the team practiced two nights a week with members of the Senior Team who weren't in school; the integration paid off. The team won the United States' first Junior World Championship title in Perth, Australia, defeating the host nation in the final.

"So then you start seeing it," Baker continued. "The 2001 Junior Team, tech-nically, would be more athletic than the 2000 Olympic Team as far as shooting and swimming speed. So you started to see the athletic ability that is in the pipeline, right away."

Several players on the 2001 Junior Team had been identified as early as 1998, and trained with the Senior Team during the years leading up to the Sydney Olympics. Amber Stachowski, Thalia Munro, and Natalie Golda were all on the gold medal-winning Junior Team before becoming National Team fixtures. All three won bronze medals as members of the 2004 Olympic Team.

Baker's focus in 2001 and 2002 was highly geared toward the athlete pipeline. He first turned his attention to the selection process of the Youth National Team, in which each USA Water Polo Zone brought a team to a Zone Championship in the summer. Baker mandated that at least one player from every Zone be selected for the Youth National Team training squad. When the Cadet National Team was created, each Zone was guaranteed two athletes on the training squad.

Baker singles out Alison Gregorka and Elsie Windes as Olympians from outside of California who began in the pipeline in 2001.

"Alison got identified and selected off the Midwest team in the summer of 2001," he recalled. "By the time the 2002 Junior Pan American Championships were happening, she's two steps ahead. She's a 'born in '85 kid' who is on the 2003 Junior World Championship Team. So she went from being the one kid picked from the Midwest Zone, to skipping the Youth Team, and going right to the Junior Team based on her ability.

In 2001, Baker also initiated a program called P.A.C.E. (Player and Coach Education). The National Team staff started running P.A.C.E. Clinics, with an eye toward getting a feel for what the water polo landscape was in different parts of the country. In Corvallis, Oregon, the staff identified the 16-year-old Windes.

"Two weeks after that, she's at the Youth National Team training camp over Thanksgiving weekend," Baker said.

Gregorka won a silver medal at the 2003 Junior World Championships; she and Windes were both on the gold medal-winning Junior World Championship Team in 2005. They teamed up again on the 2008 Olympic squad, winning a silver medal. Windes ended her National Team career with an Olympic gold medal around her neck in London in 2012.

"So it's all of that," Baker said. "It's P.A.C.E. Clinics, it's education, it's teaching our system, it's putting it in a manual, it's putting together the pipeline."

By the end of 2001, Baker had created not only a manual for the pipeline, but a roadmap to Olympic gold. Along with the entire staffs of the Senior, Junior, and Youth National Teams, Baker produced a document titled *Mission 2012*.

"*Mission 2012* was the plan to be the best women's water polo country in the world – a dominant team all the way through," Baker said. "The first goal back then was to medal all the time; the focus was to be the best by 2012."

Because the announcement of women's water polo's inclusion in the Sydney Olympics came late in 1997, the time frame for the 2000 Games was compressed; reaching the podium in Sydney fulfilled the expectations Baker brought to the position of National Team head coach. Beyond Sydney, sustainability was priority number one.

By 2001, Baker saw the new generation of players becoming the next Olympic team in front of his eyes.

"It was an explosion; it was happening so quickly, so there were going to be benefits," he said. "There were so many athletes coming into play. That 2001 Junior World Championship team – we're on the pool deck literally saying, 'We're going to select players for the 2004 Olympic Team now.' We were with them two nights a week, saying to ourselves, 'They can shoot, they have strong legs, look at what they're doing.' We became more athletic."

The 2001 Junior Worlds saw FINA switch the women's playing field from 25 meters to 30 meters. The change provided an immediate benefit to the United States.

"We would go from no advantage on the counterattack at half court, to a breakaway by the time they reached the front court," Baker said. "They were athletic as far as how they played. Then, over time, they just learned the game better, and they got more experience. Girls were playing sooner; they were playing in bigger moments."

One example is the NCAA Championship, which began in 2001. But Baker further pointed to the girls' CIF Southern Section Championships, which were played in front of packed houses.

"They're playing in front of people, they're getting that type of experience at a young age," he said. "Junior Olympics is another example – the final games are packed; kids are playing in big games."

The post-Sydney quadrennial continued with the Senior National Team reaching the final of the 2002 World Cup, falling to Hungary to claim the silver medal. The following summer, the United States women returned to the top of the podium for the first time since the 1979 World Cup in Merced. The team rolled through the 2003 World Championships in Barcelona, winning gold for the first time under Guy Baker's leadership. Less than a month later, the women qualified for the Athens Olympics by defeating Canada for gold at the 2003 Pan American Games.

In 2004, the United States won the inaugural FINA World League Super Final in Long Beach, and arrived in Athens as the favorite for Olympic gold.

Winning its preliminary group despite a loss to rival Canada, the United States advanced directly to the medal round. In its semifinal against Italy, the American team was stunned in the closing seconds, its dream of gold crushed.

Despite entering the 2008 Olympics as the reigning World Champion, the American women fell short against the Netherlands in the Olympic final in Beijing.

Following the Beijing Games, Baker took on a new position: Director of Olympic Development for USA Water Polo. Overseeing the Olympic Development Program for both men and women, Baker relinquished his duties as head coach of the Women's National Team.

UCLA's Adam Krikorian took the reins, and the program's momentum continued. Under Krikorian's guidance, the United States women won five consecutive FINA events, including the 2009 World Championships and the 2010 World Cup. A stumble at the 2011 World Championships left the Americans off the podium for the first time in five years; but the United States women had the London Olympics in their sights.

When Adam Krikorian prepared to take the team to the London Games in 2012, he kept one important tradition from past Olympics – a link to the groundbreaking Sydney team. He brought Chris Duplanty to speak to the team about the power of the circle.

Duplanty started by telling the team to believe in themselves, and recognize how far they had come.

"I told them they are members of a very elite group," Duplanty explained. "I said, 'There are over 300 million people in the United States.' And I asked them, 'How many of that number are women's water polo Olympians?' I told them, thirty-four. I told them that they were one of thirty-four. I brought that up so they could step back and understand the elite company that they are in. No matter what happens, this will never change."

A three-time Olympian, Duplanty continued by sharing some of his experiences at the Games – dealing with distractions, leading by example both in and out of the water, and managing the expectations of performance.

"Performance at the Olympics is not about being perfect," he told the 2012 Olympians. "It's about compensating and adjusting. The fear of needing to be perfect at the Olympic Games is just not true. No one is perfect; I explained to them that peak performance is not about being perfect."

Duplanty shared his own most glaring moment of imperfection – at the 1996 Olympics – when an Italian opponent scored from half pool at the end of a quarter. "Here we are at the Olympic Games, and the very first game, I get scored on from half. How do I deal with that?"

"My purpose was to take the pressure off the team – take it away from the need to be perfect – which was the same thing we talked about with the team in 2000. It's not going to be perfect. We've got to stay together as a team. At the end of all of this, Brenda asked me to lead the team in the circle."

The team got together in a circle, and held hands.

With everyone's attention locked on him, Duplanty began.

He talked about the distractions that lurk around every corner at the Olympics, seeking to separate a team. He talked about the strength of the circle, and the invincibility of a team that remains bonded through every circumstance.

Duplanty urged the group, "Don't let anyone break this team apart; there's going to be plenty of opportunities, plenty of times when you just want to break away. You want to do your own thing, whether it's for yourself, or you just get mad. Nothing breaks this circle.

"Nothing."

@/@@/@@/@

The United States. Australia. Two of the best women's water polo teams in the world, locked in a battle at the Olympic Games.

In the closing seconds of the game, an American player is excluded. With one second on the clock, confusion. The United States coach makes pleas to the referees for clarification. A shot by an Australian player skims to the right of the American goalkeeper, just out of reach. Spectators clad in yellow and green wigs burst into cheers of joy, celebrating vociferously.

It's not Sydney, in 2000. The scene is London, in 2012.

Awarded a penalty shot with one second on the clock, Ash Southern cashed in to tie the score 9-9, sending the Olympic semifinal into overtime.

Just before Southern's goal, the teams scrambled for a rebound, and United States coach Adam Krikorian was ruled to have called a timeout without his team in possession of the ball. The result was the game-tying penalty.

A distraction.

Peak performance is not about being perfect.

Nothing breaks the circle.

The American women regrouped; they held Australia scoreless in overtime, prevailing 11-9.

Two days later, the United States defeated Spain 8-5 to become Olympic champions.

Mission 2012 was accomplished.

☺☺☺☺☺☺

Maureen O'Toole's career ended on the Olympic podium in Sydney. Twelve years after receiving her silver medal alongside O'Toole in Sydney, Brenda Villa became an Olympic champion in London. Two spots to her right was Maggie Steffens, nineteen years old, the most valuable player of the London Games. The torch had been symbolically passed once again, to be carried on to Rio in 2016.

Villa, along with fellow four-time Olympic medalist Heather Petri, and two-time athlete and two-time Olympic assistant coach Heather Moody, were the last members of the Sydney team still active in London. All three moved on from the National Team following the 2012 Games.

But the United States women's water polo program surged on.

The Senior Team dropped a quarterfinal to the host team, Spain, at the 2013 World Championships in Barcelona; but the Junior Team won an unprecedented third Junior World Championship that summer. In 2014, the Seniors returned to the top of the world rankings, winning both the World League Super Final and the World Cup. That same year, the Youth National Team brought home its first gold medal, defeating Canada for the World Championship title.

The year 2015 featured golden performances for the Senior Team at the World League Super Final, the Pan American Games, and the World Championships; the Juniors repeated as World Champions, with Sydney Olympian Coralie Simmons at the helm. Simmons' all-female staff included Olympians Natalie Golda and Betsey Armstrong.

USA Water Polo dubbed the summer of 2015, "All Gold Everything."

The members of the 2000 Sydney Olympic team continue to follow the Women's National Team's accomplishments with pride.

Their journey was full of challenges that threatened to derail their dreams of the Olympics. Their achievements guaranteed those same dreams were instilled in female water polo players of all ages. The Sydney team ushered in a new era of the sport in the United States – an era of opportunity and undeniable domination on the international stage.

For the Sydney team, this is their silver lining.

Catching up with the women of the 2000 Sydney Olympic Team

Robin Beauregard • 2000 Sydney silver • 2004 Athens bronze
Robin currently lives in Southern California with her husband, her twins, and her fur baby Murphy. After Sydney, she completed her undergrad work at UCLA with double majors in Psychobiology and Physiological Sciences, before going on to play in the Athens Games. After Athens, she completed a doctorate in physical therapy from USC; she currently works as a clinical coordinator and practicing physical therapist at CHOC Children's Hospital in Orange County specializing in pediatric post-concussion, orthopedics, oncology, and rheumatology patients.

Ellen Estes Lee • 2000 Sydney silver • 2004 Athens bronze
Ellen lives on the Peninsula in the Bay Area with her family: husband Austin who is an Assistant Athletic Director at Stanford University and her two kids, Vivian (4) and Henry (2). She's looking forward to getting her kids "water safe", so she can introduce a water polo ball sooner rather than later. Ellen works at Genentech, a biotech company in South San Francisco, leading a team responsible for pricing, contracting, and distribution strategies for the infused oncology products in the portfolio. She remains involved in water polo as a member of the USA Water Polo Board of Directors.

Courtney Young Johnson • 2000 Sydney silver
Courtney lives in Moraga, California. She has four kids: Gideon (12), Ainsley (10), Maddox (8), and Emmeline (5). She has been volunteering with the USOC since 2000, serving on the USOC Athletes' Advisory Council, the USOC/NCAA Joint Task Force, and the Governance Restructure Task Force. She currently serves on the USOC Nominating and Governance Committee. She works in the athletic department at Saint Mary's College of California as a Coordinator of Compliance and Athletic Eligibility. She and husband Darren have been married for twenty years.

Ericka Lorenz • 2000 Sydney silver • 2004 Athens bronze

Ericka resides in Long Beach, California, and is currently an Ocean Lifeguard and EMT for LA County Lifeguards and Huntington Beach City Lifeguards. She is pursuing a full time career in Marine Safety.

Heather Moody • 2000 Sydney silver • 2004 Athens bronze • 2008 Beijing coach silver • 2012 London coach gold

Since the 2000 Olympics, Heather has stayed active within the water polo community. She captained the 2004 Olympic Team in Greece and then retired from competition. She continues to coach the sport she loves, and that has provided her so much joy and perspective. She currently coaches in Sacramento for the American River Water Polo Club 18-and-under girls' team and serves as the club's Performance Director. She also coaches girls' water polo at St. Francis High School.

Bernice (Orwig) O'Connor • 2000 Sydney silver

Bernice is the Director of Age Group Programs at Stanford Water Polo Club, and coaches the girls' team at Carlmont High School in Belmont. She is married to Michael O'Connor, and has two children, James and Lela.

Maureen O'Toole Purcell • 2000 Sydney silver

Maureen lives in Danville, California with husband Jim Purcell. She and Jim started the girl's program at Diablo Water Polo Club in 2002, and the club now has about 150 girls. Maureen established a non-profit organization, Pursuit of Excellence for Youth, and along with Sue Peterson, wrote a book titled, *Becoming a Better You*. She is also a realtor for Village Associates. Maureen's daughter, Kelly Mendoza, graduated from USC, where she played water polo. At USC, Kelly became an NCAA Champion and earned All-American honors. Following her college career, she trained and competed with the United States National Team. Now, at age 24, Kelly has returned to Sydney, where she cheered for her mom at the 2000 Olympics as an eight-year-old, to play water polo for Sydney Uni in the National Water Polo League. She remains in Sydney, working as a graphic designer. She also started her own swim suit and sunglass company, NAEKD.

Nicolle Payne • 2000 Sydney silver • 2004 Athens bronze

Nicolle currently resides in Berkeley, California, and started a company with Heather Petri called Teammates 4 Lyfe, which focuses on mentoring young athletes.

Heather Petri • 2000 Sydney silver • 2004 Athens bronze • 2008 Beijing silver • 2012 London gold

Heather is back living in Northern California, teaching, working in sales, and making time for philanthropy. She is also loving the opportunity to collaborate with fellow Sydney (and Athens) teammate Nicolle Payne on a new project called Teammates 4 Lyfe. In addition, Heather also coaches private water polo lessons and attends water polo clinics all over the United States.

Rachel (Scott) Ruano • 2004 Athens coach bronze

Rachel currently lives in Sacramento, California, with her husband Rafael and their four boys: Mateo, Lucas, Nicolas, and Andres. Rachel is humbled by the opportunities water polo has given her, and continues to be actively involved as a coach and the primary administrator of American River Water Polo Club. She is also the girls' coach at Rio Americano High School.

Kathy "Gubba" Sheehy • 2000 Sydney silver

Gubba is retired and lives in Lake Tahoe.

Coralie Simmons • 2000 Sydney silver

Coralie resides with her family in Sonoma County, California. She coaches water polo at Sonoma State University and with the United States National Teams (Youth and Junior). She is running out her career playing on the NYAC water polo team.

Julie (Swail) Ertel • 2000 Sydney silver • 2008 Beijing Triathlon

Julie currently lives in Irvine, California, with her husband Greg and her twin six-year-olds Catherine and Jackson. After Sydney, she coached Division I college water polo for three years and high school water polo for five years. She took a break between coaching to compete in the 2008 Olympic Games in Beijing and develop her talents in the sport of triathlon. Julie eventually competed in triathlon at two Pan American Games and won three national championships in addition to competing in the Beijing Olympics. Julie worked for NBC as a color commentator for women's water polo at the Athens and London Olympics, and will do so again in Rio. She currently stays involved in water polo by giving private lessons and playing with a pick-up masters men's team twice a week.

Brenda Villa • 2000 Sydney silver • 2004 Athens bronze • 2008 Beijing silver • 2012 London gold

Brenda lives in Palo Alto, California. She is married to Gino Medina and is expecting a daughter this summer. Brenda coaches water polo at Castilleja School and Mavericks Water Polo in Menlo Park. She is a co-founder of Project 2020, a non-profit organization aiming to provide low income youths of the San Francisco mid-peninsula with the opportunity to learn to swim and play water polo.

1984 Los Angeles Olympic Games

Author's Note

When I was 11 years old, my prized possession was an oversized book that told the story of the 1984 Olympic Games – both the winter edition in Sarajevo, and the summer blockbuster that took place in Los Angeles, close to my home in Fullerton. The book contained large full-color photo spreads of all the sports, and, most importantly to me, listings of all the medal winners, their time or score, and their nationality. I was fascinated by the athletes, the magnitude of their competitive spirit, and the concept of nations competing for athletic glory.

The Los Angeles Olympic Games captured my attention completely. I remember waking up basically in the middle of the night, and catching a bus near Disneyland to head to USC to watch Olympic swimming with my family. We did the same to get to the water polo competition at Pepperdine with some of my 12-and-under teammates from our club, STOP.

Olympic fever hit close to home again in 1988 when Tom Milich, my coach at El Dorado High School, was on the men's water polo staff – we all followed along as the United States earned the silver medal in Seoul. But the most famous Golden Hawk at the 1988 Games brought home gold – Janet Evans swam to Olympic victories in the 400 meter individual medley, the 400 meter freestyle, and the 800 meter freestyle. (Her world record 4:03.85 in the 400 freestyle stood for nearly eighteen years.)

The elements of the Olympics that thrilled me as a kid never ceased to grab my attention whenever the Games rolled around. Little did I know that watching Olympic water polo at Pepperdine in 1984 was just the beginning.

My Olympic journey, like anyone else's – athletes, staff, family members, spectators – is unique in its own right, studded with a handful of uncommon experiences. But all of these experiences, each unpredictable moment, all combined to set me upon a path to Guy Baker and the Women's National Team – which I witnessed transform into the 2000 Women's Olympic Team:

❖ My first full Olympic experience came in 1996 in Atlanta. I worked with Scott Ball, Simon Perez, and Vicki Gorman on the media team for the Atlanta Committee for the Olympic Games (ACOG) at the water polo competition. After writing match reports and getting flash quotes from athletes and coaches for the entire tournament, I was on the deck the day Olympic legend Manuel Estiarte and Spain captured the gold. After the medal ceremony, Croatia's Dubravko Šimenc grabbed me in the tunnel behind the pool to proudly show me his silver medal. He explained how one side was the same as the gold medal he earned playing for Yugoslavia in Seoul, and the other was unique to the Atlanta Games. Before running off to celebrate with his teammates, he said to me, "See you in Sydney!"

❖ In Atlanta, our credentials allowed us entry to any venue, with no restrictions. The night after the water polo final, we went to Athletics, and found empty seats at field level, just beyond the finish line of the 400 meters. That night, we saw three Americans win gold medals: Allen Johnson in the 110 meter hurdles, Carl Lewis in the long jump, and Michael Johnson in the 400 meters. At one point, I used my credential to go to the media room to get a drink – and bumped smack into Lewis walking into his press conference. When the night's competition ended, we tried to find our way to the bus to head back to our accommodations. We ended up getting lost in the bowels of Centennial Olympic Stadium. As we walked through the tunnel, Allen Johnson came running right toward us, gold medal swinging from his neck. I casually high-fived the Olympic champion – who was all smiles – with a, "Great job, man!" When we finally found our way above ground, we popped up in the dugout of the stadium, which would become the Atlanta Braves' Turner Field after the Games. Before heading home for the night, we stood on the Olympic track for photos with the Olympic flame dancing in the background.

❖ Atlanta was also where I first met an important friend – a man with no team. Everybody in the FINA water polo circle knows Australian Russell McKinnon – and Russell knows everyone. Russell was in Atlanta, but the Aussie men were not. He had booked his flight and accommodation well in advance of the Games – so far, in fact, that it was before he could have known his country-men would miss out on qualification for Atlanta. Russell was the Media Manager for Australian Water Polo Inc., and I was about to begin my first job, as Editor of *Water Polo Scoreboard* magazine.

Russell, ultra-friendly and always generous, invited me to assist him with media at the 1998 FINA World Championships, held in his hometown of Perth. So I arrived in Western Australia on New Year's Eve 1998, and stayed with Russell and his lovely wife, Shirley. It was the first of many stays with the McKinnons in the paradise that is Perth. We celebrated the 2005 Junior World Championship with a barbeque at their home, and it was the first place I went to begin my research for *Sydney's Silver Lining* in the fall of 2015.

❖ The 1998 World Championships in Perth was my first major event work-ing with the Women's National Team. The next time I traveled to cover the team, it was to Winnipeg for the 1999 FINA World Cup – the first Olympic qualifier. The World Cup, held once every four years, is a great tournament for spectators and athletes alike. It features the best eight teams in the world and four high-quality games a day. There's a lot of time to hang around at the World Cup. Susan Ortwein and Lynn Wittstock made the most of being in Winnipeg, playing tennis on a court with a chain link net, and taking an airplane tour above the city, after which Susan declared Winnipeg to be "flat as a pancake."

There was no streaming video back then. I tried to convince broadcast.com that we should provide an audio webcast of the critical match versus Canada, to no avail. Instead, I was on the phone with Paul Rosenberg in San Mateo through-out the game, relaying play-by-play, which he loaded to uswp.org. It was my first attempt at live-blogging, and it ended with a thud when the United States fell to Canada. It was going to be off to Europe to try to qualify, and people weren't giving us much of a chance. When I was working in the media room after the game, a very nice Canadian volunteer consoled me with, "I'm sorry your team won't get to go to the Olympics."

❖ I didn't believe that happy Canadian, and I went to Italy with Craig and Wendy Rosenberg to report on the Olympic Qualification Tournament. Before heading to Palermo, we toured Rome and Naples. We got to Rome in the evening – it was dark. We took a taxi to Hotel Forum, dropped off our bags, and got into another taxi to go to dinner. When we woke up in the morning, we went upstairs for the typical European hotel breakfast, then got ready to go sightseeing. We asked the man at the front desk, "Which way to the Colosseum?"

This guy stared at us for a few seconds – *then leaned forward as if he were checking if it were still there* – and when satisfied that he was giving us accurate information, pointed out the door and said, "One hundred meters. Colosseum."

We stepped outside to see a humongous ancient structure looming above us. As I said, it was dark when we rolled into town.

❖ Making our way to Palermo by boat, we settled in at the same hotel as the United States women's team. As described in the book, it was good living – seaside location, easy trams into town, and great food. We enjoyed *arancini* (Sicilian rice balls), incredible pizza, and the local specialty, *ricci di mare* (sea urchin). We also shared a great meal with Alan Cima, his daughter Bekki, and her future husband, Adam Lyon. Alan and I ended up sharing many meals together all over the world as staff on the Junior National Team.

❖ At the Olympic Qualifying Tournament, the fourth quarter of the game between the USA and Hungary was probably my most nerve-wracking water polo experience ever. When the final shot was saved, and the win secured, it was a joy to see the team celebrate. They did lose the tournament final to Russia – I still have the handwritten post-game interview notes in which Guy Baker points out areas that needed to improve. ("I am so proud we qualified, but this game showed we have a lot of work to do.")

❖ In July of 2000, the United States and Russia came up to Stanford for the Sendoff to Sydney, the last international friendly before the Olympics in September. After both teams had a chance to loosen-out in the pool at Menlo, we all gathered for a picnic lunch on the grass. We took the advice of the internationally savvy Andy Burke, who had plenty of experience with the Russian men's teams. "Russians love fruit. Get a lot of fruit." There was probably no amount of fruit that would have been too much. The Russians descended upon and devoured it all.

The other part of lunch was a burrito bar, catered by the water polo family that owned La Costeña in Mountain View. The Russians patiently watched, nodding their heads, as they received lessons in burrito-wrapping. When they sat down to eat, they immediately unwrapped the tortillas to eat the fillings with a fork.

❖ After working the 1998 World Championships with Russell, the two of us hooked up with the Sydney Organising Committee for the Olympic Games (SOCOG). We worked side-by-side at the 1999 FINA World Cup in Sydney, the Olympic test event. A year later, we logged double-duty, as the Sydney Olympics included both women's and men's competitions for the first time. For the second consecutive Olympics, I watched every game – this time culminating in two gold medal finals.

❖ In Sydney, I had a great time living in a suburb called Ryde, home of the water polo venue, with Wayne Rosenberg and his kids Chloe (6) and Jed (2) whom I met through the Goss family. Faith Goss was a freshman on the team at Menlo School, which Maureen Eger coached in my absence. Barry Goss made the trip to Sydney – his recollections of the gold medal game include being absolutely drowned out every time the small pocket of American fans started a *USA!* cheer, and calling his wife Claire while walking out of the Sydney International Aquatic Centre. He had lost his voice from screaming for the United States to pull out the gold. Awakened by Barry's call, Claire pieced together that the United States lost, but there was as much confusion in the conversation as there was on the pool deck an hour earlier. When Faith woke up for school and was told that her hero Brenda Villa and the United States team lost, she cried. Not because of the result, but because she had met all the players at the Sendoff to Sydney. She wanted her new heroes to win and be happy.

❖ Two memories of the women's water polo tournament stick out in my mind. One was watching the end of the USA-Canada game on a monitor in the media room. For some reason, I left the press tribune. I hate to say, but it was probably because I thought Canada had wrapped up the win. But I clearly recall looking up at the monitor as Brenda grabbed the rebound and dropped a dime to Mo – thinking, "It's a two-on-one." And silently willing Robin to catch the ball.

"*Don't drop it. Don't drop it.*" The other is something that struck me – this was relatively early in my coaching career – as really cool. I watched the United States team practice on the morning of the semifinal at Ryde. Later, coaching internationally, I would learn that you really can't do much in one hour of pool time. But that day, I was totally impressed by how calm everyone was as they ran through their plays. Guy was satisfied. They were ready. The work was done.

Women's water polo gold medal match – September 23, 2000

❖ The women's team played the first week of the Sydney Games – they had another full week of being Olympic spectators and enjoying the festivities. It was the only time the women's and men's tournaments were played that way – starting in Athens, FINA used the current system of alternating days. Russell and I covered the rest of the men's tournament and were treated to a wonderful surprise at the men's final. Our friend Erica Hua, who worked with us at the '98 World Champs in Perth, asked if we were going to the closing ceremony, scheduled for just after the water polo medals were awarded. When we said we weren't, she handed us two VIP tickets to the closing ceremony, courtesy of the Olympic Committee of Nigeria. It's the only closing ceremony I've attended, and it was fantastic.

These are just a few of my favorite memories from my days of traveling the world as a water polo journalist. There are so many more from my days as a coach, working with Guy Baker, pursuing the mission of the women's pipeline, and Olympic gold, alongside him. On a personal level, walking into the opening ceremonies in Athens and Beijing are unforgettable experiences, clear cases of sensory overload. And as a coach, as someone who loves seeing a plan, a vision, come together, watching players who developed into Olympians through the Youth and Junior National Teams achieve their dreams is incomparably gratifying.

All of this was made possible because of the dedication and perseverance of the people whose stories are told in *Sydney's Silver Lining*. My life in water polo – at the club, collegiate, and international level – is highly indebted to them.

I want to thank all of the great water polo people who helped me tell the story of the 2000 Women's Olympic Team. Specifically, I am appreciative of all the athletes and staff who so willingly and generously shared their time. I knew your story was a good one. I had no idea how good.

This entire experience for me has been solid gold.

All-Time United States Women's National Team Rosters

FINA World Championships • FINA World Cup
FINA World League Super Final • Olympic Games

1978	1979	1980
World Championships	World Cup	World Cup
Berlin, West Germany	Merced, United States	Breda, Netherlands
3rd	1st	2nd
Nancy Bishop	Lynn Comer	Carmen Bejarano
Amy Caulkins	Laura Cox	Becky Black
Lynn Comer	Dion Dickinson	Lynn Comer
Laura Cox	Vaune Kadlubek	Laura Cox
Dion Dickinson	Debbi Kemp	Ruth Cox
Leslie Entwistle	Simone La Pay	Dion Dickinson
Kathy Horne	Marsha McCuen-Kavanagh	Vaune Kadlubek
Vaune Kadlubek	Susie McIntyre	Robin Linn
Simone La Pay	Maureen O'Toole	Susie McIntyre-Henry
Marsha McCuen	Lyn Taylor	Maureen O'Toole
Susie McIntyre	Sallie Thomas	Marla Smith
Maureen O'Toole		
Kristi Shepard		
Lyn Taylor		Head coach: Sandy Nitta
	Head coach: Flip Hassett	Asst coach: Kelly Kemp
Head coach: Stan Sprague	Asst coach: Kelly Kemp	Team leader: Jennie Jacobsen
Team leader: Jennie Jacobsen	Team leader: Jennie Jacobsen	Doctor: Dr. Ralph Hale

1981	1982	1983
World Cup	World Championships	World Cup
Brisbane, Australia	Guyaquil, Ecuador	Sainte Foy, Canada
4th	3rd	2nd
Laura Cox	Susan Arnold	Theresa Breckon
Dion Dickinson	Carmen Bejarano	Lynn Comer
Leslie Entwistle	Lynn Comer	Laura Cox
Karen Hastie	Dion Dickinson	Yolanda Gascon
Pam Hendricks	Robin Linn Dressel	Dion Gray
Vaune Kadlubek	Yolanda Gascon	Vaune Kadlubek
Robin Linn	Vaune Kadlubek	Simone La Pay
Marla Smith	Simone La Pay	Laura Laughlin
Lyn Taylor	Laura Laughlin	Robin Linn
Debbie Witt	Susie McIntyre	Margo Miranda
Nancy Wright	Maureen OToole	Maureen O'Toole
	Marla Smith	Marla Smith
	Diane Stein	Lynn Taylor
Head coach: Sandy Nitta	Head coach: Sandy Nitta	Head coach: Sandy Nitta
Team leader: Lynn Cox	Asst coach: Rich Corso	Asst coach: Richard Hunkler
	Team leader: Jane Hale	Team leader: Jane Hale
	Doctor: Dr. Ralph Hale	Doctor: Dr. Ralph Hale

1984	1986	1988
World Cup	World Championships	World Cup
Irvine, United States	Madrid, Spain	Christchurch, New Zealand
2nd	3rd	4th

Theresa Breckon	Theresa Breckon	Kelli Billish
Lynn Comer	Lynn Comer	Theresa Breckon
Val Dominguez	Yolanda Gascon	Nancy Corstophine
Yolanda Gascon	Dion Gray	Amber Drury
Dion Gray	Vaune Kadlubek	Pam Hendricks
Simone La Pay	Mary Beth Kolding	Maggi Kelly
Laura Laughlin	Simone La Pay	Susie McIntyre
Susie McIntyre	Laura Laughlin	Maureen Mendoza
Margo Miranda	Maureen O'Toole	Margo Miranda
Maureen O'Toole	Marla Smith	Shari Smart
Marla Smith	Jill Sterkel	Sandy Vessey
Sandy Vessey	Lyn Taylor	Jocelyn Wilkie
Lynn Wittstock	Lynn Wittstock	Lynn Wittstock

Head coach: Sandy Nitta	Head coach: Sandy Nitta	Head coach: Sandy Nitta
Asst coach: Richard Hunkler	Asst coach: Scott Hinman	Asst coach: Scott Hinman
	Team leader: Jane Hale	Team leader: Jane Hale
	Doctor: Dr. Ralph Hale	Doctor: Dr. Ralph Hale
		Referee: Gary Robinett

1989	1991	1991
World Cup	World Championships	World Cup
Eindhoven, Netherlands	Perth, Australia	Long Beach, United States
2nd	3rd	3rd

Laura Baker	Erika Billish	Amber Alatorre
Anabel Barragan	Kelli Billish	Katherine Florio
Serena Bucholz	Theresa Breckon	Jenny Hodge
Kelli Billish	Amber Drury	Sarah Johnston
Theresa Breckon	Megan Hernandez	Maggi Kelly
Amber Drury	Jenny Hodge	Tricia McGuire
Jenny Hodge	Maggi Kelly	Margo Miranda
Maggi Kelly	Margo Miranda	Susan Ortwein
Margo Miranda	Maureen O'Toole	Maureen O'Toole-Mendoza
Maureen O'Toole-Mendoza	Sandy Vessey	Brenda Reiton
Maria Patullo	Jocelyn Wilkie	Suzanne Shriner
Sandy Vessey	Lynn Wittstock	Jocelyn Wilkie
Lynn Wittstock	Nancy Wright	Lynn Wittstock

Head coach: Sandy Nitta	Head coach: Sandy Nitta	Head coach: Sandy Nitta
Asst coach: Scott Hinman	Asst coach: Vaune Kadlubek	Asst coach: Vaune Kadlubek
Team leader: Janice O'Toole	Asst coach: Lynn Comer	Team leader: Becky Shaw
Doctor: Dr. Ralph Hale	Team leader: Becky Shaw	Referee: Bob Lee
Referee: Bob Lee	Doctor: Dr. Ralph Hale	
	Trainer: Kam Knoll	
	Referee: Bob Lee	
	Referee: Andy Takata	

1993	1994	1995
World Cup	World Championships	World Cup
Catania, Italy	Rome, Italy	Sydney, Australia
5th	4th	6th
Amber Alatorre	Amber Alatorre	Danielle Dabbaghian
Anabel Barragan	Erika Billish	Jaimi Doan
Carrie Bayse	Jamey Dailey	Katherine Florio
Jamey Dailey	Jaimi Doan	Heather Kohler
Katherine Florio	Maggi Kelly	Heather Moody
Maggi Kelly	Jadene Kramer	Nicolle Payne
Jadene Kramer	Heidi McElhaney	Tracy Proietti
Heidi McElhaney	Maureen O'Toole	Gubba Sheehy
Maureen Mendoza	Maria Patullo	Coralie Simmons
Maria Patullo	Brenda Reiton	Dana Simon
Brenda Reiton	Gubba Sheehy	Julie Swail
Gubba Sheehy	Julie Swail	Lynn Wittstock
Lynn Wittstock	Lynn Wittstock	Courtney Young-Johnson

Head coach: Sandy Nitta — Head coach: Sandy Nitta — Head coach: Vaune Kadlubek
Asst coach: Vaune Kadlubek — Asst coach: Vaune Kadlubek — Asst coach: Amber Drury
Team leader: Becky Shaw — Asst coach: Dion Gray — Asst coach: Sandy Vessey
Team leader: Becky Shaw
Trainer: Robyn Johnson

1996	1997	1998
Olympic Year Tournament	World Cup	World Championships
Emmen, Netherlands	Nancy, France	Perth, Australia
7th	7th	8th
Danielle Dabbaghian	Danielle Dabbaghian	Courtney Johnson
Jaimi Doan	Jaimi Doan	Maggi Kelly
Liz Garcia	Courtney Johnson	Heather Kohler
Courtney Johnson	Heather Kohler	Heather Moody
Heather Kohler	Heather Moody	Maureen O'Toole
Heather Moody	Nicolle Payne	Nicolle Payne
Nicolle Payne	Rachel Scott	Rachel Scott
Kimberlie Rawlings	Gubba Sheehy	Gubba Sheehy
Gubba Sheehy	Coralie Simmons	Coralie Simmons
Coralie Simmons	Julie Swail	Julie Swail
Julie Swail	Brenda Villa	Brenda Villa
Brenda Villa	Alisa von Hartitzsch	Alisa von Hartitzsch
Lynn Wittstock	Lynn Wittstock	Lynn Wittstock

Head coach: Vaune Kadlubek — Head coach: Vaune Kadlubek — Head coach: Sandy Nitta
Asst coach: Amber Drury — Asst coach: Amber Drury — Asst coach: Amber Drury
Asst coach: Sandy Vessey — Asst coach: Sandy Vessey — Asst coach: Sandy Vessey

1999	2000	2001
World Cup	Olympic Games	World Championships
Winnipeg, Canada	Sydney, Australia	Fukuoka, Japan
6th	2nd	4th
Robin Beauregard	Robin Beauregard	Margie Dingeldein
Ellen Estes	Ellen Estes	Courtney Johnson
Jackie Frank	Courtney Johnson	Ericka Lorenz
Courtney Johnson	Ericka Lorenz	Heather Moody
Heather Moody	Heather Moody	Bernice Orwig
Maureen O'Toole	Bernice Orwig	Nicolle Payne
Nicolle Payne	Maureen O'Toole	Heather Petri
Rachel Scott	Nicolle Payne	Gubba Sheehy
Gubba Sheehy	Heather Petri	Coralie Simmons
Coralie Simmons	Gubba Sheehy	Amber Stachowski
Julie Swail	Coralie Simmons	Ashley Stachowski
Brenda Villa	Julie Swail	Brenda Villa
Alisa von Hartitzsch	Brenda Villa	Catherine von Schwarz

1999	2000	2001
Head coach: Guy Baker	Head coach: Guy Baker	Head coach: Guy Baker
Asst coach: Chris Duplanty	Asst coach: Chris Duplanty	Asst coach: Kyle Kopp
Asst coach: Ken Lindgren	Asst coach: Ken Lindgren	Team leader: Michelle Pickering
Team leader: Michelle Pickering	Team leader: Michelle Pickering	

2002	2003	2004
World Cup	World Championships	World League Super Final
Perth, Australia	Barcelona, Spain	Long Beach, United States
2nd	1st	1st
Robin Beauregard	Robin Beauregard	Robin Beauregard
Margie Dingeldein	Gabrielle Domanic	Margie Dingeldein
Gabrielle Domanic	Ellen Estes	Ellen Estes
Ellen Estes	Jackie Frank	Jackie Frank
Jackie Frank	Natalie Golda	Natalie Golda
Ericka Lorenz	Ericka Lorenz	Ericka Lorenz
Heather Moody	Heather Moody	Heather Moody
Thalia Munro	Thalia Munro	Thalia Munro
Nicolle Payne	Nicolle Payne	Nicolle Payne
Heather Petri	Heather Petri	Heather Petri
Coralie Simmons	Kelly Rulon	Kelly Rulon
Amber Stachowski	Amber Stachowski	Amber Stachowski
Brenda Villa	Brenda Villa	Brenda Villa

2002	2003	2004
Head coach: Guy Baker	Head coach: Guy Baker	Head coach: Guy Baker
Asst coach: Kyle Kopp	Asst coach: Kyle Kopp	Asst coach: Kyle Kopp
Asst coach: Rachel Scott	Asst coach: Rachel Scott	Asst coach: Rachel Scott
Team leader: Michelle Pickering	Team leader: Michelle Pickering	Team leader: Michelle Pickering

2004	2005	2005
Olympic Games	World Championships	World League Super Final
Athens, Greece	Montreal, Canada	Kirishi, Russia
3rd	2nd	5th
Robin Beauregard	Emily Feher	Katie Hansen
Margie Dingeldein	Erika Figge	Jaime Hipp
Ellen Estes	Natalie Golda	Erika Figge
Jackie Frank	Jaime Hipp	Natalie Golda
Natalie Golda	Kristina Kunkel	Brittany Hayes
Ericka Lorenz	Ericka Lorenz	Kristina Kunkel
Heather Moody	Thalia Munro	Ericka Lorenz
Thalia Munro	Heather Petri	Heather Petri
Nicolle Payne	Kelly Rulon	Aimee Stachowski
Heather Petri	Moriah van Norman	Brenda Villa
Kelly Rulon	Brenda Villa	Moriah Van Norman
Amber Stachowski	Drue Wawrzynski	Drue Wawrzynski
Brenda Villa	Lauren Wenger	Lauren Wenger
Head coach: Guy Baker	Head coach: Heather Moody	Head coach: Heather Moody
Asst coach: Kyle Kopp	Asst coach: Bernice Orwig	Asst coach: Bernice Orwig
Asst coach: Rachel Scott	Team leader: Michelle Pickering	Team leader: Michelle Pickering
Team leader: Michelle Pickering		

2006	2006	2007
World League Super Final	World Cup	World Championships
Cosenza, Italy	Tianjing, China	Melbourne, Australia
1st	4th	1st
Betsey Armstrong	Betsey Armstrong	Betsey Armstrong
Patty Cardenas	Patty Cardenas	Patty Cardenas
Kami Craig	Kami Craig	Kami Craig
Emily Feher	Emily Feher	Natalie Golda
Erika Figge	Erika Figge	Alison Gregorka
Natalie Golda	Natalie Golda	Brittany Hayes
Alison Gregorka	Alison Gregorka	Jaime Hipp
Ericka Lorenz	Ericka Lorenz	Ericka Lorenz
Heather Petri	Heather Petri	Heather Petri
Jessica Steffens	Moriah van Norman	Moriah van Norman
Moriah van Norman	Brenda Villa	Brenda Villa
Brenda Villa	Lauren Wenger	Lauren Wenger
Lauren Wenger	Elsie Windes	Elsie Windes
Elsie Windes		
Head coach: Guy Baker	Head coach: Guy Baker	Head coach: Guy Baker
Asst coach: Kyle Kopp	Asst coach: Kyle Kopp	Asst coach: Kyle Kopp
Asst coach: Heather Moody	Asst coach: Heather Moody	Asst coach: Heather Moody
Team leader: Bernice Orwig	Team leader: Bernice Orwig	Team leader: Bernice Orwig

2007	2008	2008
World League Super Final	World League Super Final	Olympic Games
Montreal, Canada	Tenerife, Spain	Beijing, China
1st	2nd	2nd

Betsey Armstrong	Betsey Armstrong	Betsey Armstrong
Patty Cardenas	Patty Cardenas	Patty Cardenas
Kami Craig	Kami Craig	Kami Craig
Erika Figge	Erika Figge	Natalie Golda
Natalie Golda	Natalie Golda	Alison Gregorka
Alison Gregorka	Alison Gregorka	Brittany Hayes
Jaime Hipp	Brittany Hayes	Jaime Hipp
Heather Petri	Jaime Hipp	Heather Petri
Jessica Steffens	Heather Petri	Jessica Steffens
Moriah van Norman	Jessica Steffens	Moriah van Norman
Brenda Villa	Moriah van Norman	Brenda Villa
Lauren Wenger	Brenda Villa	Lauren Wenger
Elsie Windes	Lauren Wenger	Elsie Windes
	Elsie Windes	

Head coach: Guy Baker		Head coach: Guy Baker
Asst coach: Kyle Kopp	Head coach: Guy Baker	Asst coach: Kyle Kopp
Asst coach: Heather Moody	Asst coach: Kyle Kopp	Asst coach: Heather Moody
Team leader: Bernice Orwig	Asst coach: Heather Moody	Team leader: Bernice Orwig
	Team leader: Bernice Orwig	

2009	2009	2010
World League Super Final	World Championships	World League Super Final
Kirishi, Russia	Rome, Italy	La Jolla, United States
1st	1st	1st

Betsey Armstrong	Betsey Armstrong	Betsey Armstrong
Kami Craig	Kami Craig	Kami Craig
Annika Dries	Tanya Gandy	Annika Dries
Erika Figge	Alison Gregorka	Emily Feher
Tanya Gandy	Brittany Hayes	Erika Figge
Alison Gregorka	Jaime Hipp	Tanya Gandy
Brittany Hayes	Heather Petri	Courtney Mathewson
Jaime Hipp	Kelly Rulon	Heather Petri
Heather Petri	Jessica Steffens	Kelly Rulon
Kelly Rulon	Moriah van Norman	Melissa Seidemann
Lauren Silver	Brenda Villa	Lauren Silver
Jessica Steffens	Lauren Wenger	Maggie Steffens
Brenda Villa	Elsie Windes	Brenda Villa
Lauren Wenger		Elsie Windes
Elsie Windes	Head coach: Adam Krikorian	Lauren Wenger
	Asst coach: Coralie Simmons	
Head coach: Adam Krikorian	Asst coach: Brandon Brooks	Head coach: Adam Krikorian
Asst coach: Coralie Simmons	Asst coach: Aaron Chaney	Asst coach: Heather Moody
Asst coach: Brandon Brooks	Team leader: Serela Kay	Asst coach: Dan Klatt
Asst coach: Aaron Chaney		Team leader: Jen Adams
Team leader: Serela Kay		

2010	2011	2011
World Cup	World League Super Final	World Championships
Christchurch, New Zealand	Tianjin, China	Shanghai, China
1st	1st	6th
Betsey Armstrong	Tumua Anae	Tumua Anae
Anne Belden	Betsey Armstrong	Betsey Armstrong
Kami Craig	Anne Belden	Kami Craig
Annika Dries	Kami Craig	Annika Dries
Emily Feher	Annika Dries	Courtney Mathewson
Courtney Mathewson	Courtney Mathewson	Heather Petri
Juliet Moss	Heather Petri	Kelly Rulon
Kelly Rulon	Kelly Rulon	Melissa Seidemann
Melissa Seidemann	Melissa Seidemann	Jessica Steffens
Lauren Silver	Lauren Silver	Meggie Steffens
Maggie Steffens	Jessica Steffens	Brenda Villa
Brenda Villa	Meggie Steffens	Lauren Wenger
Elsie Windes	Brenda Villa	Elsie Windes
	Lauren Wenger	
Head coach: Adam Krikorian	Elsie Windes	Head coach: Adam Krikorian
Asst coach: Heather Moody		Asst coach: Heather Moody
Asst coach: Dan Klatt	Head coach: Adam Krikorian	Asst coach: Dan Klatt
Team leader: Jen Adams	Asst coach: Heather Moody	Team leader: Jen Adams
	Asst coach: Dan Klatt	
	Team leader: Jen Adams	

2012	2012	2013
World League Super Final	Olympic Games	World League Super Final
Changshu, China	London, Great Britain	Beijing, China
1st	1st	3rd
Tumua Anae	Tumua Anae	Tumua Anae
Betsey Armstrong	Betsey Armstrong	Betsey Armstrong
Kami Craig	Kami Craig	KK Clark
Annika Dries	Annika Dries	Kami Craig
Courtney Mathewson	Courtney Mathewson	Annika Dries
Heather Petri	Heather Petri	Jillian Kraus
Kelly Rulon	Kelly Rulon	Courtney Mathewson
Melissa Seidemann	Melissa Seidemann	Kiley Neushul
Jessica Steffens	Jessica Steffens	Kelly Rulon
Meggie Steffens	Meggie Steffens	Lauren Silver
Brenda Villa	Brenda Villa	Melissa Seidemann
Lauren Wenger	Lauren Wenger	Maggie Steffens
Elsie Windes	Elsie Windes	Danielle Warde
Head coach: Adam Krikorian	Head coach: Adam Krikorian	Head coach: Adam Krikorian
Asst coach: Heather Moody	Asst coach: Heather Moody	Asst coach: Dan Klatt
Asst coach: Dan Klatt	Asst coach: Dan Klatt	Asst coach: Chris Oeding
Team leader: Jen Adams	Team leader: Jen Adams	Team leader: Jen Funakura

2013	2014	2014
World Championships	World League Super Final	World Cup
Barcelona, Spain	Kunshan, China	Khanty-Mansiysk, Russia
5th	1st	1st
Tumua Anae	KK Clark	KK Clark
Betsey Armstrong	Kami Craig	Kami Craig
KK Clark	Annika Dries	Annika Dries
Kami Craig	Rachel Fattal	Rachel Fattal
Annika Dries	Makenzie Fischer	Kaleigh Gilchrist
Rachel Fattal	Kaleigh Gilchrist	Sami Hill
Jillian Kraus	Sami Hill	Ashleigh Johnson
Courtney Mathewson	EB Keeve	Jillian Kraus
Kiley Neushul	Jillian Kraus	Courtney Mathewson
Kelly Rulon	Kiley Neushul	Kiley Neushul
Melissa Seidemann	Melissa Seidemann	Melissa Seidemann
Lauren Silver	Maggie Steffens	Maggie Steffens
Maggie Steffens	Alys Williams	Alys Williams

Head coach: Adam Krikorian	Head coach: Adam Krikorian	Head coach: Adam Krikorian
Asst coach: Dan Klatt	Asst coach: Dan Klatt	Asst coach: Dan Klatt
Asst coach: Chris Oeding	Asst coach: Chris Oeding	Asst coach: Chris Oeding
Team leader: Jen Funakura	Team leader: Jen Funakura	Team leader: Jen Funakura

2015	2015	2016
World League Super Final	World Championships	World League Super Final
Shanghai, China	Kazan, Russia	Shanghai, China
1st	1st	
KK Clark	Kami Craig	KK Clark
Kami Craig	Rachel Fattal	Kami Craig
Rachel Fattal	Makenzie Fischer	Rachel Fattal
Makenzie Fischer	Kaleigh Gilchrist	Aria Fischer
Kaleigh Gilchrist	Ashley Grossman	Makenzie Fischer
Ashley Grossman	Sami Hill	Kaleigh Gilchrist
Sami Hill	Ashleigh Johnson	Sami Hill
Ashleigh Johnson	Courtney Mathewson	Ashleigh Johnson
Courtney Mathewson	Maddie Musselman	Courtney Mathewson
Maddie Musselman	Kiley Neushul	Maddie Musselman
Kiley Neushul	Melissa Seidemann	Kiley Neushul
Melissa Seidemann	Maggie Steffens	Melissa Seidemann
Maggie Steffens	Alys Williams	Maggie Steffens
		Alys Williams

Head coach: Adam Krikorian	Head coach: Adam Krikorian	Head coach: Adam Krikorian
Asst coach: Dan Klatt	Asst coach: Dan Klatt	Asst coach: Dan Klatt
Asst coach: Chris Oeding	Asst coach: Chris Oeding	Asst coach: Chris Oeding
Team leader: Jen Funakura	Team leader: Jen Funakura/ Liz Grimes	Team leader: Jen Funakura

2016
Olympic Games
Rio de Janiero, Brazil

KK Clark
Kami Craig
Rachel Fattal
Aria Fischer
Makenzie Fischer
Kaleigh Gilchrist
Sami Hill
Ashleigh Johnson
Courtney Mathewson
Maddie Musselman
Kiley Neushul
Melissa Seidemann
Maggie Steffens

Head coach: Adam Krikorian
Asst coach: Dan Klatt
Asst coach: Chris Oeding
Team leader: Jen Funakura

United States Water Polo Junior and Youth World Champions

2001	2005	2013
Junior World Champions	Junior World Champions	Junior World Champions
Perth, Australia	Perth, Australia	Volos, Greece

2001	2005	2013
Lauren Dennis	Kami Craig	Mackenzie Barr
Gabrielle Domanic	Gabrielle Domanic	Eike Daube
Emily Feher	Emily Feher	Emily Donohoe
Mo Flanagan	Erika Figge	Rachel Fattal
Julie Gardner	Alison Gregorka	Mackenzie Fischer
Natalie Golda	Katie Hansen	Ashley Grossman
Lauren Heineck	Brittany Hayes	Kodi Hill
Kristina Kunkel	Christina Hewko	Ashleigh Johnson
Ericka Lorenz	Jillian Kraus	Kiley Neushul
Thalia Munro	Kacy Kunkel	Tierra Schroeder
Scotti Shafer	Meredith McColl	Monica Vavic
Amber Stachowski	Aimee Stachowski	Alys Williams
Ashley Stachowski	Elsie Windes	Jillian Yocum

2001	2005	2013
Head coach: John Wright	Head coach: Kyle Utsumi	Head coach: Dan Klatt
Assistant coach: Nicolle Payne	Assistant coach: Kim Everist	Assistant coach: Brandon Brooks
Assistant coach: Mark Walsh	Assistant coach: Bernice Orwig	Assistant coach: Aaron Chaney
Team manager: Kim Everist	Team manager: Alan Cima	Team manager: Kendra Klein

2014	2015
Youth World Champions	Junior World Champions
Madrid, Spain	Volos, Greece

2014	2015
Madison Berggren	Mackenzie Barr
Mary Brooks	Mary Brooks
Brianna Daboub	Emalia Eichelberger
Aria Fischer	Aria Fischer
Mackenzie Fischer	Alexis Liebowitz
Devin Grab	Amanda Longan
Carlee Kapana	Stephanie Mutafyan
Kat Klass	Jamie Neushul
Cana Manzella	Tara Prentice
Maddie Musselman	Jordan Raney
Jordan Raney	Emily Louglin
Helena Van Brande	
Haley Wan	

2014	2015
	Head coach: Coralie Simmons
	Assistant coach: Natalie Benson
Head coach: Marcello Leonardi	Assistant coach: Betsey Armstrong
Assistant coach: Coralie Simmons	Team manager: Lori Verdegaal
Assistant coach: Ethan Damato	
Team manager: Jen Gudmundsson	

All-Time FINA Results

Senior Events

World Cup • World Championships • World League Super Final • Olympic Games

World Champs Berlin, FRG	1978	NED	AUS	USA	CAN	FRG			
World Cup Merced, USA	1979	USA	NED	AUS	CAN	NZL			
World Cup Breda, NED	1980	NED	USA	CAN	AUS				
World Cup Brisbane, AUS	1981	CAN	NED	AUS	USA				
World Champs Guyaquil, ECU	1982	NED	AUS	USA	CAN				
World Cup Sainte Foy, CAN	1983	NED	USA	AUS	CAN				
World Cup Irvine, USA	1984	AUS	USA	NED	NZL				
World Champs Madrid, ESP	1986	AUS GBR	NED	USA	CAN	HUN	FRG	NOR	BEL
World Cup Christchurch, NZL	1988	NED	HUN	CAN	USA	AUS	NZL	PUR	
World Cup Eindhoven, NED	1989	NED	USA	HUN	CAN	AUS	FRG	FRA	ITA
World Champs Perth, AUS	1991	NED FRA	CAN	USA	HUN	AUS	GER	NZL	BRA
World Cup Long Beach, USA	1991	NED	AUS	USA	CAN	ITA	JPN	NZL	BRA
World Cup Catania, ITA	1993	NED	ITA	HUN	AUS	USA	CAN	JPN	KAZ
World Champs Rome, ITA	1994	HUN FRA	NED NZL	ITA BRA	USA KAZ	CAN	AUS	RUS	GER
World Cup Sydney, AUS	1995	AUS	NED	HUN	RUS	ITA	USA	FRA	NZL
Olympic Year Tourn Emmen, NED	1996	NED	AUS	ITA	GRE	CAN	RUS	USA	FRA
World Cup Nancy, FRA	1997	NED	RUS	AUS	ITA	CAN	GRE	USA	FRA

Event	Year	1	2	3	4	5	6	7	8
World Champs Perth, AUS	1998	ITA	NED	AUS	RUS	GRE	CAN	HUN	USA
		ESP	BRA	NZL	KAZ				
World Cup Winnipeg, CAN	1999	NED	AUS	ITA	HUN	CAN	USA	RUS	GRE
Olympic Games Sydney, AUS	2000	AUS	USA	RUS	NED	CAN	KAZ		
World Champs Fukuoka, JPN	2001	ITA	HUN	CAN	USA	AUS	RUS	GRE	KAZ
		NED	BRA	JPN	NZL				
World Cup Perth, AUS	2002	HUN	USA	CAN	RUS	ITA	AUS	GRE	KAZ
World Champs Barcelona, ESP	2003	USA	ITA	RUS	CAN	HUN	NED	AUS	ESP
		GRE	GER	JPN	BRA	KAZ	VEN	FRA	GBR
World League Long Beach, USA	2004	USA	HUN	ITA	RUS	CAN	GRE	AUS	KAZ
Olympic Games Athens, GRE	2004	ITA	GRE	USA	AUS	RUS	HUN	CAN	KAZ
World League Kirishi, RUS	2005	GRE	RUS	AUS	HUN	USA	CAN	NED	ITA
World Champs Montreal, CAN	2005	HUN	USA	CAN	RUS	GRE	AUS	ITA	GER
		CUB	NED	ESP	NZL	BRA	VEN	UZB	CHN
World League Athens, GRE	2006	USA	ITA	RUS	AUS	NED	CAN		
World Cup Tianjing, CHN	2006	AUS	ITA	RUS	USA	HUN	GRE	CAN	CHN
World League Montreal, CAN	2007	USA	AUS	GRE	CAN	ESP	CHN		
World Champs Melbourne, AUS	2007	USA	AUS	RUS	HUN	ITA	CAN	ESP	GRE
		NED	BRA	GER	NZL	KAZ	CHN	CUB	PUR
World League Tenerife, ESP	2008	RUS	USA	AUS	CAN	CHN	ESP		
Olympic Games Beijing, CHN	2008	NED	USA	AUS	HUN	CHN	ITA	RUS	GRE
World League Kirishi, RUS	2009	USA	CAN	AUS	ESP	CHN	RUS	GRE	ITA
World Champs Rome, ITA	2009	USA	CAN	RUS	GRE	NED	AUS	HUN	ESP
		ITA	GER	CHN	NZL	BRA	KAZ	UZB	RSA
World League La Jolla, USA	2010	USA	AUS	GRE	RUS	CHN	HUN	GRE	CAN

World Cup Christchurch, NZL	2010	USA	AUS	CHN	RUS	CAN	HUN	GRE	NZL
World League Kirishi, RUS	2011	USA	CAN	AUS	ESP	CHN	RUS	GRE	ITA
		RUS	GRE	ITA					
World Champs Shanghai, CHN	2011	GRE	CHN	RUS	ITA	AUS	USA	NED	CAN
		HUN	CUB	ESP	NZL	KAZ	BRA	RSA	UZB
World League Changshu, CHN	2012	USA	AUS	GRE	CHN	RUS	GER	CAN	ITA
Olympic Games London, GBR	2012	USA	ESP	AUS	HUN	CHN	RUS	ITA	GBR
World League Beijing, CHN	2013	CHN	RUS	USA	HUN	ESP	ITA	AUS	CAN
World Champs Barcelona, ESP	2013	ESP	AUS	HUN	RUS	USA	GRE	NED	CAN
		CHN	ITA	KAZ	NZL	GBR	BRA	RSA	UZB
World League Kunshan, CHN	2014	USA	ITA	AUS	CHN	ESP	CAN	RUS	BRA
World Cup Khanty-Mansiysk, RUS	2014	USA	AUS	ESP	CHN	HUN	RUS	RSA	SIN
World League Shanghai, CHN	2015	USA	AUS	NED	CHN	RUS	CAN	ITA	BRA
World Champs Kazan, RUS	2015	USA	NED	ITA	AUS	CHN	GRE	ESP	RUS
		HUN	BRA	CAN	KAZ	NZL	FRA	JPN	RSA
World League Shanghai, CHN	2016	USA	ESP	AUS	CHN	ITA	RUS	CAN	BRA
Olympic Games Rio de Janeiro, BRA	2016								

Junior World Champiomships

Location	Year	1	2	3	4	5	6	7	8
Sainte Foy, CAN	1995	NED	AUS	USA	GRE	CAN	BRA	KAZ	CZE
Prague, CZE	1997	GRE	AUS	USA	HUN	CAN	NED	ITA	GER
		BRA	CZE	FRA	KAZ				
Messina, ITA	1999	AUS	CAN	HUN	RUS	USA	GER	GRE	BRA
		ITA	RSA	GBR	UZB				
Perth, AUS	2001	USA	AUS	RUS	HUN	GER	NZL	GRE	CAN
		BRA	ITA	VEN	RSA				
Calgary, CAN	2003	CAN	USA	ESP	RUS	GER	AUS	NED	BRA
		CZE	GRE	NZL	MEX	FRA	SUI		
Perth, AUS	2005	USA	RUS	AUS	GRE	NED	CAN	ESP	NZL
		ITA	GER	HUN	PUR	JPN	CHN	BRA	
Porto, POR	2007	AUS	CHN	HUN	USA	ITA	ESP	NED	NZL
		RUS	CAN	JPN	GER	GRE	PUR	BRA	POR
Khanty-Mansiysk, RUS	2009	RUS	NED	USA	HUN	ITA	CAN	AUS	
		ESP	GRE	GER	NZL	RSA	KAZ	BRA	UZB
Trieste, ITA	2011	ESP	HUN	AUS	RUS	ITA	GRE	NED	USA
		CAN	UZB	CHN	GER	BRA	RSA	MEX	INA
Volos, GRE	2013	USA	ESP	GRE	RUS	ITA	HUN	AUS	GBR
		CAN	NZL	UZB	UKR	BRA	KAZ	RSA	
Volos, GRE	2015	USA	ESP	RUS	CAN	GRE	ITA	HUN	BRA
		AUS	NZL	JPN	MEX	NED	GBR	RSA	UKR

Youth World Championships

Location	Year	1	2	3	4	5	6	7	8
Perth, AUS	2012	GRE	HUN	RUS	USA	CAN	NZL	AUS	BRA
		ITA	CZE	RSA	UZB	INA	ZIM	IND	
Madrid, ESP	2014	USA	CAN	HUN	GRE	ITA	NED	ESP	CHN
		RUS	JPN	AUS	RSA	NZL	BRA	PUR	GER

Sydney's Silver Lining Backers

BRONZE

Blunt Family, Melbourne, Australia • Paul Rosenberg • Brenda Villa, Project 2020 • Michi
Rocky Mountain Neptunes • Raney Family • The Dillon Family, Stanford Water Polo Club
Bridgette Harper • John Abdou • Bruce Wigo, ISHOF • The Jacobsen Family
Hathaway & Katherine Moore, Stanford Water Polo Club 2004-2014 • Erin Gillett
Danny Boyer • The Quintero Family • Diane & Brandy Sikic • Meri & Andrew Klingelhofer
Tom, Traci & Katie Dudley • Santa Clara University Women's Water Polo
The Grossman Family • Cathy, Maura & Susan Cantoni
Abigail Schechter, Bakersfield Water Polo Club • The Mandelbaum-Dorosin Family
Laurie Burmeister • Menlo Water Polo Team 2005-06 • Shin & Gaby • Andy Burke
Michelle Bacolini Scaduto & Lindsey Bacolini, Stanford Water Polo Club
Sylvia Lacock Marino • Lucy Grossman • American River Water Polo Club
Sofia Carrera-Justiz • The Dodson Family • The Sandell Family • Josh & Judy Green
SNB Breakers Water Polo Club • Carole & Gary Estes • Steve Yancey • Kai Burke
Patrick Galligan, Menlo Mavericks • Paquin Family • The Hilsabeck Family
Akashi Grimes Family • The Xu-Wu Family, Stanford Water Polo Club • The Walker Family
The Tocchini Family • Carl, Denise & Terez Touhey
Heather Kohler Flynn, Oakland Masters Water Polo • Bruce Awad • Heather Moody
The Cousineau Family • Dana Saign, Stanford Water Polo Club
Amy Amanda Chinn • Artyn & Max Gardner, Stanford Water Polo Club • Bob Averill
The Reynolds Family • Becca Corb • Lauren Lesyna Family • Atherton Family
Rebecca Koshy & Koshy Family • The Watkins Family • The Brockstahler Family • Julia Stone
The Krueger Family • Melanie vonHartitzsch, Go Bears! • The Burmeister Family
Christy Medigovich • The Cima Family • Jenna MacAulay, Stanford Water Polo Club
LFL: Lefties for Life • Maggie & Jessica Heilman • Maureen O'Toole Purcell
Mike Wallen, Puget Sound Water Polo • Sharf Family • Grace Curry
Kristen Hong & Family, Diablo Water Polo • Andrea Hackett Henningsen • Joelle Elliott
The Vazquez-Azpiri Family • Akuiyibo Family • UC Davis Women's Water Polo 1994-1999
Michael and Vicki O'Connor • Enumclaw Water Polo
The Billish Family, Slippery Rock University Water Polo
Mackenzie Rosenthal, Stanford Water Polo Club • Alyssa, Michelle, Mike & Keiko Meyer
Bekki Lyon • Tammy Cook-Endres